Microsoft®
Excel® 2013
for Medical Professionals

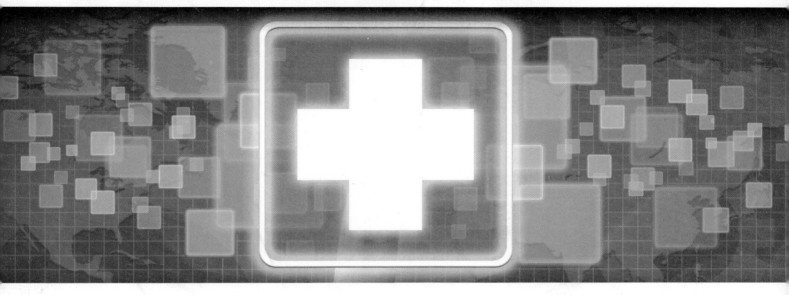

Microsoft® Excel® 2013
for Medical Professionals

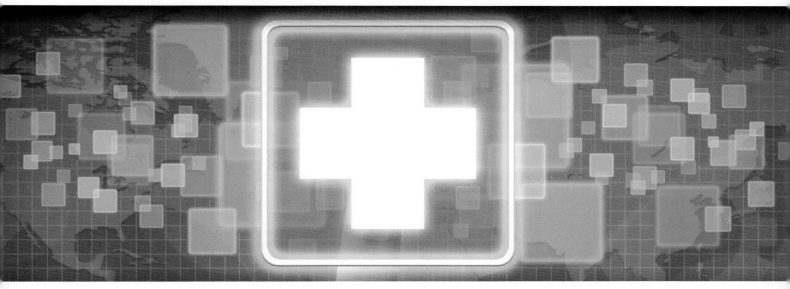

Elizabeth Eisner Reding/Lynn Wermers

 CENGAGE
Learning·

Australia • Brazil • Mexico • Singapore • United Kingdom • United States

CENGAGE
Learning·

Microsoft® Excel® 2013 for Medical Professionals
Elizabeth Eisner Reding/Lynn Wermers

Senior Product Manager: Marjorie Hunt

Associate Product Manager: Amanda Lyons

Senior Content Developer: Christina Kling-Garrett

Content Developer: Megan Chrisman

Marketing Manager: Gretchen Swan

Developmental Editor: Marj Hopper

Full-Service Project Management: GEX Publishing
    Services

Print Buyer: Fola Orekoya

Proofreader: Nancy Lamm

Indexer: Alexandra Nickerson

QA Manuscript Reviewers: John Freitas,
    Jeff Schwartz, Danielle Shaw, Susan Pedicini,
    Susan Whalen

Cover Designer: GEX Publishing Services

Cover Artist: GEX Publishing Services

Cover Image: ©Nonnakrit/Shutterstock

Composition: GEX Publishing Services

For product information and technology assistance, contact us at
Cengage Learning Customer & Sales Support, 1-800-354-9706

For permission to use material from this text or product, submit all
requests online at **www.cengage.com/permissions**
Further permissions questions can be emailed to
permissionrequest@cengage.com

Library of Congress Control Number: 2013951071
ISBN-13: 978-1-285-09333-8
ISBN-10: 1-285-09333-X

Cengage Learning
200 First Stamford Place, 4th Floor
Stamford, CT 06902
USA

Cengage Learning is a leading provider of customized learning solutions
with office locations around the globe, including Singapore, the United
Kingdom, Australia, Mexico, Brazil, and Japan. Locate your local office at:
www.cengage.com/global

Cengage Learning products are represented in Canada by
Nelson Education, Ltd.

For your course and learning solutions, visit **www.cengage.com**

Purchase any of our products at your local college store or at our
preferred online store **www.cengagebrain.com**

Trademarks:
Some of the product names and company names used in this book have
been used for identification purposes only and may be trademarks or
registered trademarks of their respective manufacturers and sellers.

Microsoft and the Windows logo are registered trademarks of Microsoft
Corporation in the United States and/or other countries. Cengage Learning
is an independent entity from Microsoft Corporation, and not affiliated with
Microsoft in any manner.

Printed in the United States of America
1 2 3 4 5 6 7 19 18 17 16 15 14

Brief Contents

Preface x

Office 2013

Unit A: Getting Started with Microsoft Office 2013 ....Office 1

Excel 2013

Unit A: Getting Started with Excel 2013 .... Excel 1
Unit B: Working with Formulas and Functions .... Excel 25
Unit C: Formatting a Worksheet... Excel 51
Unit D: Working with Charts.. Excel 79
Unit E: Analyzing Data Using Formulas .... Excel 105
Unit F: Managing Workbook Data .... Excel 129
Unit G: Managing Data Using Tables .... Excel 153
Unit H: Analyzing Table Data .... Excel 177

Cloud

Appendix: Working in the Cloud ....Cloud 1

Glossary..Glossary 1
Index.. Index 6

Contents

Preface x

Office 2013

Unit A: Getting Started with Microsoft Office 2013 .... **Office 1**
    Understand the Office 2013 Suite.. Office 2
        What is Office 365?
    Start an Office App.. Office 4
        Starting an app using Windows 7
        Using shortcut keys to move between Office programs
        Using the Office Clipboard
    Identify Office 2013 Screen Elements.. Office 6
        Using Backstage view
    Create and Save a File... Office 8
        Saving files to SkyDrive
    Open a File and Save It with a New Name .... Office 10
        Exploring File Open options
        Working in Compatibility Mode
    View and Print Your Work... Office 12
        Customizing the Quick Access toolbar
        Creating a screen capture
    Get Help, Close a File, and Exit an App... Office 14
        Enabling touch mode
        Recovering a document
    Practice Office 16

Excel 2013

Unit A: Getting Started with Excel 2013 .... **Excel 1**
    Understand Spreadsheet Software...Excel 2
    Identify Excel 2013 Window Components ....Excel 4
        Using SkyDrive and Web Apps
    Understand Formulas..Excel 6
    Enter Labels and Values and Use the AutoSum Button..............................Excel 8
        Navigating a worksheet
    Edit Cell Entries ....Excel 10
        Recovering unsaved changes to a workbook file
    Enter and Edit a Simple Formula ....Excel 12
        Understanding named ranges
    Switch Worksheet Views..Excel 14
    Choose Print Options...Excel 16
        Printing worksheet formulas
        Scaling to fit
    Practice ....Excel 18

Unit B: Working with Formulas and Functions .... Excel 25

Create a Complex Formula .... Excel 26
　　Using Apps for Office to improve worksheet functionality
　　Reviewing the order of precedence
Insert a Function .... Excel 28
Type a Function .... Excel 30
　　Using the COUNT and COUNTA functions
Copy and Move Cell Entries .... Excel 32
　　Inserting and deleting selected cells
Understand Relative and Absolute Cell References .... Excel 34
　　Using a mixed reference
Copy Formulas with Relative Cell References .... Excel 36
　　Using Paste Preview
　　Using Auto Fill options
Copy Formulas with Absolute Cell References .... Excel 38
　　Using the fill handle for sequential text or values
Round a Value with a Function .... Excel 40
　　Creating a new workbook using a template
Practice .... Excel 42

Unit C: Formatting a Worksheet .... Excel 51

Format Values .... Excel 52
　　Formatting as a table
Change Font and Font Size .... Excel 54
　　Inserting and adjusting online pictures and other images
Change Font Styles and Alignment .... Excel 56
　　Rotating and indenting cell entries
Adjust the Column Width .... Excel 58
　　Changing row height
Insert and Delete Rows and Columns .... Excel 60
　　Hiding and unhiding columns and rows
　　Adding and editing comments
Apply Colors, Patterns, and Borders .... Excel 62
　　Working with themes and cell styles
Apply Conditional Formatting .... Excel 64
　　Managing conditional formatting rules
Rename and Move a Worksheet .... Excel 66
　　Copying, Adding, and Deleting worksheets
Check Spelling .... Excel 68
　　Emailing a workbook
Practice .... Excel 70

Unit D: Working with Charts .... Excel 79

Plan a Chart .... Excel 80
Create a Chart .... Excel 82
　　Creating sparklines
Move and Resize a Chart .... Excel 84
　　Moving an embedded chart to a sheet
Change the Chart Design .... Excel 86
　　Creating a combination chart
　　Working with a 3-D chart

Change the Chart Format ....Excel 88
    Adding data labels to a chart
Format a Chart ....Excel 90
    Previewing a chart
    Changing alignment and angle in axis labels and titles
Annotate and Draw on a Chart ....Excel 92
    Adding SmartArt graphics
Create a Pie Chart ....Excel 94
Practice .... Excel 96

Unit E: Analyzing Data Using Formulas ....Excel 105

Format Data Using Text Functions ....Excel 106
    Working with text in other ways
Sum a Data Range Based on Conditions...Excel 108
    Entering date and time functions
Consolidate Data Using a Formula ....Excel 110
    Linking data between workbooks
Check Formulas for Errors...Excel 112
    Correcting circular references
Construct Formulas Using Named Ranges ....Excel 114
    Consolidating data using named ranges
    Managing workbook names
Build a Logical Formula with the IF Function ....Excel 116
Build a Logical Formula with the AND Function ....Excel 118
    Using the OR and NOT logical functions
    Inserting an equation into a worksheet
Calculate Payments with the PMT Function ....Excel 120
    Calculating future value with the FV function
Practice .... Excel 122

Unit F: Managing Workbook Data ....Excel 129

View and Arrange Worksheets ....Excel 130
    Splitting the worksheet into multiple panes
Protect Worksheets and Workbooks ....Excel 132
    Freezing rows and columns
Save Custom Views of a Worksheet ....Excel 134
    Using Page Break Preview
Add a Worksheet Background ....Excel 136
    Working with Screenshots in Excel
Prepare a Workbook for Distribution..Excel 138
    Sharing a workbook using SkyDrive
Insert Hyperlinks...Excel 140
    Working with Headers and Footers
    Using research tools
Save a Workbook for Distribution...Excel 142
    Understanding Excel file formats
Group Worksheets..Excel 144
    Adding a digital signature to a workbook
Practice .... Excel 146

Unit G: Managing Data Using Tables ....**Excel 153**

    Plan a Table ....Excel 154

    Create and Format a Table ....Excel 156
        Changing table style options

    Add Table Data ....Excel 158
        Selecting table elements

    Find and Replace Table Data ....Excel 160
        Using Find and Select features

    Delete Table Data ....Excel 162

    Sort Table Data ....Excel 164
        Sorting conditionally formatted data
        Specifying a custom sort order

    Use Formulas in a Table ....Excel 166
        Using structured references

    Print a Table ....Excel 168
        Setting a print area

    Practice ....Excel 170

Unit H: Analyzing Table Data ....**Excel 177**

    Filter a Table ....Excel 178

    Create a Custom Filter ....Excel 180
        Using more than one rule when conditionally formatting data

    Filter a Table with the Advanced Filter ....Excel 182
        Using advanced conditional formatting options

    Extract Table Data ....Excel 184
        Understanding the criteria range and the copy-to location

    Look Up Values in a Table ....Excel 186
        Finding records using the DGET function
        Using the HLOOKUP and MATCH functions

    Summarize Table Data ....Excel 188

    Validate Table Data ....Excel 190
        Restricting cell values and data length
        Adding input messages and error alerts

    Create Subtotals ....Excel 192

    Practice ....Excel 194

Cloud

Appendix: Working in the Cloud ....**Cloud 1**

    Understand Office 2013 in the Cloud ....Cloud 2

    Work Online ....Cloud 4
        Getting a Microsoft account

    Explore SkyDrive ....Cloud 6
        How to disable default saving to Skydrive

    Manage Files on SkyDrive ....Cloud 8

    Share Files ....Cloud 10
        Co-authoring documents

    Explore Office Web Apps ....Cloud 12
        Exploring other Office Web Apps

    Team Project ....Cloud 14

Glossary ....**Glossary 1**

Index ....**Index 6**

Preface

Welcome to *Microsoft Excel 2013 for Medical Professionals*. This book helps students learn Excel skills within the context of a medical setting. This book also has a unique design: each skill is presented on two facing pages, with steps on the left and screens on the right. The layout makes it easy to learn a skill without having to read a lot of text and flip pages to see an illustration.

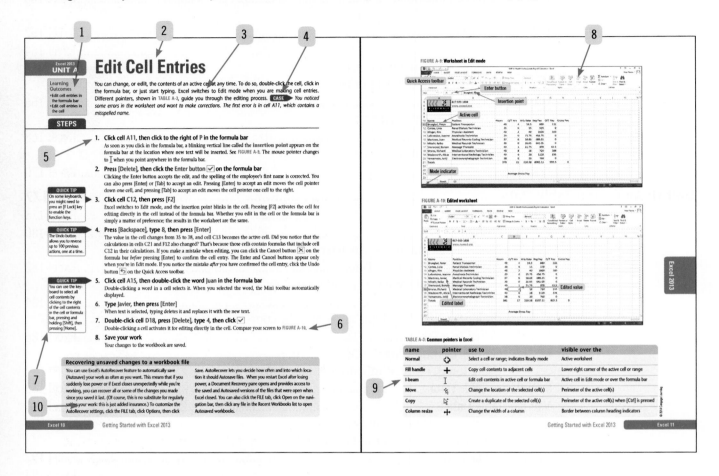

1 New! Learning Outcomes box lists measurable learning goals for which a student is accountable in that lesson.

2 Each two-page lesson focuses on a single skill.

3 Introduction briefly explains why the lesson skill is important.

4 A case scenario featuring the Riverwalk Medical Clinic motivates the steps and puts learning in a real-world medical context.

5 Step-by-step instructions and brief explanations guide students through each hands-on lesson activity.

6 New! Figure references are now in red bold to help students refer back and forth between the steps and screenshots.

7 Tips and troubleshooting advice, right where you need it—next to the step itself.

8 New! Larger screenshots with green callouts keep students on track as they complete steps.

9 Tables provide summaries of helpful information such as button references or keyboard shortcuts.

10 Clues to Use yellow boxes provide useful information related to the lesson skill.

Each example in the lessons and exercises features a spreadsheet or chart from a medical setting, providing context to help students succeed in the workplace. This book is an ideal learning tool for a wide range of learners—the "rookies" will find the clean design easy to follow and focused with only essential information presented, and the "hotshots" will appreciate being able to move quickly through the lessons to find the information they need without reading a lot of text. The design also makes this a great reference after the course is over! See the illustration on the left to learn more about the pedagogical and design elements of a typical lesson.

What's New in this Edition

- **Coverage** — This book helps students learn how to use Microsoft Excel 2013 including step-by-step instructions on creating worksheets, working with formulas and functions, and creating charts. Working in the Cloud appendix helps students learn to use SkyDrive to save, share, and manage files in the cloud and to use Office Web Apps.

- **New! Learning Outcomes** — Each lesson displays a green Learning Outcomes box that lists skills-based or knowledge-based learning goals for which students are accountable. Each Learning Outcome maps to a variety of learning activities and assessments. (See the *New! Learning Outcomes* section on page xiii for more information.)

- **New! Updated Design** — This edition features many new design improvements to engage students — including larger lesson screenshots with green callouts placed on top, and a refreshed Unit Opener page.

- **New! Independent Challenge 4: Explore** — This new case-based assessment activity allows students to explore new skills and use creativity to solve a problem or create a project.

Assignments

This book includes a wide variety of high quality assignments you can use for practice and assessment. Assignments include:

- **Concepts Review** — Multiple choice, matching, and screen identification questions.

- **Skills Review** — Step-by-step, hands-on review of every skill covered in the unit.

- **Independent Challenges 1–3** — Case projects requiring critical thinking and application of the unit skills. The Independent Challenges increase in difficulty. The first one in each unit provides the most hand-holding; the subsequent ones provide less guidance and require more critical thinking and independent problem solving.

- **Independent Challenge 4: Explore** — Case projects that let students explore new skills that are related to the core skills covered in the unit and are often more open ended, allowing students to use creativity to complete the assignment.

- **Visual Workshop** — Critical thinking exercises that require students to create a project by looking at a completed solution; they must apply the skills they've learned in the unit and use critical thinking skills to create the project from scratch.

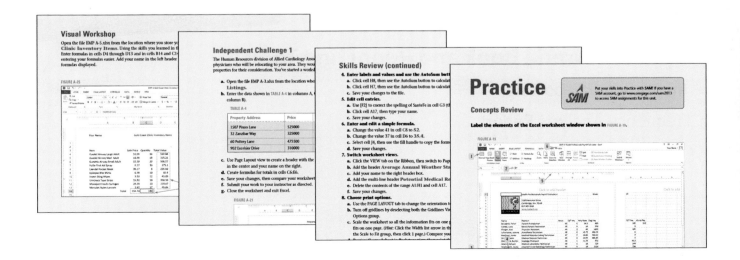

WHAT'S NEW FOR SAM 2013?

Get your students workplace ready with  **SAM**

The market-leading assessment and training solution for Microsoft Office

SAM 2013

Exciting New Features and Content

➤ Computer Concepts Trainings and Assessments *(shown on monitor)*

➤ Student Assignment Calendar

➤ Mac Hints

➤ More MindTap Readers

More Efficient Course Setup and Management Tools

➤ Individual Assignment Tool

➤ Video Playback of Student Clickpaths

➤ Express Assignment Creation Tool

Improved Grade Book and Reporting Tools

➤ Institutional Reporting

➤ Frequency Analysis Report

➤ Grade Book Enhancements

SAM's active, hands-on environment helps students master Microsoft Office skills and computer concepts that are essential to academic and career success.

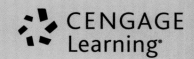
CENGAGE Learning

New! Learning Outcomes

Every 2-page lesson in this book now contains a green **Learning Outcomes box** that states the learning goals for that lesson.

- **What is a learning outcome?** A learning outcome states what a student is expected to know or be able to do after completing a lesson. Each learning outcome is skills-based or knowledge-based and is *measurable*. Learning outcomes map to learning activities and assessments.

- **How do students benefit from learning outcomes?** Learning outcomes tell students exactly what skills and knowledge they are *accountable* for learning in that lesson. This helps students study more efficiently and effectively and makes them more active learners.

- **How do instructors benefit from learning outcomes?** Learning outcomes provide clear, measurable, skills-based learning goals that map to various high-quality learning activities and assessments. A **Learning Outcomes Map**, available for each unit in this book, maps every learning outcome to the learning activities and assessments shown below.

Learning Outcomes Map to These Learning Activities:

1. **Book lessons:** Step-by-step tutorial on one skill presented in a two-page learning format
2. **SAM Training:** Short animations and hands-on practice activities in simulated environment

Learning Outcomes Map to These Assessments:

1. **End-of-Unit Exercises: Concepts Review** (screen identification, matching, multiple choice); **Skills Review** (hands-on review of each lesson); **Independent Challenges** (hands-on, case-based review of specific skills); **Visual Workshop** (activity that requires student to build a project by looking at a picture of the final solution).
2. **Exam View Test Banks:** Objective-based questions you can use for online or paper testing.
3. **SAM Assessment:** Performance-based assessment in a simulated environment (SAM sold separately.)
4. **Extra Independent Challenges:** Extra case-based exercises available in the Instructor Resources that cover various skills.

Learning Outcomes Map

A **Learning Outcomes Map**, contained in the Instructor Resources, provides a listing of learning activities and assessments for each learning outcome in the book.

Learning Outcomes Map
Microsoft Excel 2013 for Medical Professionals
Unit B

KEY:
IC=Independent Challenge   EIC=Extra Independent Challenge
VW=Visual Workshop   CS=Capstone

	Concepts Review	Skills Review	IC1	IC2	IC3	IC4	VW	EIC 1	EIC 2	Test Bank	SAM Assessment	SAM Training
Create a Complex Formula												
Create a Complex Formula by pointing		✓	✓		✓	✓	✓			✓	✓	✓
Use the fill handle and Auto Fill	✓	✓	✓	✓	✓	✓	✓			✓		
Insert a Function												
Use the Insert Function button		✓	✓	✓	✓	✓	✓			✓	✓	✓
Select a range for use in a function		✓	✓	✓	✓	✓	✓			✓	✓	✓
Select a function from the Sum list arrow		✓	✓	✓	✓	✓	✓				✓	
Type a Function												
Select a fun...					✓							

Instructor Resources

This book comes with a wide array of high-quality technology-based, teaching tools to help you teach and to help students learn. The following teaching tools are available for download at our Instructor Companion Site. Simply search for this text at *login.cengage.com*. An instructor login is required.

- **New! Learning Outcomes Map** — A detailed grid for each unit (in Excel format) shows the learning activities and assessments that map to each learning outcome in that unit.

- **Instructor's Manual** — Available as an electronic file, the Instructor's Manual includes lecture notes with teaching tips for each unit.

- **Sample Syllabus** — Prepare and customize your course easily using this sample course outline.

- **PowerPoint Presentations** — Each unit has a corresponding PowerPoint presentation covering the skills and topics in that unit that you can use in lectures, distribute to your students, or customize to suit your course.

- **Figure Files** — The figures in the text are provided on the Instructor Resources site to help you illustrate key topics or concepts. You can use these to create your own slide shows or learning tools.

- **Solution Files** — Solution Files are files that contain the finished project that students create or modify in the lessons or end-of-unit material.

- **Solutions Document** — This document outlines the solutions for the end-of-unit Concepts Review, Skills Review, Independent Challenges and Visual Workshops. An Annotated Solution File and Grading Rubric accompany each file and can be used together for efficient grading.

- **ExamView Test Banks** — ExamView is a powerful testing software package that allows you to create and administer printed, computer (LAN-based), and Internet exams. Our ExamView test banks include questions that correspond to the skills and concepts covered in this text, enabling students to generate detailed study guides that include page references for further review. The computer-based and Internet testing components allow students to take exams at their computers, and also save you time by grading each exam automatically.

Key Facts About Using This Book

Data Files are needed: To complete many of the lessons and end-of-unit assignments, students need to start from partially completed Data Files, which help students learn more efficiently. By starting out with a Data File, students can focus on performing specific tasks without having to create a file from scratch. All Data Files are available as part of the Instructor Resources. Students can also download Data Files themselves for free at cengagebrain.com. (For detailed instructions, go to www.cengage.com/ct/studentdownload.)

System requirements: This book was developed using Microsoft Office 2013 Professional running on Windows 8. Note that Windows 8 is not a requirement for the units on Microsoft Office; Office 2013 runs virtually the same on Windows 7 and Windows 8. Please see Important Notes for Windows 7 Users on the next page for more information.

Screen resolution: This book was written and tested on computers with monitors set at a resolution of 1366 x 768. If your screen shows more or less information than the figures in this book, your monitor is probably set at a higher or lower resolution. If you don't see something on your screen, you might have to scroll down or up to see the object identified in the figure.

Tell Us What You Think!

We want to hear from you! Please email your questions, comments, and suggestions to the Illustrated Series team at: **illustratedseries@cengage.com**

Important Notes for Windows 7 Users

The screenshots in this book show Microsoft Office 2013 running on Windows 8. However, if you are using Microsoft Windows 7, you can still use this book because Office 2013 runs virtually the same on both platforms. There are only two differences that you will encounter if you are using Windows 7. Read this section to understand the differences.

Dialog boxes

If you are a Windows 7 user, dialog boxes shown in this book will look slightly different than what you see on your screen. Dialog boxes for Windows 7 have a light blue title bar, instead of a medium blue title bar. However, beyond this superficial difference in appearance, the options in the dialog boxes across platforms are the same. For instance, the screen shots below show the Font dialog box running on Windows 7 and the Font dialog box running on Windows 8.

FIGURE 1: **Font dialog box in Windows 7**

FIGURE 2: **Font dialog box in Windows 8**

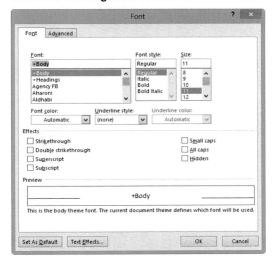

Alternate Steps for Starting an App in Windows 7

Nearly all of the steps in this book work exactly the same for Windows 7 users. However, starting an app (or program/application) requires different steps for Windows 7. The steps below show the Windows 7 steps for starting an app. (Note: Windows 7 alternate steps also appear in red Trouble boxes next to any step in the book that requires starting an app.)

Starting an app (or program/application) using Windows 7

1. Click the **Start button** on the taskbar to open the Start menu.
2. Click **All Programs**, then click the **Microsoft Office 2013 folder**. See Figure 3.
3. Click the app you want to use (such as **Excel 2013**).

FIGURE 3: **Starting an app using Windows 7**

Acknowledgements

Author Acknowledgements

Creating a book of this magnitude is a team effort. I would like to thank my husband, Michael, as well as Christina Kling-Garrett, the project manager, and my development editor, Marj Hopper, for her suggestions and corrections. I would also like to thank the production and editorial staff for all their hard work that made this project a reality.

–Elizabeth Eisner Reding

Thanks to Barbara Clemens for her insightful contributions, invaluable feedback, great humor, and patience. Thanks also to Christina Kling-Garrett for her encouragement and support in guiding and managing this project.

–Lynn Wermers

Advisory Board Acknowledgements

We thank our Illustrated Advisory Board who gave us their opinions and guided our decisions as we developed all of the new editions for Microsoft Office 2013.

Merlin Amirtharaj, Stanly Community College

Londo Andrews, J. Sargeant Reynolds Community College

Rachelle Hall, Glendale Community College

Terri Helfand, Chaffey Community College

Sheryl Lenhart, Terra Community College

Dr. Jose Nieves, Lord Fairfax Community College

Getting Started with Microsoft Office 2013

CASE ▶ This unit introduces you to the most frequently used programs in Office, as well as common features they all share.

Unit Objectives

After completing this unit, you will be able to:

- Understand the Office 2013 suite
- Start an Office app
- Identify Office 2013 screen elements
- Create and save a file

- Open a file and save it with a new name
- View and print your work
- Get Help, close a file, and exit an app

File You Will Need

OFFICE A-1.xlsx

©Dimec/Shutterstock

Understand the Office 2013 Suite

Learning
Outcomes
• Identify Office
  suite components
• Describe the
  features of each
  program

Microsoft Office 2013 is a group of programs--which are also called applications or apps--designed to help you create documents, collaborate with coworkers, and track and analyze information. You use different Office programs to accomplish specific tasks, such as writing a letter or producing a presentation, yet all the programs have a similar look and feel. Microsoft Office 2013 apps feature a common, context-sensitive user interface, so you can get up to speed faster and use advanced features with greater ease. The Office apps are bundled together in a group called a **suite**. The Office suite is available in several configurations, but all include Word, Excel, and PowerPoint. Other configurations include Access, Outlook, Publisher, and other programs. **CASE** ➤ As part of your job, you need to understand how each Office app is best used to complete specific tasks.

DETAILS

The Office apps covered in this book include:

QUICK TIP
The terms "program" and "app" are used interchangeably.

- ### Microsoft Word 2013
  When you need to create any kind of text-based document, such as a memo, newsletter, or multipage report, Word is the program to use. You can easily make your documents look great by inserting eye-catching graphics and using formatting tools such as themes, which are available in most Office programs. **Themes** are predesigned combinations of color and formatting attributes you can apply to a document. The Word document shown in FIGURE A-1 was formatted with the Organic theme.

- ### Microsoft Excel 2013
  Excel is the perfect solution when you need to work with numeric values and make calculations. It puts the power of formulas, functions, charts, and other analytical tools into the hands of every user, so you can analyze sales projections, calculate loan payments, and present your findings in a professional manner. The Excel worksheet shown in FIGURE A-1 tracks personal expenses. Because Excel automatically recalculates results whenever a value changes, the information is always up to date. A chart illustrates how the monthly expenses are broken down.

- ### Microsoft PowerPoint 2013
  Using PowerPoint, it's easy to create powerful presentations complete with graphics, transitions, and even a soundtrack. Using professionally designed themes and clip art, you can quickly and easily create dynamic slide shows such as the one shown in FIGURE A-1.

- ### Microsoft Access 2013
  Access is a relational database program that helps you keep track of large amounts of quantitative data, such as product inventories or employee records. The form shown in FIGURE A-1 was created for a grocery store inventory database. Employees use the form to enter data about each item. Using Access enables employees to quickly find specific information such as price and quantity.

Microsoft Office has benefits beyond the power of each program, including:

QUICK TIP
In Word, Excel, and PowerPoint, the interface can be modified to automatically open a blank document, workbook, or presentation. To do this, click the FILE tab, click Options, click Show the Start screen when this application starts (to deselect it), then click OK. The next time the program opens, it will open a blank document.

- ### Common user interface: Improving business processes
  Because the Office suite programs have a similar **interface**, or look and feel, your experience using one program's tools makes it easy to learn those in the other programs. In addition, Office documents are **compatible** with one another, meaning that you can easily incorporate, or **integrate**, an Excel chart into a PowerPoint slide, or an Access table into a Word document.

- ### Collaboration: Simplifying how people work together
  Office recognizes the way people do business today, and supports the emphasis on communication and knowledge sharing within companies and across the globe. All Office programs include the capability to incorporate feedback—called **online collaboration**—across the Internet or a company network.

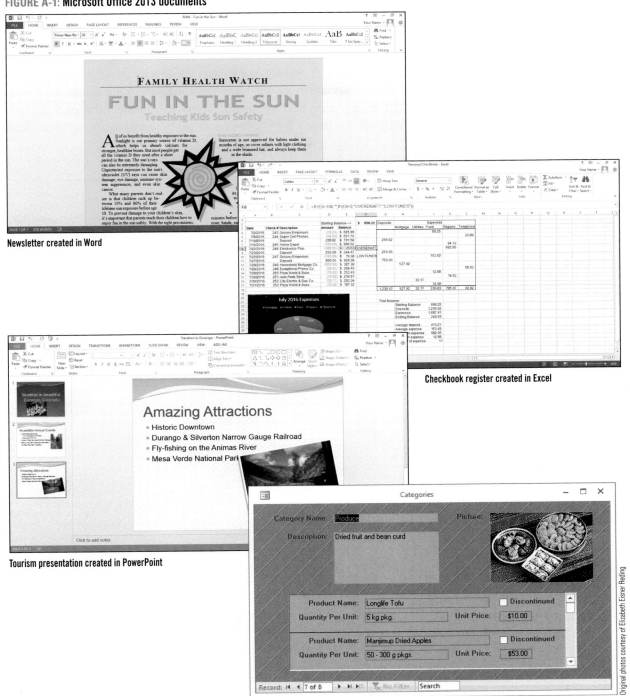

Newsletter created in Word

Checkbook register created in Excel

Tourism presentation created in PowerPoint

Store inventory form created in Access

What is Office 365?

Until the release of Microsoft Office 2013, most consumers purchased Microsoft Office in a traditional way: by buying a retail package from a store or downloading it from Microsoft.com. You can still purchase Microsoft Office 2013 in this traditional way--but you can also now purchase it as a subscription service called Microsoft Office 365 (for businesses) and Microsoft Office 365 Home Premium (for consumers). Office 365 requires businesses to pay a subscription fee for each user. Office 365 Home Premium Edition allows households to install Office on up to 5 devices. These subscription versions of Office provide extra services and are optimized for working in the cloud.

Start an Office App

Learning Outcomes
• Start an Office app
• Explain the purpose of a template
• Start a new blank document

To get started using Microsoft Office, you need to start, or **launch**, the Office app you want to use. If you are running Microsoft Office on Windows 8, an easy way to start the app you want is to go to the Start screen, type the app name you want to search for, then click the app name In the Results list. If you are running Windows 7, you start an app using the Start menu. (If you are running Windows 7, follow the Windows 7 steps at the bottom of this page.) **CASE** *You decide to familiarize yourself with Office by starting Microsoft Word.*

STEPS

1. **Go to the** Windows 8 Start screen

   Your screen displays a variety of colorful tiles for all the apps on your computer. You could locate the app you want to open by scrolling to the right until you see it, or you can type the app name to search for it.

2. **Type** word

   Your screen now displays "Word 2013" under "Results for 'word'", along with any other app that has "word" as part of its name (such as WordPad). See FIGURE A-2.

3. **Click** Word 2013

   Word 2013 launches, and the Word **start screen** appears, as shown in FIGURE A-3. The start screen is a landing page that appears when you first start an Office app. The left side of this screen displays recent files you have opened. (If you have never opened any files, then there will be no files listed under Recent.) The right side displays images depicting different templates you can use to create different types of documents. A **template** is a file containing professionally designed content that you can easily replace with your own. You can also start from scratch using the Blank Document option.

Starting an app using Windows 7

1. Click the Start button 🪟 on the taskbar
2. Click All Programs on the Start menu, click the Microsoft Office 2013 folder as shown in FIGURE A-4, then click Word 2013

Word 2013 launches, and the Word start screen appears, as shown previously in FIGURE A-3. The start screen is a landing page that appears when you first start an Office app. The left side of this screen displays recent files you have opened. (If you have never opened any files, then there will be no files listed under Recent.) The right side displays images depicting different templates you can use to create different types of documents. A **template** is a file containing professionally designed content that you can easily replace with your own. Using a template to create a document can save time and ensure that your document looks great. You can also start from scratch using the Blank Document option.

Using shortcut keys to move between Office programs

You can switch between open apps using a keyboard shortcut. The [Alt][Tab] keyboard combination lets you either switch quickly to the next open program or file or choose one from a gallery. To switch immediately to the next open program or file, press [Alt][Tab]. To choose from all open programs and files, press and hold [Alt], then press and release [Tab] without releasing [Alt]. A gallery opens on screen, displaying the filename and a thumbnail image of each open program and file, as well as of the desktop. Each time you press [Tab] while holding [Alt], the selection cycles to the next open file or location. Release [Alt] when the program, file, or location you want to activate is selected.

FIGURE A-2: Searching for Word app from the Start screen in Windows 8

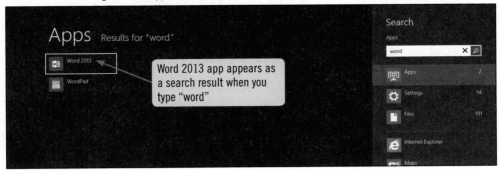

Word 2013 app appears as a search result when you type "word"

FIGURE A-3: Word start screen

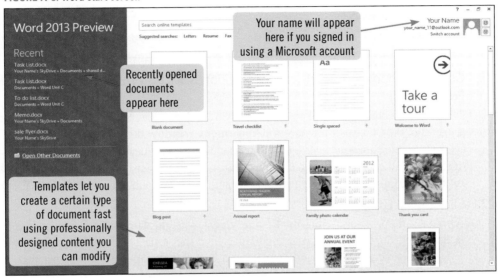

Your name will appear here if you signed in using a Microsoft account

Recently opened documents appear here

Templates let you create a certain type of document fast using professionally designed content you can modify

FIGURE A-4: Starting an app using Windows 7

Using the Office Clipboard

You can use the Office Clipboard to cut and copy items from one Office program and paste them into others. The Office Clipboard can store a maximum of 24 items. To access it, open the Office Clipboard task pane by clicking the dialog box launcher ⬚ in the Clipboard group on the HOME tab. Each time you copy a selection, it is saved in the Office Clipboard. Each entry in the Office Clipboard includes an icon that tells you the program it was created in. To paste an entry, click in the document where you want it to appear, then click the item in the Office Clipboard. To delete an item from the Office Clipboard, right-click the item, then click Delete.

Identify Office 2013 Screen Elements

Learning Outcomes
• Identify basic components of the user interface
• Display and use Backstage view
• Adjust the Zoom level

One of the benefits of using Office is that the programs have much in common, making them easy to learn and making it simple to move from one to another. Individual Office programs have always shared many features, but the innovations in the Office 2013 user interface mean even greater similarity among them all. That means you can also use your knowledge of one program to get up to speed in another. A **user interface** is a collective term for all the ways you interact with a software program. The user interface in Office 2013 provides intuitive ways to choose commands, work with files, and navigate in the program window. **CASE** *Familiarize yourself with some of the common interface elements in Office by examining the PowerPoint program window.*

STEPS

1. **Go to the Windows 8 Start screen, type pow, click PowerPoint 2013, then click Blank Presentation**

   PowerPoint becomes the active program displaying a blank slide. Refer to **FIGURE A-5** to identify common elements of the Office user interface. The **document window** occupies most of the screen. At the top of every Office program window is a **title bar** that displays the document name and program name. Below the title bar is the **Ribbon**, which displays commands you're likely to need for the current task. Commands are organized onto **tabs**. The tab names appear at the top of the Ribbon, and the active tab appears in front.

2. **Click the FILE tab**

   The FILE tab opens, displaying **Backstage view**. It is called Backstage view becausee the commands available here are for working with the files "behind the scenes." The navigation bar on the left side of Backstage view contains commands to perform actions common to most Office programs.

3. **Click the Back button ⊙ to close Backstage view and return to the document window, then click the DESIGN tab on the Ribbon**

   To display a different tab, click its name. Each tab contains related commands arranged into **groups** to make features easy to find. On the DESIGN tab, the Themes group displays available design themes in a **gallery**, or visual collection of choices you can browse. Many groups contain a **dialog box launcher**, which you can click to open a dialog box or pane from which to choose related commands.

4. **Move the mouse pointer ⤧ over the Ion theme in the Themes group as shown in FIGURE A-6, but *do not click* the mouse button**

   The Ion theme is temporarily applied to the slide in the document window. However, because you did not click the theme, you did not permanently change the slide. With the **Live Preview** feature, you can point to a choice, see the results, then decide if you want to make the change. Live Preview is available throughout Office.

5. **Move ⤧ away from the Ribbon and towards the slide**

   If you had clicked the Ion theme, it would be applied to this slide. Instead, the slide remains unchanged.

6. **Point to the Zoom slider | — | + | 100% | on the status bar, then drag to the right until the Zoom level reads 166%**

   The slide display is enlarged. Zoom tools are located on the status bar. You can drag the slider or click the Zoom In or Zoom Out buttons to zoom in or out on an area of interest. **Zooming in** (a higher percentage), makes a document appear bigger on screen but less of it fits on the screen at once; **zooming out** (a lower percentage) lets you see more of the document at a reduced size.

7. **Click the Zoom Out button − on the status bar to the left of the Zoom slider until the Zoom level reads 120%**

Getting Started with Microsoft Office 2013

FIGURE A-5: PowerPoint program window

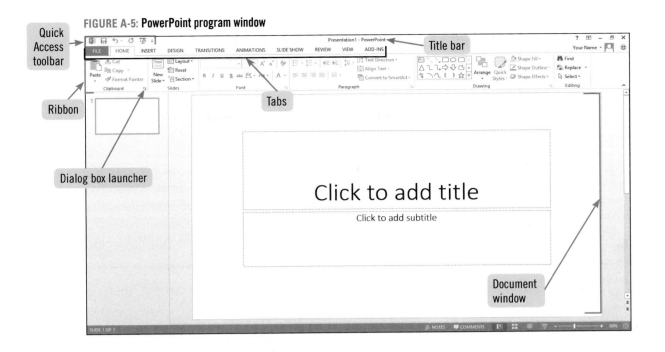

FIGURE A-6: Viewing a theme with Live Preview

Using Backstage view

Backstage view in each Microsoft Office program offers "one stop shopping" for many commonly performed tasks, such as opening and saving a file, printing and previewing a document, defining document properties, sharing information, and exiting a program. Backstage view opens when you click the FILE tab in any Office program, and while features such as the Ribbon, Mini toolbar, and Live Preview all help you work *in* your documents, the FILE tab and Backstage view help you work *with* your documents. You can return to your active document by pressing the Back button.

Office 2013

Create and Save a File

Learning Outcomes
• Create a file
• Save a file
• Explain SkyDrive

When working in an Office program, one of the first things you need to do is to create and save a file. A **file** is a stored collection of data. Saving a file enables you to work on a project now, then put it away and work on it again later. In some Office programs, including Word, Excel, and PowerPoint, you can open a new file when you start the program, then all you have to do is enter some data and save it. In Access, you must create a file before you enter any data. You should give your files meaningful names and save them in an appropriate location, such as a folder on your hard drive or SkyDrive so they're easy to find. **SkyDrive** is the Microsoft cloud storage system that lets you easily save, share, and access your files from anywhere you have Internet access. See "Saving Files to SkyDrive" for more information on this topic. **CASE** *Use Word to familiarize yourself with creating and saving a document. First you'll type some notes about a possible location for a corporate meeting, then you'll save the information for later use.*

STEPS

1. **Click the Word program button** 🔲 **on the taskbar, click Blank document, then click the Zoom In button** ➕ **until the level is 120%, if necessary**

2. **Type Locations for Corporate Meeting, then press [Enter] twice**
   The text appears in the document window, and the **insertion point** blinks on a new blank line. The insertion point indicates where the next typed text will appear.

3. **Type Las Vegas, NV, press [Enter], type San Diego, CA, press [Enter], type Seattle, WA, press [Enter] twice, then type your name**

4. **Click the Save button** 🔲 **on the Quick Access toolbar**
   Backstage view opens showing various options for saving the file, as shown in FIGURE A-7.

5. **Click Computer, then click Browse**
   Because this is the first time you are saving this document, the Save As command is displayed. Once you choose a location where you will save the file, the Save As dialog box displays, as shown in FIGURE A-8. Once a file is saved, clicking 🔲 saves any changes to the file *without* opening the Save As dialog box. The Address bar in the Save As dialog box displays the default location for saving the file, but you can change it to any location. The File name field contains a suggested name for the document based on text in the file, but you can enter a different name.

6. **Type OF A-Potential Corporate Meeting Locations**
   The text you type replaces the highlighted text. (The "OF A-" in the filename indicates that the file is created in Office Unit A. You will see similar designations throughout this book when files are named.)

7. **In the Save As dialog box, use the Address bar or Navigation Pane to navigate to the location where you store your Data Files**
   You can store files on your computer, a network drive, your SkyDrive, or any acceptable storage device.

8. **Click Save**
   The Save As dialog box closes, the new file is saved to the location you specified, and the name of the document appears in the title bar, as shown in FIGURE A-9. (You may or may not see the file extension ".docx" after the filename.) See TABLE A-1 for a description of the different types of files you create in Office, and the file extensions associated with each.

TABLE A-1: Common filenames and default file extensions

file created in	is called a	and has the default extension
Word	document	.docx
Excel	workbook	.xlsx
PowerPoint	presentation	.pptx
Access	database	.accdb

© 2014 Cengage Learning

FIGURE A-7: Save As screen in Backstage view

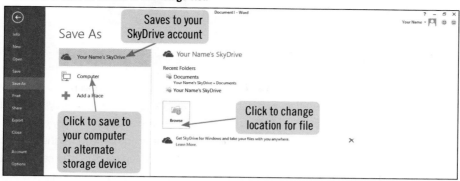

Saves to your SkyDrive account

Click to save to your computer or alternate storage device

Click to change location for file

FIGURE A-8: Save As dialog box

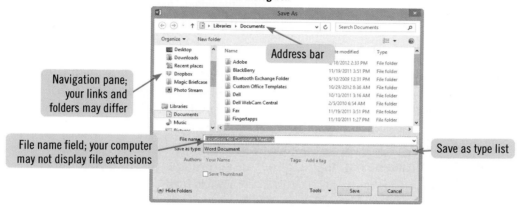

Address bar

Navigation pane; your links and folders may differ

File name field; your computer may not display file extensions

Save as type list

FIGURE A-9: Saved and named Word document

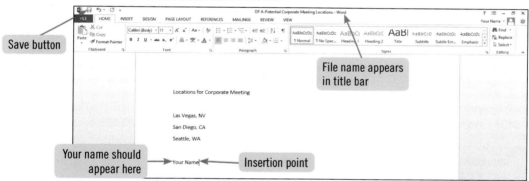

Save button

File name appears in title bar

Your name should appear here

Insertion point

Saving files to SkyDrive

All Office programs include the capability to incorporate feedback—called **online collaboration**—across the Internet or a company network. Using **cloud computing** (work done in a virtual environment), you can take advantage of commonly shared features such as a consistent interface. Using SkyDrive, a free file storage service from Microsoft, you and your colleagues can create and store documents in the cloud and make the documents available anywhere there is Internet access to whomever you choose. To use SkyDrive, you need a free Microsoft Account, which you obtain at the signup.live.com website. You can find more information about SkyDrive in the "Working in the Cloud" appendix. When you are logged into your Microsoft account and you save a file in any of the Office apps, the first option in the Save As screen is your SkyDrive. Double-click your SkyDrive option and the Save As dialog box opens displaying a location in the address bar unique to your SkyDrive account. Type a name in the File name text box, then click Save and your file is saved to your SkyDrive. To sync your files with SkyDrive, you'll need to download and install the SkyDrive for Windows app. Then, when you open Explorer, you'll notice a new folder called SkyDrive has been added to the Users folder. In this folder is a sub-folder called Documents, in which an updated copy of your Office app files resides. This means if your Internet connection fails, you can work on your files offline. The SkyDrive folder also displays Explorer in the list of Favorites folders.

Office 2013

Open a File and Save It with a New Name

Learning
Outcomes
• Open an existing
file
• Save a file with a
new name

In many cases as you work in Office, you start with a blank document, but often you need to use an existing file. It might be a file you or a coworker created earlier as a work in progress, or it could be a complete document that you want to use as the basis for another. For example, you might want to create a budget for this year using the budget you created last year; instead of typing in all the categories and information from scratch, you could open last year's budget, save it with a new name, and just make changes to update it for the current year. By opening the existing file and saving it with the Save As command, you create a duplicate that you can modify to suit your needs, while the original file remains intact. **CASE** *Use Excel to open an existing workbook file, and save it with a new name so the original remains unchanged.*

STEPS

TROUBLE
If you are running
WIndows 7, click
the Start button on
the taskbar, type
excel, then click
Excel 2013.

1. **Go to the Windows 8 Start screen, type exc, click Excel 2013, click Open Other Workbooks, click Computer on the navigation bar, then click Browse**

   The Open dialog box opens, where you can navigate to any drive or folder accessible to your computer to locate a file. You can click Recent Workbooks on the navigation bar to display a list of recent workbooks; click a file in the list to open it.

2. **In the Open dialog box, navigate to the location where you store your Data Files**

   The files available in the current folder are listed, as shown in FIGURE A-10. This folder displays one file.

TROUBLE
Click Enable Editing
on the Protected
View bar near the
top of your docu-
ment window if
prompted.

3. **Click OFFICE A-1.xlsx, then click Open**

   The dialog box closes, and the file opens in Excel. An Excel file is an electronic spreadsheet, so the new file displays a grid of rows and columns you can use to enter and organize data.

4. **Click the FILE tab, click Save As on the navigation bar, then click Browse**

   The Save As dialog box opens, and the current filename is highlighted in the File name text box. Using the Save As command enables you to create a copy of the current, existing file with a new name. This action preserves the original file and creates a new file that you can modify.

5. **Navigate to the location where you store your Data Files if necessary, type OF A-Budget for Corporate Meeting in the File name text box, as shown in FIGURE A-11, then click Save**

   A copy of the existing workbook is created with the new name. The original file, Office A-1.xlsx, closes automatically.

6. **Click cell A19, type your name, then press [Enter], as shown in FIGURE A-12**

   In Excel, you enter data in cells, which are formed by the intersection of a row and a column. Cell A19 is at the intersection of column A and row 19. When you press [Enter], the cell pointer moves to cell A20.

7. **Click the Save button 🖫 on the Quick Access toolbar**

   Your name appears in the workbook, and your changes to the file are saved.

Exploring File Open options

You might have noticed that the Open button in the Open dialog box includes a list arrow to the right of the button. In a dialog box, if a button includes a list arrow you can click the button to invoke the command, or you can click the list arrow to see a list of related commands that you can apply to a selected file in the file list. The Open list arrow includes several related commands, including Open Read-Only and Open as Copy.

Clicking Open Read-Only opens a file that you can only save with a new name; you cannot make changes to the original file. Clicking Open as Copy creates and opens a copy of the selected file and inserts the word "Copy" in the file's title. Like the Save As command, these commands provide additional ways to use copies of existing files while ensuring that original files do not get changed by mistake.

FIGURE A-10: Open dialog box

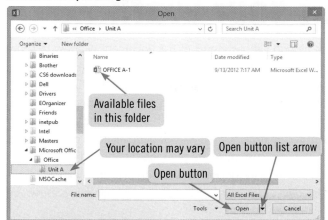

FIGURE A-11: Save As dialog box

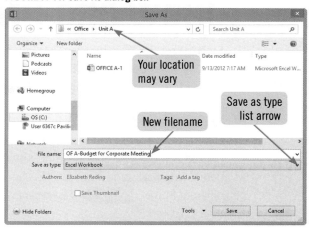

FIGURE A-12: Your name added to the workbook

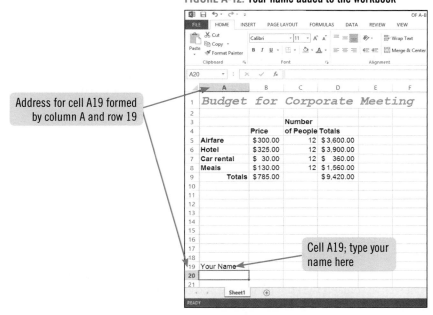

Working in Compatibility Mode

Not everyone upgrades to the newest version of Office. As a general rule, new software versions are **backward compatible**, meaning that documents saved by an older version can be read by newer software. To open documents created in older Office versions, Office 2013 includes a feature called Compatibility Mode. When you use Office 2013 to open a file created in an earlier version of Office, "Compatibility Mode" appears in the title bar, letting you know the file was created in an earlier but usable version of the program. If you are working with someone who may not be using the newest version of the software, you can avoid possible incompatibility problems by saving your file in another, earlier format. To do this in an Office program, click the FILE tab, click Save As on the navigation bar, click the location where you want to save the file, then click Browse. In the Save As dialog box, click the Save as type list arrow in the Save As dialog box, then click an option on the list. For example, if you're working in Excel, click Excel 97-2003 Workbook format in the Save as type list to save an Excel file so it can be opened in Excel 97 or Excel 2003.

View and Print Your Work

Each Microsoft Office program lets you switch among various **views** of the document window to show more or fewer details or a different combination of elements that make it easier to complete certain tasks, such as formatting or reading text. Changing your view of a document does not affect the file in any way, it affects only the way it looks on screen. If your computer is connected to a printer or a print server, you can easily print any Office document using the Print button on the Print tab in Backstage view. Printing can be as simple as **previewing** the document to see exactly what a document will look like when it is printed and then clicking the Print button. Or, you can customize the print job by printing only selected pages. The Backstage view can also be used to share your document with others, or to export it in a different format. **CASE** ▸ *Experiment with changing your view of a Word document, and then preview and print your work.*

STEPS

1. **Click the Word program button 🔲 on the taskbar**

   Word becomes the active program, and the document fills the screen.

2. **Click the VIEW tab on the Ribbon**

   In most Office programs, the VIEW tab on the Ribbon includes groups and commands for changing your view of the current document. You can also change views using the View buttons on the status bar.

3. **Click the Read Mode button in the Views group on the VIEW tab**

   The view changes to Read Mode view, as shown in FIGURE A-13. This view shows the document in an easy-to-read, distraction-free reading mode. Notice that the Ribbon is no longer visible on screen.

4. **Click the Print Layout button 🔲 on the Status bar**

   You return to Print Layout view, the default view in Word.

5. **Click the FILE tab, then click Print on the navigation bar**

   The Print tab opens in Backstage view. The preview pane on the right side of the window displays a preview of how your document will look when printed. Compare your screen to FIGURE A-14. Options in the Settings section enable you to change margins, orientation, and paper size before printing. To change a setting, click it, and then click a new setting. For instance, to change from Letter paper size to Legal, click Letter in the Settings section, then click Legal on the menu that opens. The document preview updates as you change the settings. You also can use the Settings section to change which pages to print. If your computer is connected to multiple printers, you can click the current printer in the Printer section, then click the one you want to use. The Print section contains the Print button and also enables you to select the number of copies of the document to print.

6. **If your school allows printing, click the Print button in the Print section (otherwise, click the Back button ⊖)**

   If you chose to print, a copy of the document prints, and Backstage view closes.

Customizing the Quick Access toolbar

You can customize the Quick Access toolbar to display your favorite commands. To do so, click the Customize Quick Access Toolbar button ⩢ in the title bar, then click the command you want to add. If you don't see the command in the list, click More Commands to open the Quick Access Toolbar tab of the current program's Options dialog box. In the Options dialog box, use the Choose commands from list to choose a category, click the desired command in the list on the left, click Add to add it to the Quick Access toolbar, then click OK. To remove a button from the toolbar, click the name in the list on the right in the Options dialog box, then click Remove. To add a command to the Quick Access toolbar as you work, simply right-click the button on the Ribbon, then click Add to Quick Access Toolbar on the shortcut menu. To move the Quick Access toolbar below the Ribbon, click the Customize Quick Access Toolbar button, and then click Show Below the Ribbon.

FIGURE A-13: Web Layout view

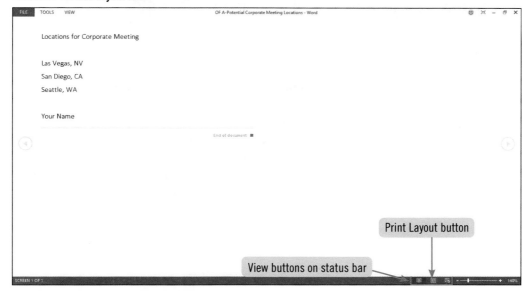

FIGURE A-14: Print settings on the FILE tab

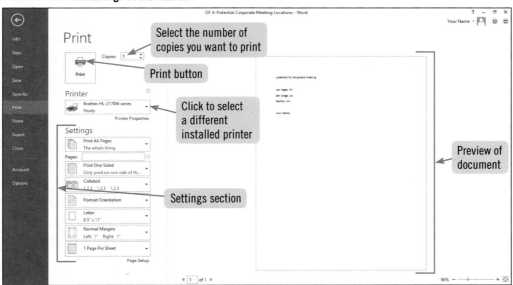

Creating a screen capture

A **screen capture** is a digital image of your screen, as if you took a picture of it with a camera. For instance, you might want to take a screen capture if an error message occurs and you want a Technical Support person to see exactly what's on the screen. You can create screen capture using features found in Windows 8 or Office 2013. Both Windows 7 and Windows 8 come with the Snipping Tool, a separate program designed to capture whole screens or portions of screens. To open the Snipping Tool, click the Start screen thumbnail, type "sni", then click the Snipping Tool when it appears in the left panel. After opening the Snipping Tool, click New, then drag the pointer on the screen to select the area of the screen you want to capture. When you release the mouse button, the screen capture opens in the Snipping Tool window, and you can save, copy, or send it in an email. In Word, Excel, and PowerPoint 2013, you can capture screens or portions of screens and insert them in the current document using the Screenshot button in the Illustrations group on the INSERT tab. And finally, you can create a screen capture by pressing [PrtScn]. (Keyboards differ, but you may find the [PrtScn] button in or near your keyboard's function keys.) Pressing this key places a digital image of your screen in the Windows temporary storage area known as the **Clipboard**. Open the document where you want the screen capture to appear, click the HOME tab on the Ribbon (if necessary), then click the Paste button in the Clipboard group on the HOME tab. The screen capture is pasted into the document.

Learning Outcomes
• Display a ScreenTip
• Use Help
• Close a file
• Exit an app

Get Help, Close a File, and Exit an App

You can get comprehensive help at any time by pressing [F1] in an Office app or clicking the Help button on the right end of the title bar. You can also get help in the form of a ScreenTip by pointing to almost any icon in the program window. When you're finished working in an Office document, you have a few choices regarding ending your work session. You close a file by clicking the FILE tab, then clicking Close; you exit a program by clicking the Close button on the title bar. Closing a file leaves a program running, while exiting a program closes all the open files in that program as well as the program itself. In all cases, Office reminds you if you try to close a file or exit a program and your document contains unsaved changes. **CASE** *Explore the Help system in Microsoft Office, and then close your documents and exit any open programs.*

STEPS

1. **Point to the Zoom button in the Zoom group on the VIEW tab of the Ribbon**
   A ScreenTip appears that describes how the Zoom button works and explains where to find other zoom controls.

QUICK TIP
You can also open Help (in any of the Office apps) by pressing [F1].

2. **Click the Microsoft Word Help (F1) button ⍰ in the upper-right corner of the title bar**
   The Word Help window opens, as shown in FIGURE A-15, displaying the home page for help in Word. Each entry is a hyperlink you can click to open a list of topics. The Help window also includes a toolbar of useful Help commands such as printing and increasing the font size for easier readability, and a Search field. If you are not connected to Office.com, a gold band is displayed telling you that you are not connected. Office.com supplements the help content available on your computer with a wide variety of up-to-date topics, templates, and training. If you are not connected to the Internet, the Help window displays only the help content available on your computer.

3. **Click the Learn Word basics link in the Getting started section of the Word Help window**
   The Word Help window changes, and a list of basic tasks appears below the topic.

4. **If necessary, scroll down until the Choose a template topic fills the Word Help window**
   The topic is displayed in the pane of the Help window, as shown in FIGURE A-16. The content in the window explains that you can create a document using a template (a pre-formatted document) or just create a blank document.

QUICK TIP
You can print the entire current topic by clicking the Print button 🖶 on the Help toolbar, then clicking Print in the Print dialog box.

5. **Click in the Search online help text box, type Delete, then press [Enter]**
   The Word Help window now displays a list of links to topics about different types of deletions that are possible within Word.

6. **Click the Keep Help on Top button ⍏ in the upper-right corner (below the Close button)**
   The Pin Help button rotates so the pin point is pointed towards the bottom of the screen: this allows you to read the Help window while you work on your document.

7. **Click the Word document window, then notice the Help window remains visible**

8. **Click a blank area of the Help window, click ⍏ to Unpin Help, click the Close button ☒ in the Help window, then click the Close button ☒ in the upper-right corner of the screen**
   Word closes, and the Excel program window is active.

9. **Click the Close button ☒ to exit Excel, click the Close button ☒ to exit the remaining Excel workbook, click the PowerPoint program button 🖳 on the taskbar if necessary, then click the Close button ☒ to exit PowerPoint**
   Excel and PowerPoint both close.

FIGURE A-15: Word Help window

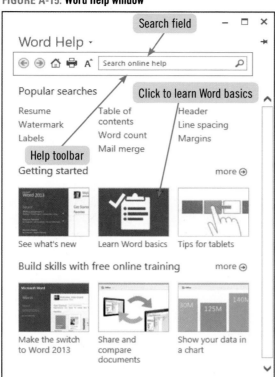

FIGURE A-16: Create a document Help topic

Enabling touch mode

If you are using a touch screen with any of the Office 2013 apps, you can enable the touch mode to give the user interface a more spacious look. Enable touch mode by clicking the Quick Access toolbar list arrow, then clicking Touch/Mouse Mode to select it. Then you'll see the Touch Mode button 👆 in the Quick Access toolbar. Click 👆, and you'll see the interface spread out.

Recovering a document

Each Office program has a built-in recovery feature that allows you to open and save files that were open at the time of an interruption such as a power failure. When you restart the program(s) after an interruption, the Document Recovery task pane opens on the left side of your screen displaying both original and recovered versions of the files that were open. If you're not sure which file to open (original or recovered), it's usually better to open the recovered file because it will contain the latest information. You can, however, open and review all versions of the file that were recovered and save the best one. Each file listed in the Document Recovery task pane displays a list arrow with options that allow you to open the file, save it as is, delete it, or show repairs made to it during recovery.

Practice

Concepts Review

Label the elements of the program window shown in FIGURE A-17.

FIGURE A-17

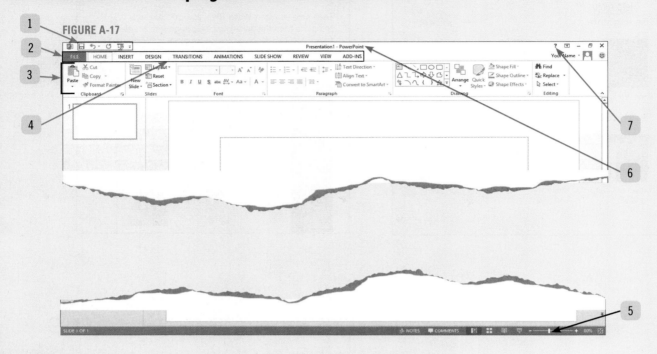

Match each project with the program for which it is best suited.

8. Microsoft Access   a. Corporate convention budget with expense projections

9. Microsoft Excel   b. Presentation for city council meeting

10. Microsoft Word   c. Business cover letter for a job application

11. Microsoft PowerPoint   d. Department store inventory

Independent Challenge 1

You just accepted an administrative position with a local independently owned produce vendor that has recently invested in computers and is now considering purchasing Microsoft Office for the company. You are asked to propose ways Office might help the business. You produce your document in Word.

a. Start Word, create a new Blank document, then save the document as **OF A-Microsoft Office Document** in the location where you store your Data Files.

b. Change the zoom factor to 120%, type **Microsoft Word**, press [Enter] twice, type **Microsoft Excel**, press [Enter] twice, type **Microsoft PowerPoint**, press [Enter] twice, type **Microsoft Access**, press [Enter] twice, then type your name.

c. Click the line beneath each program name, type at least two tasks you can perform using that program (each separated by a comma), then press [Enter].

d. Save the document, then submit your work to your instructor as directed.

e. Exit Word.

Getting Started with Excel 2013

CASE You have been hired as an assistant at Riverwalk Medical Clinic (RMC), a large outpatient medical facility staffed by family physicians, specialists, nurses, and other allied health professionals. You report to Tony Sanchez, R.N., the office manager. As Tony's assistant, you create worksheets to analyze data from various departments, so you can help him make sound decisions on company expansion and investments, as well as day-to-day operations.

Unit Objectives

After completing this unit, you will be able to:

- Understand spreadsheet software
- Identify Excel 2013 window components
- Understand formulas
- Enter labels and values and use the AutoSum button

- Edit cell entries
- Enter and edit a simple formula
- Switch worksheet views
- Choose print options

Files You Will Need

EMP A-1.xlsx
EMP A-2.xlsx
EMP A-3.xlsx
EMP A-4.xlsx
EMP A-5.xlsx

Understand Spreadsheet Software

Microsoft Excel is the electronic spreadsheet program within the Microsoft Office suite. An **electronic spreadsheet** is an application you use to perform numeric calculations and to analyze and present numeric data. One advantage of a spreadsheet program over pencil and paper is that your calculations are updated automatically, so you can change entries without having to manually recalculate. TABLE A-1 shows some of the common business tasks people accomplish using Excel. In Excel, the electronic spreadsheet you work in is called a **worksheet**, and it is contained in a file called a **workbook**, which has the file extension .xlsx. **CASE** ▶ *At Riverwalk Medical Clinic, you use Excel extensively to track finances and manage corporate data.*

DETAILS

When you use Excel, you have the ability to:

• **Enter data quickly and accurately**

With Excel, you can enter information faster and more accurately than with pencil and paper. FIGURE A-1 shows a payroll worksheet created using pencil and paper. FIGURE A-2 shows the same worksheet created using Excel. Equations were added to calculate the hours and pay. You can use Excel to recreate this information for each week by copying the worksheet's structure and the information that doesn't change from week to week, then entering unique data and formulas for each week.

• **Recalculate data easily**

Fixing typing errors or updating data is easy in Excel. In the payroll example, if you receive updated hours for an employee, you just enter the new hours and Excel recalculates the pay.

• **Perform what-if analysis**

The ability to change data and quickly view the recalculated results gives you the power to make informed business decisions. For instance, if you're considering raising the hourly rate for an entry-level tour guide from $12.50 to $15.00, you can enter the new value in the worksheet and immediately see the impact on the overall payroll as well as on the individual employee. Any time you use a worksheet to ask the question "What if?" you are performing **what-if analysis**. Excel also includes a Scenario Manager where you can name and save different what-if versions of your worksheet.

• **Change the appearance of information**

Excel provides powerful features, such as the Quick Analysis tool, for making information visually appealing and easier to understand. Format text and numbers in different fonts, colors, and styles to make it stand out.

• **Create charts**

Excel makes it easy to create charts based on worksheet information. Charts are updated automatically in Excel whenever data changes. The worksheet in FIGURE A-2 includes a 3-D pie chart.

• **Share information**

It's easy for everyone at RMC to collaborate in Excel using the company intranet, the Internet, or a network storage device. For example, you can complete the weekly payroll that your boss, Tony Sanchez, started creating. You can also take advantage of collaboration tools such as shared workbooks, so that multiple people can edit a workbook simultaneously.

• **Build on previous work**

Instead of creating a new worksheet for every project, it's easy to modify an existing Excel worksheet. When you are ready to create next week's payroll, you can open the file for last week's payroll, save it with a new filename, and modify the information as necessary. You can also use predesigned, formatted files called **templates** to create new worksheets quickly. Excel comes with many templates that you can customize.

FIGURE A-1: Traditional paper worksheet

Riverwalk Medical Clinic
Health Professionals Payroll Calculator

Name	Position	Hours	O/T Hours	Hrly Rate	Reg Pay	O/T Pay	Gross Pay
Brueghel, Pieter	Patient Transporter	40	4	16.50	666.00	132.00	792.00
Cortez, Livia	Renal Dialysis Technician	35	0	15.00	525.00	0.00	525.00
Klinger, Kim	Physician Assistant	40	2	40.00	1,600.00	160.00	1,760.00
Lafontaine, Jeanne	Anesthesia Technician	29	0	15.75	456.75	0.00	456.75
Martinez, Juan	Medical Records Coding Technician	37	0	18.63	689.31	0.00	689.31
Mioshi, Keiko	Medical Records Technician	39	0	16.95	661.05	0.00	661.05
Sherwood, Burton	Massage Therapist	40	1	21.75	870.00	43.50	913.50
Strano, Richard	Medical Laboratory Technician	40	8	18.00	720.00	288.00	1,008.00
Wadsworth, Alicia	Interventional Radiology Technician	40	5	28.00	1,120.00	280.00	1,400.00
Yamamoto, Johji	Electroencephalograph Technician	38	0	20.00	760.00	0.00	760.00

FIGURE A-2: Excel worksheet

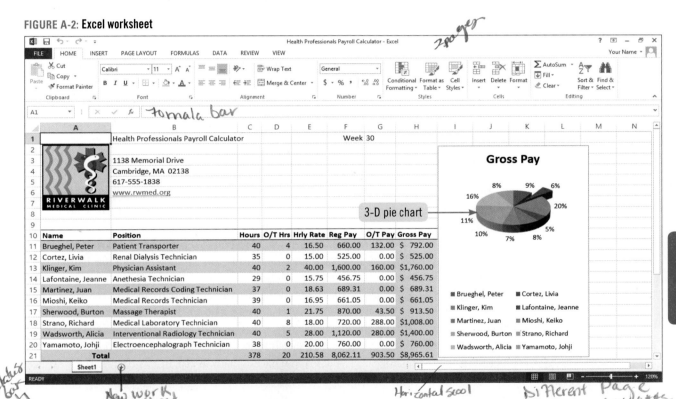

TABLE A-1: Business tasks you can accomplish using Excel

you can use spreadsheets to	by
Perform calculations	Adding formulas and functions to worksheet data; for example, adding a list of sales results or calculating a car payment
Represent values graphically	Creating charts based on worksheet data; for example, creating a chart that displays expenses
Generate reports	Creating workbooks that combine information from multiple worksheets, such as summarized sales information from multiple stores
Organize data	Sorting data in ascending or descending order; for example, alphabetizing a list of products or customer names, or prioritizing orders by date
Analyze data	Creating data summaries and short lists using PivotTables or AutoFilters; for example, making a list of the top 10 customers based on spending habits
Create what-if data scenarios	Using variable values to investigate and sample different outcomes, such as changing the interest rate or payment schedule on a loan

Identify Excel 2013 Window Components

Learning Outcomes
• Open and save an Excel file
• Identify Excel window elements

To start Excel, Microsoft Windows must be running. Similar to starting any program in Office, you can use the Start screen thumbnail on the Windows taskbar, the Start button on your keyboard, or you may have a shortcut on your desktop you prefer to use. If you need additional assistance, ask your instructor or technical support person. **CASE** ▶ *You decide to start Excel and familiarize yourself with the worksheet window.*

STEPS

1. **Start Excel, click Open Other Workbooks on the navigation bar, click Computer, then click Browse to open the Open dialog box**

2. **In the Open dialog box, navigate to the location where you store your Data Files, click EMP A-1.xlsx, then click Open**

   The file opens in the Excel window.

3. **Click the FILE tab, click Save As on the navigation bar, click Computer, then click Browse to open the Save As dialog box**

4. **In the Save As dialog box, navigate to the location where you store your Data Files, type EMP A-Health Professionals Payroll Calculator in the File name text box, then click Save**

   Using **FIGURE A-3** as a guide, identify the following items:

   • The **Name box** displays the active cell address. "A1" appears in the Name box.
   • The **formula bar** allows you to enter or edit data in the worksheet.
   • The **worksheet window** contains a grid of columns and rows. Columns are labeled alphabetically and rows are labeled numerically. The worksheet window can contain a total of 1,048,576 rows and 16,384 columns. The intersection of a column and a row is called a **cell**. Cells can contain text, numbers, formulas, or a combination of all three. Every cell has its own unique location or **cell address**, which is identified by the coordinates of the intersecting column and row. The column and row indicators are shaded to make identifying the cell address easy.
   • The **cell pointer** is a dark rectangle that outlines the cell you are working in. This cell is called the **active cell**. In **FIGURE A-3**, the cell pointer outlines cell A1, so A1 is the active cell. The column and row headings for the active cell are highlighted, making it easier to locate.
   • **Sheet tabs** below the worksheet grid let you switch from sheet to sheet in a workbook. By default, a workbook file contains one worksheet—but you can have as many as 255, in a workbook. The New sheet button to the right of Sheet 1 allows you to add worksheets to a workbook. **Sheet tab scrolling buttons** let you navigate to additional sheet tabs when available.
   • You can use the **scroll bars** to move around in a worksheet that is too large to fit on the screen at once.
   • The **status bar** is located at the bottom of the Excel window. It provides a brief description of the active command or task in progress. The **mode indicator** in the lower-left corner of the status bar provides additional information about certain tasks.

5. **Click cell D4**

   Cell D4 becomes the active cell. To activate a different cell, you can click the cell or press the arrow keys on your keyboard to move to it.

6. **Click cell C11, press and hold the mouse button, drag ⤢ to cell C20, then release the mouse button**

   You selected a group of cells and they are highlighted, as shown in **FIGURE A-4**. A selection of two or more cells such as C11:C20 is called a **range**; you select a range when you want to perform an action on a group of cells at once, such as moving them or formatting them. When you select a range, the status bar displays the average, count (or number of items selected), and sum of the selected cells as a quick reference.

FIGURE A-3: Open workbook

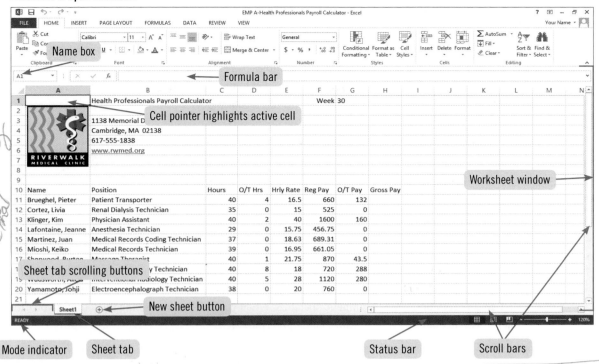

Name box
Formula bar
Cell pointer highlights active cell
Worksheet window
Sheet tab scrolling buttons
New sheet button
Mode indicator
Sheet tab
Status bar
Scroll bars

(handwritten note: Identify thing on the top ...)

FIGURE A-4: Selected range

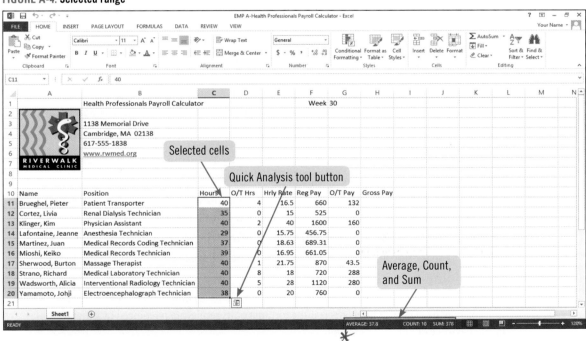

Selected cells
Quick Analysis tool button
Average, Count, and Sum

Using SkyDrive and Web Apps

If you have a free Microsoft account, you can save your Excel files to SkyDrive, a free cloud-based service from Microsoft. When you save files to SkyDrive, you can access them on other devices–such as a tablet or smart phone. SkyDrive is available as an app on smart phones, which makes access very easy. You can open files to view them on any device and you can even make edits to them using **Office Web Apps**, which are simplified versions of the apps found in the Office 2013 suite. Because the Web Apps are online, they take up no computer disk space, and you can use them on any Internet-connected device. You can find more information in the "Working in the Cloud" appendix.

Understand Formulas

Excel is a truly powerful program because users at every level of mathematical expertise can make calculations with accuracy. To do so, you use formulas. A **formula** is an equation in a worksheet. You use formulas to make calculations as simple as adding a column of numbers, or as complex as creating profit-and-loss projections for a global corporation. To tap into the power of Excel, you should understand how formulas work. **CASE** ▸ *Managers at RMC use the Health Professionals Payroll Calculator workbook to keep track of employee hours prior to submitting them to the Payroll Department. You'll be using this workbook regularly, so you need to understand the formulas it contains and how Excel calculates the results.*

STEPS

1. **Click cell F11**

   The active cell contains a formula, which appears on the formula bar. All Excel formulas begin with the equal sign (=). If you want a cell to show the result of adding 4 plus 2, the formula in the cell would look like this: =4+2. If you want a cell to show the result of multiplying two values in your worksheet, such as the values in cells C11 and E11, the formula would look like this: =C11*E11, as shown in **FIGURE A-5**. While you're entering a formula in a cell, the cell references and arithmetic operators appear on the formula bar. See **TABLE A-2** for a list of commonly used arithmetic operators. When you're finished entering the formula, you can either click the Enter button on the formula bar or press [Enter].

2. **Click cell G11**

   An example of a more complex formula is the calculation of overtime pay. At RMC, overtime pay is calculated at twice the regular hourly rate times the number of overtime hours. The formula used to calculate overtime pay for the employee in row 11 is:

   O/T Hrs times (2 times Hrly Rate)

   In the worksheet cell, you would enter: =D11*(2*E11), as shown in **FIGURE A-6**. The use of parentheses creates groups within the formula and indicates which calculations to complete first—an important consideration in complex formulas. In this formula, first the hourly rate is multiplied by 2, because that calculation is within the parentheses. Next, that value is multiplied by the number of overtime hours. Because overtime is calculated at twice the hourly rate, managers are aware that they need to closely watch this expense.

DETAILS

In creating calculations in Excel, it is important to:

- **Know where the formulas should be**

  An Excel formula is created in the cell where the formula's results should appear. This means that the formula calculating Gross Pay for the employee in row 11 will be entered in cell G11.

- **Know exactly what cells and arithmetic operations are needed**

  Don't guess; make sure you know exactly what cells are involved before creating a formula.

- **Create formulas with care**

  Make sure you know exactly what you want a formula to accomplish before it is created. An inaccurate formula may have far-reaching effects if the formula or its results are referenced by other formulas, as shown in the payroll example in **FIGURE A-6**.

- **Use cell references rather than values**

  The beauty of Excel is that whenever you change a value in a cell, any formula containing a reference to that cell is automatically updated. For this reason, it's important that you use cell references in formulas, rather than actual values, whenever possible.

- **Determine what calculations will be needed**

  Sometimes it's difficult to predict what data will be needed within a worksheet, but you should try to anticipate what statistical information may be required. For example, if there are columns of numbers, chances are good that both column and row totals should be present.

FIGURE A-5: Viewing a formula

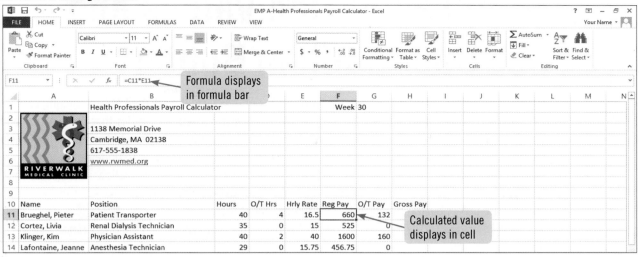

FIGURE A-6: Formula with multiple operators

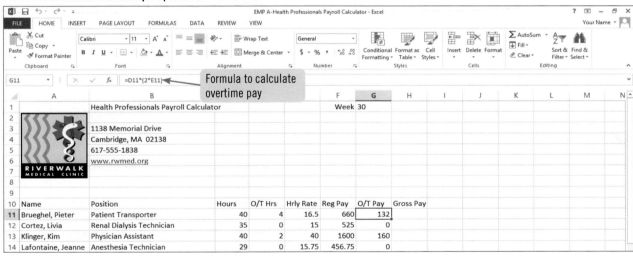

TABLE A-2: Excel arithmetic operators

operator	purpose	example
+	Addition	=A5+A7
-	Subtraction or negation	=A5-10
*	Multiplication	=A5*A7
/	Division	=A5/A7
%	Percent	=35%
^ (caret)	Exponent	=6^2 (same as 6^2)

Learning Outcomes
- Build formulas with the AutoSum button
- Copy formulas with the fill handle

Enter Labels and Values and Use the AutoSum Button

To enter content in a cell, you can type in the formula bar or directly in the cell itself. When entering content in a worksheet, you should start by entering all the labels first. **Labels** are entries that contain text and numerical information not used in calculations, such as "2016 Revenue" or "Travel Expenses". Labels help you identify data in worksheet rows and columns, making your worksheet easier to understand. **Values** are numbers, formulas, and functions that can be used in calculations. To enter a calculation, you type an equal sign (=) plus the formula for the calculation; some examples of an Excel calculation are "=2+2" and "=C5+C6". Functions are Excel's built-in formulas; you learn more about them in the next unit. **CASE** ▶ *You want to enter some information in the Health Professionals Payroll Calculator workbook, and use a very simple function to total a range of cells.*

STEPS

1. **Click cell A21, then click in the formula bar**

   Notice that the **mode indicator** on the status bar now reads "Edit," indicating you are in Edit mode. You are in Edit mode any time you are entering or changing the contents of a cell.

   QUICK TIP
   If you change your mind and want to cancel an entry in the formula bar, click the Cancel button ✖ on the formula bar.

2. **Type Totals, then click the Enter button ✔ on the formula bar**

   Clicking the Enter button accepts the entry. The new text is left-aligned in the cell. Labels are left-aligned by default, and values are right-aligned by default. Excel recognizes an entry as a value if it is a number or it begins with one of these symbols: +, -, =, @, #, or $. When a cell contains both text and numbers, Excel recognizes it as a label.

3. **Click cell C21**

   You want this cell to total the hours worked by all the trip advisors. You might think you need to create a formula that looks like this: =B11+B12+B13+B14+B15+B16+B17+B18+B19+B20. However, there's an easier way to achieve this result.

4. **Click the AutoSum button ∑ in the Editing group on the HOME tab on the Ribbon**

   The SUM function is inserted in the cell, and a suggested range appears in parentheses, as shown in FIGURE A-7. A **function** is a built-in formula; it includes the **arguments** (the information necessary to calculate an answer) as well as cell references and other unique information. Clicking the AutoSum button sums the adjacent range (that is, the cells next to the active cell) above or to the left, although you can adjust the range if necessary by selecting a different range before accepting the cell entry. Using the SUM function is quicker than entering a formula, and using the range C11:C20 is more efficient than entering individual cell references.

   QUICK TIP
   You can create formulas in a cell even before you enter the values to be calculated; the results will be recalculated as soon as the data is entered.

5. **Click ✔ on the formula bar**

   Excel calculates the total contained in cells C11:C20 and displays the result, 378, in cell C21. The cell actually contains the formula =SUM(C11:C20), and the result is displayed.

6. **Click cell D19, type 6, then press [Enter]**

   The number 6 replaces the cell's contents, the cell pointer moves to cell D20, and the value in cell G19 changes.

7. **Scroll down to cell D24, type Average Gross Pay, then press [Enter]**

   The new label is entered in cell D24. The contents appear to spill into the empty cells to the right.

   QUICK TIP
   You can also press [Tab] to complete a cell entry and move the cell pointer to the right.

8. **Click cell C21, position the pointer on the lower-right corner of the cell (the fill handle) so that the pointer changes to ✚, drag the ✚ to cell H21, then release the mouse button**

   Dragging the fill handle across a range of cells copies the contents of the first cell into the other cells in the range. In the range C21:H21, each filled cell now contains a function that sums the range of cells above, as shown in FIGURE A-8.

9. **Save your work**

FIGURE A-7: Creating a formula using the Sum button

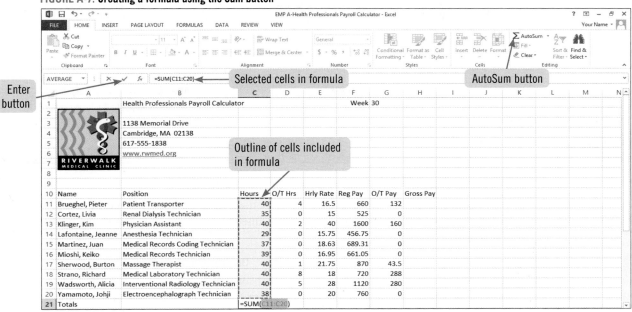

FIGURE A-8: Results of copied SUM functions

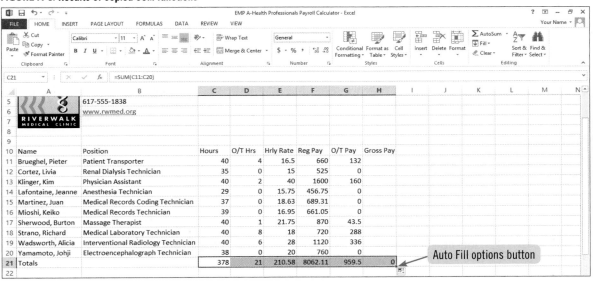

Navigating a worksheet

With over a million cells available in a worksheet, it is important to know how to move around in, or **navigate**, a worksheet. You can use the arrow keys on the keyboard ↑, ↓, →, or ← to move one cell at a time, or press [Page Up] or [Page Down] to move one screen at a time. To move one screen to the left press [Alt][Page Up]; to move one screen to the right press

[Alt][Page Down]. You can also use the mouse pointer to click the desired cell. If the desired cell is not visible in the worksheet window, use the scroll bars or use the Go To command by clicking the Find & Select button in the Editing group on the HOME tab on the Ribbon. To quickly jump to the first cell in a worksheet press [Ctrl][Home]; to jump to the last cell, press [Ctrl][End].

Getting Started with Excel 2013

Edit Cell Entries

Learning Outcomes
- Edit cell entries in the formula bar
- Edit cell entries in the cell

You can change, or **edit**, the contents of an active cell at any time. To do so, double-click the cell, click in the formula bar, or just start typing. Excel switches to Edit mode when you are making cell entries. Different pointers, shown in **TABLE A-3**, guide you through the editing process. **CASE** ▶ *You noticed some errors in the worksheet and want to make corrections. The first error is in cell A11, which contains a misspelled name.*

STEPS

1. **Click cell A11, then click to the right of P in the formula bar**

   As soon as you click in the formula bar, a blinking vertical line called the **insertion point** appears on the formula bar at the location where new text will be inserted. See **FIGURE A-9**. The mouse pointer changes to I when you point anywhere in the formula bar.

2. **Press [Delete], then click the Enter button ✓ on the formula bar**

   Clicking the Enter button accepts the edit, and the spelling of the employee's first name is corrected. You can also press [Enter] or [Tab] to accept an edit. Pressing [Enter] to accept an edit moves the cell pointer down one cell, and pressing [Tab] to accept an edit moves the cell pointer one cell to the right.

   QUICK TIP
   On some keyboards, you might need to press an [F Lock] key to enable the function keys.

3. **Click cell C12, then press [F2]**

   Excel switches to Edit mode, and the insertion point blinks in the cell. Pressing [F2] activates the cell for editing directly in the cell instead of the formula bar. Whether you edit in the cell or the formula bar is simply a matter of preference; the results in the worksheet are the same.

   QUICK TIP
   The Undo button allows you to reverse up to 100 previous actions, one at a time.

4. **Press [Backspace], type 8, then press [Enter]**

   The value in the cell changes from 35 to 38, and cell C13 becomes the active cell. Did you notice that the calculations in cells C21 and F12 also changed? That's because those cells contain formulas that include cell C12 in their calculations. If you make a mistake when editing, you can click the Cancel button ✕ on the formula bar *before* pressing [Enter] to confirm the cell entry. The Enter and Cancel buttons appear only when you're in Edit mode. If you notice the mistake *after* you have confirmed the cell entry, click the Undo button ↺ on the Quick Access toolbar.

   QUICK TIP
   You can use the keyboard to select all cell contents by clicking to the right of the cell contents in the cell or formula bar, pressing and holding [Shift], then pressing [Home].

5. **Click cell A15, then double-click the word Juan in the formula bar**

   Double-clicking a word in a cell selects it. When you selected the word, the Mini toolbar automatically displayed.

6. **Type Javier, then press [Enter]**

   When text is selected, typing deletes it and replaces it with the new text.

7. **Double-click cell D18, press [Delete], type 4, then click ✓**

   Double-clicking a cell activates it for editing directly in the cell. Compare your screen to **FIGURE A-10**.

8. **Save your work**

   Your changes to the workbook are saved.

Recovering unsaved changes to a workbook file

You can use Excel's AutoRecover feature to automatically save (Autosave) your work as often as you want. This means that if you suddenly lose power or if Excel closes unexpectedly while you're working, you can recover all or some of the changes you made since you saved it last. (Of course, this is no substitute for regularly saving your work: this is just added insurance.) To customize the AutoRecover settings, click the FILE tab, click Options, then click Save. AutoRecover lets you decide how often and into which location it should Autosave files. When you restart Excel after losing power, a Document Recovery pane opens and provides access to the saved and Autosaved versions of the files that were open when Excel closed. You can also click the FILE tab, click Open on the navigation bar, then click any file in the Recent Workbooks list to open Autosaved workbooks.

FIGURE A-9: Worksheet in Edit mode

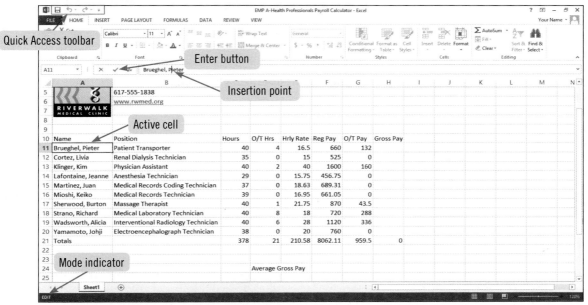

Quick Access toolbar

Enter button

Insertion point

Active cell

Mode indicator

FIGURE A-10: Edited worksheet

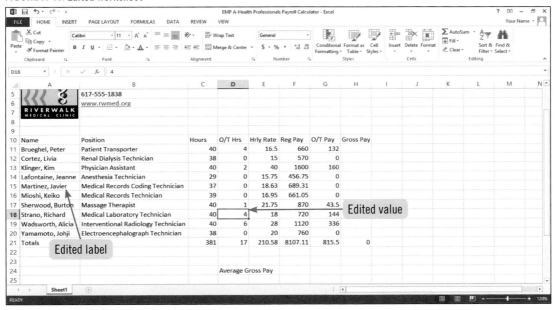

Edited value

Edited label

TABLE A-3: Common pointers in Excel

name	pointer	use to	visible over the
Normal	⬧	Select a cell or range; indicates Ready mode	Active worksheet
Fill handle	+	Copy cell contents to adjacent cells	Lower-right corner of the active cell or range
I-beam	I	Edit cell contents in active cell or formula bar	Active cell in Edit mode or over the formula bar
Move	⬧	Change the location of the selected cell(s)	Perimeter of the active cell(s)
Copy	⬧	Create a duplicate of the selected cell(s)	Perimeter of the active cell(s) when [Ctrl] is pressed
Column resize	++	Change the width of a column	Border between column heading indicators

Enter and Edit a Simple Formula

Learning Outcomes
• Enter a formula
• Use cell references to create a formula

You use formulas in Excel to perform calculations such as adding, multiplying, and averaging. Formulas in an Excel worksheet start with the equal sign (=), also called the **formula prefix**, followed by cell addresses, range names, values, and **calculation operators**. Calculation operators indicate what type of calculation you want to perform on the cells, ranges, or values. They can include **arithmetic operators**, which perform mathematical calculations (see TABLE A-2 in the "Understand Formulas" lesson); **comparison operators**, which compare values for the purpose of true/false results; **text concatenation operators**, which join strings of text in different cells; and **reference operators**, which enable you to use ranges in calculations. **CASE** *You want to create a formula in the worksheet that calculates gross pay for each employee.*

STEPS

1. **Click cell H11**

   This is the first cell where you want to insert the formula. To calculate gross pay, you need to add regular pay and overtime pay. For employee Peter Brueghel, regular pay appears in cell F11 and overtime pay appears in cell G11.

   QUICK TIP
   You can reference a cell in a formula either by typing the cell reference or clicking the cell in the worksheet; when you click a cell to add a reference, the Mode indicator changes to "Point."

2. **Type =, click cell F11, type +, then click cell G11**

   Compare your formula bar to **FIGURE A-11**. The blue and red cell references in cell H11 correspond to the colored cell outlines. When entering a formula, it's a good idea to use cell references instead of values whenever you can. That way, if you later change a value in a cell (if, for example, Peter's regular pay changes to 690), any formula that includes this information reflects accurate, up-to-date results.

3. **Click the Enter button** **on the formula bar**

   The result of the formula =F11+G11, 792, appears in cell H11. This same value appears in cell H21 because cell H21 contains a formula that totals the values in cells H11:H20, and there are no other values at this time.

4. **Click cell G11**

   The formula in this cell calculates overtime pay by multiplying overtime hours (D11) times twice the regular hourly rate (2*E11). You want to edit this formula to reflect a new overtime pay rate.

5. **Click to the right of 2 in the formula bar, then type .5 as shown in FIGURE A-12**

   The formula that calculates overtime pay has been edited.

6. **Click** ✓ **on the formula bar**

   Compare your screen to **FIGURE A-13**. Notice that the calculated values in cells G21, H11, and H21 have all changed to reflect your edits to cell G11.

7. **Save your work**

Understanding named ranges

It can be difficult to remember the cell locations of critical information in a worksheet, but using cell names can make this task much easier. You can name a single cell or range of contiguous, or touching, cells. For example, you might name a cell that contains data on average gross pay "AVG_GP" instead of trying to remember the cell address C18. A named range must begin with a letter or an underscore. It cannot contain any spaces or be the same as a built-in name, such as a function or another object (such as a different named range) in the workbook. To name a range, select the cell(s) you want to name, click the Name box in the formula bar, type the name you want to use, then press [Enter]. You can also name a range by clicking the FORMULAS tab, then clicking the Define Name button in the Defined Names group. Type the new range name in the Name text box in the New Name dialog box, verify the selected range, then click OK. When you use a named range in a formula, the named range appears instead of the cell address. You can also create a named range using the contents of a cell already in the range. Select the range containing the text you want to use as a name, then click the Create from Selection button in the Defined Names group. The Create Names from Selection dialog box opens. Choose the location of the name you want to use, then click OK.

FIGURE A-11: Simple formula in a worksheet

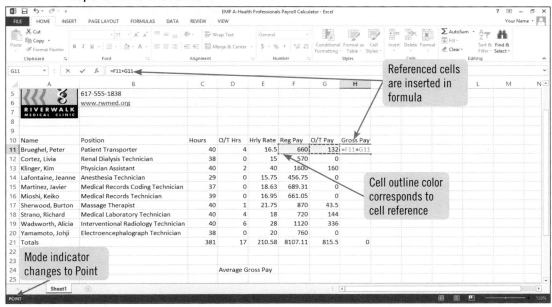

FIGURE A-12: Edited formula in a worksheet

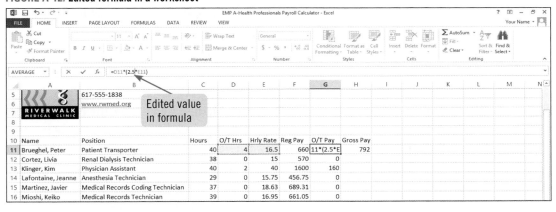

FIGURE A-13: Edited formula with changes

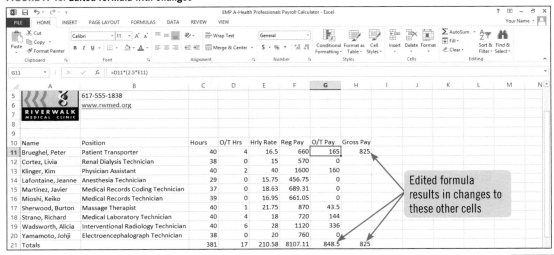

Switch Worksheet Views

Learning Outcomes
• Change worksheet views
• Create a header/footer
• Select a range

You can change your view of the worksheet window at any time, using either the VIEW tab on the Ribbon or the View buttons on the status bar. Changing your view does not affect the contents of a worksheet; it just makes it easier for you to focus on different tasks, such as entering content or preparing a worksheet for printing. The VIEW tab includes a variety of viewing options, such as View buttons, zoom controls, and the ability to show or hide worksheet elements such as gridlines. The status bar offers fewer View options but can be more convenient to use. **CASE** ▶ *You want to make some final adjustments to your worksheet, including adding a header so the document looks more polished.*

STEPS

QUICK TIP

Although a worksheet can contain more than a million rows and thousands of columns, the current document contains only as many pages as necessary for the current project.

1. **Press [Ctrl][Home] to return to cell A1, click the VIEW tab on the Ribbon, then click the Page Layout button in the Workbook Views group**

   The view switches from the default view, Normal, to Page Layout view. **Normal view** shows the worksheet without including certain details like headers and footers, or tools like rulers and a page number indicator; it's great for creating and editing a worksheet, but may not be detailed enough when you want to put the finishing touches on a document. **Page Layout view** provides a more accurate view of how a worksheet will look when printed, as shown in FIGURE A-14. The margins of the page are displayed, along with a text box for the header. A footer text box appears at the bottom of the page, but your screen may not be large enough to view it without scrolling. Above and to the left of the page are rulers. Part of an additional page appears to the right of this page. If the contents fit on a single page, the page to the right would appear dimmed, indicating that it does not contain any data. A page number indicator on the status bar tells you the current page and the total number of pages in this worksheet.

2. **Move the pointer ℞ over the header *without clicking***

   The header is made up of three text boxes: left, center, and right. Each text box is outlined in green as you pass over it with the pointer.

QUICK TIP

You can change header and footer information using the HEADER & FOOTER TOOLS DESIGN tab that opens on the Ribbon when a header or footer is active. For example, you can insert the date by clicking the Current Date button in the Header & Footer Elements group, or insert the time by clicking the Current Time button.

3. **Click the left header text box, type Riverwalk Medical Clinic, click the center header text box, type Health Prof Payroll Calculator, click the right header text box, then type Week 30**

   The new text appears in the text boxes, as shown in FIGURE A-15. You can also press the [Tab] key to advance from one header box to the next.

4. **Select the range B1:G1, then press [Delete]**

   The duplicate information you just entered in the header is deleted from cells in the worksheet.

5. **Click the VIEW tab if necessary, click the Ruler check box in the Show group, then click the Gridlines check box in the Show group**

   The rulers and the gridlines are hidden. By default, gridlines in a worksheet do not print, so hiding them gives you a more accurate image of your final document.

6. **Click the Page Break Preview button ▦ on the status bar**

   Your view changes to Page Break Preview, which displays a reduced view of each page of your worksheet, along with page break indicators that you can drag to include more or less information on a page.

7. **Drag the pointer ⬌ from the solid vertical page break indicator to the right of column I**

   See FIGURE A-16. When you're working on a large worksheet with multiple pages, sometimes you need to adjust where pages break; in this worksheet, however, you want the information to fit on one page.

QUICK TIP

Once you view a worksheet in Page Break Preview, the page break indicators appear as dotted lines after you switch back to Normal view or Page Layout view.

8. **Click the Page Layout button in the Workbook Views group, click the Ruler check box in the Show group, then click the Gridlines check box in the Show group**

   The rulers and gridlines are no longer hidden. You can show or hide VIEW tab items in any view.

9. **Save your work**

FIGURE A-14: Page Layout view

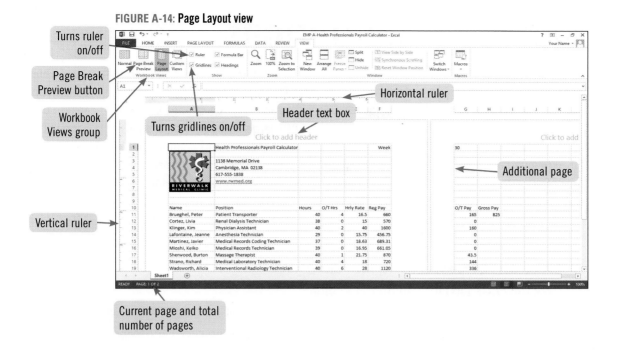

Turns ruler on/off

Page Break Preview button

Workbook Views group

Turns gridlines on/off

Header text box

Horizontal ruler

Additional page

Vertical ruler

Current page and total number of pages

FIGURE A-15: Header text entered

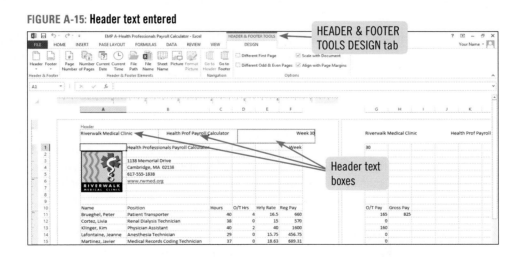

HEADER & FOOTER TOOLS DESIGN tab

Header text boxes

FIGURE A-16: Page Break Preview

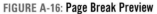

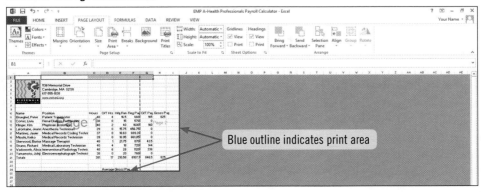

Blue outline indicates print area

Choose Print Options

Learning Outcomes
• Change the page orientation
• Hide/view gridlines when printing
• Preview and print a worksheet

Before printing a document, you may want to review it using the PAGE LAYOUT tab to fine-tune your printed output. You can use tools on the PAGE LAYOUT tab to adjust print orientation (the direction in which the content prints across the page), paper size, and location of page breaks. You can also use the Scale to Fit options on the PAGE LAYOUT tab to fit a large amount of data on a single page without making changes to individual margins, and to turn gridlines and column/row headings on and off. When you are ready to print, you can set print options such as the number of copies to print and the correct printer, and you can preview your document in Backstage view using the FILE tab. You can also adjust page layout settings from within Backstage view and immediately see the results in the document preview. **CASE** *You are ready to prepare your worksheet for printing.*

STEPS

1. **Click cell A24, type your name, then click** ✓

2. **Click the PAGE LAYOUT tab on the Ribbon**
   Compare your screen to FIGURE A-17. The solid outline indicates the default **print area**, the area to be printed.

3. **Click the Orientation button in the Page Setup group, then click Landscape**
   The paper orientation changes to **landscape**, so the contents will print across the length of the page instead of across the width.

   You could return to the **portrait** orientation, so the contents would print across the width of the page by clicking the Orientation button in the Page Setup group, then clicking Portrait.

4. **Click the Gridlines View check box in the Sheet Options group on the PAGE LAYOUT tab, click the Gridlines Print check box to select it if necessary, then save your work**
   Printing gridlines makes the data easier to read, but the gridlines will not print unless the Gridlines Print check box is checked.

5. **Click the FILE tab, then click Print on the navigation bar**
   The Print tab in Backstage view displays a preview of your worksheet exactly as it will look when it is printed. To the left of the worksheet preview, you can also change a number of document settings and print options. To open the Page Setup dialog box and adjust page layout options, click the Page Setup link in the Settings section. Compare your preview screen to FIGURE A-18. You can print from this view by clicking the Print button, or return to the worksheet without printing by clicking the Back button ⬅. You can also print an entire workbook from the Backstage view by clicking the Print button in the Settings section, then selecting the active sheet or entire workbook.

6. **Compare your settings to FIGURE A-18, then click the Print button**
   One copy of the worksheet prints.

7. **Submit your work to your instructor as directed, then exit Excel**

Printing worksheet formulas

Sometimes you need to keep a record of all the formulas in a worksheet. You might want to do this to see exactly how you came up with a complex calculation, so you can explain it to others. To prepare a worksheet to show formulas rather than results when printed, open the workbook containing the formulas you want to print. Click the FORMULAS tab, then click the Show Formulas button in the Formula Auditing group to select it. When the Show Formulas button is selected, formulas rather than resulting values are displayed in the worksheet on screen and when printed. (The Show Formulas button is a *toggle*: click it again to hide the formulas.)

FIGURE A-17: Worksheet with Portrait orientation

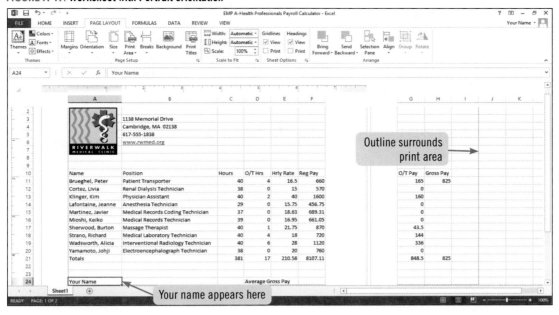

FIGURE A-18: Worksheet in Backstage view

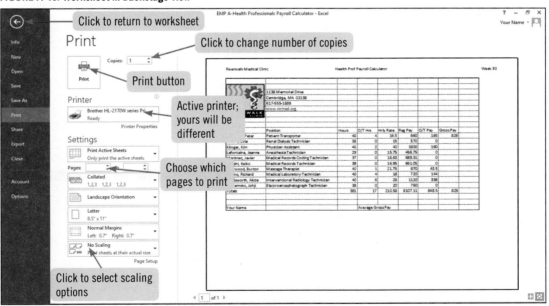

Scaling to fit

If you have a large amount of data that you want to fit to a single sheet of paper, but you don't want to spend a lot of time trying to adjust the margins and other settings, you have several options. You can easily print your work on a single sheet by clicking the No Scaling list arrow in the Settings section on the Print button in Backstage view, then clicking Fit Sheet on One Page. Another method for fitting worksheet content onto one page is to click the PAGE LAYOUT tab, then change the Width and Height settings in the Scale to Fit group each to 1 Page. You can also use the Fit to option in the Page Setup dialog box to fit a worksheet on one page. To open the Page Setup dialog box, click the dialog box launcher in the Scale to Fit group on the PAGE LAYOUT tab, or click the Page Setup link on the Print tab in Backstage view. Make sure the Page tab is selected in the Page Setup dialog box, then click the Fit to option button.

Practice

Concepts Review

Label the elements of the Excel worksheet window shown in FIGURE A-19.

FIGURE A-19

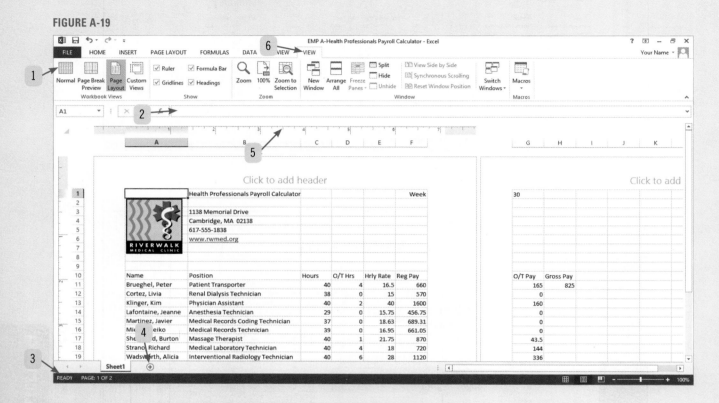

Match each term with the statement that best describes it.

7. **Cell**

8. **Orientation**

9. **Normal view**

10. **Formula prefix**

11. **Workbook**

12. **Name box**

a. Part of the Excel program window that displays the active cell address

b. Default view in Excel

c. Direction in which contents of page will print

d. Equal sign preceding a formula

e. File consisting of one or more worksheets

f. Intersection of a column and a row

Select the best answer from the list of choices.

13. The maximum number of worksheets you can include in a workbook is:
  a. 3.   **c.** 255.
  b. 250.   **d.** Unlimited.

14. Which feature could be used to print a very long worksheet on a single sheet of paper?
  a. Show Formulas   **c.** Page Break Preview
  b. Scale to fit   **d.** Named Ranges

15. Using a cell address in a formula is known as:
  a. Formularizing.   **c.** Cell referencing.
  b. Prefixing.   **d.** Cell mathematics.

16. A selection of multiple cells is called a:
  a. Group.   **c.** Reference.
  b. Range.   **d.** Package.

17. In which area can you see a preview of your worksheet?
  a. Page Setup   **c.** Printer Setup
  b. Backstage view   **d.** VIEW tab

18. Which worksheet view shows how your worksheet will look when printed?
  a. Page Layout   **c.** Review
  b. Data   **d.** View

19. Which key can you press to switch to Edit mode?
  a. [F1]   **c.** [F4]
  b. [F2]   **d.** [F6]

20. In which view can you see the header and footer areas of a worksheet?
  a. Normal view   **c.** Page Break Preview
  b. Page Layout view   **d.** Header/Footer view

21. Which view shows you a reduced view of each page of your worksheet?
  a. Normal   **c.** Thumbnail
  b. Page Layout   **d.** Page Break Preview

Skills Review

1. Understand spreadsheet software.
  a. What is the difference between a workbook and a worksheet?
  b. Identify five common business uses for electronic spreadsheets.
  c. What is what-if analysis?

2. Identify Excel 2013 window components.
  a. Start Excel.
  b. Open the file EMP A-2.xlsx from the location where you store your Data Files, then save it as
     EMP A-Weather Statistics.
  c. Locate the formula bar, the Sheet tabs, the mode indicator, and the cell pointer.

3. Understand formulas.
  a. What is the average high temperature of the listed cities? (*Hint*: Select the range B5:G5 and use the status bar.)
  b. What formula would you create to calculate the difference in altitude between Atlanta and Phoenix? Enter your answer (as an equation) in cell D13.

Skills Review (continued)

4. **Enter labels and values and use the AutoSum button.**
   a. Click cell H8, then use the AutoSum button to calculate the total snowfall.
   b. Click cell H7, then use the AutoSum button to calculate the total rainfall.
   c. Save your changes to the file.

5. **Edit cell entries.**
   a. Use [F2] to correct the spelling of SanteFe in cell G3 (the correct spelling is Santa Fe).
   b. Click cell A17, then type your name.
   c. Save your changes.

6. **Enter and edit a simple formula.**
   a. Change the value 41 in cell C8 to **52**.
   b. Change the value 37 in cell D6 to **35.4**.
   c. Select cell J4, then use the fill handle to copy the formula in cell J4 to cells J5:J8.
   d. Save your changes.

7. **Switch worksheet views.**
   a. Click the VIEW tab on the Ribbon, then switch to Page Layout view.
   b. Add the header **Average Annual Weather Statistics** to the center header text box.
   c. Add your name to the right header box.
   d. Add the multi-line header **Potential Medical Research Locations** to the left header box.
   e. Delete the contents of the range A1:H1 and cell A17.
   f. Save your changes.

8. **Choose print options.**
   a. Use the PAGE LAYOUT tab to change the orientation to Portrait.
   b. Turn off gridlines by deselecting both the Gridlines View and Gridlines Print check boxes (if necessary) in the Sheet Options group.
   c. Scale the worksheet so all the information fits on one page. If necessary, scale the worksheet so all the information fits on one page. (*Hint*: Click the Width list arrow in the Scale to Fit group, click 1 page, click the Height list arrow in the Scale to Fit group, then click 1 page.) Compare your screen to FIGURE A-20.
   d. Preview the worksheet in Backstage view, then print the worksheet.
   e. Save your changes, submit your work to your instructor as directed, then close the workbook and exit Excel.

FIGURE A-20

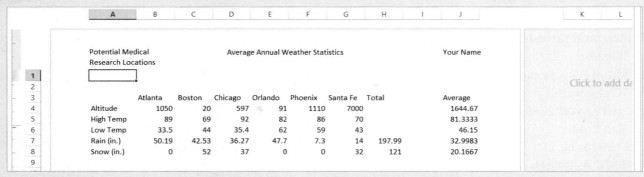

Independent Challenge 1

The Human Resources division of Allied Cardiology Associates has just notified you that they have hired two new physicians who will be relocating to your area. They would like you to create a workbook that contains real estate properties for their consideration. You've started a worksheet for this project that contains labels but no data.

a. Open the file EMP A-3.xlsx from the location where you store your Data Files, then save it as **EMP A-Property Listings**.

b. Enter the data shown in TABLE A-4 in columns A, C, D, and E (the property address information should spill into column B).

TABLE A-4

Property Address	Price	Bedrooms	Bathrooms
1507 Pinon Lane	525000	4	2.5
32 Zanzibar Way	325000	3	4
60 Pottery Lane	475500	2	2
902 Excelsior Drive	310000	4	3

© 2014 Cengage Learning

c. Use Page Layout view to create a header with the following components: the title **Property Listings** in the center and your name on the right.

d. Create formulas for totals in cells C6:E6.

e. Save your changes, then compare your worksheet to FIGURE A-21.

f. Submit your work to your instructor as directed.

g. Close the worksheet and exit Excel.

FIGURE A-21

Independent Challenge 2

You are the General Manager for Top Flight Medical Supplies, a small auto parts supplier. Although the company is just five years old, it is expanding rapidly, and you are continually looking for ways to save time. You recently began using Excel to manage and maintain data on inventory and sales, which has greatly helped you to track information accurately and efficiently.

a. Start Excel.

b. Save a new workbook as **EMP A-Top Flight Medical Supplies** in the location where you store your Data Files.

c. Switch to an appropriate view, then add a header that contains your name in the left header text box and the title **Top Flight Medical Supplies** in the center header text box.

Independent Challenge 2 (continued)

d. Using FIGURE A-22 as a guide, create labels for at least seven car manufacturers and sales for three months. Include other labels as appropriate. The car make should be in column A and the months should be in columns C, D, and E. A Total row should be beneath the data, and a Total column should be in column F.

FIGURE A-22

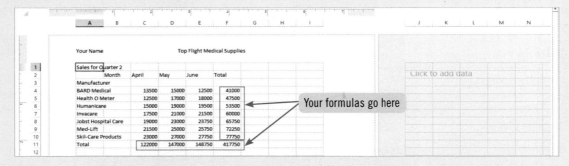

e. Enter values of your choice for the monthly sales for each manufacturer.

f. Add formulas in the Total column to calculate total quarterly sales for each make. Add formulas at the bottom of each column of values to calculate the total for that column. Remember that you can use the AutoSum button and the fill handle to save time.

g. Save your changes, preview the worksheet in Backstage view, then submit your work to your instructor as directed.

h. Close the workbook and exit Excel.

Independent Challenge 3

This Independent Challenge requires an Internet connection.

Some of the research staff at Great Plains Hospital prefer to use Celsius, rather than Fahrenheit temperatures, so you thought it would be helpful to create a worksheet that can be used to convert Fahrenheit temperatures to Celsius, to help employees who are unfamiliar with this type of temperature measurement.

a. Start Excel, then save a blank workbook as **EMP A-Temperature Conversions** in the location where you store your Data Files.

b. Create column headings using FIGURE A-23 as a guide. (*Hint*: You can widen column B by clicking cell B1, clicking the Format button in the Cells group on the HOME tab, then clicking AutoFit Column Width.)

c. Create row labels for each of the seasons.

d. In the appropriate cells, enter what you determine to be a reasonable indoor temperature for each season.

e. Use your Web browser to find out the conversion rate for Fahrenheit to Celsius. (*Hint*: Use your favorite search engine to search on a term such as **temperature conversion formula**.)

f. In the appropriate cells, create a formula that calculates the conversion of the Fahrenheit temperature you entered into a Celsius temperature.

g. In Page Layout View, add your name and the title **Temperature Conversions** to the header.

h. Save your work, then submit your work to your instructor as directed.

i. Close the file, then exit Excel.

Independent Challenge 3 (continued)

FIGURE A-23

Independent Challenge 4: Explore

You recently started working as a bookkeeper at the Cuba, NM Clinic. You've set up a sample Excel worksheet to keep track of the many start-up expenses.

a. Start Excel, open the file EMP A-4.xlsx from the location where you store your Data Files, then save it as **EMP A-Cuba Clinic Expenses**.

b. There is an error in cell E5: please use the Help feature to find out what is wrong. If you need additional assistance, search Help on *overview of formulas*.

c. Correct the error in the formula in cell E5, then copy the corrected formula into cells E6:E7.

d. Correct the error in the formula in cell E11: then copy the corrected formula into cells E12 and E13.

e. Cells E8 and E14 each contain incorrect formulas. Cell E8 should contain a formula that calculates the total personnel expense and cell E14 should calculate the total supplies used.

f. Cell F17 should contain a formula that adds the Invoice subtotal (total personnel and total supplies).

g. Cell F18 should calculate the sales tax by multiplying the Subtotal (cell F17) and the Sales tax (cell B18).

h. The Invoice Total (cell F19) should contain a formula that adds the Invoice subtotal (cell F17) and Sales tax (cell F18).

i. Switch to the Page Layout view and make the following changes to the Header: Week 42 (in the left header box), Cuba, NM Clinic Expenses (in the center header box), and your name (in the right header box).

j. Delete the contents of A1:A2, switch to the Normal view, then compare your worksheet to FIGURE A-24.

k. Save your work.

Excel 2013

FIGURE A-24

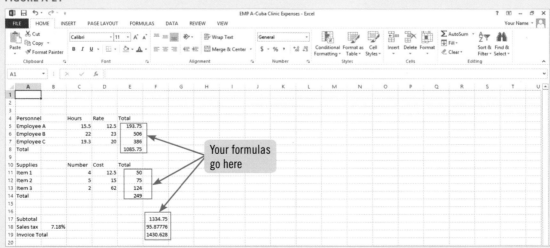

Visual Workshop

Open the file EMP A-5.xlsx from the location where you store your Data Files, then save it as **EMP A-Gold Coast Clinic Inventory Items**. Using the skills you learned in this unit, modify your worksheet so it matches FIGURE A-25. Enter formulas in cells D4 through D13 and in cells B14 and C14. Use the AutoSum button and fill handle to make entering your formulas easier. Add your name in the left header text box, then print one copy of the worksheet with the formulas displayed.

FIGURE A-25

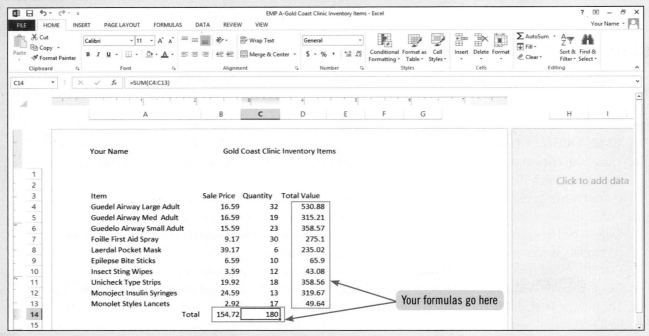

Working with Formulas and Functions

CASE ▶ Tony Sanchez, R.N., office manager at Riverwalk Medical Clinic, needs to analyze departmental insurance reimbursements for the current year. He has asked you to prepare a worksheet that summarizes this reimbursement data and includes some statistical analysis. He would also like you to perform some what-if analysis, to see what quarterly revenues would look like with various projected increases.

Unit Objectives

After completing this unit, you will be able to:

- Create a complex formula
- Insert a function
- Type a function
- Copy and move cell entries
- Understand relative and absolute cell references

- Copy formulas with relative cell references
- Copy formulas with absolute cell references
- Round a value with a function

Files You Will Need

EMP B-1.xlsx
EMP B-2.xlsx
EMP B-3.xlsx
EMP B-4.xlsx

Create a Complex Formula

Finale Question

A **complex formula** is one that uses more than one arithmetic operator. You might, for example, need to create a formula that uses addition and multiplication. In formulas containing more than one arithmetic operator, Excel uses the standard **order of precedence** rules to determine which operation to perform first. You can change the order of precedence in a formula by using parentheses around the part you want to calculate first. For example, the formula =4+2*5 equals 14, because the order of precedence dictates that multiplication is performed before addition. However, the formula =(4+2)*5 equals 30, because the parentheses cause 4+2 to be calculated first. **CASE** *You want to create a formula that calculates a 20% increase in insurance reimbursements.*

STEPS

1. **Start Excel, open the file EMP B-1.xlsx from the location where you store your Data Files, then save it as EMP B-Insurance Reimbursement Analysis**

2. **Select the range B9:B16, click the Quick Analysis tool 📧, then click the TOTALS tab**
   The TOTALS tab in the Quick Analysis tool displays commonly used functions, as seen in **FIGURE B-1**.

3. **Click the Sum button 📊 in the Quick Analysis tool**
   The newly calculated value displays in cell B17 and has a darker appearance than the figures in the selected range.

4. **Click cell B17, then drag the fill handle to cell E17**
   The formula in cell B17 is copied to cells C17:E17. The copied cells have the same dark appearance as that of cell B17.

5. **Click cell B19, type =, click cell B17, then type +**
   In this first part of the formula, you are using a reference to the total insurance reimbursements for Quarter 1.

6. **Click cell B17, then type *.2**
   The second part of this formula adds a 20% increase (B17*.2) to the original value of the cell (the total insurance reimbursements for Quarter 1).

7. **Click the Enter button ✔ on the formula bar**
   The result, 417895.56, appears in cell B19.

8. **Press [Tab], type =, click cell C17, type +, click cell C17, type *.2, then click ✔**
   The result, 413529.12, appears in cell C19.

9. **Drag the fill handle from cell C19 to cell E19**
   The calculated values appear in the selected range, as shown in **FIGURE B-2**. Dragging the fill handle on a cell copies the cell's contents or continues a series of data (such as Quarter 1, Quarter 2, etc.) into adjacent cells. This option is called **Auto Fill**.

10. **Save your work**

Using Apps for Office to improve worksheet functionality

Excel has more functionality than simple and complex math computations. Using the Apps for Office feature (found in the Apps group in the INSERT tab), you can insert an app into your worksheet that accesses the web and adds functionality to your work. Many of the available apps are free and can be used to create an email, appointment, meeting, contact, or task, or be a reference source, such as the Mini Calendar and Date Picker. When you click the Apps for Office button arrow, you'll see any Recently Used Apps. Click See All to display the featured apps and to go to the Office store to view available apps. When you find an app you want, make sure you're logged in to Office.com (you may need to log in again), click the app, click Add, then follow the prompts to download the app. Click the Apps for Office button arrow, click See All, click the app you just added, then click Insert. The app will display as an embedded object in your worksheet and will also appear in the Recently Used Apps palette when you click the Apps for Office button.

FIGURE B-6: MAX function in progress

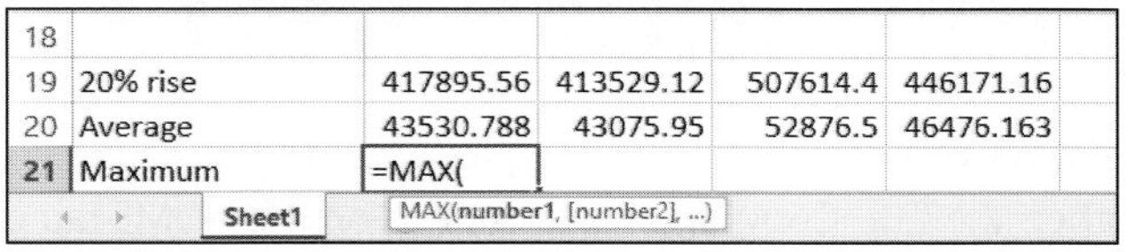

18					
19	20% rise	417895.56	413529.12	507614.4	446171.16
20	Average	43530.788	43075.95	52876.5	46476.163
21	Maximum	=MAX(			

Sheet1   MAX(**number1**, [number2], ...)

FIGURE B-7: Completing the MAX function

FIGURE B-8: Completed MAX and MIN functions

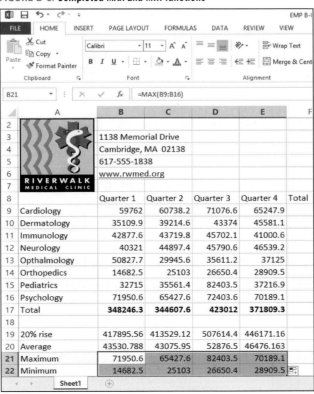

Copy and Move Cell Entries

Learning Outcomes
- Copy a range to the Clipboard
- Paste a Clipboard entry
- Empty cell contents
- Copy cell contents

There are three ways you can copy or move cells and ranges (or the contents within them) from one location to another: the Cut, Copy, and Paste buttons on the HOME tab on the Ribbon; the fill handle in the lower-right corner of the active cell or range; or the drag-and-drop feature. When you copy cells, the original data remains in the original location; when you cut or move cells, the original data is deleted from its original location. You can also cut, copy, and paste cells or ranges from one worksheet to another. **CASE** *In addition to the 20% rise in insurance reimbursements, you also want to show a 30% rise. Rather than retype this information, you copy and move the labels in these cells.*

STEPS

QUICK TIP

To cut or copy selected cell contents, activate the cell, then select the characters within the cell that you want to cut or copy.

1. **Select the range B8:E8, then click the Copy button 📋 in the Clipboard group on the HOME tab**

   The selected range (B8:E8) is copied to the **Clipboard**, a temporary Windows storage area that holds the selections you copy or cut. A moving border surrounds the selected range until you press [Esc] or copy an additional item to the Clipboard.

2. **Click the dialog box launcher 📑 in the Clipboard group**

   The Office Clipboard opens in the Clipboard task pane, as shown in FIGURE B-9. When you copy or cut an item, it is cut or copied both to the Clipboard provided by Windows and to the Office Clipboard. Unlike the Windows Clipboard, which holds just one item at a time, the Office Clipboard contains up to 24 of the most recently cut or copied items from any Office program. Your Clipboard task pane may contain more items than shown in the figure.

QUICK TIP

Once the Office Clipboard contains 24 items, the oldest existing item is automatically deleted each time you add an item.

3. **Scroll down so row 27 is visible, click cell B25, then click the Paste button in the Clipboard group**

   A copy of the contents of range B8:E8 is pasted into the range B25:E25. When pasting an item from the Office Clipboard or Clipboard into a worksheet, you only need to specify the upper-left cell of the range where you want to paste the selection. Notice that the information you copied remains in the original range B8:E8; if you had cut instead of copied, the information would have been deleted from its original location once it was pasted.

4. **Press [Delete]**

   The selected cells are empty. You have decided to paste the cells in a different row. You can repeatedly paste an item from the Office Clipboard as many times as you like, as long as the item remains in the Office Clipboard.

QUICK TIP

You can also close the Office Clipboard pane by clicking the dialog box launcher in the Clipboard group.

5. **Click cell B24, click the first item in the Office Clipboard, then click the Close button ✖ on the Clipboard task pane**

   Cells B24:E24 contain the copied labels.

6. **Click cell A19, press and hold [Ctrl], point to any edge of the cell until the pointer changes to ▨, drag cell A19 to cell A25, release the mouse button, then release [Ctrl]**

   The copy pointer ▨ continues to appear as you drag, as shown in FIGURE B-10. When you release the mouse button, the contents of cell A19 are copied to cell A25.

7. **Click to the right of 2 in the formula bar, press [Backspace], type 3, then press [Tab]**

8. **Type =, click cell B17, type *1.3, click the Enter button ✔ on the formula bar, then save your work**

   This new formula calculates a 30% increase of the reimbursements for Quarter 1, though using a different method from what you previously used. Anything you multiply by 1.3 returns an amount that is 130% of the original amount, or a 30% increase. Compare your screen to FIGURE B-11.

FIGURE B-9: Copied data in Office Clipboard

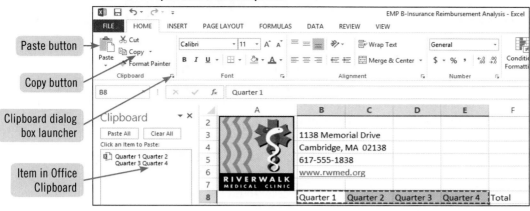

FIGURE B-10: Copying cell contents with drag-and-drop

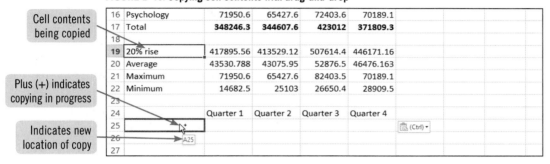

FIGURE B-11: Formula entered to calculate a 30% increase

	A	B	C	D		G	H
7	RIVERWALK MEDICAL CLINIC						
8		Quarter 1	Quarter 2	Quarter 3	Quarter 4	Total	
9	Cardiology	59762	60738.2	71076.6	65247.9		
10	Dermatology	35109.9	39214.6	43374	45581.1		
11	Immunology	42877.6	43719.8	45702.1	41000.6		
12	Neurology	40321	44897.4	45790.6	46539.2		
13	Opthalmology	50827.7	29945.6	35611.2	37125		
14	Orthopedics	14682.5	25103	26650.4	28909.5		
15	Pediatrics	32715	35561.4	82403.5	37216.9		
16	Psychology	71950.6	65427.6	72403.6	70189.1		
17	Total	**348246.3**	**344607.6**	**423012**	**371809.3**		
18							
19	20% rise	417895.56	413529.12	507614.4	446171.16		
20	Average	43530.788	43075.95	52876.5	46476.163		
21	Maximum	71950.6	65427.6	82403.5	70189.1		
22	Minimum	14682.5	25103	26650.4	28909.5		
23							
24		Quarter 1	Quarter 2	Quarter 3	Quarter 4		
25	30% rise	452720.19					
26							

B25 = B17*1.3

Formula calculates 30% increase

Inserting and deleting selected cells

As you add formulas to your workbook, you may need to insert or delete cells. When you do this, Excel automatically adjusts cell references to reflect their new locations. To insert cells, click the Insert list arrow in the Cells group on the HOME tab, then click Insert Cells. The Insert dialog box opens, asking if you want to insert a cell and move the current active cell down or to the right of the new one. To delete one or more selected cells, click the Delete list arrow in the Cells group, click Delete Cells, and in the Delete dialog box, indicate which way you want to move the adjacent cells. When using this option, be careful not to disturb row or column alignment that may be necessary to maintain the accuracy of cell references in the worksheet. Click the Insert button or Delete button in the Cells group to insert or delete a single cell.

Understand Relative and Absolute Cell References

Learning Outcomes
• Identify cell referencing
• Identify when to use absolute or relative cell references

As you work in Excel, you may want to reuse formulas in different parts of a worksheet to reduce the amount of data you have to retype. For example, you might want to include a what-if analysis in one part of a worksheet showing a set of sales projections if sales increase by 10%. To include another analysis in another part of the worksheet showing projections if sales increase by 50%, you can copy the formulas from one section to another and simply change the "1" to a "5". But when you copy formulas, it is important to make sure that they refer to the correct cells. To do this, you need to understand the difference between relative and absolute cell references. **CASE** ▶ *You plan to reuse formulas in different parts of your worksheets, so you want to understand relative and absolute cell references.*

DETAILS

Answer to the Question

3k #5

Final

Consider the following when using relative and absolute cell references:

- **Use relative references when you want to preserve the relationship to the formula location**

  When you create a formula that references another cell, Excel normally does not "record" the exact cell address for the cell being referenced in the formula. Instead, it looks at the relationship that cell has to the cell containing the formula. For example, in **FIGURE B-12**, cell F5 contains the formula: =SUM(B5:E5). When Excel retrieves values to calculate the formula in cell F5, it actually looks for "the four cells to the left of the formula," which in this case is cells B5:E5. This way, if you copy the cell to a new location, such as cell F6, the results will reflect the new formula location, and will automatically retrieve the values in cells B6, C6, D6, and E6. These are **relative cell references**, because Excel is recording the input cells *in relation to* or *relative to* the formula cell.

  In most cases, you want to use relative cell references when copying or moving, so this is the Excel default. In **FIGURE B-12**, the formulas in F5:F12 and in B13:F13 contain relative cell references. They total the "four cells to the left of" or the "eight cells above" the formulas.

- **Use absolute cell references when you want to preserve the exact cell address in a formula**

  There are times when you want Excel to retrieve formula information from a specific cell, and you don't want the cell address in the formula to change when you copy it to a new location. For example, you might have a price in a specific cell that you want to use in all formulas, regardless of their location. If you use relative cell referencing, the formula results would be incorrect, because Excel would use a different cell every time you copy the formula. Therefore you need to use an **absolute cell reference**, which is a reference that does not change when you copy the formula.

  You create an absolute cell reference by placing a $ (dollar sign) in front of both the column letter and the row number of the cell address. You can either type the dollar sign when typing the cell address in a formula (for example, "=C12*$B$16"), or you can select a cell address on the formula bar and then press [F4] and the dollar signs are added automatically. **FIGURE B-13** shows formulas containing both absolute and relative references. The formulas in cells B19 to E26 use absolute cell references to refer to a potential sales increase of 50%, shown in cell B16.

FIGURE B-12: Formulas containing relative references

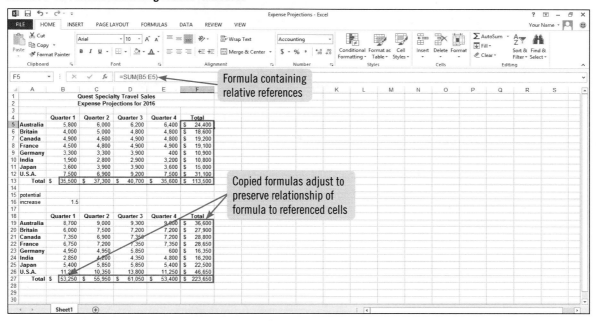

Formula containing relative references

Copied formulas adjust to preserve relationship of formula to referenced cells

FIGURE B-13: Formulas containing absolute and relative references

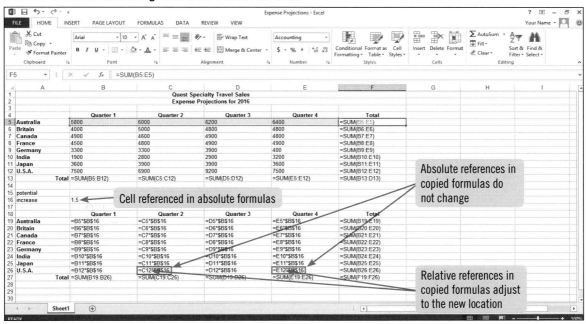

Absolute references in copied formulas do not change

Cell referenced in absolute formulas

Relative references in copied formulas adjust to the new location

Excel 2013

Using a mixed reference

Sometimes when you copy a formula, you want to change the row reference, but keep the column reference the same. This type of cell referencing combines elements of both absolute and relative referencing and is called a **mixed reference**. For example, when copied, a formula containing the mixed reference C$14 would change the column letter relative to its new location, but not the row number. In the mixed reference $C14, the column letter would not change, but the row number would be updated relative to its location. Like an absolute reference, a mixed reference can be created by pressing the [F4] function key with the cell reference selected. With each press of the [F4] key, you cycle through all the possible combinations of relative, absolute, and mixed references (C14, $C$14, C$14, and $C14).

Working with Formulas and Functions

Copy Formulas with Relative Cell References

Learning Outcomes
- Copy and Paste formulas with relative cell references
- Examine Auto Fill and Paste Options
- Use the Fill button

Copying and moving a cell allows you to reuse a formula you've already created. Copying cells is usually faster than retyping the formulas in them and helps to prevent typing errors. If the cells you are copying contain relative cell references and you want to maintain the relative referencing, you don't need to make any changes to the cells before copying them. **CASE** ▸ *You want to copy the formula in cell B25, which calculates the 30% increase in quarterly insurance reimbursements for Quarter 1, to cells C25 through E25. You also want to create formulas to calculate total reimbursements for each department.*

STEPS

1. **Click cell B25, if necessary, then click the Copy button 📋 in the Clipboard group on the HOME tab**

   The formula for calculating the 30% expense increase during Quarter 1 is copied to the Clipboard. Notice that the formula =B17*1.3 appears in the formula bar, and a moving border surrounds the active cell.

QUICK TIP

To paste only specific components of a copied cell or range, click the Paste button arrow in the Clipboard group, then click Paste Special. You can selectively copy formats, formulas, values, comments, validation rules, transpose columns and rows, paste a link, or add, subtract, multiply, or divide using the Paste Special dialog box.

2. **Click cell C25, then click the Paste button** *(not the list arrow)* **in the Clipboard group**

   The formula from cell B25 is copied into cell C25, where the new result of 447989.88 appears. Notice in the formula bar that the cell references have changed, so that cell C17 is referenced in the formula. This formula contains a relative cell reference, which tells Excel to substitute new cell references within the copied formulas as necessary. This maintains the same relationship between the new cell containing the formula and the cell references within the formula. In this case, Excel adjusted the formula so that cell C17—the cell reference nine rows above C25—replaced cell B17, the cell reference nine rows above B25.

3. **Drag the fill handle from cell C25 to cell E25**

   A formula similar to the one in cell C25 now appears in cells D25 and E25. After you use the fill handle to copy cell contents, the **Auto Fill Options button** appears, as seen in **FIGURE B-14**. You can use the Auto Fill Options button to fill the cells with only specific elements of the copied cell if you wish.

4. **Scroll up, click cell F9, click the AutoSum button Σ in the Editing group, then click the Enter button ✓ on the formula bar**

5. **Click 📋 in the Clipboard group, select the range F10:F11, then click the Paste button**

   See **FIGURE B-15**. After you click the Paste button, the **Paste Options button** appears, which you can use to paste only specific elements of the copied selection if you wish. The formula for calculating total reimbursements for dermatology appears in the formula bar. You would like totals to appear in cells F12:F16. The Fill button in the Editing group can be used to copy the formula into the remaining cells.

6. **Select the range F11:F16**

7. **Click the Fill button 🔽 in the Editing group, then click Down**

   The formulas containing relative references are copied to each cell. Compare your worksheet to **FIGURE B-16**.

8. **Save your work**

FIGURE B-14: Formula copied using the fill handle

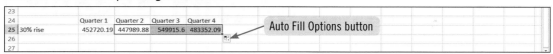

FIGURE B-15: Formulas pasted in the range F5:F6

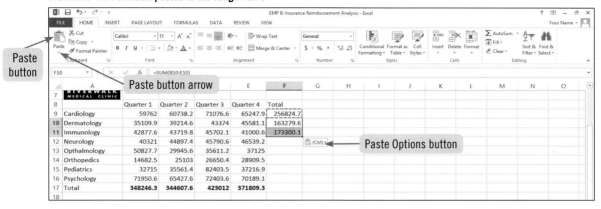

FIGURE B-16: Formula copied using Fill Down

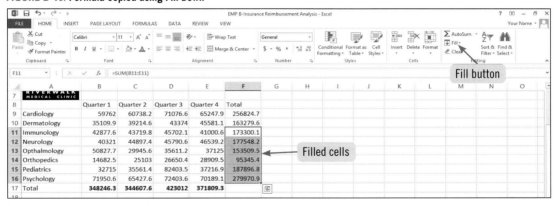

Using Paste Preview

You can selectively copy formulas, values, or other choices using the Paste button arrow, and you can see how the pasted contents will look using the Paste Preview feature. When you click the Paste button arrow, a gallery of paste option icons opens. When you point to an icon, a preview of how the content will be pasted using that option is shown in the worksheet. Options include pasting values only, pasting values with number formatting, pasting formulas only, pasting formatting only, pasting transposed data so that column data appears in rows and row data appears in columns, and pasting with no borders (to remove any borders around pasted cells).

Using Auto Fill options

When you use the fill handle to copy cells, the Auto Fill Options button appears. Auto Fill options differ depending on what you are copying. If you had selected cells containing a series (such as "Monday" and "Tuesday") and then used the fill handle, you would see options for continuing the series (such as "Wednesday" and "Thursday") or for simply pasting the copied cells. Clicking the Auto Fill Options button opens a list that lets you choose from the following options: Copy Cells, Fill Series (if applicable), Fill Formatting Only, Fill Without Formatting, or Flash Fill. Choosing Copy Cells means that the cell's contents and its formatting will be copied. The Fill Formatting Only option copies only the formatting attributes, but not cell contents. The Fill Without Formatting option copies the cell contents, but no formatting attributes. Copy Cells is the default option when using the fill handle to copy a cell, so if you want to copy the cell's contents and its formatting, you can ignore the Auto Fill Options button. The Flash Fill option allows you to create customized fill ranges on the fly, such as 2, 4, 6, 8, 10 by entering at least two values in a pattern: Excel automatically senses the pattern.

Copy Formulas with Absolute Cell References

Learning Outcomes
- Create an absolute cell reference
- Use the fill handle to copy absolute cell references

When copying formulas, you might want one or more cell references in the formula to remain unchanged in relation to the formula. In such an instance, you need to apply an absolute cell reference before copying the formula to preserve the specific cell address when the formula is copied. You create an absolute reference by placing a dollar sign ($) before the column letter and row number of the address (for example, $A$1). **CASE** *You need to do some what-if analysis to see how various percentage increases might affect total reimbursements. You decide to add a column that calculates a possible increase in the total reimbursements, and then change the percentage to see various potential results.*

STEPS

1. **Press [Ctrl][Home], click cell G6, type Change, then press [Enter]**

2. **Type 1.1, then press [Enter]**

   You store the increase factor that will be used in the what-if analysis in this cell (G7). The value 1.1 can be used to calculate a 10% increase: anything you multiply by 1.1 returns an amount that is 110% of the original amount.

3. **Click cell H8, type What if?, then press [Enter]**

4. **In cell H9, type =, click cell F9, type *, click cell G7, then click the Enter button ✓ on the formula bar**

   The result, 282507, appears in cell H9. This value represents the total annual insurance reimbursements for the cardiology department if there is a 10% increase. You want to perform a what-if analysis for all the departments.

   QUICK TIP
   Before you copy or move a formula, always check to see if you need to use an absolute cell reference.

5. **Drag the fill handle from cell H9 to cell H16**

   The resulting values in the range H9:H16 are all zeros, which is not the result you wanted. Because you used relative cell addressing in cell H9, the copied formula adjusted so that the formula in cell H10 is =F10*G8. Because there is no value in cell G8, the result is 0, an error. You need to use an absolute reference in the formula to keep the formula from adjusting itself. That way, it will always reference cell G7.

   QUICK TIP
   When changing a cell reference to an absolute reference, make sure the reference is selected or the insertion point is next to it in the cell before pressing [F4].

6. **Click cell H9, press [F2] to change to Edit mode, then press [F4]**

   When you press [F2], the range finder outlines the arguments of the equation in blue and red. The insertion point appears next to the G7 cell reference in cell H9. When you press [F4], dollar signs are inserted in the G7 cell reference, making it an absolute reference. See **FIGURE B-17**.

7. **Click ✓, then drag the fill handle from cell H9 to cell H16**

   Because the formula correctly contains an absolute cell reference, the correct values for a 10% increase appear in cells H9:H16. You now want to see what a 20% increase in expenses looks like.

8. **Click cell G7, type 1.2, then click ✓**

   The values in the range H9:H16 change to reflect the 20% increase. Compare your worksheet to **FIGURE B-18**.

9. **Save your work**

FIGURE B-17: Absolute reference created in formula

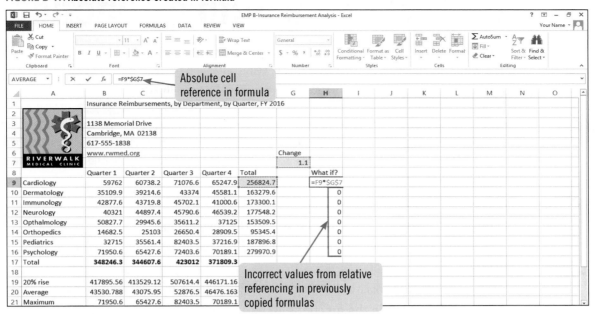

Absolute cell reference in formula

Incorrect values from relative referencing in previously copied formulas

FIGURE B-18: What-if analysis with modified change factor

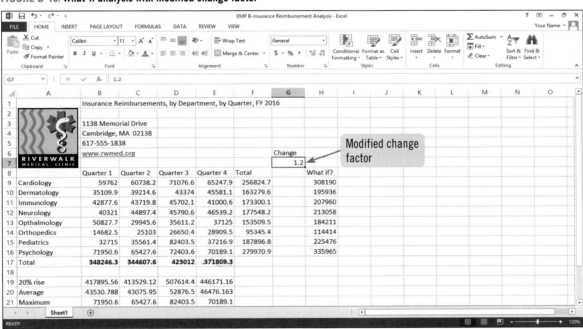

Modified change factor

Using the fill handle for sequential text or values

Often, you need to fill cells with sequential text: months of the year, days of the week, years, or text plus a number (Quarter 1, Quarter 2,...). For example, you might want to create a worksheet that calculates data for every month of the year. Using the fill handle, you can quickly and easily create labels for the months of the year just by typing "January" in a cell. Drag the fill handle from the cell containing "January" until you have all the monthly labels you need. You can also easily fill cells with a date sequence by dragging the fill handle on a single cell containing a date. You can

fill cells with a number sequence (such as 1, 2, 3,...) by dragging the fill handle on a selection of two or more cells that contain the sequence. To create a number sequence using the value in a single cell, press and hold [Ctrl] as you drag the fill handle of the cell. As you drag the fill handle, Excel automatically extends the existing sequence into the additional cells. (The content of the last filled cell appears in the ScreenTip.) To examine all the fill series options for the current selection, click the Fill button in the Editing group on the HOME tab, then click Series to open the Series dialog box.

Round a Value with a Function

Learning
Outcomes
• Use Formula
  AutoComplete to
  insert a function
• Copy an edited
  formula

The more you explore features and tools in Excel, the more ways you'll find to simplify your work and convey information more efficiently. For example, cells containing financial data are often easier to read if they contain fewer decimal places than those that appear by default. You can round a value or formula result to a specific number of decimal places by using the ROUND function. **CASE** ▶ *In your worksheet, you'd like to round the cells showing the 20% rise in reimbursements to show fewer digits; after all, it's not important to show cents in the projections, only whole dollars. You want Excel to round the calculated value to the nearest integer. You decide to edit cell B14 so it includes the ROUND function, and then copy the edited formula into the other formulas in this row.*

STEPS

1. **Click cell B19, then click to the right of = in the formula bar**

   You want to position the function at the beginning of the formula, before any values or arguments.

QUICK TIP
In the Insert Function
dialog box, the
ROUND function is
in the Math & Trig
category.

2. **Type RO**

   Formula AutoComplete displays a list of functions beginning with RO beneath the formula bar.

3. **Double-click ROUND in the functions list**

   The new function and an opening parenthesis are added to the formula, as shown in **FIGURE B-19**. A few additional modifications are needed to complete your edit of the formula. You need to indicate the number of decimal places to which the function should round numbers and you also need to add a closing parenthesis around the set of arguments that comes after the ROUND function.

TROUBLE
If you have too
many or too few
parentheses, the
extraneous paren-
thesis is displayed in
red, or a warning
dialog box opens
with a suggested
solution to the error.

4. **Press [END], type ,0), then click the Enter button ✓ on the formula bar**

   The comma separates the arguments within the formula, and 0 indicates that you don't want any decimal places to appear in the calculated value. When you complete the edit, the parentheses at either end of the formula briefly become bold, indicating that the formula has the correct number of open and closed parentheses and is balanced.

5. **Drag the fill handle from cell B19 to cell E19**

   The formula in cell B19 is copied to the range C19:E19. All the values are rounded to display no decimal places. Compare your worksheet to **FIGURE B-20**.

6. **Scroll down so row 27 is visible, click cell A27, type your name, then click ✓ on the formula bar**

7. **Save your work, preview the worksheet in Backstage view, then submit your work to your instructor as directed**

8. **Exit Excel**

FIGURE B-19: ROUND function added to an existing formula

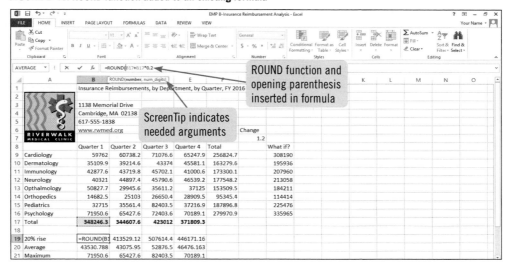

FIGURE B-20: Completed worksheet

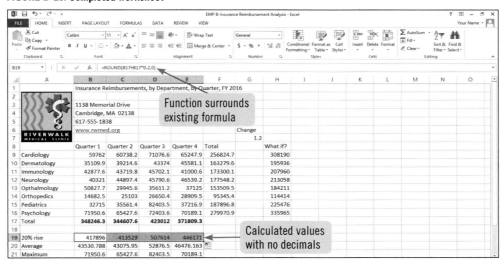

Creating a new workbook using a template

Excel **templates** are predesigned workbook files intended to save time when you create common documents such as balance sheets, budgets, or time cards. Templates contain labels, values, formulas, and formatting, so all you have to do is customize them with your own information. Excel comes with many templates, and you can also create your own or find additional templates on the Web. Unlike a typical workbook, which has the file extension .xlsx, a template has the extension .xltx. To create a workbook using a template, click the FILE tab, then click New on the navigation bar. The New pane in Backstage view lists templates available through Office.com. The Blank workbook template is selected by default and is used to create a blank workbook with no content or special formatting. A preview of the selected template appears in a separate window on top of the New pane. To select a template, click one of the selections in the New pane, then click Create. **FIGURE B-21** shows an Office.com template. (Your list of templates may differ.) When you click Create, a new

workbook is created based on the template; when you save the new file in the default format, it has the regular .xlsx extension. To save a workbook of your own as a template, open the Save As dialog box, click the Save as type list arrow, then change the file type to Excel Template.

FIGURE B-21: EXPENSE TRENDS template selected in Backstage view

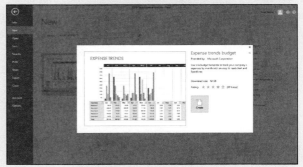

Practice

Concepts Review

Label each element of the Excel worksheet window shown in FIGURE B-22.

FIGURE B-22

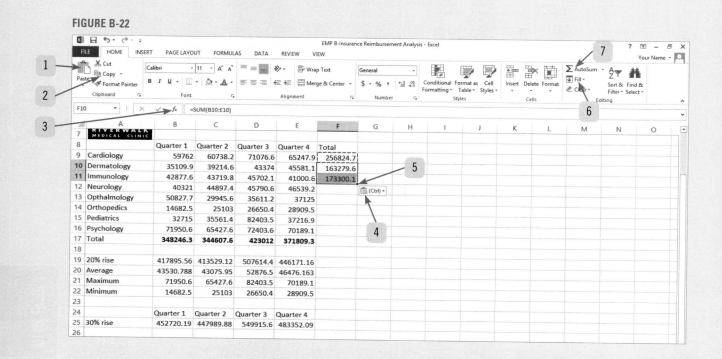

Match each term or button with the statement that best describes it.

8. **Fill handle**

9. **[Delete]**

10. **Dialog box launcher**

11. **Formula AutoComplete**

12. **Drag-and-drop method**

a. Clears the contents of selected cells

b. Item on the Ribbon that opens a dialog box or task pane

c. Lets you move or copy data from one cell to another without using the Clipboard

d. Displays an alphabetical list of functions from which you can choose

e. Lets you copy cell contents or continue a series of data into a range of selected cells

Select the best answer from the list of choices.

13. **What type of cell reference changes when it is copied?**
    a. Circular
    b. Absolute
    c. Relative
    d. Specified

14. **What type of cell reference is C$19?**
    a. Relative
    b. Absolute
    c. Mixed
    d. Certain

15. **Which key do you press to copy while dragging and dropping selected cells?**
    a. [Alt]
    b. [Ctrl]
    c. [F2]
    d. [Tab]

16. **You can use any of the following features to enter a function *except*:**
    a. Insert Function button.
    b. Formula AutoComplete.
    c. AutoSum list arrow.
    d. Clipboard.

17. **Which key do you press to convert a relative cell reference to an absolute cell reference?**
    a. [F2]
    b. [F4]
    c. [F5]
    d. [F6]

Skills Review

1. **Create a complex formula.**
   a. Open the file EMP B-2.xlsx from the location where you store your Data Files, then save it as **EMP B-Medical Supply Company Inventory**.
   b. Select the range B4:B8, click the TOTALS tab in the Quick Analysis tool, then click the Sum button.
   c. Use the fill handle to copy the formula in cell B9 to cells C9:E9.
   d. In cell B11, create a complex formula that calculates a 30% decrease in the total number of cases of masks.
   e. Use the fill handle to copy this formula into cell C11 through cell E11.
   f. Save your work.

2. **Insert a function.**
   a. Use the AutoSum list arrow to create a formula in cell B13 that averages the number of cases of masks in each storage area.
   b. Use the Insert Function button to create a formula in cell B14 that calculates the maximum number of cases of masks in a storage area.
   c. Use the AutoSum list arrow to create a formula in cell B15 that calculates the minimum number of cases of masks in a storage area.
   d. Save your work.

3. **Type a function.**
   a. In cell C13, type a formula that includes a function to average the number of cases of tubes in each storage area. (*Hint*: Use Formula AutoComplete to enter the function.)
   b. In cell C14, type a formula that includes a function to calculate the maximum number of cases of tubes in a storage area.
   c. In cell C15, type a formula that includes a function to calculate the minimum number of cases of tubes in a storage area.
   d. Save your work.

Skills Review (continued)

4. Copy and move cell entries.

a. Select the range B3:F3.

b. Copy the selection to the Clipboard.

c. Open the Clipboard task pane, then paste the selection into cell B17.

d. Close the Clipboard task pane, then select the range A4:A9.

e. Use the drag-and-drop method to copy the selection to cell A18. (*Hint*: The results should fill the range A18:A23.)

f. Save your work.

5. Understand relative and absolute cell references.

a. Write a brief description of the difference between relative and absolute references.

b. List at least three situations in which you think a business might use an absolute reference in its calculations. Examples can include calculations for different types of worksheets, such as time cards, invoices, and budgets.

6. Copy formulas with relative cell references.

a. Calculate the total in cell F4.

b. Use the Fill button to copy the formula in cell F4 down to cells F5:F8.

c. Select the range C13:C15.

d. Use the fill handle to copy these cells to the range D13:E15.

e. Save your work.

7. Copy formulas with absolute cell references.

a. In cell H1, enter the value **1.575**.

b. In cell H4, create a formula that multiplies F4 and an absolute reference to cell H1.

c. Use the fill handle to copy the formula in cell H4 to cells H5 and H6.

d. Use the Copy and Paste buttons to copy the formula in cell H4 to cells H7 and H8.

e. Change the amount in cell H1 to **2.3**.

f. Save your work.

8. Round a value with a function.

a. Click cell H4.

b. Edit this formula to include the ROUND function showing one decimal places.

c. Use the fill handle to copy the formula in cell H4 to the range H5:H8.

d. Enter your name in cell A25, then compare your work to **FIGURE B-23**.

e. Save your work, preview the worksheet in Backstage view, then submit your work to your instructor as directed.

f. Close the workbook, then exit Excel.

FIGURE B-23

	A	B	C	D	E	F	G	H	I	J
1	Medical Supply Company						Change	2.3		
2	Inventory, in cases									
3		O2 Masks	O2 Tubes	Syringes	Gowns	Total		What if?		
4	Storage 1	57	55	57	38	207		476.1		
5	Storage 2	29	43	47	52	171		393.3		
6	Storage 3	40	34	59	23	156		358.8		
7	Storage 4	23	79	46	29	177		407.1		
8	Storage 5	28	32	41	43	144		331.2		
9	Total	177	243	250	185					
10										
11	30% drop	123.9	170.1	175	129.5					
12										
13	Average	35.4	48.6	50	37					
14	Maximum	57	79	59	52					
15	Minimum	23	32	41	23					
16										
17		O2 Masks	O2 Tubes	Syringes	Gowns	Total				
18	Storage 1									
19	Storage 2									
20	Storage 3									
21	Storage 4									

Your formulas go here

Independent Challenge 1

You keep the accounts for a local charity that wants to start a small clinic in an underserved area. Before you begin, you need to evaluate what you think your monthly expenses will be. You've started a workbook, but need to complete the entries and add formulas.

a. Open the file EMP B-3.xlsx from the location where you store your Data Files, then save it as **EMP B-Estimated Clinic Expenses**.

b. Make up your own expense data, and enter it in cells B4:B10. (Monthly reimbursements are already included in the worksheet.)

c. Create a formula in cell C4 that calculates the annual rent.

d. Copy the formula in cell C4 to the range C5:C10.

e. Move the label in cell A15 to cell A14.

f. Create formulas in cells B11 and C11 that total the monthly and annual expenses.

g. Create a formula in cell C13 that calculates annual reimbursements.

h. Create a formula in cell B14 that determines whether you will make a profit or loss, then copy the formula into cell C14.

i. Copy the labels in cells B3:C3 to cells E3:F3.

j. Type **Projection Increase** in cell G1, then type **.2** in cell I1.

k. Create a formula in cell E4 that calculates an increase in the monthly rent by the amount in cell H2. You will be copying this formula to other cells, so you'll need to use an absolute reference.

l. Create a formula in cell F4 that calculates the increased annual rent expense based on the calculation in cell E4.

m. Copy the formulas in cells E4:F4 into cells E5:F10 to calculate the remaining monthly and annual expenses.

n. Create a formula in cell E11 that calculates the total monthly expenses, then copy that formula to cell F11.

o. Copy the contents of cells B13:C13 into cells E13:F13.

p. Create formulas in cells E14 and F14 that calculate profit/loss based on the projected increase in monthly and annual expenses.

q. Change the projected increase to **.17**, then compare your work to the sample in FIGURE B-24.

r. Enter your name in a cell in the worksheet.

s. Save your work, preview the worksheet in Backstage view, submit your work to your instructor as directed, close the workbook, and exit Excel.

FIGURE B-24

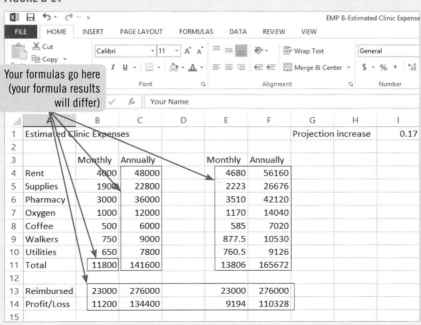

Excel 2013

Independent Challenge 2

The Flight Nurse Training Academy is a small, growing nursing education center that has hired you to organize its accounting records using Excel. The owners want you to track the company's expenses. Before you were hired, one of the bookkeepers began entering last year's expenses in a workbook, but the analysis was never completed.

a. Start Excel, open the file EMP B-4.xlsx from the location where you store your Data Files, then save it as **EMP B-Flight Nurse Training Academy**. The worksheet includes labels for functions such as the average, maximum, and minimum amounts of each of the expenses in the worksheet.

b. Think about what information would be important for the bookkeeping staff to know.

c. Using the Quick Analysis tool, create a formula in the Quarter 1 column that uses the SUM function, then copy that formula into the Total row for the remaining Quarters.

d. Use the SUM function to create formulas for each expense in the Total column.

e. Create formulas for each expense and each quarter in the Average, Maximum, and Minimum columns and rows using the method of your choice.

f. Compare your worksheet to the sample shown in FIGURE B-25.

g. Enter your name in cell A25, then save your work.

h. Preview the worksheet, then submit your work to your instructor as directed.

i. Close the workbook and exit Excel.

FIGURE B-25

	A	B	C	D	E	F	G	H	I	J	K
1	Flight Nurse Training Academy										
2											
3	Operating Expenses for 2016										
4											
5	Expense	Quarter 1	Quarter 2	Quarter 3	Quarter 4	Total	Average	Maximum	Minimum		
6	Rent	9240	9240	9240	9240	36960	9240	9240	9240		
7	Utilities	9000	7982	7229	8096	32307	8076.75	9000	7229		
8	Payroll	23456	26922	25876	29415	105669	26417.3	29415	23456		
9	Insurance	8550	8194	8225	8327	33296	8324	8550	8194		
10	Education	3000	3081	6552	4006	16639	4159.75	6552	3000		
11	Inventory	29986	27115	25641	32465	115207	28801.8	32465	25641		
12	Total	**83232**	**82534**	**82763**	**91549**	340078					
13											
14	Average	13872	13755.7	13793.8	15258.2				Your formulas go here		
15	Maximum	29986	27115	25876	32465						
16	Minimum	3000	3081	6552	4006						
17											

Working with Formulas and Functions

Independent Challenge 3

As the accounting manager of a locally owned business, it is your responsibility to calculate accrued sales tax payments on a monthly basis and then submit the payments to the state government. You've decided to use an Excel workbook to make these calculations.

a. Start Excel, then save a new, blank workbook to the drive and folder where you store your Data Files as **EMP B-Sales Tax Calculations**.

b. Decide on the layout for all columns and rows. The worksheet will contain data for six stores, which you can name by store number, neighborhood, or another method of your choice. For each store, you will calculate total sales tax based on the local sales tax rate. You'll also calculate total tax owed for all six stores.

c. Make up sales data for all six stores.

d. Enter the rate to be used to calculate the sales tax, using your own local rate.

e. Create formulas to calculate the sales tax owed for each store. If you don't know the local tax rate, use **6.5%**.

f. Create a formula to total all the accrued sales tax.

g. Use the ROUND function to eliminate any decimal places in the sales tax figures for each store and the total due.

h. Add your name to the header, then compare your work to the sample shown in FIGURE B-26.

i. Save your work, preview the worksheet, and submit your work to your instructor as directed.

j. Close the workbook and exit Excel.

FIGURE B-26

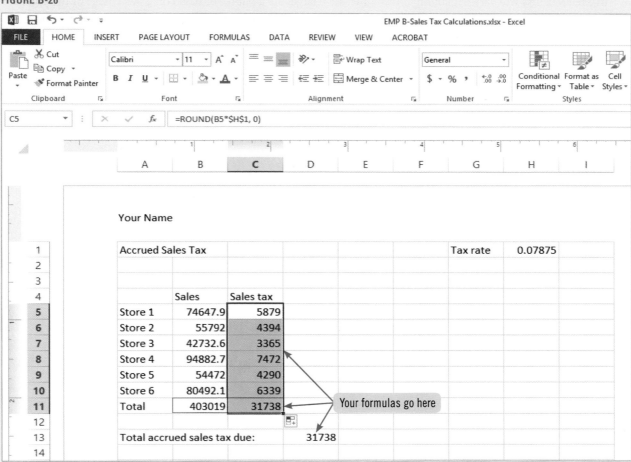

Independent Challenge 4: Explore

Since your recent promotion at work, you have started thinking about purchasing a home. As you begin the round of open houses and realtors' listings, you notice that there are many fees associated with buying a home. Some fees are based on a percentage of the purchase price, and others are a flat fee; overall, they seem to represent a substantial amount above the purchase prices you see listed. You've seen five houses so far that interest you; one is easily affordable, and the remaining four are all nice, but increasingly more expensive. Although you will be financing the home, the bottom line is still important to you, so you decide to create an Excel workbook to figure out the real cost of buying each one.

a. Find out the typical cost or percentage rate of at least three fees that are usually charged when buying a home and taking out a mortgage. (*Hint*: If you have access to the Internet you can research the topic of home buying on the Web, or you can ask friends about standard rates or percentages for items such as title insurance, credit reports, and inspection fees.)

b. Start Excel, then save a new, blank workbook to the location where you store your Data Files as **EMP B-Home Purchase Costs**.

c. Create labels and enter data for at least three homes. If you enter this information across the columns in your worksheet, you should have one column for each house, with the purchase price in the cell below each label. Be sure to enter a different purchase price for each house.

d. Create labels for the Fees column and for an Amount or Rate column. Enter the information for each of the fees you have researched.

e. In each house column, enter formulas that calculate the fee for each item. The formulas (and use of absolute or relative referencing) will vary depending on whether the charges are a flat fee or based on a percentage of the purchase price. Make sure that the formulas for items that are based on a percentage of the purchase price (such as the fees for the Title Insurance Policy, Loan Origination, and Underwriter) contain absolute references.

Independent Challenge 4: Explore (continued)

f. Total the fees for each house, then create formulas that add the total fees to the purchase price. A sample of what your workbook might look like is shown in FIGURE B-27.

g. Enter a title for the worksheet in the header.

h. Enter your name in the header, save your work, preview the worksheet, then submit your work to your instructor as directed.

i. Close the file and exit Excel.

FIGURE B-27

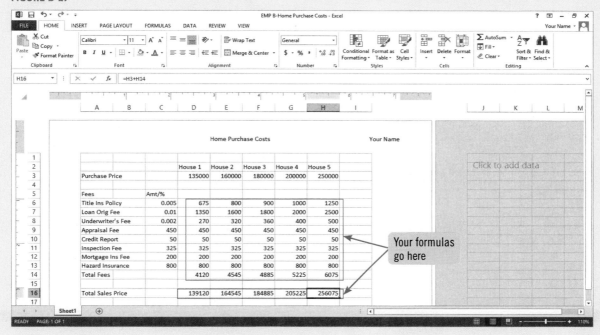

Excel 2013

Visual Workshop

Create the worksheet shown in **FIGURE B-28** using the skills you learned in this unit. Save the workbook as **EMP B-Health Insurance Cost Analysis** to the location where you store your Data Files. Enter your name and worksheet title in the header as shown, hide the gridlines, preview the worksheet, and then submit your work to your instructor as directed. (*Hint:* Change the Zoom factor to 90% by clicking the Zoom out button once.)

FIGURE B-28

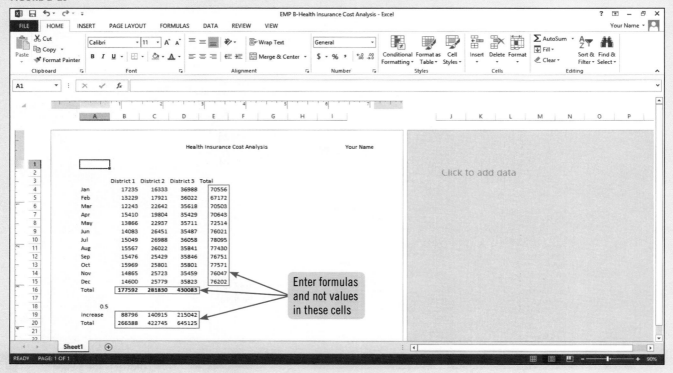

Formatting a Worksheet

CASE ▶ The administrators at RMC have requested data for expenses incurred during the first quarter of this year. Tony Sanchez has created a worksheet listing this information. He asks you to format the worksheet to make it easier to read and to call attention to important data.

Unit Objectives

After completing this unit, you will be able to:

- Format values
- Change font and font size
- Change font styles and alignment
- Adjust the column width
- Insert and delete rows and columns

- Apply colors, patterns, and borders
- Apply conditional formatting
- Rename and move a worksheet
- Check spelling

Files You Will Need

EMP C-1.xlsx
EMP C-2.xlsx
EMP C-3.xlsx
EMP C-4.xlsx
EMP C-5.xlsx

Format Values

**Learning
Outcomes**
• Format a number
• Format a date
• Increase/decrease
  decimals

The **format** of a cell determines how the labels and values look—for example, whether the contents appear boldfaced, italicized, or with dollar signs and commas. Formatting changes only the appearance of a value or label; it does not alter the actual data in any way. To format a cell or range, first you select it, then you apply the formatting using the Ribbon, Mini toolbar, or a keyboard shortcut. You can apply formatting before or after you enter data in a cell or range. **CASE** *Tony has provided you with a worksheet that details emergency room expenses, and you're ready to improve its appearance and readability. You start by formatting some of the values so they are displayed as currency, percentages, and dates.*

STEPS

1. **Start Excel, open the file EMP C-1.xlsx from the location where you store your Data Files, then save it as EMP C-RMC Emergency Room Expenses**

   This worksheet is difficult to interpret because all the information is crowded and looks the same. In some columns, the contents appear cut off because there is too much data to fit given the current column width. You decide not to widen the columns yet, because the other changes you plan to make might affect column width and row height. The first thing you want to do is format the data showing the cost of each expense.

QUICK TIP
You can use a different type of currency, such as Euros or British pounds, by clicking the Number Format list arrow, then clicking a different currency type.

2. **Select the range D11:D39, then click the Accounting Number Format button $ in the Number group on the HOME tab**

   The default Accounting **number format** adds dollar signs and two decimal places to the data, as shown in **FIGURE C-1**. Formatting this data in Accounting format makes it clear that its values are monetary values. Excel automatically resizes the column to display the new formatting. The Accounting and Currency number formats are both used for monetary values, but the Accounting format aligns currency symbols and decimal points of numbers in a column.

QUICK TIP
Select any range of contiguous cells by clicking the upper-left cell of the range, pressing and holding [Shift], then clicking the lower-right cell of the range. Add a column to the selected range by continuing to hold down [Shift] and pressing ➡; add a row by pressing ⬇.

3. **Select the range F11:H39, then click the Comma Style button 🔹 in the Number group**

   The values in columns F, G, and H display the Comma Style format, which does not include a dollar sign but can be useful for some types of accounting data.

4. **Select the range J11:J39, click the Number Format list arrow, click Percentage, then click the Increase Decimal button in the Number group**

   The data in the % of Total column is now formatted with a percent sign (%) and three decimal places. The Number Format list arrow lets you choose from popular number formats and shows an example of what the selected cell or cells would look like in each format (when multiple cells are selected, the example is based on the first cell in the range). Each time you click the Increase Decimal button, you add one decimal place; clicking the button twice would add two decimal places.

5. **Click the Decrease Decimal button in the Number group twice**

   Two decimal places are removed from the percentage values in column J.

6. **Select the range B11:B38, then click the dialog box launcher in the Number group**

   The Format Cells dialog box opens with the Date category already selected on the Number tab.

7. **Select the first 14-Mar-12 format in the Type list box as shown in FIGURE C-2, then click OK**

   The dates in column B appear in the 14-Mar-12 format. The second 14-Mar-12 format in the list (visible if you scroll down the list) displays all days in two digits (it adds a leading zero if the day is only a single-digit number), while the one you chose displays single-digit days without a leading zero.

QUICK TIP
Make sure you examine formatted data to confirm that you have applied the appropriate formatting; for example, dates should not have a currency format, and monetary values should not have a date format.

8. **Select the range C11:C38, right-click the range, click Format Cells on the shortcut menu, click 14-Mar in the Type list box in the Format Cells dialog box, then click OK**

   Compare your worksheet to **FIGURE C-3**.

9. **Press [Ctrl][Home], then save your work**

FIGURE C-1: Accounting number format applied to range

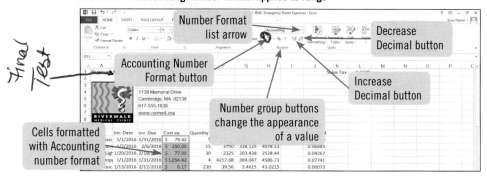

FIGURE C-2: Format Cells dialog box

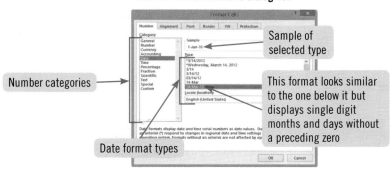

FIGURE C-3: Worksheet with formatted values

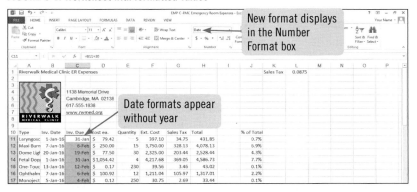

Formatting as a table

Excel includes 60 predefined **table styles** to make it easy to format selected worksheet cells as a table. You can apply table styles to any range of cells that you want to format quickly, or even to an entire worksheet, but they're especially useful for those ranges with labels in the left column and top row, and totals in the bottom row or right column. To apply a table style, select the data to be formatted or click anywhere within the intended range (Excel can automatically detect a range of cells filled with data), click the Format as Table button in the Styles group on the HOME tab, then click a style in the gallery, as shown in **FIGURE C-4**. Table styles are organized in three categories: Light, Medium, and Dark. Once you click a style, Excel asks you to confirm the range selection, then applies the style. Once you have formatted a range as a table, you can use Live Preview to preview the table in other styles by pointing to any style in the Table Styles gallery.

FIGURE C-4: Table Styles gallery

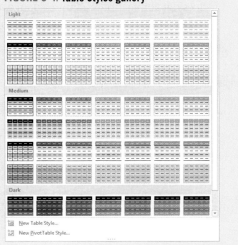

Change Font and Font Size

Learning Outcomes
- Change a font
- Change a font size
- Use the Mini toolbar

A **font** is the name for a collection of characters (letters, numbers, symbols, and punctuation marks) with a similar, specific design. The **font size** is the physical size of the text, measured in units called points. A **point** is equal to 1/72 of an inch. The default font and font size in Excel is 11-point Calibri. **TABLE C-1** shows several fonts in different font sizes. You can change the font and font size of any cell or range using the Font and Font Size list arrows. The Font and Font Size list arrows appear on the HOME tab on the Ribbon and on the Mini toolbar, which opens when you right-click a cell or range. **CASE** *You want to change the font and font size of the labels and the worksheet title so that they stand out more from the data.*

STEPS

QUICK TIP
When you point to an option in the Font or Font Size list, Live Preview shows the selected cells with the option temporarily applied.

1. **Click the Font list arrow in the Font group on the HOME tab, scroll down in the Font list to see an alphabetical listing of the fonts available on your computer, then click Times New Roman, as shown in FIGURE C-5**

   The font in cell A1 changes to Times New Roman. Notice that the font names on the list are displayed in the font they represent.

QUICK TIP
You can format an entire row by clicking the row indicator button to select the row before formatting (or select an entire column by clicking the column indicator button before formatting).

2. **Click the Font Size list arrow in the Font group, then click 20**

   The worksheet title appears in 20-point Times New Roman, and the Font and Font Size list boxes on the HOME tab display the new font and font size information.

3. **Click the Increase Font Size button A˄ in the Font group twice**

   The font size of the title increases to 24 point.

4. **Select the range A10:J10, right-click, then click the Font list arrow on the Mini toolbar**

   The Mini toolbar includes the most commonly used formatting tools, so it's great for making quick formatting changes.

QUICK TIP
To quickly move to a font in the Font list, type the first few characters of its name.

5. **Scroll through in the Font list and click Times New Roman, click the Font Size list arrow on the Mini toolbar, then click 14**

   The Mini toolbar closes when you move the pointer away from the selection. Compare your worksheet to **FIGURE C-6**. Notice that some of the column labels are now too wide to appear fully in the column. Excel does not automatically adjust column widths to accommodate cell formatting; you have to adjust column widths manually. You'll learn to do this in a later lesson.

6. **Save your work**

TABLE C-1: Examples of fonts and font sizes

font	12 point	24 point
Calibri	Excel	Excel
Playbill	Excel	Excel
Comic Sans MS	Excel	Excel
Times New Roman	Excel	Excel

© 2014 Cengage Learning

FIGURE C-5: Font list

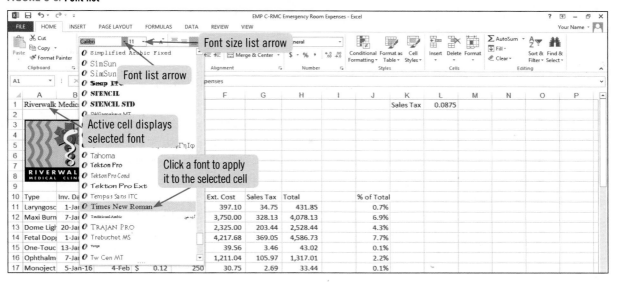

FIGURE C-6: Worksheet with formatted title and column labels

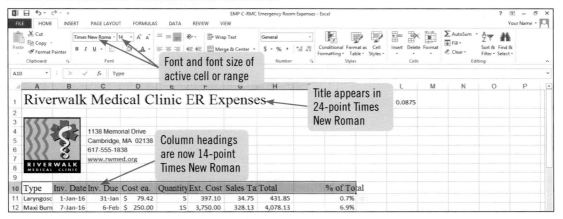

Inserting and adjusting online pictures and other images

You can illustrate your worksheets using online pictures and other images. Office.com makes many photos and animations available for your use. To add a picture to a worksheet, click the Online Pictures button in the Illustrations group on the INSERT tab. The Insert Pictures window opens. Here you can search for online pictures (or Clip Art) in Office.com, through the Bing search engine, or on your SkyDrive by typing one or more **keywords** (words related to your subject) in the appropriate Search text box, then press [Enter]. For example, pictures that relate to the keyword health in a search of Office.com appear in the Office.com window, as shown in **FIGURE C-7**. When you double-click the image you want in the window, the image is inserted at the location of the active cell. To add images on your computer (or computers on your network) to a worksheet, click the INSERT tab on the Ribbon, then click the Pictures button in the Illustrations group. Navigate to the file you want, then click Insert. To resize an image, drag any corner sizing handle. To move an image, point inside the clip until the pointer changes to ⁺⇖, then drag it to a new location.

FIGURE C-7: Results of Online Picture search

Change Font Styles and Alignment

Font styles are formats such as bold, italic, and underlining that you can apply to affect the way text and numbers look in a worksheet. You can also change the **alignment** of labels and values in cells to position them in relation to the cells' edges—such as left-aligned, right-aligned, or centered. You can apply font styles and alignment options using the HOME tab, the Format Cells dialog box, or the Mini toolbar. See TABLE C-2 for a description of common font style and alignment buttons that are available on the HOME tab and the Mini toolbar. Once you have formatted a cell the way you want it, you can "paint" or copy the cell's formats into other cells by using the Format Painter button in the Clipboard group on the HOME tab. This is similar to using copy and paste, but instead of copying cell contents, it copies only the cell's formatting. **CASE** *You want to further enhance the worksheet's appearance by adding bold and underline formatting and centering some of the labels.*

STEPS

1. **Press [Ctrl][Home], then click the Bold button Ⓑ in the Font group on the HOME tab**
   The title in cell A1 appears in bold.

2. **Click cell A10, then click the Underline button ⒰ in the Font group**
   The column label is now underlined, though this may be difficult to see with the cell selected.

3. **Click the Italic button Ⓘ in the Font group, then click Ⓑ**
   The heading now appears in boldface, underlined, italic type. Notice that the Bold, Italic, and Underline buttons in the Font group are all selected.

4. **Click the Italic button Ⓘ to deselect it**
   The italic font style is removed from cell A10, but the bold and underline font styles remain.

5. **Click the Format Painter button ⊛ in the Clipboard group, then select the range B10:J10**
   The formatting in cell A10 is copied to the rest of the column labels. To paint the formats on more than one selection, double-click the Format Painter button to keep it activated until you turn it off. You can turn off the Format Painter by pressing [Esc] or by clicking ⊛. You decide the title would look better if it were centered over the data columns.

6. **Select the range A1:H1, then click the Merge & Center button ▤ in the Alignment group**
   The Merge & Center button creates one cell out of the eight cells across the row, then centers the text in that newly created, merged cell. The title "Riverwalk Medical Clinic ER Expenses" is centered across the eight columns you selected. To split a merged cell into its original components, select the merged cell, then click the Merge & Center button to deselect it. The merged and centered text might look awkward now, but you'll be changing the column widths shortly. Occasionally, you may find that you want cell contents to wrap within a cell. You can do this by selecting the cells containing the text you want to wrap, then clicking the Wrap Text button ▤ in the Alignment group on the HOME tab on the Ribbon.

7. **Select the range A10:J10, right-click, then click the Center button ▤ on the Mini toolbar**
   Compare your screen to FIGURE C-8. Although they may be difficult to read, notice that all the headings are centered within their cells.

8. **Save your work**

FIGURE C-8: Worksheet with font styles and alignment applied

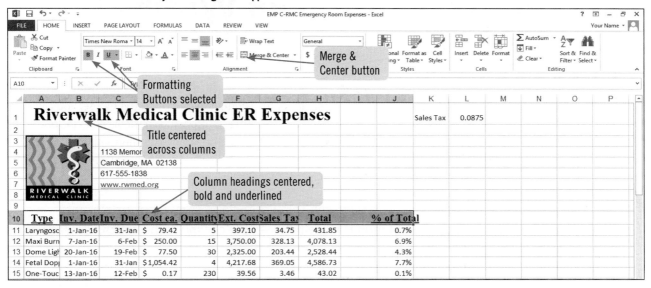

TABLE C-2: Common font style and alignment buttons

button	description
B	Bolds text
I	Italicizes text
U	Underlines text
	Centers text across columns, and combines two or more selected, adjacent cells into one cell
	Aligns text at the left edge of the cell
	Centers text horizontally within the cell
	Aligns text at the right edge of the cell
	Wraps long text into multiple lines

© 2014 Cengage Learning

Rotating and indenting cell entries

In addition to applying fonts and font styles, you can rotate or indent data within a cell to further change its appearance. You can rotate text within a cell by altering its alignment. To change alignment, select the cells you want to modify, then click the dialog box launcher ⬂ in the Alignment group to open the Alignment tab of the Format Cells dialog box. Click a position in the Orientation box or type a number in the Degrees text box to rotate text from its default horizontal orientation, then click OK. You can indent cell contents using the Increase Indent button ⬆ in the Alignment group, which moves cell contents to the right one space, or the Decrease Indent button ⬅, which moves cell contents to the left one space.

Adjust the Column Width

As you format a worksheet, you might need to adjust the width of one or more columns to accommodate changes in the amount of text, the font size, or font style. The default column width is 8.43 characters, a little less than 1". With Excel, you can adjust the width of one or more columns by using the mouse, the Format button in the Cells group on the HOME tab, or the shortcut menu. Using the mouse, you can drag or double-click the right edge of a column heading. The Format button and shortcut menu include commands for making more precise width adjustments. TABLE C-3 describes common column formatting commands. **CASE** ▶ *You have noticed that some of the labels in columns A through J don't fit in the cells. You want to adjust the widths of the columns so that the labels appear in their entirety.*

STEPS

1. **Position the mouse pointer on the line between the column A and column B headings until it changes to ↔**

   See FIGURE C-9. The **column heading** is the box at the top of each column containing a letter. Before you can adjust column width using the mouse, you need to position the pointer on the right edge of the column heading for the column you want to adjust. The cell entry "TV commercials" is the widest in the column.

2. **Click and drag the ↔ to the right until the column displays the "Monoject Syringes" cell entries fully (approximately 16.43 characters, 1.31", or 120 pixels)**

   As you change the column width, a ScreenTip is displayed listing the column width. In Normal view, the ScreenTip lists the width in characters and pixels; in Page Layout view, the ScreenTip lists the width in inches and pixels.

3. **Position the pointer on the line between columns B and C until it changes to ↔, then double-click**

   Double-clicking the right edge of a column heading activates the **AutoFit** feature, which automatically resizes the column to accommodate the widest entry in the column. Column B automatically widens to fit the widest entry, which is the column label "Inv. Date".

4. **Use AutoFit to resize columns D, and J, and resize column C so it has a width of 10 characters**

5. **Select the range E12:H12**

   You can change the width of multiple columns at once, by first selecting either the column headings or at least one cell in each column.

6. ▶ **Click the Format button in the Cells group, then click Column Width**

   The Column Width dialog box opens. Column width measurement is based on the number of characters that will fit in the column when formatted in the Normal font and font size (in this case, 11 pt Calibri).

7. **Drag the dialog box by its title bar if its placement obscures your view of the worksheet, type 11 in the Column width text box, then click OK**

   The widths of columns E, F, G, and H change to reflect the new setting. See FIGURE C-10.

8. **Save your work**

TABLE C-3: Common column formatting commands

command	description	available using
Column Width	Sets the width to a specific number of characters	Format button; shortcut menu
AutoFit Column Width	Fits to the widest entry in a column	Format button; mouse
Hide & Unhide	Hides or displays hidden column(s)	Format button; shortcut menu
Default Width	Resets column to worksheet's default column width	Format button

FIGURE C-9: Preparing to change the column width

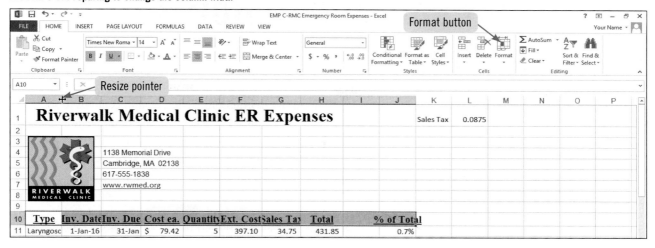

FIGURE C-10: Worksheet with column widths adjusted

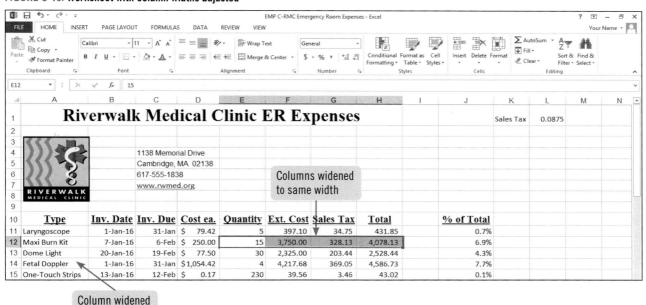

Changing row height

Changing row height is as easy as changing column width. Row height is calculated in points, the same units of measure used for fonts. The row height must exceed the size of the font you are using. Normally, you don't need to adjust row heights manually, because row heights adjust automatically to accommodate font size changes. If you format something in a row to be a larger point size, Excel adjusts the row to fit the largest point size in the row. However, you have just as many options for changing row height as you do column width. Using the mouse, you can place the ✛ pointer on the line dividing a row heading from the heading below, and then drag to the desired height; double-clicking the line AutoFits the row height where necessary. You can also select one or more rows, then use the Row Height command on the shortcut menu, or click the Format button on the HOME tab and click the Row Height or AutoFit Row Height command.

Insert and Delete Rows and Columns

As you modify a worksheet, you might find it necessary to insert or delete rows and columns to keep your worksheet current. For example, you might need to insert rows to accommodate new inventory products or remove a column of yearly totals that are no longer necessary. When you insert a new row, the row is inserted above the cell pointer and the contents of the worksheet shift down from the newly inserted row. When you insert a new column, the column is inserted to the left of the cell pointer and the contents of the worksheet shift to the right of the new column. To insert multiple rows, select the same number of row headings as you want to insert before using the Insert command. **CASE** *You want to improve the overall appearance of the worksheet by inserting a row between the last row of data and the totals. Also, you have learned that row 34 and column J need to be deleted from the worksheet.*

STEPS

1. **Right-click cell A39, then click Insert on the shortcut menu**

   The Insert dialog box opens. See **FIGURE C-11**. You can choose to insert a column or a row; insert a single cell and shift the cells in the active column to the right; or insert a single cell and shift the cells in the active row down. An additional row between the last row of data and the totals will visually separate the totals.

2. **Click the Entire row option button, then click OK**

   A blank row appears between the emergency room supplies data and the totals, and the formula result in cell E40 has not changed. The Insert Options button ⬦ appears beside cell A40. Pointing to the button displays a list arrow, which you can click and then choose from the following options: Format Same As Above (the default setting, already selected), Format Same As Below, or Clear Formatting.

3. **Click the row 34 heading**

   All of row 34 is selected, as shown in **FIGURE C-12**.

4. **Click the Delete button in the Cells group;** *do not click the list arrow*

   Excel deletes row 34, and all rows below it shift up one row. You must use the Delete button or the Delete command on the shortcut menu to delete a row or column; pressing [Delete] on the keyboard removes only the *contents* of a selected row or column.

5. **Click the column J heading**

   The percentage information is calculated elsewhere and is no longer necessary in this worksheet.

6. **Click the Delete button in the Cells group**

   Excel deletes column J. The remaining columns to the right shift left one column.

7. **Use AutoFit to resize columns F and H, then save your work**

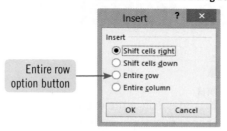

FIGURE C-11: Insert dialog box

FIGURE C-12: Worksheet with row 34 selected

	A	B	C	D	E	F	G	H	I	J	K	L	M	N
25	One-Touch Strips	28-Feb-16	29-Mar	$ 0.17	275	47.30	4.14	51.44		0.1%				
26	Ophthalmoscope	27-Feb-16	28-Mar	$ 100.92	12	1,211.04	105.97	1,317.01		2.2%				
27	Dome Light	22-Feb-16	23-Mar	$ 77.50	30	2,325.00	203.44	2,528.44		4.3%				
28	Maxi Burn Kit	1-Feb-16	2-Mar	$ 250.00	30	7,500.00	656.25	8,156.25		13.8%				
29	Laryngoscope	25-Feb-16	26-Mar	$ 79.42	6	476.52	41.70	518.22		0.9%				
30	One-Touch Strips	-Mar-16	9-Apr	$ 0.17	275	47.30	4.14	51.44		0.1%				
31		-Feb-16	16-Mar	$ 250.00	25	6,250.00	546.88	6,796.88		11.5%				
32	Monoject Syringes	15-Mar-16	14-Apr	$ 0.12	250	30.75	2.69	33.44		0.1%				
33	Fetal Doppler	1-Mar-16	31-Mar	$1,054.44	4	4,217.76	369.05	4,586.81		7.7%				
34	Penlights	20-Mar-16	19-Apr	$ 7.20	250	1,800.00	157.50	1,957.50		3.3%				
35	Dome Light	20-Mar-16	19-Apr	$ 75.50	30	2,265.00	198.19	2,463.19		4.2%				
36	Laryngoscope	1-Apr-16	1-May	$ 79.42	2	158.84	13.90	172.74		0.3%				
37	Dome Light	10-Apr-16	10-May	$ 77.50	30	2,325.00	203.44	2,528.44		4.3%				
38	Otoscope Set	28-Mar-16	27-Apr	$ 101.87	20	2,037.40	178.27	2,215.67		3.7%				
39														
40				$5,311.50	2034	54,485.30	4,767.46	59,252.76		100.0%				
41														
42														

Delete button

Row 34 heading

Inserted row

Insert Options button

Hiding and unhiding columns and rows

When you don't want data in a column or row to be visible, but you don't want to delete it, you can hide the column or row. To hide a selected column, click the Format button in the Cells group on the HOME tab, point to Hide & Unhide, then click Hide Columns. A hidden column is indicated by a dark green vertical line in its original position. This green line disappears when you click elsewhere in the worksheet. You can display a hidden column by selecting the columns on either side of the hidden column, clicking the Format button in the Cells group, pointing to Hide & Unhide, and then clicking Unhide Columns. (To hide or unhide one or more rows, substitute Hide Rows and Unhide Rows for the Hide Columns and Unhide Columns commands.)

Adding and editing comments

Much of your work in Excel may be in collaboration with teammates with whom you share worksheets. You can share ideas with other worksheet users by adding comments within selected cells. To include a comment in a worksheet, click the cell where you want to place the comment, click the REVIEW tab on the Ribbon, then click the New Comment button in the Comments group. You can type your comments in the resizable text box that opens containing the computer user's name. A small, red triangle appears in the upper-right corner of a cell containing a comment. If comments are not already displayed in a workbook, other users can point to the triangle to display the comment. To see all worksheet comments, as shown in FIGURE C-13, click the Show All Comments button in the Comments group. To edit a comment, click the cell containing the comment, then click the Edit Comment button in the Comments group. To delete a comment, click the cell containing the comment, then click the Delete button in the Comments group.

FIGURE C-13: Comments displayed in a worksheet

19	Otoscope Set	12-Jan-16	11-Feb	$ 101.87	20	2,037.40
20	Laryngoscope	25-Jan-16	24-Feb	$ 72.34	6	434.04
21	Laryngoscope	1-Feb-16	2-Mar	$ 23.91	2	47.82
22	Ring Cutter	3-Feb-16	4-Mar	$ 5.67	Tony Sanchez:	
23	Fetal Doppler	1-Feb-16	2-Mar	$ 1,054.42	These items are very costly. How can we	
24	Laryngoscope	1-Mar-16	31-Mar	$ 23.91	economize?	
25	One-Touch Strips	28-Feb-16	29-Mar	$ 0.17		
26	Ophthalmoscope	27-Feb-16	28-Mar	$ 100.92	12	1,211.04
27	Dome Light	22-Feb-16	23-Mar	$ 75.50	30	2,265.00
28	Maxi Burn Kit	1-Feb-16	2-Mar	$ 250.00	30	7,500.00
29	Laryngoscope	25-Feb-16	26-Mar	$ 72.34	Tony Sanchez:	
30	One-Touch Strips	10-Mar-16	9-Apr	$ 0.17	We've gotten a great price on these!	
31	Maxi Burn Kit	15-Feb-16	16-Mar	$ 250.00		
32	Monoject Syringes	15-Mar-16	14-Apr	$ 0.12		

Apply Colors, Patterns, and Borders

Learning Outcomes
• Use Live Preview to apply color to cells
• Format cells using the shortcut menu
• Apply a border and pattern to a cell

You can use colors, patterns, and borders to enhance the overall appearance of a worksheet and make it easier to read. You can add these enhancements by using the Borders, Font Color, and Fill Color buttons in the Font group on the HOME tab of the Ribbon and on the Mini toolbar, or by using the Fill tab and the Border tab in the Format Cells dialog box. You can open the Format Cells dialog box by clicking the dialog box launcher in the Font, Alignment, or Number group on the HOME tab, or by right-clicking a selection, then clicking Format Cells on the shortcut menu. You can apply a color to the background of a cell or a range or to cell contents (such as letters and numbers), and you can apply a pattern to a cell or range. You can apply borders to all the cells in a worksheet or only to selected cells to call attention to selected information. To save time, you can also apply **cell styles**, predesigned combinations of formats. **CASE** ▶ *You want to add a pattern, a border, and color to the title of the worksheet to give the worksheet a more professional appearance.*

STEPS

1. **Select cell A1, click the Fill Color list arrow 🔲 ▾ in the Font group, then hover the pointer over the Turquoise, Accent 2 color (first row, sixth column from the left)**
   See **FIGURE C-14**. Live Preview shows you how the color will look *before* you apply it. (Remember that cell A1 spans columns A through H because the Merge & Center command was applied.)

2. **Click the Turquoise, Accent 2 color**
   The color is applied to the background (or fill) of this cell. When you change fill or font color, the color on the Fill Color or Font Color button changes to the last color you selected.

3. **Right-click cell A1, then click Format Cells on the shortcut menu**
   The Format Cells dialog box opens.

4. **Click the Fill tab, click the Pattern Style list arrow, click the 6.25% Gray style (first row, sixth column from the left), then click OK**

5. **Click the Borders list arrow 🔲 ▾ in the Font group, then click Thick Bottom Border**
   Unlike underlining, which is a text-formatting tool, borders extend to the width of the cell, and can appear at the bottom of the cell, at the top, on either side, or on any combination of the four sides. It can be difficult to see a border when the cell is selected.

6. **Select the range A10:H10, click the Font Color list arrow 🔲 ▾ in the Font group, then click the Blue, Accent 1 color (first Theme color row, fifth column from the left) on the palette**
   The new color is applied to the labels in the selected range.

7. **Select the range J1:K1, click the Cell Styles button in the Styles group, click the Neutral cell style (first row, fourth column from the left) in the gallery, then AutoFit column J**
   The font and color change in the range is shown in **FIGURE C-15**.

8. **Save your work**

FIGURE C-14: Live Preview of fill color

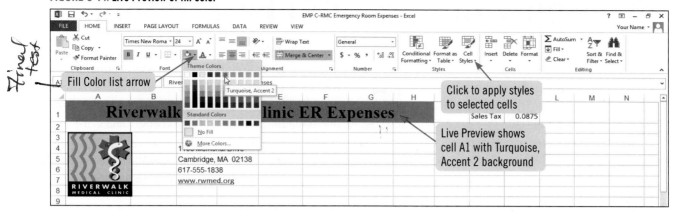

FIGURE C-15: Worksheet with color, patterns, border, and cell style applied

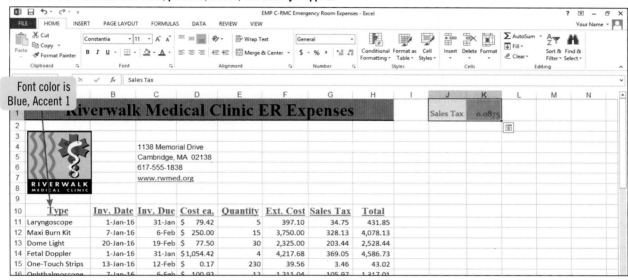

Working with themes and cell styles

Using themes and cell styles makes it easier to ensure that your worksheets are consistent. A **theme** is a predefined set of formats that gives your Excel worksheet a professional look. Formatting choices included in a theme are colors, fonts, and line and fill effects. To apply a theme, click the Themes button in the Themes group on the PAGE LAYOUT tab to open the Themes gallery, as shown in **FIGURE C-16**, then click a theme in the gallery. **Cell styles** are sets of cell formats based on themes, so they are automatically updated if you change a theme. For example, if you apply the 20% - Accent1 cell style to cell A1 in a worksheet that has no theme applied, the fill color changes to light blue with no pattern, and the font changes to Constantia. If you change the theme of the worksheet to Ion Boardroom, cell A1's fill color changes to red and the font changes to Century Gothic, because these are the new theme's associated formats.

FIGURE C-16: Themes gallery

Apply Conditional Formatting

Learning Outcomes
• Create conditional formatting in a range
• Change formatting and parameters in conditional formatting

So far, you've used formatting to change the appearance of different types of data, but you can also use formatting to highlight important aspects of the data itself. For example, you can apply formatting that changes the font color to red for any cells where ad costs exceed $100 and to green where ad costs are below $50. This is called **conditional formatting** because Excel automatically applies different formats to data if the data meets conditions you specify. The formatting is updated if you change data in the worksheet. You can also copy conditional formats the same way you copy other formats. **CASE** ▶ *Tony is concerned about advertising costs exceeding the yearly budget. You decide to use conditional formatting to highlight certain trends and patterns in the data so that it's easy to spot the most expensive advertising.*

STEPS

QUICK TIP
You can also use the Quick Analysis tool to create data bars, but with fewer choices.

1. **Select the range H11:H37, click the Conditional Formatting button in the Styles group on the HOME tab, point to Data Bars, then point to the Light Blue Data Bar (second row, second from left)**

   Data bars are colored horizontal bars that visually illustrate differences between values in a range of cells. Live Preview shows how this formatting will appear in the worksheet, as shown in FIGURE C-17.

QUICK TIP
You can apply an Icon Set to a selected range by clicking the Conditional Formatting button in the Styles group, then pointing to Icon Sets; icons appear within the cells to illustrate differences in values.

2. **Point to the Green Data Bar (first row, second from left), then click it**

3. **Select the range F11:F37, click the Conditional Formatting button in the Styles group, then point to Highlight Cells Rules**

   The Highlight Cells Rules submenu displays choices for creating different formatting conditions. For example, you can create a rule for values that are greater than or less than a certain amount, or between two amounts.

4. **Click Between on the submenu**

   The Between dialog box opens, displaying input boxes you can use to define the condition and a default format (Light Red Fill with Dark Red Text) selected for cells that meet that condition. Depending on the condition you select in the Highlight Cells Rules submenu (such as "Greater Than" or "Less Than"), this dialog box displays different input boxes. You define the condition using the input boxes and then assign the formatting you want to use for cells that meet that condition. Values used in input boxes for a condition can be constants, formulas, cell references, or dates.

QUICK TIP
To define custom formatting for data that meets the condition, click Custom Format at the bottom of the with list, and then use the Format Cells dialog box to set the formatting to be applied.

5. **Type 2000 in the first text box, type 4000 in the second text box, click the with list arrow, click Light Red Fill, compare your settings to FIGURE C-18, then click OK**

   All cells with values between 2000 and 4000 in column F appear with a light red fill.

6. **Click cell F14, type 3975.55, then press [Enter]**

   When the value in cell F14 changes, the formatting also changes because the new value meets the condition you set. Compare your results to FIGURE C-19.

7. **Press [Ctrl][Home] to select cell A1, then save your work**

Managing conditional formatting rules

If you create a conditional formatting rule and then want to change the condition to reflect a different value or format, you don't need to create a new rule; instead, you can modify the rule using the Rules Manager. Select the cell(s) containing conditional formatting, click the Conditional Formatting button in the Styles group, then click Manage Rules. The Conditional Formatting Rules Manager dialog box opens. Select the rule you want to edit, click Edit Rule, and then modify the settings in the Edit the Rule Description area in the Edit Formatting Rule dialog box. To change the formatting for a rule, click the Format button in the Edit the Rule Description area, select the formatting styles you want the text to have, then click OK three times to close the Format Cells dialog box, the Edit Formatting Rule dialog box, and then the Conditional Formatting Rules Manager dialog box. The rule is modified, and the new conditional formatting is applied to the selected cells. To delete a rule, select the rule in the Conditional Formatting Rules Manager dialog box, then click the Delete Rule button.

FIGURE C-17: Previewing data bars in a range

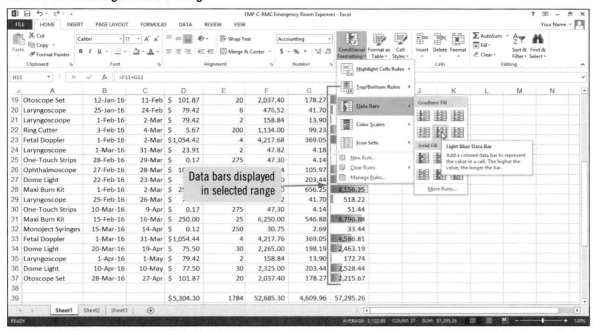

FIGURE C-18: Between dialog box

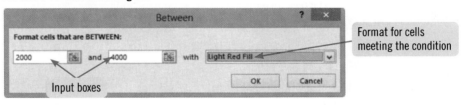

FIGURE C-19: Worksheet with conditional formatting

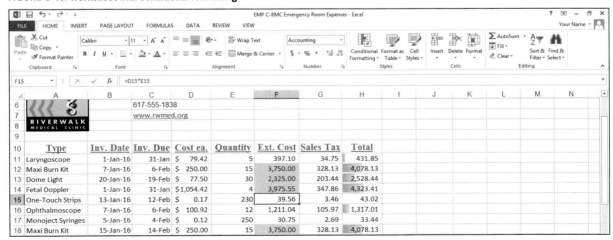

Rename and Move a Worksheet

By default, an Excel workbook initially contains one worksheet named Sheet1, although you can add sheets at any time. Each sheet name appears on a sheet tab at the bottom of the worksheet. When you open a new workbook, the first worksheet, Sheet1, is the active sheet. To move from sheet to sheet, you can click any sheet tab at the bottom of the worksheet window. The sheet tab scrolling buttons, located to the left of the sheet tabs, are useful when a workbook contains too many sheet tabs to display at once. To make it easier to identify the sheets in a workbook, you can rename each sheet and add color to the tabs. You can also organize them in a logical way. For instance, to better track performance goals, you could name each workbook sheet for an individual salesperson, and you could move the sheets so they appear in alphabetical order. **CASE** *In the current workbook, Sheet1 contains information about actual advertising expenses. Sheet2 contains an advertising budget, and Sheet3 contains no data. You want to rename the two sheets in the workbook to reflect their contents, add color to a sheet tab to easily distinguish one from the other, and change their order.*

STEPS

1. **Click the Sheet2 tab**

   Sheet2 becomes active, appearing in front of the Sheet1 tab; this is the worksheet that contains the budgeted advertising expenses. See FIGURE C-20.

2. **Click the Sheet1 tab**

   Sheet1, which contains the actual advertising expenses, becomes active again.

3. **Double-click the Sheet2 tab, type Budget, then press [Enter]**

   The new name for Sheet2 automatically replaces the default name on the tab. Worksheet names can have up to 31 characters, including spaces and punctuation.

4. **Right-click the Budget tab, point to Tab Color on the shortcut menu, then click the Bright Green, Accent 4, Lighter 40% color (fourth row, third column from the right) as shown in FIGURE C-21**

5. **Double-click the Sheet1 tab, type Actual, then press [Enter]**

   Notice that the color of the Budget tab changes depending on whether it is the active tab; when the Actual tab is active, the color of the Budget tab changes to the green tab color you selected. You decide to rearrange the order of the sheets, so that the Budget tab is to the left of the Actual tab.

6. **Click the Budget tab, hold down the mouse button, drag it to the left of the Actual tab, as shown in FIGURE C-22, then release the mouse button**

   As you drag, the pointer changes to ▯, the sheet relocation pointer, and a small, black triangle just above the tabs shows the position the moved sheet will be in when you release the mouse button. The first sheet in the workbook is now the Budget sheet. See FIGURE C-23. You can move multiple sheets by pressing and holding [Shift] while clicking the sheets you want to move, then dragging the sheets to their new location.

7. **Click the Actual sheet tab, click the Page Layout button 🖩 on the status bar to open Page Layout view, enter your name in the left header text box, then click anywhere in the worksheet to deselect the header**

8. **Click the PAGE LAYOUT tab on the Ribbon, click the Orientation button in the Page Setup group, then click Landscape**

9. **Right-click the Sheet3 tab, click Delete on the shortcut menu, press [Ctrl][Home], then save your work**

FIGURE C-20: **Sheet tabs in workbook**

FIGURE C-21: **Tab Color palette**

Sheet2 renamed

FIGURE C-22: **Moving the Budget sheet**

Sheet relocation pointer

FIGURE C-23: **Reordered sheets**

Budget sheet comes
before Actual sheet

Copying, Adding, and Deleting worksheets

There are times when you may want to copy a worksheet. For example, a workbook might contain a sheet with Quarter 1 expenses, and you want to use that sheet as the basis for a sheet containing Quarter 2 expenses. To copy a sheet within the same workbook, press and hold [Ctrl], drag the sheet tab to the desired tab location, release the mouse button, then release [Ctrl]. A duplicate sheet appears with the same name as the copied sheet followed by "(2)" indicating it is a copy. You can then rename the sheet to a more meaningful name. To copy a sheet to a different workbook, both the source and destination workbooks must be open. Select the sheet to copy or move, right-click the sheet tab, then click Move or Copy in the shortcut menu. Complete the information in the Move or Copy dialog

box. Be sure to click the Create a copy check box if you are copying rather than moving the worksheet. Carefully check your calculation results whenever you move or copy a worksheet. You can add multiple worksheets to a workbook by clicking the HOME tab on the Ribbon, pressing and holding [Shift], then clicking the number of existing worksheet tabs that correspond with the number of sheets you want to add, clicking the Insert list arrow in the Cells group on the HOME tab, then clicking Insert Sheet. You can delete multiple worksheets from a workbook by clicking the HOME tab on the Ribbon, pressing and holding [Shift], clicking the sheet tabs of the worksheets you want to delete, clicking the Delete list arrow in the Cells group on the HOME tab, then clicking Delete Sheet.

Excel 2013

Check Spelling

Excel includes a spell checker to help you ensure that the words in your worksheet are spelled correctly. The spell checker scans your worksheet, displays words it doesn't find in its built-in dictionary, and suggests replacements when they are available. To check all of the sheets in a multiple-sheet workbook, you need to display each sheet individually and run the spell checker for each one. Because the built-in dictionary cannot possibly include all the words that anyone needs, you can add words to the dictionary, such as your company name, an acronym, or an unusual technical term. Once you add a word or term, the spell checker no longer considers that word misspelled. Any words you've added to the dictionary using Word, Access, or PowerPoint are also available in Excel. **CASE** ▶ *Before you distribute this workbook to Tony and the marketing managers, you check its spelling.*

STEPS

QUICK TIP
The Spelling dialog box lists the name of the language currently being used in its title bar.

1. **Click the REVIEW tab on the Ribbon, then click the Spelling button in the Proofing group**

   The Spelling: English (United States) dialog box opens, as shown in FIGURE C-24, with "Riverwalk" selected as the first misspelled word in the worksheet. For any word, you have the option to Ignore this case of the flagged word, Ignore All cases of the flagged word, Change the word to the selected suggestion, Change All instances of the flagged word to the selected suggestion, or add the flagged word to the dictionary using Add to Dictionary.

2. **Click Ignore All, then click Ignore All for the next two cases (Monoject and Otoscope)**

   Next, the spell checker finds the word "Laryngoscoope" and suggests "Laryngoscope" as an alternative.

3. **Verify that the word Laryngoscope is selected in the Suggestions list, then click Change**

   When no more incorrect words are found, Excel displays a message indicating that the spell check is complete.

4. **Click OK**

5. **Click the HOME tab, click Find & Select in the Editing group, then click Replace**

   The Find and Replace dialog box opens. You can use this dialog box to replace a word or phrase. It might be a misspelling of a proper name that the spell checker didn't recognize as misspelled, or it could simply be a term that you want to change throughout the worksheet. Tony has just told you that each instance of "Maxi" in the worksheet should be changed to "ACE."

6. **Type Maxi in the Find what text box, press [Tab], then type ACE in the Replace with text box**

   Compare your dialog box to FIGURE C-25.

7. **Click Replace All, click OK to close the Microsoft Excel dialog box, then click Close to close the Find and Replace dialog box**

   Excel has made four replacements.

8. **Click the FILE tab, click Print on the navigation bar, click the No Scaling setting in the Settings section on the Print tab, then click Fit Sheet on One Page**

9. **Click the Return button to return to your worksheet, save your work, submit it to your instructor as directed, close the workbook, then exit Excel**

   The completed worksheet is shown in FIGURE C-26.

Emailing a workbook

You can send an entire workbook from within Excel using your installed email program, such as Microsoft Outlook. To send a workbook as an email message attachment, open the workbook, click the FILE tab, then click Share on the navigation bar. With the Email option selected in the Share section in Backstage view, click Send as Attachment in the right pane. An email message opens in your default email program with the workbook automatically attached; the filename appears in the Attached field. Complete the To and optional Cc fields, include a message if you wish, then click Send.

FIGURE C-24: Spelling: English (United States) dialog box

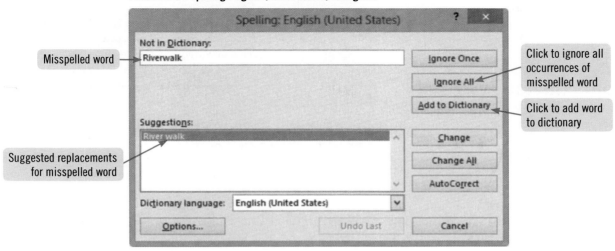

Misspelled word

Suggested replacements for misspelled word

Click to ignore all occurrences of misspelled word

Click to add word to dictionary

FIGURE C-25: Find and Replace dialog box

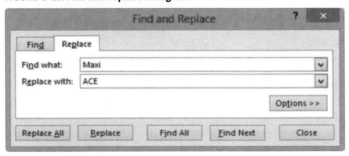

FIGURE C-26: Completed worksheet

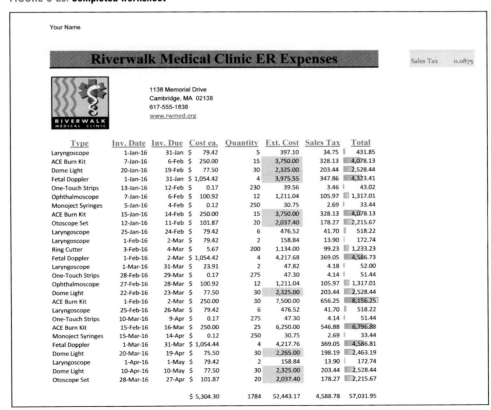

Excel 2013

Practice

Concepts Review

Label each element of the Excel worksheet window shown in FIGURE C-27.

FIGURE C-27

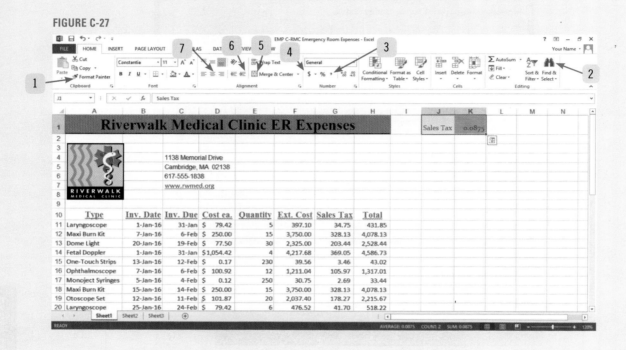

Match each command or button with the statement that best describes it.

8. **Conditional formatting**
9. $
10. **Spelling button**
11. **[Ctrl][Home]**
12. ⊞
13. 🪣 ▾

a. Checks for apparent misspellings in a worksheet
b. Adds dollar signs and two decimal places to selected data
c. Centers cell contents over multiple cells
d. Changes formatting of a cell that meets a certain rule
e. Moves cell pointer to cell A1
f. Displays background color options for a cell

Select the best answer from the list of choices.

14. **Which button increases the number of decimal places in selected cells?**
    - **a.** [icon]
    - **b.** [icon]
    - **c.** [icon]
    - **d.** [icon]

15. **What feature is used to delete a conditional formatting rule?**
    - **a.** Rules Reminder
    - **b.** Conditional Formatting Rules Manager
    - **c.** Condition Manager
    - **d.** Format Manager

16. **Which button removes the italic font style from selected cells?**
    - **a.** [I icon]
    - **b.** [B icon]
    - **c.** [I icon]
    - **d.** [U icon]

17. **Which button copies multiple formats from selected cells to other cells?**
    - **a.** [icon]
    - **b.** [icon]
    - **c.** [A icon]
    - **d.** [icon]

18. **What is the name of the feature used to resize a column to accommodate its widest entry?**
    - **a.** AutoFormat
    - **b.** AutoFit
    - **c.** AutoResize
    - **d.** AutoRefit

19. **Which of the following is an example of Accounting number format?**
    - **a.** 5555
    - **b.** $5,555.55
    - **c.** 55.55%
    - **d.** 5,555.55

Skills Review

1. **Format values.**
   a. Start Excel, open the file EMP C-2.xlsx from the location where you store your Data Files, then save it as **EMP C-Health Insurance Premiums**.
   b. Use the Sum function to enter a formula in cell B10 that totals the number of employees.
   c. Create a formula in cell C5 that calculates the monthly insurance premium for the accounting department. (*Hint*: Make sure you use the correct type of cell reference in the formula. To calculate the department's monthly premium, multiply the number of employees by the monthly premium in cell B14.)
   d. Copy the formula in cell C5 to the range C6:C10.
   e. Format the range C5:C10 using Accounting number format.
   f. Change the format of the range C6:C9 to the Comma Style.
   g. Reduce the number of decimals in cell B14 to 0 using a button in the Number group on the HOME tab.
   h. Save your work.

2. **Change font and font sizes.**
   a. Select the range of cells containing the column labels (in row 4).
   b. Change the font of the selection to Times New Roman.
   c. Increase the font size of the selection to 12 points.
   d. Increase the font size of the label in cell A1 to 14 points.
   e. Save your changes.

3. **Change font styles and alignment.**
   a. Apply the bold and italic font styles to the worksheet title in cell A1.
   b. Use the Merge & Center button to center the Health Insurance Premiums label over columns A through C.
   c. Apply the italic font style to the Health Insurance Premiums label.
   d. Add the bold font style to the labels in row 4.
   e. Use the Format Painter to copy the format in cell A4 to the range A5:A10.
   f. Apply the format in cell C10 to cell B14.
   g. Change the alignment of cell A10 to Align Right using a button in the Alignment group.

Skills Review (continued)

    h. Select the range of cells containing the column labels, then center them.

    i. Remove the italic font style from the Health Insurance Premiums label, then increase the font size to 14.

    j. Move the Health Insurance Premiums label to cell A3, then add the bold and underline font styles.

    k. Save your changes.

4. Adjust the column width.

    a. Resize column C to a width of 10.71 characters.

    b. Use the AutoFit feature to resize columns A and B.

    c. Clear the contents of cell A13 (do not delete the cell).

    d. Change the text in cell A14 to **Monthly Insurance Premium**, then change the width of the column to 25 characters.

    e. Save your changes.

5. Insert and delete rows and columns.

    a. Insert a new row between rows 5 and 6.

    b. Add a new department, **Charity**, in the newly inserted row. Enter **6** as the number of employees in the department.

    c. Copy the formula in cell C7 to C6.

    d. Add the following comment to cell A6: **New department**. Display the comment, then drag to move it out of the way, if necessary.

    e. Add a new column between the Department and Employees columns with the label **Family Coverage**, then resize the column using AutoFit.

    f. Delete the Legal row from the worksheet.

    g. Move the value in cell C14 to cell B14.

    h. Save your changes.

6. Apply colors, patterns, and borders.

    a. Add Outside Borders around the range A4:D10.

    b. Add a Bottom Double Border to cells C9 and D9 (above the calculated employee and premium totals).

    c. Apply the Aqua, Accent 5, Lighter 80% fill color to the labels in the Department column (do not include the Total label).

    d. Apply the Orange, Accent 6, Lighter 60% fill color to the range A4:D4.

    e. Change the color of the font in the range A4:D4 to Red, Accent 2, Darker 25%.

    f. Add a 12.5% Gray pattern style to cell A1.

    g. Format the range A14:B14 with a fill color of Dark Blue, Text 2, Lighter 40%, change the font color to White, Background 1, then apply the bold font style.

    h. Save your changes.

7. Apply conditional formatting.

    a. Select the range D5:D9, then create a conditional format that changes cell contents to green fill with dark green text if the value is between 150 and 275.

    b. Select the range C5:C9, then create a conditional format that changes cell contents to red text if the number of employees exceeds 10.

    c. Apply a purple gradient-filled data bar to the range C5:C9. (*Hint*: Click Purple Data Bar in the Gradient Fill section.)

    d. Use the Conditional Formatting Rules Manager to modify the conditional format in cells C5:C9 to display values greater than 10 in bold dark red text.

    e. Merge and center the title (cell A1) over columns A through D.

    f. Save your changes.

8. Rename and move a worksheet.

    a. Name the Sheet1 tab **Insurance Data**.

    b. Add a sheet to the workbook, then name the new sheet **Employee Data**.

    c. Change the Insurance Data tab color to Red, Accent 2, Lighter 40%.

Skills Review (continued)

d. Change the Employee Data tab color to Aqua, Accent 5, Lighter 40%.

e. Move the Employee Data sheet so it comes before (to the left of) the Insurance Data sheet.

f. Make the Insurance Data sheet active, enter your name in cell A20, then save your work.

9. Check spelling.

a. Move the cell pointer to cell A1.

b. Use the Find & Select feature to replace the Accounting label in cell A5 with Accounting/Legal.

c. Check the spelling in the worksheet using the spell checker, and correct any spelling errors if necessary.

d. Save your changes, then compare your Insurance Data sheet to FIGURE C-28.

e. Preview the Insurance Data sheet in Backstage view, submit your work to your instructor as directed, then close the workbook and exit Excel.

FIGURE C-28

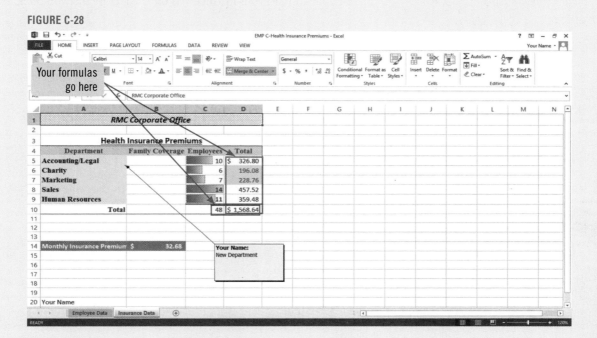

Independent Challenge 1

You run a wholesale medical supply distribution business, and one of your newest clients is Montebello, a small assisted living facility. Now that you've converted the store's accounting records to Excel, the manager would like you to work on an analysis of the Montebello inventory. Although more items will be added later, the worksheet has enough items for you to begin your modifications.

a. Start Excel, open the file EMP C-3.xlsx from the location where you store your Data Files, then save it as **EMP C-Medical Supply Inventory**.

b. Create a formula in cell E4 that calculates the value of the items in stock based on the price paid per item in cell B4. Format the cell in the Comma Style.

c. In cell F4, calculate the sale price of the items in stock using an absolute reference to the markup value shown in cell H1.

d. Copy the formulas created above into the range E5:F14.

e. Apply bold to the column labels, and italicize the inventory items in column A.

f. Make sure all columns are wide enough to display the data and labels.

g. Format the values in the Sale Price column as Accounting number format with two decimal places.

h. Format the values in the Price Paid column as Comma Style with two decimal places.

Independent Challenge 1 (continued)

i. Add a row under Thera-Band Assists for **Nail files**, price paid **$0.31**, sold individually (**each**), with **24** on hand. Copy the appropriate formulas to cells E5:F5.

j. Verify that all the data in the worksheet is visible and formulas are correct. Adjust any items as needed, and check the spelling of the entire worksheet.

k. Use conditional formatting to apply yellow fill with dark yellow text to items with a quantity of less than 20 on hand.

l. Use an icon set of your choosing in the range D4:D15 to illustrate the relative differences between values in the range.

m. Add an outside border around the data in the Item column (*do not* include the Item column label).

n. Delete the row containing the Pins entry.

o. Enter your name in an empty cell below the labels, then save the file. Compare your worksheet to the sample in **FIGURE C-29**.

p. Preview the worksheet in Backstage view, submit your work to your instructor as directed, close the workbook, then exit Excel.

FIGURE C-29

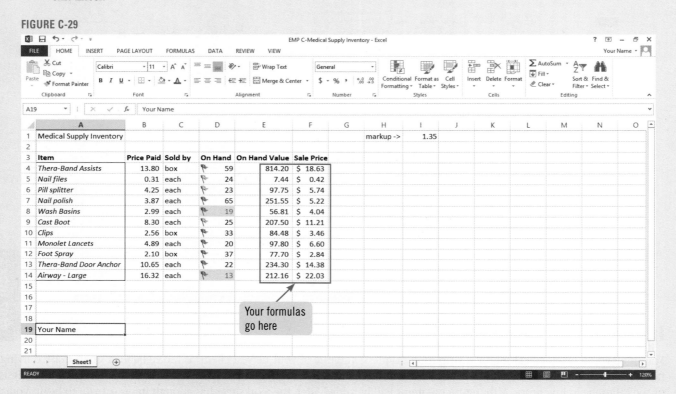

Independent Challenge 2

You volunteer several hours each week with the Assistance League of San Antonio, and you are in charge of maintaining the membership list. You're currently planning a mailing campaign to members in certain regions of the city. You also want to create renewal letters for members whose membership expires soon. You decide to format the list to enhance the appearance of the worksheet and make your upcoming tasks easier to plan.

a. Start Excel, open the file EMP C-4.xlsx from the location where you store your Data Files, then save it as **EMP C-Houston Association of Medical Clinics**.

b. Remove any blank columns.

c. Create a conditional format in the Zip Code column so that entries greater than 98149 appear in light red fill with dark red text.

d. Make all columns wide enough to fit their data and labels. (*Hint*: You can use any method to size the columns.)

e. Use formatting enhancements, such as fonts, font sizes, font styles, and fill colors, to make the worksheet more attractive.

Formatting a Worksheet

Independent Challenge 2 (continued)

f. Center the column labels.

g. Use conditional formatting so that entries for Year of Membership Expiration that are between 2017 and 2019 appear in green fill with bold black text. (*Hint*: Create a custom format for cells that meet the condition.)

h. Adjust any items as necessary, then check the spelling.

i. Change the name of the Sheet1 tab to one that reflects the sheet's contents, then add a tab color of your choice.

j. Enter your name in an empty cell, then save your work.

FIGURE C-30

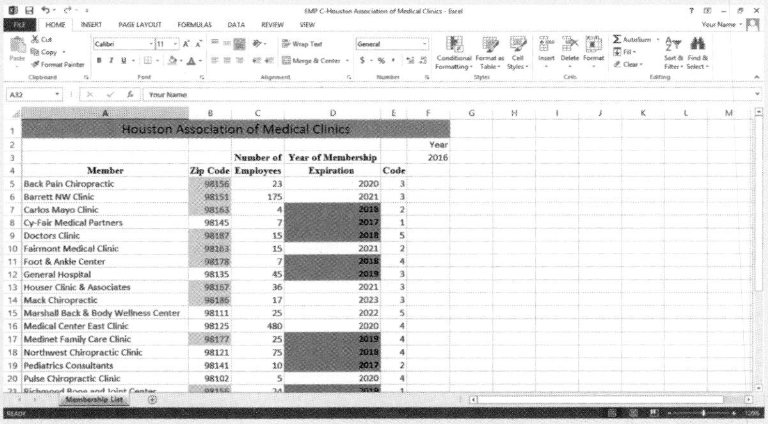

k. Preview the worksheet in Backstage view, make any final changes you think necessary, then submit your work to your instructor as directed. Compare your work to the sample shown in **FIGURE C-30**.

l. Close the workbook, then exit Excel.

Independent Challenge 3

Emergent Health Care Systems is a Boston-based healthcare provider that offers clinic and urgent-care services. As the finance manager for the company, one of your responsibilities is to analyze the monthly reports from the five district sales offices. Your boss, Joanne Bennington, has just asked you to prepare a quarterly sales report for an upcoming meeting. Because several top executives will be attending this meeting, Joanne reminds you that the report must look professional. In particular, she asks you to emphasize the company's surge in profits during the last month and to highlight the fact that the Northeastern district continues to outpace the other districts.

a. Plan a worksheet that shows the company's sales during the first quarter. Assume that all client visits are the same price. Make sure you include the following:
   - The number of patients seen (clients seen) and the associated revenues (revenue) for each of the five district sales offices. The five sales districts are Northeastern, Midwestern, Southeastern, Southern, and Western.
   - Calculations that show month-by-month totals for January, February, and March, and a 3-month cumulative total.
   - Calculations that show each district's share of sales (percent of Total Sales).
   - Labels that reflect the month-by-month data as well as the cumulative data.
   - Formatting enhancements such as data bars that emphasize the recent month's sales surge and the Northeastern district's sales leadership.

b. Ask yourself the following questions about the organization and formatting of the worksheet: What worksheet title and labels do you need, and where should they appear? How can you calculate the totals? What formulas can you copy to save time and keystrokes? Do any of these formulas need to use an absolute reference? How do you show dollar amounts? What information should be shown in bold? Do you need to use more than one font? Should you use more than one point size?

c. Start Excel, then save a new, blank workbook as **EMP C-Emergent Health Care Systems** to the location where you store your Data Files.

Independent Challenge 3 (continued)

d. Build the worksheet with your own price and sales data. Enter the titles and labels first, then enter the numbers and formulas. You can use the information in **TABLE C-4** to get started.

TABLE C-4

Emergent Health Care Systems											
1st Quarter Sales Report											
		January		February		March		Total			
Office	Price	Clients Seen	Revenue	Clients Seen	Revenue	Clients Seen	Revenue	Clients Seen	Revenue	Total % of Revenue	
Northeastern											
Midwestern											
Southeastern											
Southern											
Western											

e. Add a row beneath the data containing the totals for each column.

f. Adjust the column widths as necessary.

g. Change the height of row 1 to 33 points.

h. Format labels and values to enhance the look of the worksheet, and change the font styles and alignment if necessary.

i. Resize columns and adjust the formatting as necessary.

j. Add data bars for the monthly Clients Seen columns.

k. Add a column that calculates a 25% increase in total sales dollars. Use an absolute cell reference in this calculation. (*Hint*: Make sure the current formatting is applied to the new information.)

l. Delete the contents of cells J4:K4 if necessary, then merge and center cell I4 over column I:K.

m. Add a bottom double border to cells I10:L10.

n. Enter your name in an empty cell.

o. Check the spelling in the workbook, change to a landscape orientation, save your work, then compare your work to **FIGURE C-31**.

p. Preview the worksheet in Backstage view, then submit your work to your instructor as directed.

q. Close the workbook file, then exit Excel.

FIGURE C-31

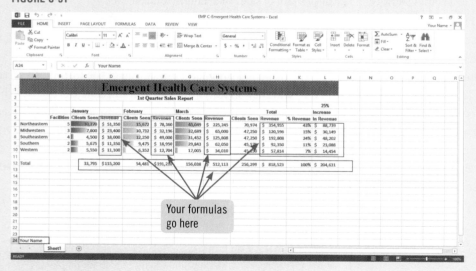

Formatting a Worksheet

Independent Challenge 4: Explore

This Independent Challenge requires an Internet connection.

You have been notified that your research grant to study the spread of airborne diseases has been approved. You plan to visit seven different countries over the course of 2 months, and you have budgeted an identical spending allowance in each country. You want to create a worksheet that calculates the amount of native currency you will have in each country based on the budgeted amount. You want the workbook to reflect the currency information for each country.

a. Start Excel, then save a new, blank workbook as **EMP C-Research Grant Travel Budget** to the location where you store your Data Files.

b. Add a title at the top of the worksheet.

c. Think of seven countries you would like to visit, then enter column and row labels for your worksheet. (*Hint*: You may wish to include row labels for each country, plus column labels for the country, the $1 equivalent in native currency, the total amount of native currency you'll have in each country, and the name of each country's monetary unit.)

d. Decide how much money you want to bring to each country (for example, $1,000), and enter that in the worksheet.

e. Use your favorite search engine to find your own information sources on currency conversions for the countries you plan to visit.

f. Enter the cash equivalent to $1 in U.S. dollars for each country in your list.

g. Create an equation that calculates the amount of native currency you will have in each country, using an absolute cell reference in the formula.

h. Format the entries in the column containing the native currency $1 equivalent as Number number format with three decimal places, and format the column containing the total native currency budget with two decimal places, using the correct currency symbol for each country. (*Hint*: Use the Number tab in the Format cells dialog box; choose the appropriate currency number format from the Symbol list.)

i. Create a conditional format that changes the font style and color of the calculated amount in the $1,000 US column to light red fill with dark red text if the amount exceeds **1000** units of the local currency.

j. Merge and center the worksheet title over the column headings.

k. Add any formatting you want to the column headings, and resize the columns as necessary.

l. Add a background color to the title and change the font color if you choose.

m. Enter your name in the header of the worksheet.

n. Spell check the worksheet, save your changes, compare your work to FIGURE C-32, then preview the worksheet in Backstage view, and submit your work to your instructor as directed.

o. Close the workbook and exit Excel.

FIGURE C-32

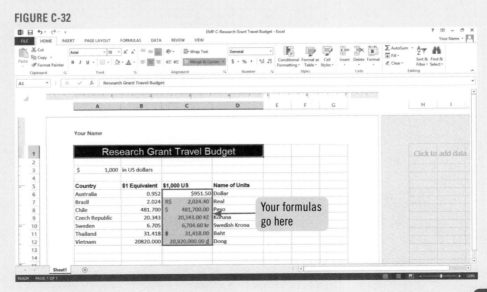

Visual Workshop

Open the file EMP C-5.xlsx from the location where you store your Data Files, then save it as **EMP C-Portland General Hospital Administrative Staff**. Use the skills you learned in this unit to format the worksheet so it looks like the one shown in FIGURE C-33. Create a conditional format in the Level column so that entries greater than 3 appear in light red fill with dark red text. Create an additional conditional format in the Review Cycle column so that any value equal to 3 appears in black fill with white bold text. Replace the Accounting department label with **Paralegal**. (*Hint*: The only additional font used in this exercise is 18-point Times New Roman in row 1.) Enter your name in the upper-right part of the header, check the spelling in the worksheet, save your changes, then submit your work to your instructor as directed. (*Hint*: Zoom out until the Zoom level is 100%.)

FIGURE C-33

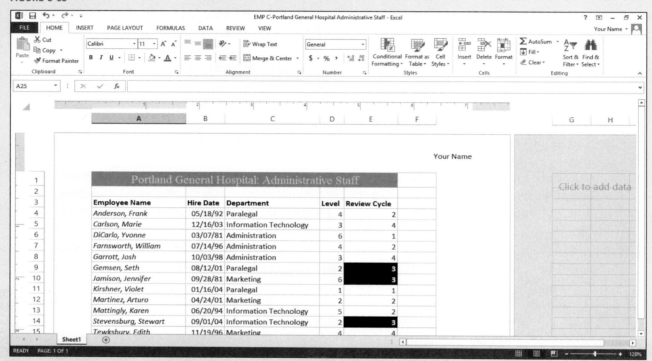

Formatting a Worksheet

Working with Charts

CASE At the upcoming annual meeting, Tony Sanchez wants to emphasize spending patterns at Riverwalk Medical Clinic. He asks you to create a chart showing the trends in insurance reimbursements over the past four quarters.

Unit Objectives

After completing this unit, you will be able to:

- Plan a chart
- Create a chart
- Move and resize a chart
- Change the chart design
- Change the chart format
- Format a chart
- Annotate and draw on a chart
- Create a pie chart

Files You Will Need

EMP D-1.xlsx	EMP D-4.xlsx
EMP D-2.xlsx	EMP D-5.xlsx
EMP D-3.xlsx	EMP D-6.xlsx

Plan a Chart

Learning Outcomes
- Prepare to create a chart
- Identify chart elements
- Explore common chart types

Before creating a chart, you need to plan the information you want your chart to show and how you want it to look. Planning ahead helps you decide what type of chart to create and how to organize the data. Understanding the parts of a chart makes it easier to format and to change specific elements so that the chart best illustrates your data. **CASE** ▶ *In preparation for creating the chart for Tony's presentation, you identify your goals for the chart and plan its layout.*

DETAILS

Use the following guidelines to plan the chart:

- **Determine the purpose of the chart, and identify the data relationships you want to communicate graphically**

  You want to create a chart that shows quarterly insurance reimbursements throughout Riverwalk Medical Clinic. This worksheet data is shown in **FIGURE D-1**. In the first quarter, the Ophthalmology department settled a dispute with a large insurance carrier, which resulted in greatly increased reimbursements starting in the third quarter. You also want the chart to illustrate whether the quarterly reimbursements for each department increased or decreased from quarter to quarter.

- **Determine the results you want to see, and decide which chart type is most appropriate**

  Different chart types display data in distinctive ways. For example, a pie chart compares parts to the whole, so it's useful for showing what proportion of a budget amount was spent on print ads relative to what was spent on direct mail or radio commercials. A line chart, in contrast, is best for showing trends over time. To choose the best chart type for your data, you should first decide how you want your data displayed and interpreted. **TABLE D-1** describes several different types of charts you can create in Excel and their corresponding buttons on the INSERT tab on the Ribbon. Because you want to compare RMC reimbursements in multiple departments over a period of four quarters, you decide to use a column chart.

- **Identify the worksheet data you want the chart to illustrate**

  Sometimes you use all the data in a worksheet to create a chart, while at other times you may need to select a range within the sheet. The worksheet from which you are creating your chart contains expense data for each of the past four quarters and the totals for the past year. You will need to use all the quarterly data contained in the worksheet except the quarterly totals.

- **Understand the elements of a chart**

  The chart shown in **FIGURE D-2** contains basic elements of a chart. In the figure, RMC departments are on the horizontal axis (also called the **x-axis**) and expense dollar amounts are on the vertical axis (also called the **y-axis**). The horizontal axis is also called the **category axis** because it often contains the names of data groups, such as locations, months, or years. The vertical axis is also called the **value axis** because it often contains numerical values that help you interpret the size of chart elements. (3-D charts also contain a **z-axis**, for comparing data across both categories and values.) The area inside the horizontal and vertical axes is the **plot area**. The **tick marks**, on the vertical axis, and **gridlines** (extending across the plot area) create a scale of measure for each value. Each value in a cell you select for your chart is a **data point**. In any chart, a **data marker** visually represents each data point, which in this case is a column. A collection of related data points is a **data series**. In this chart, there are four data series (Quarter 1, Quarter 2, Quarter 3, and Quarter 4). Each is made up of column data markers of a different color, so a **legend** is included to make it easy to identify them.

FIGURE D-1: Worksheet containing reimbursement data

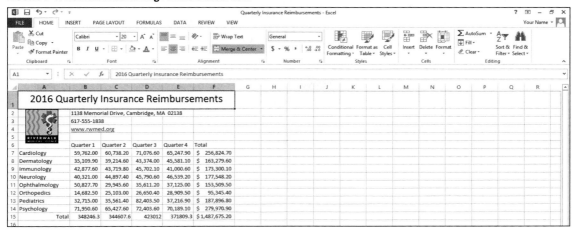

FIGURE D-2: Chart elements

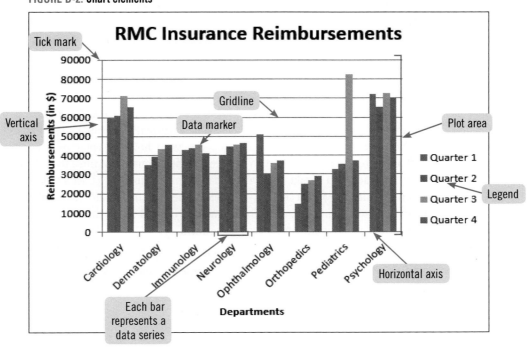

TABLE D-1: Common chart types

type	button	description
Column		Compares data using columns; the Excel default; sometimes referred to as a bar chart in other spreadsheet programs
Line		Compares trends over even time intervals; looks similar to an area chart, but does not emphasize total
Pie		Compares sizes of pieces as part of a whole; used for a single series of numbers
Bar		Compares data using horizontal bars; sometimes referred to as a horizontal bar chart in other spreadsheet programs
Area		Shows how individual volume changes over time in relation to total volume
Scatter		Compares trends over uneven time or measurement intervals; used in scientific and engineering disciplines for trend spotting and extrapolation

Create a Chart

Learning Outcomes
• Create a chart
• Switch a chart's columns/rows
• Add a chart title

To create a chart in Excel, you first select the range in a worksheet containing the data you want to chart. Once you've selected a range, you can use buttons on the INSERT tab on the Ribbon to create a chart based on the data in the range. **CASE** ➤ *Using the worksheet containing the quarterly reimbursement data, you create a chart that shows how the reimbursements in each department varied across the quarters.*

STEPS

1. **Start Excel, open the file EMP D-1.xlsx from the location where you store your Data Files, then save it as EMP D-Quarterly Insurance Reimbursements**

   You want the chart to include the quarterly insurance reimbursement values, as well as quarter and department labels. You don't include the Total column and row because the figures in these cells would skew the chart.

2. **Select the range A6:E14, then click the Quick Analysis tool 📧 in the lower-right corner of the range**

   The Quick Analysis tool contains a tab that lets you quickly insert commonly used charts. The CHARTS tab includes buttons for each major chart type, plus a More Charts button for additional chart types, such as stock charts for charting stock market data.

3. **Click the CHARTS tab, as shown in FIGURE D-3, then click Clustered Column**

   The chart is inserted in the center of the worksheet, and two contextual CHART TOOLS tabs appear on the Ribbon: DESIGN, and FORMAT. On the DESIGN tab, which is currently in front, you can quickly change the chart type, chart layout, and chart style, and you can swap how the columns and rows of data in the worksheet are represented in the chart. When seen in the Normal view, three tools display to the right of the chart: these enable you to add, remove, or change chart elements ➕, set a style and color scheme 🖌, and filter the results shown in a chart ▼. Currently, the departments are charted along the horizontal x-axis, with the quarterly reimbursement dollar amounts charted along the y-axis. This lets you easily compare the quarterly reimbursements for each department.

4. **Click the Switch Row/Column button in the Data group on the CHART TOOLS DESIGN tab**

   The quarters are now charted along the x-axis. The expense amounts per department are charted along the y-axis, as indicated by the updated legend. See FIGURE D-4.

5. **Click the Undo button ↶ on the Quick Access toolbar**

   The chart returns to its original design.

6. **Click the Chart Title placeholder to show the text box, click anywhere in the Chart Title text box, press [Ctrl][A] to select the text, type Quarterly Insurance Reimbursements, then click anywhere in the chart to deselect the title**

   Adding a title helps identify the chart. The border around the chart and the chart's **sizing handles**, the small series of dots at the corners and sides of the chart's border, indicate that the chart is selected. See FIGURE D-5. Your chart might be in a different location on the worksheet and may look slightly different; you will move and resize it in the next lesson. Any time a chart is selected, as it is now, a blue border surrounds the worksheet data range on which the chart is based, a purple border surrounds the cells containing the category axis labels, and a red border surrounds the cells containing the data series labels. This chart is known as an **embedded chart** because it is inserted directly in the current worksheet and doesn't exist in a separate file. Embedding a chart in the current sheet is the default selection when creating a chart, but you can also embed a chart on a different sheet in the workbook, or on a newly created chart sheet. A **chart sheet** is a sheet in a workbook that contains only a chart that is linked to the workbook data.

7. **Save your work**

Working with Charts

FIGURE D-3: CHARTS tab in Quick Analysis tool

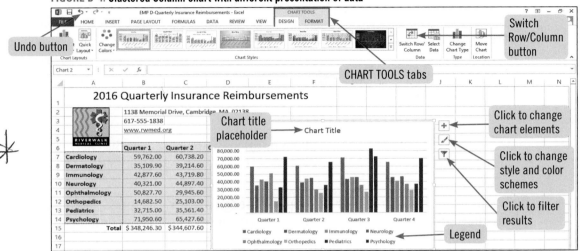

FIGURE D-4: Clustered Column chart with different presentation of data

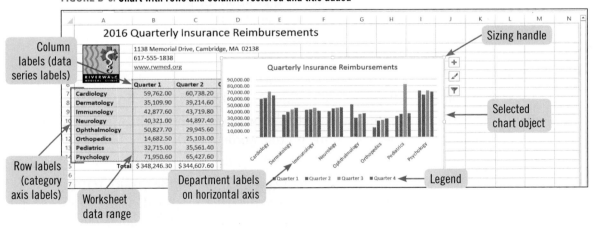

FIGURE D-5: Chart with rows and columns restored and title added

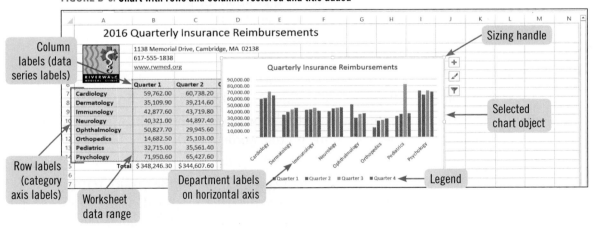

Creating sparklines

You can quickly create a miniature chart called a **sparkline** that serves as a visual indicator of data trends. You can create a sparkline by selecting a range of data, clicking the Quick Analysis tool, clicking the SPARKLINES tab, then clicking the type of sparkline you want. (The sparkline appears in the cell immediately adjacent to the selected range.) You can also select a range, click the INSERT tab, then click the Line, Column, or Win/Loss button in the Sparklines group. In the Create Sparklines dialog box that opens, enter the cell in which you want the sparkline to appear, then click OK.

FIGURE D-6 shows a sparkline created in a cell. Any changes to data in the range are reflected in the sparkline. To delete a selected sparkline from a cell, click the Clear button in the Group group on the SPARKLINE TOOLS DESIGN tab.

FIGURE D-6: Sparklines in cells

Move and Resize a Chart

Learning Outcomes
- Reposition a chart
- Resize a chart
- Modify a legend
- Modify chart data

A chart is an **object**, or an independent element on a worksheet, and is not located in a specific cell or range. You can select an object by clicking it; sizing handles around the object indicate it is selected. (When a chart is selected in Excel, the Name box, which normally tells you the address of the active cell, tells you the chart number.) You can move a selected chart anywhere on a worksheet without affecting formulas or data in the worksheet. Any data changed in the worksheet is automatically updated in the chart. You can even move a chart to a different sheet in the workbook and it will still reflect the original data. You can resize a chart to improve its appearance by dragging its sizing handles. You can reposition chart objects (such as a title or legend) to predefined locations using the Chart Elements button or the Add Chart Element button on the CHART TOOLS DESIGN tab, or you can freely move any chart object by dragging it or by cutting and pasting it to a new location. When you point to a chart object, the name of the object appears as a ScreenTip. **CASE** ▸ *You want to resize the chart, position it below the worksheet data, and move the legend.*

STEPS

QUICK TIP
To delete a selected chart, press [Delete].

1. **Make sure the chart is still selected, then position the pointer over the chart**

   The pointer shape ⬚ indicates that you can move the chart. For a table of commonly used object pointers, refer to **TABLE D-2**.

TROUBLE
If you do not drag a blank area on the chart, you might inadvertently move a chart element instead of the whole chart; if this happens, undo the action and try again.

2. **Position ⬚ on a blank area near the upper-left edge of the chart, press and hold the left mouse button, drag the chart until its upper-left corner is at the upper-left corner of cell A18, then release the mouse button**

   As you drag the chart, you can see the chart being dragged. When you release the mouse button, the chart appears in the new location.

3. **Scroll down so you can see the whole chart, position the pointer on the right-middle sizing handle until it changes to ↔, then drag the right border of the chart to the right edge of column F**

   The chart is widened. See **FIGURE D-7**.

QUICK TIP
To resize a selected chart to an exact specification, click the CHART TOOLS FORMAT tab, then enter the desired height and width in the Size group.

4. **Position the pointer over the upper-middle sizing handle until it changes to ↕, then drag the top border of the chart to the top edge of row 17**

5. **Position the pointer over the lower-middle sizing handle until it changes to ↕, then drag the bottom border of the chart to the bottom border of row 30**

   You can move any object on a chart. You want to align the top of the legend with the top of the plot area.

QUICK TIP
You can move a legend to the right, top, left, or bottom of a chart by clicking Legend in the Add Chart Element button in the Chart Layouts group on the CHART TOOLS DESIGN tab, then clicking a location option.

6. **Click the Quick Layout button in the Chart Layouts group of the CHART TOOLS DESIGN tab, click Layout 1 (in the upper-left corner of the palette), click the legend to select it, press and hold [Shift], drag the legend up using ⬚ so the dotted outline is approximately 1/4" above the top of the plot area, then release [Shift]**

   When you click the legend, sizing handles appear around it and "Legend" appears as a ScreenTip when the pointer hovers over the object. As you drag, a dotted outline of the legend border appears. Pressing and holding the [Shift] key holds the horizontal position of the legend as you move it vertically. Although the sizing handles on objects within a chart look different from the sizing handles that surround a chart, they function the same way.

7. **Click cell A14, type Psychiatry, click the Enter button ✓ on the formula bar, use AutoFit to resize column A, then save your work**

   The axis label changes to reflect the updated cell contents, as shown in **FIGURE D-8**. Changing any data in the worksheet modifies corresponding text or values in the chart. Because the chart is no longer selected, the CHART TOOLS tabs no longer appear on the Ribbon.

Working with Charts

FIGURE D-7: Moved and resized chart

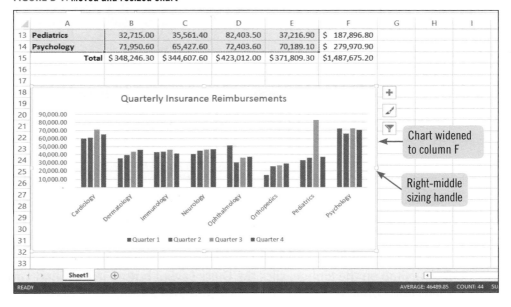

FIGURE D-8: Worksheet with modified legend and label

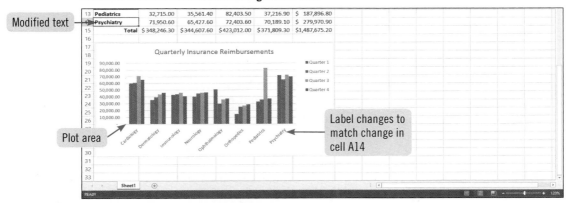

TABLE D-2: Common object pointers

name	pointer	use	name	pointer	use
Diagonal resizing	⬈ or ⬊	Change chart shape from corners	I-beam	I	Edit object text
Draw	+	Draw an object	Move	⤧	Move object
Horizontal resizing	⬌	Change object width	Vertical resizing	⬍	Change object height

Moving an embedded chart to a sheet

Suppose you have created an embedded chart that you decide would look better on a chart sheet or in a different worksheet. You can make this change without recreating the entire chart. To do so, first select the chart, click the CHART TOOLS DESIGN tab, then click the Move Chart button in the Location group. The Move Chart dialog box opens. To move the chart to its own chart sheet, click the New sheet option button, type a name for the new sheet if desired, then click OK. If the chart is already on its own sheet, click the Object in option button, select the worksheet to where you want to move it, then click OK.

Change the Chart Design

Learning Outcomes
- Change the chart design
- Change the chart type
- Apply a chart style

Once you've created a chart, you can change the chart type, modify the data range and column/row configuration, apply a different chart style, and change the layout of objects in the chart. The layouts in the Chart Layouts group on the CHART TOOLS DESIGN tab offer arrangements of objects in your chart, such as its legend, title, or gridlines; choosing one of these layouts is an alternative to manually changing how objects are arranged in a chart. **CASE** ▸ *You discovered the data for Pediatrics and Psychiatry in Quarter 3 is incorrect. After the correction, you want to see how the data looks using different chart layouts and types.*

STEPS

1. **Click cell C13, type 39462.01, press [Enter], type 62947.18, then press [Enter]**

    In the chart, the Quarter 2 data markers for Pediatrics and Psychiatry reflect the adjusted reimbursement figures. See **FIGURE D-9**.

> **QUICK TIP**
> You can see more layout choices by clicking the More button in the Chart Styles group.

2. **Select the chart by clicking a blank area within the chart border, click the CHART TOOLS DESIGN tab on the Ribbon, click the Quick Layout button in the Chart Layouts group, then click Layout 3**

    The legend moves to the bottom of the chart. You prefer the original layout.

3. **Click the Undo button on the Quick Access toolbar, then click the Change Chart Type button in the Type group**

    The Change Chart Type dialog box opens, as shown in **FIGURE D-10**. The left pane of the dialog box lists the available categories, and the right pane shows the individual chart types. A pale green border surrounds the currently selected chart type.

4. **Click Bar in the left pane of the Change Chart Type dialog box, confirm that the first Clustered Bar chart type is selected in the right pane, then click OK**

    The column chart changes to a clustered bar chart. See **FIGURE D-11**. You look at the bar chart, then decide to see how the data looks in a three-dimensional column chart.

5. **Click the Change Chart Type button in the Type group, click Column in the left pane of the Change Chart Type dialog box, click 3-D Clustered Column (fourth from the left in the top row) in the right pane, verify that the left-most 3-D chart is selected, then click OK**

    A three-dimensional column chart appears. You notice that the three-dimensional column format gives you a sense of volume, but it is more crowded than the two-dimensional column format.

> **QUICK TIP**
> If you plan to print a chart on a black-and-white printer, you may wish to apply a black-and-white chart style to your chart so you can see how the output will look as you work.

6. **Click the Change Chart Type button in the Type group, click Clustered Column (first from the left in the top row) in the right pane of the Change Chart Type dialog box, then click OK**

7. **Click the Style 3 chart style in the Chart Styles group**

    The columns change to lighter shades of color. You prefer the previous chart style's color scheme.

8. **Click on the Quick Access toolbar, then save your work**

Creating a combination chart

A **combination chart** is two charts in one; a column chart with a line chart, for example. This type of chart is helpful when charting dissimilar but related data. For example, you can create a combination chart based on home price and home size data, showing home prices in a column chart, and related home sizes in a line chart. Here a **secondary axis** (such as a vertical axis on the right side of the chart) would supply the scale for the home sizes. To create a combination chart, select all the data you want to plot, click Recommended Charts in the Charts group in the INSERT tab, click the All Charts tab, select Combo, supply the series information that conforms to the chart you want to create, then click OK. To change an existing chart to a combination chart, select the chart, then click Change Chart Type in the Type group on the CHART TOOLS DESIGN tab. Click Combo in the Change Chart Type dialog box, select the Secondary Axis box for each data series you want to plot, then click OK.

FIGURE D-9: Worksheet with modified data

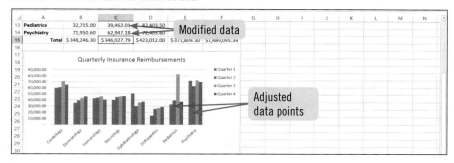

FIGURE D-10: Change Chart Type dialog box

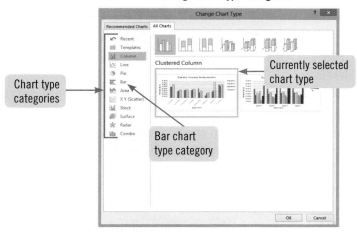

FIGURE D-11: Column chart changed to bar chart

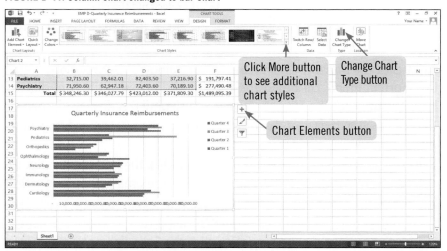

Working with a 3-D chart

Excel includes two kinds of 3-D chart types. In a true 3-D chart, a third axis, called the **z-axis**, lets you compare data points across both categories and values. The z-axis runs along the depth of the chart, so it appears to advance from the back of the chart. To create a true 3-D chart, look for chart types that begin with "3-D," such as 3-D Column. In a 3-D chart, data series can sometimes obscure other columns or bars in the same chart, but you can rotate the chart to obtain a better view. Right-click the chart, then click 3-D Rotation. The Format Chart Area pane opens with the 3-D Rotation category active. The 3-D Rotation options let you change the orientation and perspective of the chart area, plot area, walls, and floor. The 3-D Format category lets you apply three-dimensional effects to selected chart objects. (Not all 3-D Rotation and 3-D Format options are available on all charts.)

Change the Chart Format

Learning Outcomes
- Change the gridlines display
- Add axis titles
- Change the border color
- Add a shadow to an object

While the CHART TOOLS DESIGN tab contains preconfigured chart layouts you can apply to a chart, the Chart Elements button makes it easy to add, remove, and modify individual chart objects such as a chart title or legend. Using options on this shortcut menu (or using the Add Chart Element button on the CHART TOOLS DESIGN tab), you can also add text to a chart, add and modify labels, change the display of axes, modify the fill behind the plot area, create titles for the horizontal and vertical axes, and eliminate or change the look of gridlines. You can format the text in a chart object using the HOME tab or the Mini toolbar, just as you would the text in a worksheet. **CASE** ▶ *You want to change the layout of the chart by creating titles for the horizontal and vertical axes. To improve the chart's appearance, you'll add a drop shadow to the chart title.*

STEPS

1. **With the chart still selected, click the Add Chart Element button in the Chart Layouts group on the CHART TOOLS DESIGN tab, point to Gridlines, then click Primary Major Horizontal to deselect it**

   The gridlines that extend from the value axis tick marks across the chart's plot area are removed from the chart, as shown in FIGURE D-12.

2. **Click the Chart Elements button ⊞ in the upper-right corner *outside* the chart border, click the Gridlines arrow, click Primary Major Horizontal, click Primary Minor Horizontal, then click ▣ to close the Chart Elements fly-out menu**

   Both major and minor gridlines now appear in the chart. **Major gridlines** represent the values at the value axis tick marks, and **minor gridlines** represent the values between the tick marks.

3. **Click ⊞, click the Axis Titles check box to select all the axis titles options, triple-click the vertical axis title on the chart, then type Revenue (in $)**

   Descriptive text on the category axis helps readers understand the chart.

4. **Triple-click the horizontal axis title on the chart, then type Departments**

   The text "Departments" appears on the horizontal axis, as shown in FIGURE D-13.

5. **Right-click the horizontal axis labels ("Cardiology", "Dermatology", etc.), click Font on the shortcut menu, click the Latin text font list arrow in the Font dialog box, click Times New Roman, click the Size down arrow, click until 8 is displayed, then click OK**

   The font of the horizontal axis labels changes to Times New Roman, and the font size decreases, making more of the plot area visible.

6. **With the horizontal axis labels still selected, click the HOME tab, click the Format Painter button 🖌 in the Clipboard group, then click the area within the vertical axis labels**

7. **Right-click the Chart Title ("Quarterly Insurance Reimbursements"), click Format Chart Title on the shortcut menu, click the BORDER arrow ▷ in the Format Chart Title pane to display the options if necessary, then click the Solid line option button in the Format Chart Title pane**

   A solid border will appear around the chart title with the default blue color.

8. **Click the Effects button ⬡ in the Format Chart Title pane, click Shadow, click the Presets button, click Offset Diagonal Bottom Right in the Outer group (first row, first from the left), click the Format Chart Title pane Close button ✖, then save your work**

   A blue border with a drop shadow surrounds the title. Compare your work to FIGURE D-14.

Working with Charts

FIGURE D-12: Gridlines removed from chart

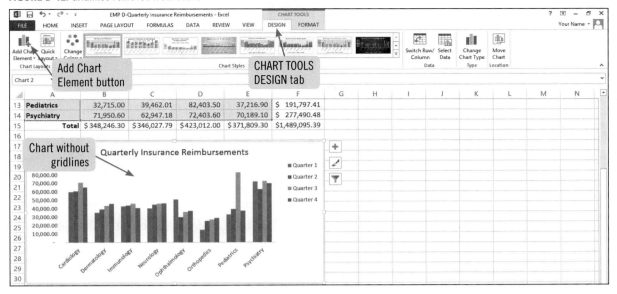

FIGURE D-13: Axis titles added to chart

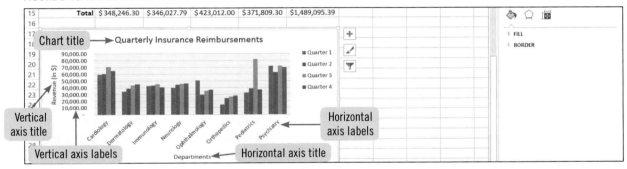

FIGURE D-14: Enhanced chart

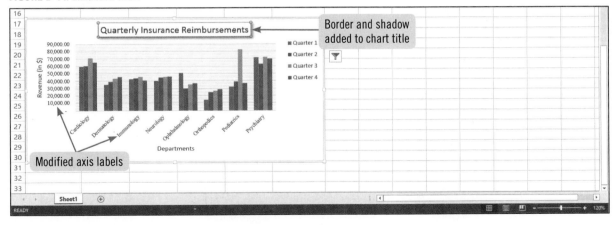

Adding data labels to a chart

There are times when your audience might benefit by seeing data labels on a chart. These labels appear next to the data markers in the chart and can indicate the series name, category name, and/or the value of one or more data points. Once your chart is selected, you can add this information to your chart by clicking the Chart Elements button in the upper-right corner outside the selected chart, clicking the Data Labels arrow, and then clicking a display option for the data labels. Once you have added the data labels, you can format them or delete individual data labels. To delete a data label, select it and then press [Delete].

Format a Chart

Formatting a chart can make it easier to read and understand. Many formatting enhancements can be made using the CHART TOOLS FORMAT tab. You can change the fill color for a specific data series, or you can apply a shape style to a title or a data series using the Shape Styles group. Shape styles make it possible to apply multiple formats, such as an outline, fill color, and text color, all with a single click. You can also apply different fill colors, outlines, and effects to chart objects using arrows and buttons in the Shape Styles group. **CASE** ➤ *You want to use a different color for one data series in the chart and apply a shape style to another to enhance the look of the chart.*

STEPS

1. **With the chart selected, click the CHART TOOLS FORMAT tab on the Ribbon, then click any column in the Quarter 4 data series**

   The CHART TOOLS FORMAT tab opens, and handles appear on each column in the Quarter 4 data series, indicating that the entire series is selected.

2. **Click the Shape Fill list arrow in the Shape Styles group on the CHART TOOLS FORMAT tab**

3. **Click Orange, Accent 6 (first row, 10th from the left) as shown in FIGURE D-15**

   All the columns for the series become orange, and the legend changes to match the new color. You can also change the color of selected objects by applying a shape style.

4. **Click any column in the Quarter 3 data series**

   Handles appear on each column in the Quarter 3 data series.

5. **Click the More button ⊽ on the Shape Styles gallery, then** *hover the pointer* **over the Moderate Effect – Olive Green, Accent 3 shape style (fifth row, fourth from the left) in the gallery, as shown in FIGURE D-16**

   Live Preview shows the data series in the chart with the shape style applied.

6. **Click the Subtle Effect – Olive Green, Accent 3 shape style (fourth row, fourth from the left) in the gallery**

   The style for the data series changes, as shown in FIGURE D-17.

7. **Save your work**

Previewing a chart

To print or preview just a chart, select the chart (or make the chart sheet active), click the FILE tab, then click Print on the navigation bar. To reposition a chart by changing the page's margins, click the Show Margins button ▦ in the lower-right corner of the Print tab to display the margins in the preview. You can drag the margin lines to the exact settings you want; as the margins change, the size and placement of the chart on the page changes too.

FIGURE D-15: New shape fill applied to data series

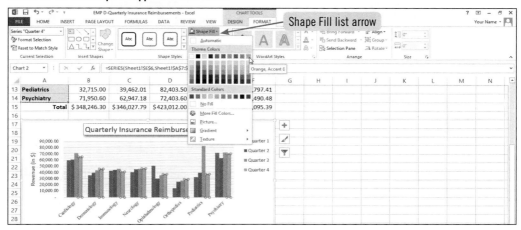

FIGURE D-16: Live Preview of new style applied to data series

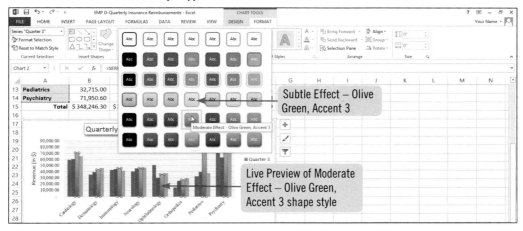

FIGURE D-17: Style of data series changed

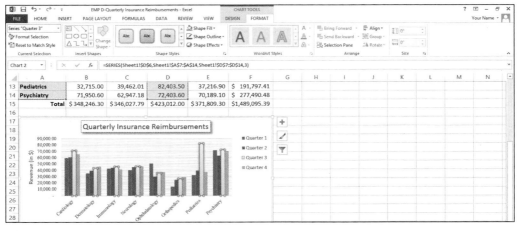

Changing alignment and angle in axis labels and titles

The buttons on the CHART TOOLS DESIGN tab provide a few options for positioning axis labels and titles, but you can customize their position and rotation to exact specifications using the Format Axis pane or Format Axis Title pane. With a chart selected, right-click the axis text you want to modify, then click Format Axis or Format Axis Title on the shortcut menu. In the pane that is displayed, click the Size & Properties button, then select the appropriate Text layout option. You can also create a custom angle by clicking the Custom angle up and down arrows. When you have made the desired changes, close the pane.

Annotate and Draw on a Chart

Learning Outcomes
• Type text in a text box
• Draw an arrow on a chart
• Modify a drawn object

You can use text annotations and graphics to point out critical information in a chart. **Text annotations** are labels that further describe your data. You can also draw lines and arrows that point to the exact locations you want to emphasize. Shapes such as arrows and boxes can be added from the Illustrations group on the INSERT tab or from the Insert Shapes group on the CHART TOOLS FORMAT tab on the Ribbon. The INSERT group is also used to insert pictures into worksheets and charts. **CASE** *You want to call attention to the Orthopedics revenue increases, so you decide to add a text annotation and an arrow to this information in the chart.*

STEPS

1. **Make sure the chart is selected with the CHART TOOLS FORMAT tab selected, click the Text Box button ⊞ in the Insert Shapes group, then move the pointer over the worksheet**

   The pointer changes to ↓, indicating that you will insert a text box where you next click.

2. **Click to the right of the chart (anywhere *outside* the chart boundary)**

   A text box is added to the worksheet, and the DRAWING TOOLS FORMAT tab appears on the Ribbon so that you can format the new object. First you need to type the text.

3. **Type Great Improvement**

   The text appears in a selected text box on the worksheet, and the chart is no longer selected, as shown in FIGURE D-18. Your text box may be in a different location; this is not important, because you'll move the annotation in the next step.

4. **Point to an edge of the text box so that the pointer changes to ⬚, drag the text box into the chart below the chart title, as shown in FIGURE D-19, then release the mouse button**

   The text box is a text annotation for the chart. You also want to add a simple arrow shape in the chart.

5. **Click the chart to select it, click the CHART TOOLS FORMAT tab, click the Arrow button ⬈ in the Insert Shapes group, then move the pointer over the text box on the chart**

   The pointer changes to ✛, and the status bar displays "Click and drag to insert an AutoShape." When ✛ is over the text box, black handles appear around the text in the text box. A black handle can act as an anchor for the arrow.

6. **Position ✛ on the black handle to the right of the "t" in the word "improvement" (in the text box), press and hold the left mouse button, drag the line to the Quarter 2 column for the Orthopedics category in the chart, then release the mouse button**

   An arrow points to the Quarter 2 revenue for Orthopedics, and the DRAWING TOOLS FORMAT tab displays options for working with the new arrow object. You can resize, format, or delete it just like any other object in a chart.

7. **Click the Shape Outline list arrow in the Shape Styles group, click the Automatic color, click the Shape Outline list arrow again, point to Weight, then click 1½ pt**

   Compare your finished chart to FIGURE D-20.

8. **Save your work**

FIGURE D-18: Text box added

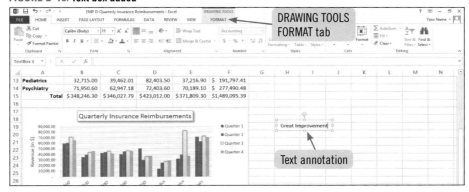

FIGURE D-19: Text annotation on the chart

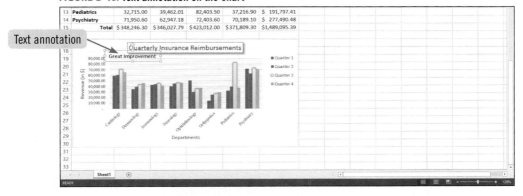

FIGURE D-20: Arrow shape added to chart

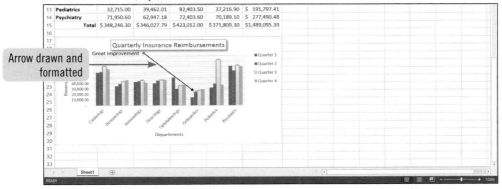

Adding SmartArt graphics

In addition to charts, annotations, and drawn objects, you can create a variety of diagrams using SmartArt graphics. **SmartArt graphics** are available in List, Process, Cycle, Hierarchy, Relationship, Matrix, and Pyramid categories. To insert SmartArt, click the Insert a SmartArt Graphic button in the Illustrations group on the INSERT tab to open the Choose a SmartArt Graphic dialog box. Click a SmartArt category in the left pane, then click the layout for the graphic in the middle pane. The right pane shows a sample of the selected SmartArt layout, as shown in **FIGURE D-21**. The SmartArt graphic appears in the worksheet as an embedded object with sizing handles. Click the Text Pane button on the SMARTART TOOLS DESIGN tab to open a text pane next to the graphic; you

can enter text into the graphic using the text pane or by typing directly in the shapes in the diagram.

FIGURE D-21: Choose a SmartArt Graphic dialog box

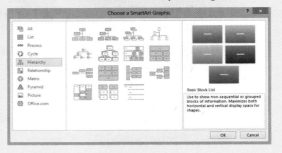

Working with Charts

Create a Pie Chart

Learning Outcomes
• Create a pie chart
• Explode a pie chart slice

You can create multiple charts based on the same worksheet data. While a column chart may illustrate certain important aspects of your worksheet data, you may find you want to create an additional chart to emphasize a different point. Depending on the type of chart you create, you have additional options for calling attention to trends and patterns. For example, if you create a pie chart, you can emphasize one data point by **exploding**, or pulling that slice away from, the pie chart. When you're ready to print a chart, you can preview it just as you do a worksheet to check the output before committing it to paper. You can print a chart by itself or as part of the worksheet. **CASE** ▸ *At an upcoming meeting, Tony plans to discuss the total reimbursement revenue and which departments need improvement. You want to create a pie chart he can use to illustrate total revenue. Finally, you want to fit the worksheet and the charts onto one worksheet page.*

STEPS

1. **Select the range A7:A14, press and hold [Ctrl], select the range F7:F14, click the INSERT tab, click the Insert Pie or Doughnut Chart button in the Charts group, then click 3-D Pie in the chart gallery**

   The new chart appears in the center of the worksheet. You can move the chart and quickly format it using a chart layout.

2. **Drag the chart so its upper-left corner is at the upper-left corner of cell G1, click the Quick Layout button in the Chart Layouts group of the CHART TOOLS DESIGN tab, then click Layout 2**

   The chart is repositioned on the page, and its layout changes so that a chart title is added, the percentages display on each slice, and the legend appears just below the chart title.

3. **Select the Chart Title text, then type Total Reimbursements, by Department**

4. **Click the slice for the Orthopedics data point, click it again so it is the only slice selected, right-click it, then click Format Data Point**

   The Format Data Point pane opens, as shown in FIGURE D-22. You can use the Point Explosion slider to control the distance a pie slice moves away from the pie, or you can type a value in the Point Explosion text box.

5. **Double-click 0 in the Point Explosion text box, type 40, then click the Close button ☒**

   Compare your chart to FIGURE D-23. You decide to preview the chart and data before you print.

6. **Click cell A1, switch to Page Layout view, type your name in the left header text box, then click cell A1**

   You decide the chart and data would fit better on the page if they were printed in landscape orientation.

7. **Click the PAGE LAYOUT tab, click the Orientation button in the Page Setup group, then click Landscape**

8. **Click the FILE tab, click Print on the navigation bar, click the No Scaling setting in the Settings section on the Print tab, then click Fit Sheet on One Page**

   The data and chart are positioned horizontally on a single page, as shown in FIGURE D-24. The printer you have selected may affect the appearance of your preview screen.

9. **Save and close the workbook, submit your work to your instructor as directed, then exit Excel**

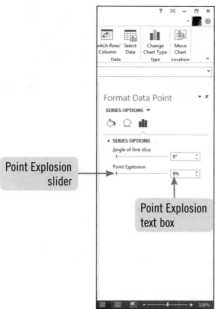

Point Explosion slider

Point Explosion text box

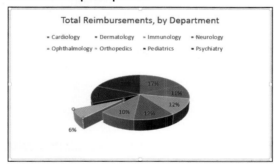

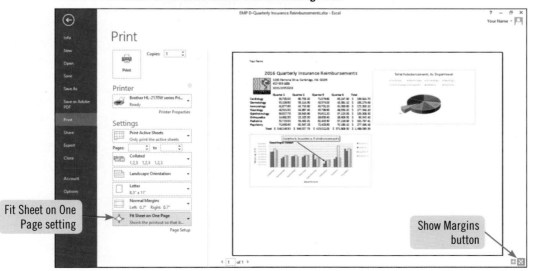

Fit Sheet on One Page setting

Show Margins button

Excel 2013

Practice

Concepts Review

Label each element of the Excel chart shown in FIGURE D-25.

FIGURE D-25

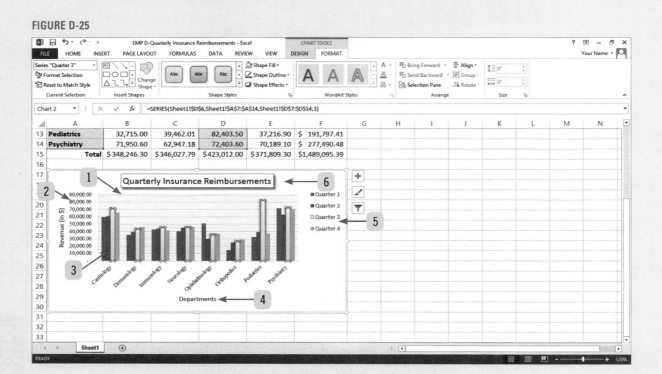

Match each chart type with the statement that best describes it.

7. **Area**	**a.** Displays a column and line chart using different scales of measurement
8. **Line**	**b.** Compares trends over even time intervals
9. **Column**	**c.** Compares data using columns
10. **Combination**	**d.** Compares data as parts of a whole
11. **Pie**	**e.** Shows how volume changes over time

Select the best answer from the list of choices.

12. **Which tab appears only when a chart is selected?**
    a. INSERT
    b. CHART TOOLS FORMAT
    c. REVIEW
    d. PAGE LAYOUT

13. **Which is *not* an example of a SmartArt graphic?**
    a. Sparkline
    b. Basic Matrix
    c. Organization Chart
    d. Basic Pyramid

14. **How do you move an embedded chart to a chart sheet?**
    a. Click a button on the CHART TOOLS DESIGN tab.
    b. Drag the chart to the sheet tab.
    c. Delete the chart, switch to a different sheet, then create a new chart.
    d. Use the Copy and Paste buttons on the Ribbon.

15. **The object in a chart that identifies the colors used for each data series is a(n):**
    a. Data marker.
    b. Data point.
    c. Organizer.
    d. Legend.

16. **A collection of related data points in a chart is called a:**
    a. Data series.
    b. Data tick.
    c. Cell address.
    d. Value title.

17. **Which tab on the Ribbon do you use to create a chart?**
    a. DESIGN
    b. INSERT
    c. PAGE LAYOUT
    d. FORMAT

Skills Review

1. **Plan a chart.**
   a. Start Excel, open the Data File EMP D-2.xlsx from the location where you store your Data Files, then save it as **EMP D-Departmental Software Usage**.
   b. Describe the type of chart you would use to plot this data.
   c. What chart type would you use to compare the number of Excel users in each department?

2. **Create a chart.**
   a. In the worksheet, select the range containing all the data and headings.
   b. Click the Quick Analysis tool.
   c. Create a Clustered Column chart, then add the chart title **Software Usage, by Department** above the chart.
   d. If necessary, click the Switch Row/Column button so the departments appear as the x-axis.
   e. Save your work.

Skills Review (continued)

3. Move and resize a chart.

   a. Make sure the chart is still selected, and close any open panes if necessary.

   b. Move the chart beneath the worksheet data.

   c. Widen the chart so it extends to the right edge of column H.

   d. Use the Quick Layout button in the CHART TOOLS DESIGN tab to move the legend to the right of the charted data. (*Hint*: Use Layout 1.)

   e. Resize the chart so its bottom edge is at the top of row 25.

   f. Save your work.

4. Change the chart design.

   a. Change the value in cell B3 to **15**. Observe the change in the chart.

   b. Select the chart.

   c. Use the Quick Layout button in the Chart Layouts group on the CHART TOOLS DESIGN tab to apply the Layout 10 layout to the chart, undo the change, then apply Layout 3.

   d. Use the Change Chart Type button on the CHART TOOLS DESIGN tab to change the chart to a Clustered Bar chart.

   e. Change the chart to a 3-D Clustered Column chart, then change it back to a Clustered Column chart.

   f. Save your work.

5. Change the chart layout.

   a. Use the Chart Elements button to turn off the primary major horizontal gridlines in the chart.

   b. Change the font used in the horizontal and vertical axes labels to Times New Roman.

   c. Turn on the primary major gridlines for both the horizontal and vertical axes.

   d. Change the chart title's font to Times New Roman if necessary, with a font size of 20, then make the chart title bold.

   e. Insert **Departments** as the primary horizontal axis title.

   f. Insert **Number of Users** as the primary vertical axis title.

   g. Change the font size of the horizontal and vertical axis titles to 10 and the font to Times New Roman, if necessary.

   h. Change "Personnel" in the worksheet column heading to **Human Resources**, then AutoFit column E.

   i. Change the font size of the legend to 14.

   j. Add a solid line border in the default color and a (preset) Offset Diagonal Bottom Right shadow to the chart title.

   k. Save your work.

6. Format a chart.

   a. Make sure the chart is selected, then select the CHART TOOLS FORMAT tab, if necessary.

   b. Change the shape fill of the Excel data series to Dark Blue, Text 2.

   c. Change the shape style of the Excel data series to Subtle Effect – Orange, Accent 6.

   d. Save your work.

7. Annotate and draw on a chart.

   a. Make sure the chart is selected, then create the text annotation **Needs more users**.

   b. Position the text annotation so the word "Needs" is just below the word "Software" in the chart title.

   c. Select the chart, then use the CHART TOOLS FORMAT tab to create a 1½ pt weight dark blue arrow that points from the bottom center of the text box to the Excel users in the Neurology department.

   d. Deselect the chart.

   e. Save your work.

Skills Review (continued)

8. Create a pie chart.

   a. Select the range A1:F2, then create a 3-D Pie chart.

   b. Drag the 3-D pie chart beneath the existing chart.

   c. Change the chart title to **Excel Users**.

   d. Apply the Style 7 chart style to the chart, then apply Layout 6 using the Quick Layout button.

   e. Explode the Human Resources slice from the pie chart at **25%**.

   f. In Page Layout view, enter your name in the left section of the worksheet header.

   g. Preview the worksheet and charts in Backstage view, make sure all the contents fit on one page, then submit your work to your instructor as directed. When printed, the worksheet should look like FIGURE D-26.

   h. Save your work, close the workbook, then exit Excel.

FIGURE D-26

Your Name

	Cardiology	Dermatology	Neurology	Human Resources	Purchasing
Excel	37	16	5	11	38
Word	10	35	17	15	10
PowerPoint	17	5	12	5	3
Access	20	25	8	10	15
Publisher	2	15	22	15	25

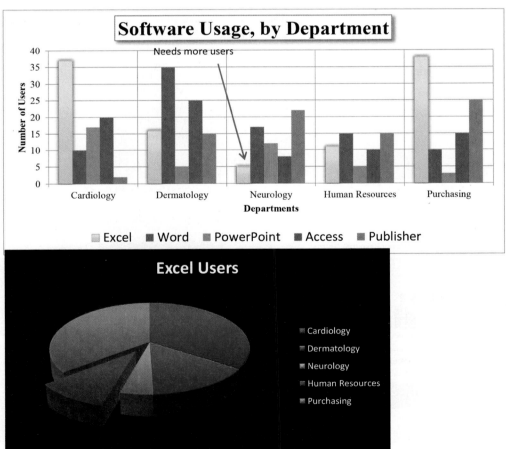

Independent Challenge 1

You are the operations manager for the Springfield Medical Research Group in Massachusetts. Each year the group applies to various state and federal agencies for matching funds. For this year's funding proposal, you need to create charts to document the number of productions in previous years.

a. Start Excel, open the file EMP D-3.xlsx from the location where you store your Data Files, then save it as **EMP D-Springfield Medical Research Group**.

b. Take some time to plan your charts. Which type of chart or charts might best illustrate the information you need to display? What kind of chart enhancements do you want to use? Will a 3-D effect make your chart easier to understand?

c. Create a Clustered Column chart for the data.

d. Change at least one of the colors used in a data series.

e. Make the appropriate modifications to the chart to make it visually attractive and easier to read and understand. Include a legend to the right of the chart, and add a chart title and horizontal and vertical axis titles using the text shown in **TABLE D-3**.

TABLE D-3

title	text
Chart title	Number of Research Grants
Vertical axis title	Number of Grants
Horizontal axis title	Departments

© 2014 Cengage Learning

f. Create at least two additional charts for the same data to show how different chart types display the same data. Reposition each new chart so that all charts are visible in the worksheet. One of the additional charts should be a pie chart; the other is up to you.

g. Modify each new chart as necessary to improve its appearance and effectiveness. A sample worksheet containing three charts based on the worksheet data is shown in **FIGURE D-27**.

h. Enter your name in the worksheet header.

i. Save your work. Before printing, preview the worksheet in Backstage view, then adjust any settings as necessary so that all the worksheet data and charts print on a single page.

j. Submit your work to your instructor as directed.

k. Close the workbook, then exit Excel.

FIGURE D-27

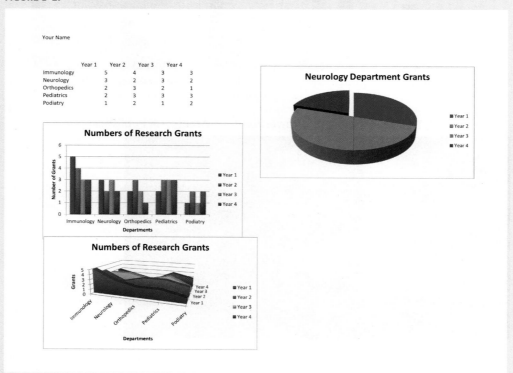

Independent Challenge 2

You work at Pinnacle Medical Consultants, a locally owned medical consortium. One of your responsibilities is to manage the company's revenues and expenses using Excel. Another is to convince the current staff that Excel can help them make daily operating decisions more easily and efficiently. To do this, you've decided to create charts using the previous year's operating expenses including rent, utilities, and payroll. The manager will use these charts at the next monthly meeting.

a. Start Excel, open the Data File EMP D-4.xlsx from the location where you store your Data Files, then save it as **EMP D-Pinnacle Medical Consultants**.

b. Decide which data in the worksheet should be charted. What chart types are best suited for the information you need to show? What kinds of chart enhancements are necessary?

c. Create a 3-D Clustered Column chart in the worksheet showing the expense data for all four quarters. (*Hint*: The expense categories should appear on the x-axis. Do not include the totals.)

d. Change the vertical axis labels (Expenses data) so that no decimals are displayed. (*Hint*: Right-click the axis labels you want to modify, click Format Axis, click the Number category in the Format Axis pane, change the number of decimal places, then close the Format Axis pane.)

e. Using the sales data, create two charts on this worksheet that compare the sales amounts. (*Hint*: Move each chart to a new location on the worksheet, then deselect it before creating the next one.)

f. In one chart of the sales data, add data labels, then add chart titles as you see fit.

g. Make any necessary formatting changes to make the charts look more attractive, then enter your name in a worksheet cell.

h. Save your work.

i. Preview each chart in Backstage view, and adjust any items as needed. Fit the worksheet to a single page, then submit your work to your instructor as directed. A sample of a printed worksheet is shown in FIGURE D-28.

j. Close the workbook, then exit Excel.

FIGURE D-28

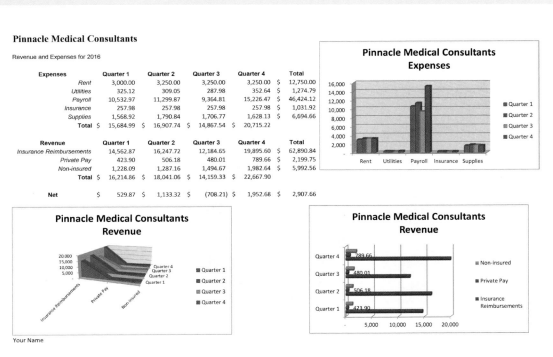

Independent Challenge 3

You are reviewing expenses for the Bethesda Medical Hospital's operating room. The board of directors wants to examine the expenses incurred recently and has asked you to prepare charts that can be used in this evaluation. In particular, you want to see how dollar amounts compare among the different expenses, and you also want to see how expenses compare with each other proportionally to the total budget.

a. Start Excel, open the Data File EMP D-5.xlsx from the location where you store your Data Files, then save it as **EMP D-OR Expenses**.

b. Identify three types of charts that seem best suited to illustrate the data in the range A16:B24. What kinds of chart enhancements are necessary?

c. Create at least two different types of charts that show the distribution of OR expenses. (*Hint*: Move each chart to a new location on the same worksheet.) One of the charts should be a 3-D pie chart.

d. In at least one of the charts, add annotated text and arrows highlighting important data, such as the largest expense.

e. Change the color of at least one data series in at least one of the charts.

f. Add chart titles and category and value axis titles where appropriate. Format the titles with a font of your choice. Apply a shadow to the chart title in at least one chart.

g. Add your name to a section of the header, then save your work.

h. Explode a slice from the 3-D pie chart.

i. Add a data label to the exploded pie slice.

j. Preview the worksheet in Backstage view. Adjust any items as needed. Be sure the charts are all visible on one page. Compare your work to the sample in FIGURE D-29.

k. Submit your work to your instructor as directed, close the workbook, then exit Excel.

FIGURE D-29

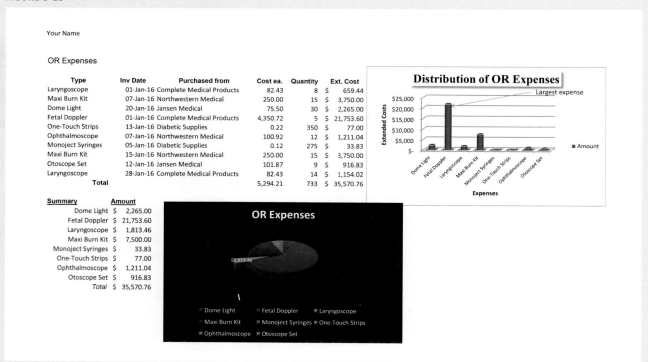

Independent Challenge 4: Explore

This Independent Challenge requires an Internet connection.

You are so indispensable in your role as financial manager at the Good Health Clinic that the company wants to move you and your family to its new location, which you get to choose. You have a good idea where you'd like to live, and you decide to use the web to find out more about houses that are currently available.

a. Start Excel, then save a new, blank workbook as **EMP D-My Dream House** to the location where you save your Data Files.

b. Decide on where you would like to live, and use your favorite search engine to find information sources on homes for sale in that area. (*Hint*: Try using realtor.com or other realtor-sponsored sites.)

c. Determine a price range and features within the home. Find data for at least five homes that meet your location and price requirements, and enter them in the worksheet. See **TABLE D-4** for a suggested data layout.

TABLE D-4

suggested data layout					
Location					
Price range					
	House 1	House 2	House 3	House 4	House 5
Asking price					
Bedrooms					
Bathrooms					
Year built					
Size (in sq. ft.)					

© 2014 Cengage Learning

d. Format the data so it looks attractive and professional.

e. Create any type of column chart using only the House and Asking Price data. Place it on the same worksheet as the data. Include a descriptive title.

f. Change the colors in the chart using the chart style of your choice.

g. Enter your name in a section of the header.

h. Create an additional chart: a combo chart that plots the asking price on one axis and the size of the home on the other axis. (*Hint*: Use Help to get tips on how to chart with a secondary axis.)

i. Save the workbook. Preview the worksheet in Backstage view and make adjustments if necessary to fit all of the information on one page. See **FIGURE D-30** for an example of what your worksheet might look like.

j. Submit your work to your instructor as directed.

k. Close the workbook, then exit Excel.

FIGURE D-30

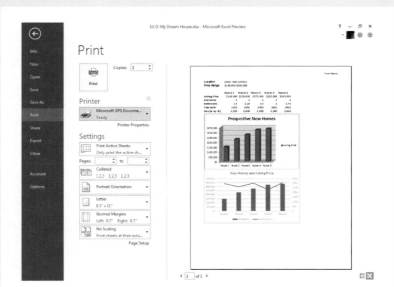

Visual Workshop

Open the Data File EMP D-6.xlsx from the location where you store your Data Files, then save it as **EMP D-Projected Diagnostics Laboratory Revenue**. Format the worksheet data so it looks like FIGURE D-31, then create and modify two charts to match the ones shown in the figure. You will need to make formatting, layout, and design changes once you create the charts. (*Hint*: The shadow used in the 3-D pie chart title is made using the Offset Diagonal Bottom Right shadow.) Enter your name in the left text box of the header, then save and preview the worksheet. Submit your work to your instructor as directed, then close the workbook and exit Excel.

FIGURE D-31

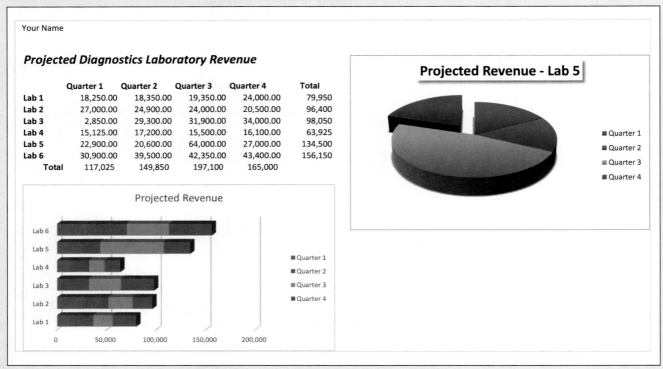

Analyzing Data Using Formulas

CASE ▶ Tony Sanchez, RMC's office manager, uses Excel formulas and functions to analyze insurance reimbursement data for the U.S. imaging company's facilities and to consolidate reimbursement data from several worksheets. Because RMC is considering adding its own imaging center, Tony asks you to estimate the loan costs for a new imaging facility and to compare the reimbursement data for the facilities RMC may acquire.

Unit Objectives

After completing this unit, you will be able to:

- Format data using text functions
- Sum a data range based on conditions
- Consolidate data using a formula
- Check formulas for errors
- Construct formulas using named ranges

- Build a logical formula with the IF function
- Build a logical formula with the AND function
- Calculate payments with the PMT function

Files You Will Need

EMP E-1.xlsx	EMP E-5.xlsx
EMP E-2.xlsx	EMP E-6.xlsx
EMP E-3.xlsx	EMP E-7.xlsx
EMP E-4.xlsx	

Format Data Using Text Functions

Often, you need to import data into Excel from an outside source, such as another program or the Internet. Sometimes you need to reformat this data to make it understandable and attractive. Instead of handling these tasks manually in each cell, you can save time by using Excel text functions to perform these tasks automatically for a range of cell data. The Convert Text to Columns feature breaks data fields in one column into separate columns. The text function PROPER capitalizes the first letter in a string of text as well as any text following a space. You can use the CONCATENATE function to join two or more strings into one text string. **CASE** *Tony has received the technicians' data from the Human Resources Department. He asks you to use text formulas to format the data into a more useful layout.*

STEPS

1. **Start Excel, open the file EMP E-1.xlsx from the location where you store your Data Files, then save it as EMP E-Imaging**

2. **On the Technicians sheet, click cell B4, type ramon silva, press [Tab], type boston, press [Tab], type 2, then click the Enter button ✓ on the Formula Bar**
   You are manually separating the data in cell A4 into the adjacent cells as shown in FIGURE E-1. You will let Excel follow your pattern for the rows below using Flash Fill. **Flash Fill** uses worksheet data you have entered as an example to predict what should be entered into similar column cells.

3. **With cell D4 selected, click the DATA tab, then click the Flash Fill button in the Data Tools group**
   The years of service number is copied from cell D4 into the range D5:D15. You will use Flash Fill to fill in the names and cities.

4. **Click cell B4, click the Flash Fill button in the Data Tools group, click cell C4, then click the Flash Fill button again**
   The column A data is separated into columns B, C and D. You want to format the letters in the names and cities to the correct cases.

5. **Click cell E4, click the FORMULAS tab, click the Text button in the Function Library group, click PROPER, with the insertion point in the Text text box, click cell B4, then click OK**
   The name is copied from cell B4 to cell E4 with the correct uppercase letters for proper names. The remaining names and the cities are still in lowercase letters.

6. **Drag the fill handle to copy the formula in cell E4 to cell F4, then copy the formulas in cells E4:F4 into the range E5:F15**
   You want to format the years data to be more descriptive.

7. **Click cell G4, click the Text button in the Function Library group, click CONCATENATE, with the insertion point in the Text1 text box, click cell D4, press [Tab], with the insertion point in the Text2 text box, press [Spacebar], type Years, then click OK**

8. **Copy the formula in cell G4 into the range G5:G15, click cell A1, compare your work to FIGURE E-2, click the INSERT tab, click the Header & Footer button in the Text group, click the Go to Footer button in the Navigation group, enter your name in the center text box, click on the worksheet, scroll up and click cell A1, then click the Normal button 🔳 in the status bar**

9. **Save your file, then preview the worksheet**

FIGURE E-1: Worksheet with data separated into columns

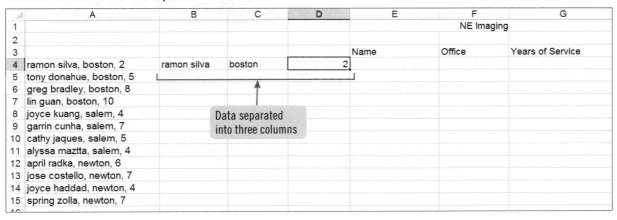

FIGURE E-2: Worksheet with data formatted in columns

	A	B	C	D	E	F	G	H
1						NE Imaging		
2								
3					Name	Office	Years of Service	
4	ramon silva, boston, 2	ramon silva	boston	2	Ramon Silva	Boston	2 Years	
5	tony donahue, boston, 5	tony donahue	boston	5	Tony Donahue	Boston	5 Years	
6	greg bradley, boston, 8	greg bradley	boston	8	Greg Bradley	Boston	8 Years	
7	lin guan, boston, 10	lin guan	boston	10	Lin Guan	Boston	10 Years	
8	joyce kuang, salem, 4	joyce kuang	salem	4	Joyce Kuang	Salem	4 Years	
9	garrin cunha, salem, 7	garrin cunha	salem	7	Garrin Cunha	Salem	7 Years	
10	cathy jaques, salem, 5	cathy jaques	salem	5	Cathy Jaques	Salem	5 Years	
11	alyssa maztta, salem, 4	alyssa maztta	salem	4	Alyssa Maztta	Salem	4 Years	
12	april radka, newton, 6	april radka	newton	6	April Radka	Newton	6 Years	
13	jose costello, newton, 7	jose costello	newton	7	Jose Costello	Newton	7 Years	
14	joyce haddad, newton, 4	joyce haddad	newton	4	Joyce Haddad	Newton	4 Years	
15	spring zolla, newton, 7	spring zolla	newton	7	Spring Zolla	Newton	7 Years	
16								

Working with text in other ways

Other useful text functions include UPPER, LOWER, and SUBSTITUTE. The UPPER function converts text to all uppercase letters, the LOWER function converts text to all lowercase letters, and SUBSTITUTE replaces text in a text string. For example, if cell A1 contains the text string "Today is Wednesday", then =LOWER(A1) would produce "today is wednesday"; =UPPER(A1) would produce "TODAY IS WEDNESDAY"; and =SUBSTITUTE(A1, "Wednesday", "Tuesday") would result in "Today is Tuesday". You can separate text data stored in one column into multiple columns by clicking the DATA tab, clicking the Text to Columns button in the Data Tools group, and specifying the delimiter for your data. A **delimiter** is a separator, such as a space, comma, or semicolon, that should separate your data. Excel then separates your data into columns at the delimiter.

If you want to copy and paste data that you have formatted using text functions, you need to select Values Only from the Paste Options drop-down list to paste the cell values rather than the text formulas.

Sum a Data Range Based on Conditions

Learning Outcomes
- Count data using the COUNTIF function
- Total data using the SUMIF function
- Summarize data using the AVERAGEIF function

You can also use Excel functions to sum, count, and average data in a range based on criteria, or conditions, you set. The SUMIF function totals only the cells in a range that meet given criteria. The COUNTIF function counts cells and the AVERAGEIF function averages cells in a range based on a specified condition. The format for the SUMIF function appears in FIGURE E-3. **CASE** ▶ *Tony asks you to analyze the Boston site's January reimbursement data to provide him with information about each procedure.*

STEPS

1. **Click the Boston sheet tab, click cell G7, click the FORMULAS tab, click the More Functions button in the Function Library group, point to Statistical, scroll down the list of functions if necessary, then click COUNTIF**

   You want to count the number of times MRI appears in the Procedure column. The formula you use will say, in effect, "Examine the range I specify, then count the number of cells in that range that contain "MRI."" You will specify absolute addresses for the range so you can copy the formula.

2. **With the insertion point in the Range text box, select the range A6:A25, press [F4], press [Tab], with the insertion point in the Criteria text box, click cell F7, then click OK**

   Your formula as shown in the formula bar in FIGURE E-4 asks Excel to search the range A6:A25, and where it finds the value shown in cell F7 (that is, when it finds the value "MRI"), add one to the total count. The number of MRI procedures, 6, appears in cell G7. You want to calculate the total insurance payments for the MRI procedures.

QUICK TIP
You can also sum, count, and average ranges with multiple criteria using the functions SUMIFS, COUNTIFS, and AVERAGEIFS.

3. **Click cell H7, click the Math & Trig button in the Function Library group, scroll down the list of functions, then click SUMIF**

   The Function Arguments dialog box opens. You want to enter two ranges and a criterion; the first range is the one where you want Excel to search for the criteria entered. The second range contains the corresponding cells that Excel will total when it finds the criterion you specify in the first range.

4. **With the insertion point in the Range text box, select the range A6:A25, press [F4], press [Tab], with the insertion point in the Criteria text box, click cell F7, press [Tab], with the insertion point in the Sum_range text box, select the range B6:B25, press [F4], then click OK**

   Your formula asks Excel to search the range A6:A25, and where it finds the value shown in cell F7 (that is, when it finds the value "MRI"), add the corresponding amounts from column B. The insurance payments for the MRI procedures, $7,445, appears in cell H7. You want to calculate the average payment for an MRI procedure.

5. **Click cell I7, click the More Functions button in the Function Library group, point to Statistical, then click AVERAGEIF**

6. **With the insertion point in the Range text box, select the range A6:A25, press [F4], press [Tab], with the insertion point in the Criteria text box, click cell F7, press [Tab], with the insertion point in the Average_range text box, select the range B6:B25, press [F4], then click OK**

   The average payment for an MRI procedure, $1,241, appears in cell I7.

TROUBLE
Follow the same steps that you used to add a footer to the Technicians worksheet in the previous lesson.

7. **Select the range G7:I7, drag the fill handle to fill the range G8:I10**

   Compare your results with those in FIGURE E-5.

8. **Add your name to the center of the footer, save the workbook, then preview the sheet**

FIGURE E-3: Format of SUMIF function

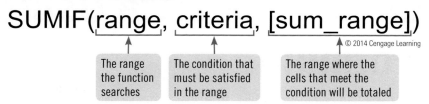

SUMIF(range, criteria, [sum_range])

© 2014 Cengage Learning

The range the function searches

The condition that must be satisfied in the range

The range where the cells that meet the condition will be totaled

FIGURE E-4: COUNTIF function in the formula bar

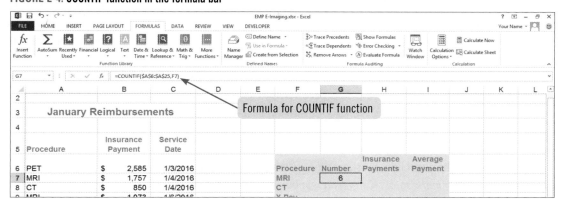

FIGURE E-5: Worksheet with conditional statistics

Procedure	Number	Insurance Payments	Average Payment
MRI	6	$ 7,445	$ 1,241
CT	5	$ 3,325	$ 665
X-Ray	5	$ 985	$ 197
PET	4	$ 10,800	$ 2,700

Entering date and time functions

Microsoft Excel stores dates as sequential serial numbers and uses them in calculations. January 1, 1900 is assigned serial number 1 and numbers are represented as the number of days following that date. You can see the serial number of a date by using the DATE function. To see the serial number of January, 1, 2016, you would enter =DATE(2016,1,1). The result would be in date format, but if you format the cell as Number, then you will see the serial number of 42370 for this date. Because Excel uses serial numbers, you can perform calculations that include dates and times using the Excel date and time functions. To enter a date or time function, click the FORMULAS tab on the Ribbon, click the Date & Time button in the Function Library group, then click the Date or Time function you want. All of the date and time functions will be displayed as dates and times unless you change the formatting to Number to see the serial date or time. See TABLE E-1 for some of the available Date and Time functions in Excel.

TABLE E-1: Date and Time functions

function	calculates the serial number of	example
TODAY	The current date	=TODAY()
NOW	The current date and time	=NOW()
DATE	A date you enter	=DATE(2016,1,2)
TIME	A time you enter	=TIME(0,0,2000)
YEAR	A year you enter	=YEAR(2016)
HOUR	An hour time you enter	=HOUR("15:30:30")
MINUTE	A time you enter	=MINUTE("15:30:30")

© 2014 Cengage Learning

Excel 2013

Consolidate Data Using a Formula

Learning Outcomes
- Consolidate data on multiple sheets using AutoSum
- Consolidate data on multiple sheets using 3-D references

When you want to summarize similar data that exists in different sheets or workbooks, you can **consolidate**, or combine and display, the data in one sheet. For example, you might have entered departmental sales figures on four different store sheets that you want to consolidate on one summary sheet, showing total departmental sales for all stores. Or, you may have quarterly sales data on separate sheets that you want to total for yearly sales on a summary sheet. The best way to consolidate data is to use cell references to the various sheets on a consolidation, or summary, sheet. Because they reference other sheets that are usually behind the summary sheet, such references effectively create another dimension in the workbook and are called **3-D references**, as shown in FIGURE E-6. You can reference, or **link** to, data in other sheets and in other workbooks. Linking to a worksheet or workbook is better than retyping calculated results from another worksheet or workbook because the data values that the calculated totals depend on might change. If you reference the values, any changes to the original values are automatically reflected in the consolidation sheet. **CASE** ▶ *Tony asks you to prepare a January reimbursement summary sheet comparing the total NE Imaging reimbursements for the procedures performed in the month.*

STEPS

1. **Click the NE Summary Jan sheet tab**

   Because the NE Summary Jan sheet (which is the consolidation sheet) will contain the reference to the data in the other sheets, the cell pointer must reside there when you begin entering the reference.

2. **Click cell B7, click the FORMULAS tab, click the AutoSum button in the Function Library group, click the Boston sheet tab, press and hold [Shift] and click the Newton sheet tab, scroll up if necessary and click cell G7, then click the Enter button ✔ on the formula bar**

   The NE Summary Jan sheet becomes active, and the formula bar reads =SUM(Boston:Newton!G7), as shown in FIGURE E-7. "Boston:Newton" references the Boston, Salem, and Newton sheets. The exclamation point (!) is an **external reference indicator**, meaning that the cells referenced are outside the active sheet; G7 is the actual cell reference you want to total in the external sheets. The result, 17, appears in cell B7 of the NE Summary Jan sheet; it is the sum of the number of MRI procedures performed and referenced in cell G7 of the Boston, Salem, and Newton sheets. Because the Insurance Payments data is in the column to the right of the Number column on the Boston, Salem, and Newton sheets, you can copy the number summary formula, with its relative addresses, into the cell that holds the insurance payment information.

3. **Drag the fill handle to copy the formula in cell B7 to cell C7, click the Auto Fill Options list arrow 🖳▾, then click the Fill Without Formatting option button**

   The result, $20,666, appears in cell C7 of the NE Summary Jan sheet, showing the sum of the MRI insurance payments referenced in cell H7 of the Boston, Salem, and Newton sheets.

4. **In the NE Summary Jan sheet, with the range B7:C7 selected, drag the fill handle to fill the range B8:C10**

   You can test a consolidation reference by changing one cell value on which the formula is based and seeing if the formula result changes.

5. **Click the Salem sheet tab, edit cell A6 to read MRI, then click the NE Summary Jan sheet tab**

   The number of MRI procedures performed is automatically updated to 18, and the insurance payments total is increased to $24,524, as shown in FIGURE E-8.

6. **Save the workbook, then preview the worksheet**

FIGURE E-6: Consolidating data from three worksheets

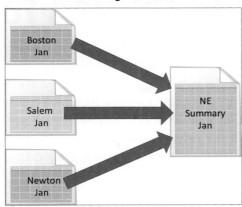

FIGURE E-7: Worksheet showing total MRI procedures

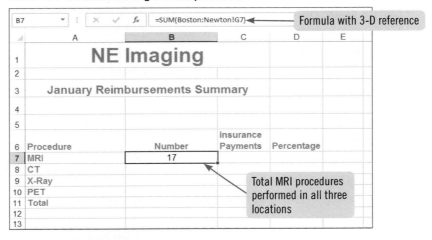

FIGURE E-8: NE Summary Jan worksheet with updated totals

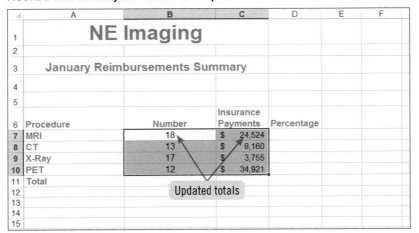

Linking data between workbooks

Just as you can link data between cells in a worksheet and between sheets in a workbook, you can link workbooks so that changes made in referenced cells in one workbook are reflected in the consolidation sheet in the other workbook. To link a single cell between workbooks, open both workbooks, select the cell to receive the linked data, type the equal sign (=), select the cell in the other workbook containing the data to be linked, then press [Enter]. Excel automatically inserts the name of the referenced workbook in the cell reference. For example, if the linked data is contained in cell C7 of the Sales worksheet in the Product workbook, the cell entry reads =[Product.xlsx]Sales!$C$7. To perform calculations, enter formulas on the consolidation sheet using cells in the supporting sheets.

Check Formulas for Errors

Learning Outcomes
- Check for formula errors using IFERROR
- Display worksheet formulas

When formulas result in errors, Excel displays an error value based on the error type. See TABLE E-2 for an explanation of the error values that might appear in worksheets. One way to check worksheet formulas for errors is to display the formulas on the worksheet rather than the formula results. You can also check for errors when entering formulas by using the IFERROR function. The IFERROR function simplifies the error-checking process for your worksheets. This function displays a message or value that you specify, rather than the one automatically generated by Excel, if there is an error in a formula. **CASE** *Tony asks you to use formulas to compare the reimbursement amounts for January. You will use the IFERROR function to help catch formula errors.*

STEPS

1. **On the NE Summary Jan sheet, click cell B11, click the FORMULAS tab, click the AutoSum button in the Function Library group, then click the Enter button ✓ on the formula bar**
   The number of procedures performed, 60, appears in cell B11.

2. **Drag the fill handle to copy the formula in cell B11 into cell C11, click the Auto Fill options list arrow ⊞ ▾, then click the Fill Without Formatting option button**
   The insurance payments total of $71,360 appears in cell C11. You decide to enter a formula to calculate the percentage of payments the MRI procedure represents by dividing the individual procedure payment amount by the total payment figure. To help with error checking, you decide to enter the formula using the IFERROR function.

3. **Click cell D7, click the Logical button in the Function Library group, click IFERROR, with the insertion point in the Value text box, click cell C7, type /, click cell C11, press [Tab], in the Value_if_error text box, type ERROR, then click OK**
   The MRI payment percentage of 34.37% appears in cell D7. You want to be sure that your error message will be displayed properly, so you decide to test it by intentionally creating an error. You copy and paste the formula—which has a relative address in the denominator, where an absolute address should be used.

4. **Drag the fill handle to copy the formula in cell D7 into the range D8:D10**
   The ERROR value appears in cells D8:D10, as shown in FIGURE E-9. The errors are a result of the relative address for C11 in the denominator of the copied formula. Changing the relative address of C11 in the copied formula to an absolute address of $C$11 will correct the errors.

5. **Double-click cell D7, select C11 in the formula, press [F4], then ✓ click on the formula bar**
   The formula now contains an absolute reference to cell C11.

6. **Copy the corrected formula in cell D7 into the range D8:D10**
   The procedure percentages now appear in all four cells, without error messages, as shown in FIGURE E-10. You want to check all of your worksheet formulas by displaying them on the worksheet.

7. **Click the Show Formulas button in the Formula Auditing group**
   The formulas appear in columns B, C, and D. You want to display the formula results again. The Show Formulas button works as a toggle, turning the feature on and off with each click.

8. **Click the Show Formulas button in the Formula Auditing group**
   The formula results appear on the worksheet.

9. **Add your name to the center section of the footer, save the workbook, preview the worksheet, close the workbook, then submit the workbook to your instructor**

FIGURE E-9: Worksheet with error codes

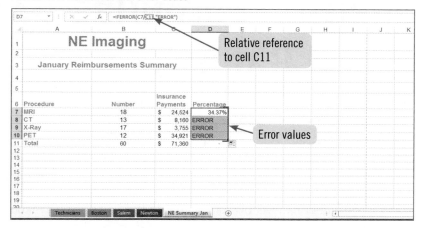

FIGURE E-10: Worksheet with procedure percentages

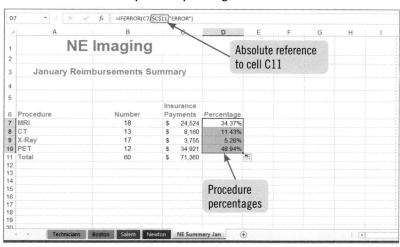

TABLE E-2: Understanding error values

error value	cause of error	error value	cause of error
#DIV/0!	A number is divided by 0	#NAME?	Formula contains text error
#NA	A value in a formula is not available	#NULL!	Invalid intersection of areas
#NUM!	Invalid use of a number in a formula	#REF!	Invalid cell reference
#VALUE!	Wrong type of formula argument or operand	#####	Column is not wide enough to display data

Correcting circular references

A cell with a circular reference contains a formula that refers to its own cell location. If you accidentally enter a formula with a circular reference, a warning box opens, alerting you to the problem. Click Help to open a Help window explaining how to find the circular reference. In simple formulas, a circular reference is easy to spot. To correct it, edit the formula to remove any reference to the cell where the formula is located.

If the circular reference is intentional, you can avoid this error by enabling the iteration feature. Excel then recalculates the formula for the number of times you specify. To enable iterative calculations, click the FILE tab on the Ribbon, click Options, click Formulas to view the options for calculations, click the Enable iterative calculation check box in the Calculation options group, enter the maximum number of iterations in the Maximum Iterations text box, enter the maximum amount of change between recalculation results in the Maximum Change text box, then click OK.

Learning
Outcomes
• Assign names to cells
• Assign names to cell ranges
• Build formulas using names

Construct Formulas Using Named Ranges

To make your worksheet easier to follow, you can assign names to cells and ranges. Then you can use the names in formulas to make them easier to build and to reduce formula errors. For example, the formula "revenue-cost" is easier to understand than the formula "A5-A8". Cell and range names can use uppercase or lowercase letters as well as digits, but cannot have spaces. After you name a cell or range, you can define its **scope**, or the worksheets where you will be able to use it. When defining a name's scope, you can limit its use to a worksheet or make it available to the entire workbook. If you move a named cell or range, its name moves with it, and if you add or remove rows or columns to the worksheet the ranges are adjusted to their new position in the worksheet. When used in formulas, names become absolute cell references by default. **CASE** ▸ *Tony asks you to calculate the number of days since each patient statement was created. You will use range names to construct the formula.*

STEPS

1. **Open the file EMP E-2.xlsx from the location where you store your Data Files, then save it as EMP E-Patient Accounts**

2. **Click cell B4, click the FORMULAS tab if necessary, then click the Define Name button in the Defined Names group**

   The New Name dialog box opens, as shown in **FIGURE E-11**. You can give a cell that contains a date a name that will make it easier to build formulas that perform date calculations.

3. **Type current_date in the Name text box, click the Scope list arrow, click Accounts, then click OK**

   The name assigned to cell B4, current_date, appears in the Name Box. Because its scope is the Accounts worksheet, the range name current_date will appear on the name list only on that worksheet. You can also name ranges that contain dates.

4. **Select the range B7:B13, click the Define Name button in the Defined Names group, enter statement_date in the Name text box, click the Scope list arrow, click Accounts, then click OK**

   Now you can use the named cell and named range in a formula. The formula =statement_date–current_date is easier to understand than =B7-$B$4.

5. **Click cell C7, type =, click the Use in Formula button in the Defined Names group, click statement_date, type –, click the Use in Formula button, click current_date, then click the Enter button ✓ on the formula bar**

   The age of the first account, 9, appears in cell C7. You can use the same formula to calculate the age of the other accounts.

6. **Drag the fill handle to copy the formula in cell C7 into the range C8:C13, then compare your formula results with those in FIGURE E-12**

7. **Save the workbook**

Consolidating data using named ranges

You can consolidate data using named cells and ranges. For example, you might have entered team sales figures using the names team1, team2, and team3 on different sheets that you want to consolidate on one summary sheet. As you enter the summary formula you can click the FORMULAS tab, click the Use in Formula button in the Defined Names group, and select the cell or range name.

FIGURE E-11: New Name dialog box

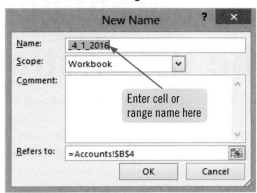

FIGURE E-12: Worksheet with statement ages

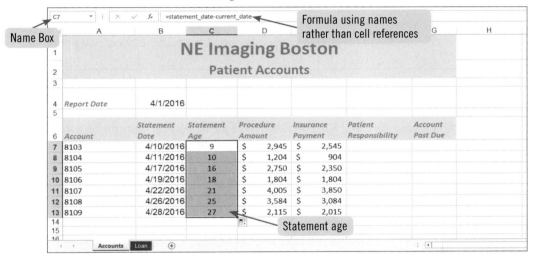

Managing workbook names

You can use the Name Manager to create, delete, and edit names in a workbook. Click the Name Manager button in the Defined Names group on the FORMULAS tab to open the Name Manager dialog box, shown in **FIGURE E-13**. Click the New button to create a new named cell or range, click Delete to remove a highlighted name, and click Filter to see options for displaying specific criteria for displaying names. Clicking Edit opens the Edit Name dialog box where you can change a highlighted cell name, edit or add comments, and change the cell or cells that the name refers to on the worksheet.

FIGURE E-13: Name Manager dialog box

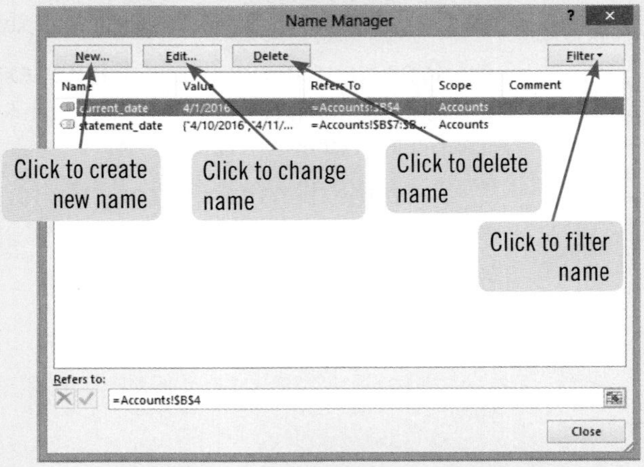

Build a Logical Formula with the IF Function

Learning Outcomes
• Build a logical formula using the IF function
• Apply comparison operators in a logical test

You can build a logical formula using an IF function. A **logical formula** makes calculations based on criteria that you create, called **stated conditions**. For example, you can build a formula to calculate bonuses based on a person's performance rating. If a person is rated a 5 (the stated condition) on a scale of 1 to 5, with 5 being the highest rating, he or she receives an additional 10% of his or her salary as a bonus; otherwise, there is no bonus. A condition that can be answered with a true or false response is called a **logical test**. The IF function has three parts, separated by commas: a condition or logical test, an action to take if the logical test or condition is true, and an action to take if the logical test or condition is false. Another way of expressing this is: IF(test_cond,do_this,else_this). Translated into an Excel IF function, the formula to calculate bonuses might look like this: IF(Rating=5,Salary*0.10,0). In other words, if the rating equals 5, multiply the salary by 0.10 (the decimal equivalent of 10%), then place the result in the selected cell; if the rating does not equal 5, place a 0 in the cell. When entering the logical test portion of an IF statement, you typically use some combination of the comparison operators listed in **TABLE E-3**. **CASE** ▸ *Tony asks you to use an IF function to calculate the amount for which the patient is responsible on each account.*

STEPS

1. **Click cell F7, on the FORMULAS tab, click the Logical button in the Function Library group, then click IF**

   The Function Arguments dialog box opens. You want the function to calculate the patient's responsibility as follows: If the procedure amount is greater than the insurance payment, calculate the amount the patient must pay (procedure amount - insurance payment), and place the result in cell F7; otherwise, place the text "None" in the cell.

2. **With the insertion point in the Logical_test text box, click cell D7, type >, click cell E7, then press [Tab]**

   The symbol (>) represents "greater than." So far, the formula reads "If the procedure amount is greater than the insurance payment,". The next part of the function tells Excel the action to take if the procedure amount exceeds the insurance payment.

3. **With the insertion point in the Value_if_true text box, click cell D7, type –, click cell E7, then press [Tab]**

   This part of the formula tells the program what you want it to do if the logical test is true. Continuing the translation of the formula, this part means "Subtract the insurance payment from the procedure amount." The last part of the formula tells Excel the action to take if the logical test is false (that is, if the procedure amount does not exceed the insurance payment).

4. **Type None in the Value_if_false text box, then click OK**

   The function is complete, and the result, $400 (the amount for which the patient is responsible), appears in cell F7, as shown in **FIGURE E-14**.

5. **Drag the fill handle to copy the formula in cell F7 into the range F8:F13**

   Compare your results with **FIGURE E-15**.

6. **Save the workbook**

FIGURE E-14: Worksheet with IF function

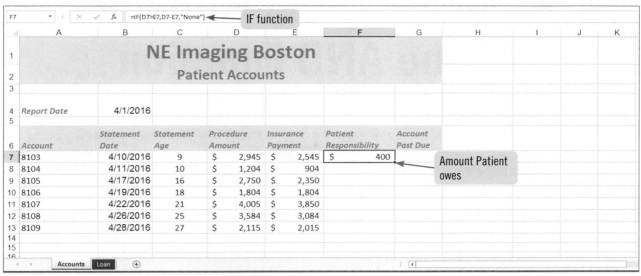

FIGURE E-15: Worksheet showing patient responsibility

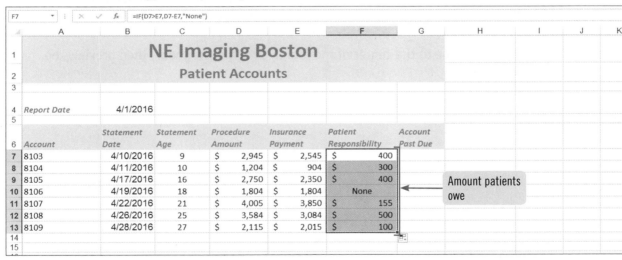

TABLE E-3: Comparison operators

operator	meaning	operator	meaning
<	Less than	<=	Less than or equal to
>	Greater than	>=	Greater than or equal to
=	Equal to	<>	Not equal to

Build a Logical Formula with the AND Function

Learning
Outcomes
• Select the AND
  function
• Apply logical tests
  using text

You can also build a logical function using the AND function. The AND function evaluates all of its arguments and **returns**, or displays, TRUE if every logical test in the formula is true. The AND function returns a value of FALSE if one or more of its logical tests is false. The AND function arguments can include text, numbers, or cell references. **CASE** ▶ *Tony wants you to analyze account data to find accounts that are past due. You will use the AND function to check for accounts that have balances and that are over 21 days old.*

STEPS

1. **Click cell G7, click the Logical button in the Function Library group, then click AND**
   The Function Arguments dialog box opens. You want the function to evaluate the past due status as follows: The patient must have a balance and the statement must be over 21 days old.

TROUBLE
If you get a formula
error, check to be
sure that you typed
the quotation marks
around None.

2. **With the insertion point in the Logical1 text box, click cell F7, type < >, type "None", then press [Tab]**
   The symbol (<>) represents "not equal to." So far, the formula reads "If the patient responsibility is not equal to None,"—in other words, if it is an integer. The next logical test checks the statement age.

3. **With the insertion point in the Logical2 text box, click cell C7, type >21, then click OK**
   The function is complete, and the result, FALSE, appears in cell G7, as shown in **FIGURE E-16**.

4. **Drag the fill handle to copy the formula in cell G7 into the range G8:G13**
   Compare your results with **FIGURE E-17**.

5. **Add your name to the center of the footer, save the workbook, then preview the worksheet**

Using the OR and NOT logical functions

The OR logical function has the same syntax as the AND function, but rather than returning TRUE if every argument is true, the OR function will return TRUE if any of its arguments are true. It will only return FALSE if all of its arguments are false. The NOT logical function reverses the value of its argument. For example NOT(TRUE) reverses its argument of TRUE and returns FALSE. This can be used in a worksheet to ensure that a cell is not equal to a particular value. See **TABLE E-4** for examples of the AND, OR, and NOT functions.

TABLE E-4: Examples of AND, OR, and NOT functions with cell values A1=10 and B1=20

function	formula	result
AND	=AND(A1>5,B1>25)	FALSE
OR	=OR(A1>5,B1>25)	TRUE
NOT	=NOT(A1=0)	TRUE

© 2014 Cengage Learning

FIGURE E-16: Worksheet with AND function

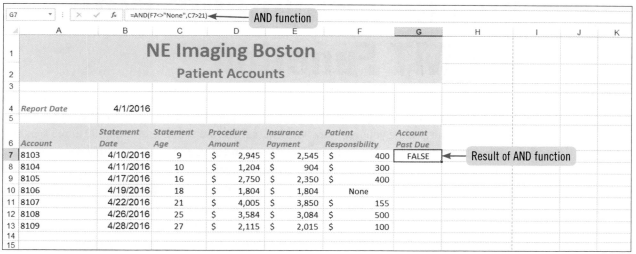

FIGURE E-17: Worksheet with accounts past due evaluated

Account	Statement Date	Statement Age	Procedure Amount	Insurance Payment	Patient Responsibility	Account Past Due
8103	4/10/2016	9	$ 2,945	$ 2,545	$ 400	FALSE
8104	4/11/2016	10	$ 1,204	$ 904	$ 300	FALSE
8105	4/17/2016	16	$ 2,750	$ 2,350	$ 400	FALSE
8106	4/19/2016	18	$ 1,804	$ 1,804	None	FALSE
8107	4/22/2016	21	$ 4,005	$ 3,850	$ 155	FALSE
8108	4/26/2016	25	$ 3,584	$ 3,084	$ 500	TRUE
8109	4/28/2016	27	$ 2,115	$ 2,015	$ 100	TRUE

Report Date: 4/1/2016

G7 =AND(F7<>"None",C7>21)

Inserting an equation into a worksheet

If your worksheet contains formulas, you might want to place an equation on the worksheet to document how you arrived at your results. First create a text box to hold the equation: Click the INSERT tab, click the Text Box button in the Text group, then click on the worksheet location where you want the equation to appear. To place the equation in the text box, click the INSERT tab again, then click the Equation button in the Symbols group. When you see "Type equation here," you can build an equation by clicking the mathematical symbols in the Structures group of the EQUATION TOOLS DESIGN tab. For example, if you wanted to enter a fraction of 2/7, you click the Fraction button, choose the first option, click the top box, enter 2, press [Tab], enter 7, then click outside of the fraction. To insert the symbol x^2 into a text box, click the Script button in the Structures group of the EQUATION TOOLS DESIGN tab, click the first option, click in the lower-left box and enter "x", press [Tab], enter 2 in the upper-right box, then click to the right of the boxes to exit the symbol. You can also add built-in equations to a text box: On the EQUATION TOOLS DESIGN tab, click the Equation button in the Tools group, then select the equation. Built-in equations include the equation for the area of a circle, the binomial theorem, Pythagorean theorem, and the quadratic equation.

Calculate Payments with the PMT Function

Learning Outcomes
- Calculate monthly payments using the PMT function
- Edit the PMT function to display payments as a positive value

PMT is a financial function that calculates the periodic payment amount for money borrowed. For example, if you want to borrow money to buy a car, and you know the principal amount, interest rate, and loan term, the PMT function can calculate your monthly payment. Say you want to borrow $20,000 at 6.5% interest and pay the loan off in 5 years. The Excel PMT function can tell you that your monthly payment will be $391.32. The main parts of the PMT function are PMT(rate, nper, pv). See **FIGURE E-18** for an illustration of a PMT function that calculates the monthly payment in the car loan example. **CASE** ▶ *The management of RMC is considering an expansion rather than acquiring a new facility. Tony has obtained quotes from three different lenders on borrowing $370,000 to begin the expansion. He obtained loan quotes from a commercial bank, a venture capitalist, and an investment banker. He wants you to summarize the information using the Excel PMT function.*

STEPS

1. **Click the Loan sheet tab, click cell F5, click the FORMULAS tab, click the Financial button in the Function Library group, scroll down the list of functions, then click PMT**

2. **With the insertion point in the Rate text box, click cell D5 on the worksheet, type /12, then press [Tab]**

   You must divide the annual interest by 12 because you are calculating monthly, not annual, payments. You need to be consistent about the units you use for rate and nper. If you express nper as the number of monthly payments, then you must express the interest rate as a monthly rate.

QUICK TIP

The Fv and Type arguments are optional: The argument Fv is the future value, or the total amount you want to obtain after all payments. If you omit it, Excel assumes you want to pay off the loan completely, so the default Fv is 0. The Type argument indicates when the payments are made; 0 is the end of the period, and 1 is the beginning of the period. The default is the end of the period.

3. **With the insertion point in the Nper text box, click cell E5; click the Pv text box, click cell B5, then click OK**

   The payment of ($6,990.84) in cell F5 appears in red, indicating that it is a negative amount. Excel displays the result of a PMT function as a negative value to reflect the negative cash flow the loan represents to the borrower. To show the monthly payment as a positive number, you can place a minus sign in front of the Pv cell reference in the function.

4. **Double-click cell F5 and edit it so it reads =PMT(D5/12,E5,-B5), then click the Enter button ✓ on the formula bar**

   A positive value of $6,990.84 now appears in cell F5, as shown in **FIGURE E-19**. You can use the same formula to generate the monthly payments for the other loans.

5. **With cell F5 selected, drag the fill handle to fill the range F6:F7**

   A monthly payment of $11,130.81 for the venture capitalist loan appears in cell F6. A monthly payment of $16,257.28 for the investment banker loan appears in cell F7. The loans with shorter terms have much higher monthly payments. But you will not know the entire financial picture until you calculate the total payments and total interest for each lender.

QUICK TIP

You can use the keyboard shortcut of [Ctrl][Enter] rather than clicking the Enter button. This enters the formula and leaves the cell selected.

6. **Click cell G5, type =, click cell E5, type *, click cell F5, then press [Tab], in cell H5, type =, click cell G5, type –, click cell B5, then click ✓**

7. **Copy the formulas in cells G5:H5 into the range G6:H7, then click cell A1**

   You can experiment with different interest rates, loan amounts, or terms for any one of the lenders; the PMT function generates a new set of values automatically.

8. **Add your name to the center section of the footer, save the workbook, preview the worksheet, then submit the workbook to your instructor**

   Your worksheet appears as shown in **FIGURE E-20**.

9. **Close the workbook and exit Excel**

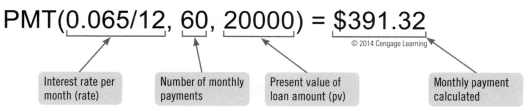

PMT(0.065/12, 60, 20000) = $391.32

© 2014 Cengage Learning

Interest rate per month (rate)

Number of monthly payments

Present value of loan amount (pv)

Monthly payment calculated

FIGURE E-19: PMT function calculating monthly loan payment

F5   fx   =PMT(D5/12,E5,-B5)

Minus sign before present value displays payment as a positive amount

Riverwalk Clinic
Imaging Center Loan Summary

Lender	Loan Amount	Term (Years)	Interest Rate	Term (Months)	Monthly Payment	Total Payments	Total Interest
Commercial Bank	$ 370,000	5	5.05%	60	$6,990.84		
Venture Capitalist	$ 370,000	3	5.25%	36			
Investment Banker	$ 370,000	2	5.15%	24			

Monthly payment calculated

FIGURE E-20: Completed worksheet

Riverwalk Clinic
Imaging Center Loan Summary

Lender	Loan Amount	Term (Years)	Interest Rate	Term (Months)	Monthly Payment	Total Payments	Total Interest
Commercial Bank	$ 370,000	5	5.05%	60	$6,990.84	$ 419,450.12	$ 49,450.12
Venture Capitalist	$ 370,000	3	5.25%	36	$11,130.81	$ 400,709.16	$ 30,709.16
Investment Banker	$ 370,000	2	5.15%	24	$16,257.28	$ 390,174.75	$ 20,174.75

Copied formula calculates total payments and interest for remaining two loan options

Calculating future value with the FV function

You can use the FV (Future Value) function to determine the amount of money a given monthly investment will amount to, at a given interest rate, after a given number of payment periods. The syntax is similar to that of the PMT function: FV(rate,nper,pmt,pv,type). The rate is the interest paid by the financial institution, the nper is the number of periods, and the pmt is the amount that you deposit. For example, suppose you want to invest $1,000 every month for the next 12 months into an account that pays 2% a year, and you want to know how much you will have at the end of 12 months (that is, its future value). You enter the function FV(.02/12,12,-1000), and Excel returns the value $12,110.61 as the future value of your investment. As with the PMT function, the units for the rate and nper must be consistent.

Practice

Put your skills into Practice with **SAM**! If you have a SAM account, go to www.cengage.com/sam2013 to access SAM assignments for this unit

Concepts Review

FIGURE E-21

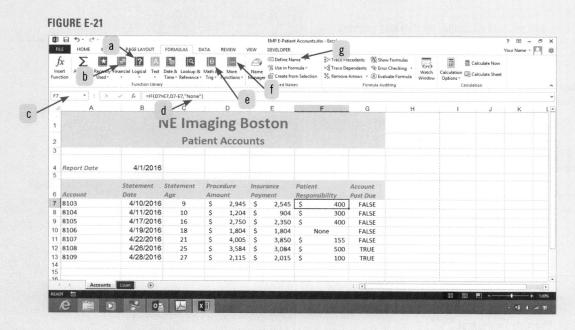

1. **Which element do you click to add a statistical function to a worksheet?**
2. **Which element do you click to name a cell or range?**
3. **Which element points to the area where the name of a selected cell or range appears?**
4. **Which element points to a logical formula?**
5. **Which element do you click to insert a PMT function into a worksheet?**
6. **Which element do you click to add a SUMIF function to a worksheet?**
7. **Which element do you click to add an IF function to a worksheet?**

Match each term with the statement that best describes it.

8. **PV**
9. **FV**
10. **PROPER**
11. **SUMIF**
12. **test_cond**

a. Function used to change the first letter of a string to uppercase
b. Function used to determine the future amount of an investment
c. Part of the PMT function that represents the loan amount
d. Part of the IF function that the conditions are stated in
e. Function used to conditionally total cells

Select the best answer from the list of choices.

13. **When you enter the rate and nper arguments in a PMT function, you must:**
   a. Be consistent in the units used.
   b. Multiply both units by 12.
   c. Divide both values by 12.
   d. Always use annual units.
14. **To express conditions such as less than or equal to, you can use a:**
   a. Text formula.
   b. Comparison operator.
   c. PMT function.
   d. Statistical function.

15. Which of the following statements is false?

a. When used in formulas, names become relative cell references by default.

b. Names cannot contain spaces.

c. Named ranges make formulas easier to build.

d. If you move a named cell or range, its name moves with it.

16. Which of the following is an external reference indicator in a formula?

a.   &

b.   :

c.   !

d.   =

17. When using text in logical tests, the text must be enclosed in:

a.   " "

b.   ( )

c.   !

d.   < >

18. Which function joins text strings into one text string?

a. Proper

b. Join

c. Combine

d. Concatenate

Skills Review

1. Format data using text functions.

a. Start Excel, open the file EMP E-3.xlsx from the location where you store your Data Files, then save it as **EMP E-Reviews**.

b. On the Managers worksheet, select cell B4 and use the Flash Fill button on the DATA tab to enter the names into column B.

c. In cell D2, enter the text formula to convert the first letter of the department in cell C2 to uppercase, then copy the formula in cell D2 into the range D3:D9.

d. In cell E2, enter the text formula to convert all letters of the department in cell C2 to uppercase, then copy the formula in cell E2 into the range E3:E9.

e. In cell F2, use the text formula to convert all letters of the department in cell C2 to lowercase, then copy the formula in cell F2 into the range F3:F9.

f. In cell G2, use the text formula to substitute "Medical Records" for "mr" if that text exists in cell F2. (*Hint*: In the Function Arguments dialog box, Text is F2, Old_text is "mr", and New_text is "Medical Records".) Copy the formula in cell G2 into the range G3:G9 to change the other cells containing "mr" to "Medical Records" and widen column G to fit the new entries. (The clinic and ultrasound entries will not change because the formula searches for the text "mr".)

g. Save your work, then enter your name in the worksheet footer. Compare your screen to FIGURE E-22.

h. Display the formulas in the worksheet.

i. Redisplay the formula results.

2. Sum a data range based on conditions.

a. Make the Clinic sheet active.

b. In cell B20, use the COUNTIF function to count the number of employees with a rating of 5.

c. In cell B21, use the AVERAGEIF function to average the salaries of those with a rating of 5.

d. In cell B22, enter the SUMIF function that totals the salaries of employees with a rating of 5.

e. Format cells B21 and B22 with the Number format using commas and no decimals. Save your work, then compare your formula results to FIGURE E-23.

FIGURE E-22

	A	B	C	D	E	F	G	H
1		Name	Department	Proper	Upper	Lower	Substitute	
2	JohnSmith@company.com	John Smith	mR	Mr	MR	mr	Medical Records	
3	PaulaJones@company.com	Paula Jones	Clinic	Clinic	CLINIC	clinic	clinic	
4	LindaKristol@company.com	Linda Kristol	mR	Mr	MR	mr	Medical Records	
5	AlMeng@company.com	Al Meng	Clinic	Clinic	CLINIC	clinic	clinic	
6	RobertDelgado@company.com	Robert Delgado	ultrasound	Ultrasound	ULTRASOUND	ultrasound	ultrasound	
7	HarryDegual@company.com	Harry Degual	ultrasound	Ultrasound	ULTRASOUND	ultrasound	ultrasound	
8	JodyWilliams@company.com	Jody Williams	clinic	Clinic	CLINIC	clinic	clinic	
9	MaryAbbott@company.com	Mary Abbott	mR	Mr	MR	mr	Medical Records	
10								
11								

FIGURE E-23

17		
18	**Department Statistics**	
19	Top Rating	
20	Number	5
21	Average Salary	31,200
22	Total Salary	156,000
23		

Skills Review (continued)

3. Consolidate data using a formula.

 a. Make the Summary sheet active.

 b. In cell B4, use the AutoSum function to total cell F15 on the Clinic and Ultrasound sheets.

 c. Format cell B4 with the Accounting Number format with two decimal places.

 d. Enter your name in the worksheet footer, then save your work. Compare your screen to FIGURE E-24.

 e. Display the formula in the worksheet, then redisplay the formula results in the worksheet.

4. Check formulas for errors.

 a. Make the Clinic sheet active.

 b. In cell I6, use the IFERROR function to display "ERROR" in the event that the formula F6/F15 results in a formula error. (*Note*: This formula will generate an intentional error after the next step, which you will correct in a moment.)

 c. Copy the formula in cell I6 into the range I7:I14.

 d. Correct the formula in cell I6 by making the denominator, F15, an absolute address.

 e. Copy the new formula in cell I6 into the range I7:I14, then save your work.

FIGURE E-24

	A	B
1	**Payroll Summary**	
2		
3		Salary
4	TOTAL	$ 566,035.00
5		

5. Construct formulas using named ranges.

 a. On the Clinic sheet, name the range C6:C14 **review_date**, and limit the scope of the name to the Clinic worksheet.

 b. In cell E6, enter the formula **=review_date+183**, using the Use in Formula button to enter the cell name.

 c. Copy the formula in cell E6 into the range E7:E14.

 d. Use the Name Manager to add a comment of **Date of last review** to the review_date name. (*Hint*: In the Name Manager dialog box, click the review_date name, then click Edit to enter the comment.) Save your work.

6. Build a logical formula with the IF function.

 a. In cell G6, use the Function Arguments dialog box to enter the formula **=IF(D6=5,F6*0.05,0)**.

 b. Copy the formula in cell G6 into the range G7:G14.

 c. In cell G15, use AutoSum to total the range G6:G14.

 d. Save your work.

7. Build a logical formula with the AND function.

 a. In cell H6, use the Function Arguments dialog box to enter the formula **=AND(G6>0,B6>5)**.

 b. Copy the formula in cell H6 into the range H7:H14.

 c. Enter your name in the worksheet footer, save your work, then compare your worksheet to FIGURE E-25.

 d. Make the Ultrasound sheet active.

 e. In cell H6, indicate if the employee needs more development hours to reach the minimum of 5. Use the Function Arguments dialog box for the NOT function to enter **B6>=5** in the Logical text box. Copy the formula in cell H6 into the range H7:H14.

 f. In cell I6, indicate if the employee needs to enroll in a quality class, as indicated by a rating less than 5 or having fewer than 5 development hours.

FIGURE E-25

	A	B	C	D	E	F	G	H	I	J
1					**Respiratory Clinic**					
2					**Merit Pay**					
3										
4										
5	Last Name	Professional Development Hours	Review Date	Rating	Next Review	Salary	Bonus	Pay Bonus	Percentage of Total	
6	Brady	6	1/5/2016	2	7/6/2016	$ 19,740.00	$0.00	FALSE	7.17%	
7	Case	8	4/1/2016	5	10/1/2016	$ 26,800.00	$1,340.00	TRUE	9.74%	
8	Donnely	1	7/1/2016	4	12/31/2016	$ 33,400.00	$0.00	FALSE	12.13%	
9	Hemsley	3	4/1/2016	5	10/1/2016	$ 25,500.00	$1,275.00	FALSE	9.26%	
10	Kim	10	3/1/2016	5	8/31/2016	$ 37,500.00	$1,875.00	TRUE	13.62%	
11	Maaley	7	5/1/2016	5	10/31/2016	$ 36,500.00	$1,825.00	TRUE	13.26%	
12	Merry	10	6/1/2016	4	12/1/2016	$ 37,500.00	$0.00	FALSE	13.62%	
13	Smith	7	1/1/2016	3	7/2/2016	$ 28,600.00	$0.00	FALSE	10.39%	
14	Storey	3	7/1/2016	5	12/31/2016	$ 29,700.00	$1,485.00	FALSE	10.79%	
15	Totals					$ 275,240.00	$7,800.00			
16										
17										

fewer than 5 development hours. Use the Function Arguments dialog box for the OR function to enter **D6<5** in the Logical1 text box and **B6<5** in the Logical2 text box. Copy the formula in cell I6 into the range I7:I14.

Skills Review (continued)

   g. Enter your name in the worksheet footer, save your work, then compare your screen to FIGURE E-26.

8. Calculate payments with the PMT function.

FIGURE E-26

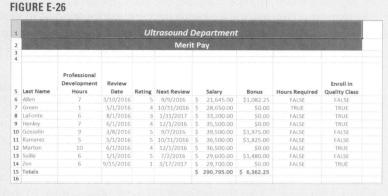

   a. Make the Loan sheet active.

   b. In cell B9, determine the monthly payment using the loan information shown: Use the Function Arguments dialog box to enter the formula **=PMT(B5/12,B6,-B4)**.

   c. In cell B10, enter a formula that multiplies the number of payments by the monthly payment.

   d. In cell B11, enter the formula that subtracts the loan amount from the total payment amount, then compare your screen to FIGURE E-27.

   e. Enter your name in the worksheet footer, save the workbook, then submit your workbook to your instructor.

   f. Close the workbook, then exit Excel.

FIGURE E-27

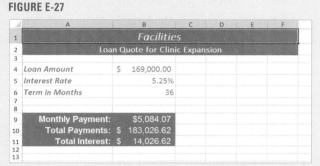

Independent Challenge 1

As the accounting manager of Community Health Clinic, you are reviewing the patient account information and prioritizing the overdue invoices for your collections service. You will analyze the invoices and use logical functions to emphasize priority accounts.

   a. Start Excel, open the file EMP E-4.xlsx from the location where you store your Data Files, then save it as **EMP E-Accounts**.

   b. Name the range B7:B13 **invoice_date**, and give the name a scope of the accounts payable worksheet.

   c. Name the cell B4 **current_date**, and give the name a scope of the accounts payable worksheet.

   d. Enter a formula using the named range invoice_date in cell E7 that calculates the invoice due date by adding 30 to the invoice date.

   e. Copy the formula in cell E7 to the range E8:E13.

   f. In cell F7, enter a formula using the named range invoice_date and the named cell current_date that calculates the invoice age by subtracting the invoice date from the current date.

   g. Copy the formula in cell F7 to the range F8:F13.

   h. In cell G7, enter an IF function that calculates the number of days an invoice is overdue, assuming that an invoice must be paid in 30 days. (*Hint*: The Logical_test should check to see if the age of the invoice is greater than 30, the Value_if_true should calculate the current date minus the invoice due date, and the Value_if_false should be 0.) Copy the IF function into the range G8:G13.

   i. In cell H7, enter an AND function to prioritize the overdue invoices that are more than $1,000 for collection services. (*Hint*: The Logical1 condition should check to see if the number of days overdue is more than 0, and the Logical2 condition should check if the amount is more than 1,000.) Copy the AND function into the range H8:H13.

   j. Use the Name Manager to name the range H7:H13 **Priority** and give the name a scope of the Accounts worksheet. (*Hint*: In the Name Manager dialog box, click New to enter the range name.)

   k. Enter your name in the worksheet footer, save the workbook, preview the worksheet, then submit the workbook to your instructor.

   l. Close the workbook, then exit Excel.

Independent Challenge 2

The management of the medical supply company where you work is interested in expanding the business and needs its sales records audited to prepare the business plan. Specifically, they want to show what percent of annual sales each category represents. You will use a formula on a summary worksheet to summarize the sales for January, February, and March and to calculate the overall first-quarter percentage of the sales categories.

a. Start Excel, open the file EMP E-5.xlsx from the location where you store your Data Files, then save it as **EMP E-Products**.

b. In cell B10 of the Jan, Feb, and Mar sheets, enter the formulas to calculate the sales totals for the month.

c. For each month, in cell C5, create a formula calculating the percent of sales for the Diagnostic sales category. Use a function to display "**INCORRECT**" if there is a mistake in the formula. Verify that the percent appears with two decimal places. Copy this formula as necessary to complete the % of sales for all sales categories on all sheets. If any cells display "**INCORRECT**", fix the formulas in those cells.

d. In column B of the Summary sheet, use formulas to total the sales categories for the Jan, Feb, and Mar worksheets.

e. Enter the formula to calculate the first quarter sales total in cell B10 using the sales totals on the Jan, Feb, and Mar worksheets.

f. Calculate the percent of each sales category on the Summary sheet. Use a function to display **MISCALCULATION** if there is a mistake in the formula. Copy this formula as necessary. If any cells display **MISCALCULATION**, fix the formulas in those cells.

g. Enter your name in the Summary worksheet footer, save the workbook, preview the worksheet, then submit it to your instructor.

h. On the Products sheet, separate the product list in cell A1 into separate columns of text data. (*Hint*: With cell A1 as the active cell, use the Text to Columns button in the Data Tools group of the DATA tab. The products are delimited with commas.) Widen the columns as necessary. Use the second row to display the products with the first letter of each word in uppercase, as shown in FIGURE E-28.

i. Enter your name in the Products worksheet footer, save the workbook, preview the worksheet, then submit the workbook to your instructor.

FIGURE E-28

	A	B	C	D	E	F	G	H	I	J
1	diagnostic	treatment	clinical	accessories	laboratory					
2	Diagnostic	Treatment	Clinical	Accessories	Laboratory					
3										
4										

Independent Challenge 3

The occupational therapy clinic where you work needs to update its equipment. It is your responsibility to research options for a $60,000 equipment loan. You check three loan sources: the Small Business Administration (SBA), your local bank, and a consortium of investors. The SBA will lend you the money at 5.5% interest, but you have to pay it off in 3 years. The local bank offers you the loan at 6.75% interest over 4 years. The consortium offers you a 7% loan, but they require you to pay it back in 2 years. To analyze all three loan options, you decide to build a loan summary worksheet. Using the loan terms provided, build a worksheet summarizing your options.

a. Start Excel, open a new workbook, save it as **EMP E-Loan**, then rename Sheet1 **Loan Summary**.

b. Using FIGURE E-29 as a guide, enter labels and worksheet data for the three loan sources in columns A through D. Use the formatting of your choice.

FIGURE E-29

	Occupational Therapy Associates						
	Loan Options						
Loan Source	Loan Amount	Interest Rate	# Payments	Monthly Payment	Total Payments	Total Interest
SBA	$ 60,000.00	5.50%	36	$ 1,811.75	$ 65,223.15	$ 5,223.15
Bank	$ 60,000.00	6.75%	48	$ 1,429.83	$ 68,631.63	$ 8,631.63
Investors	$ 60,000.00	7.00%	24	$ 2,686.35	$ 64,472.51	$ 4,472.51

Independent Challenge 3 (continued)

c. Enter the monthly payment formula for your first loan source (making sure to show the payment as a positive amount), copy the formula as appropriate, then name the range containing the monthly payment formulas **Monthly_Payment** with a scope of the workbook.

d. Name the cell range containing the number of payments **Number_Payments** with the scope of the workbook.

e. Enter the formula for total payments for your first loan source using the named ranges Monthly_Payment and Number_Payments, then copy the formula as necessary.

f. Name the cell range containing the formulas for Total payments **Total_Payments**. Name the cell range containing the loan amounts **Loan_Amount**. Each name should have the workbook as its scope.

g. Enter the formula for total interest for your first loan source using the named ranges Total_Payments and Loan_Amount, then copy the formula as necessary.

h. Format the worksheet using appropriate formatting, then enter your name in the worksheet footer.

i. Save the workbook, preview the worksheet and change it to landscape orientation on a single page, then submit the workbook to your instructor.

j. Close the workbook, then exit Excel.

Independent Challenge 4: Explore

As the heart health program manager at your clinic, you are using a weekly worksheet to log and analyze the training for each of your patients. As part of this training, you record daily running, biking, swimming, and weight training data and analyze it on a weekly basis.

a. Start Excel, open the file EMP E-6.xlsx from the location where you store your Data Files, then save it as **EMP E-Workout**.

b. Use SUMIF functions in cells G5:G8 to calculate the total minutes spent on each corresponding activity in cells F5:F8.

c. Use AVERAGEIF functions in cells H5:H8 to calculate the average number of minutes spent on each corresponding activity in cells F5:F8.

d. Use COUNTIF functions in cells I5:I8 to calculate the number of times each activity in cells F5:F8 was performed. (*Hint*: The Range of cells to count is $B$4:$B$15.)

e. Use the SUMIFS function in cell G9 to calculate the total number of minutes spent running outdoors.

f. Use the AVERAGEIFS function in cell H9 to calculate the average number of minutes spent running outdoors.

g. Use the COUNTIFS function in cell I9 to calculate the number of days spent running outdoors. Compare your worksheet to FIGURE E-30 and adjust your cell formatting as needed to match the figure.

h. Enter your name in the worksheet footer, save the workbook, preview the worksheet, then submit it to your instructor.

i. Close the workbook, then exit Excel.

FIGURE E-30

	A	B	C	D	E	F	G	H	I
1	**Total Fitness**								
2	Client Name:	Kathy Howe							
3	Date	Activity	Minutes	Location				Week of January 2nd	
4	1/2/2016	Run	30	Gym		Activity	Total Minutes	Average Minutes	Number of Workouts
5	1/2/2016	Swim	40	Aquatics Center		Run	155	38.75	4
6	1/3/2016	Run	50	Outdoors		Swim	135	45.00	3
7	1/3/2016	Bike	35	Outdoors		Bike	90	30.00	3
8	1/4/2016	Run	35	Outdoors		Weights	60	30.00	2
9	1/4/2016	Weights	30	Gym		Run Outdoors	85	42.5	2
10	1/5/2016	Swim	50	Aquatics Center					
11	1/6/2016	Weights	30	Gym					
12	1/6/2016	Bike	30	Outdoors					
13	1/7/2016	Run	40	Gym					
14	1/7/2016	Swim	45	Aquatics Center					
15	1/8/2016	Bike	25	Gym					

Visual Workshop

Open the file EMP E-7.xlsx from the location where you store your Data Files, then save it as **EMP E-Summary**. Create the worksheet shown in FIGURE E-31 using the data in columns B, C, and D along with the following criteria:

- The employee is eligible for a bonus if:
  - The person is under 40.

    AND
  - The person does not smoke.
- If the person is eligible for a discount, the discount amount is calculated as 5% of the monthly premium. Otherwise the discount amount is 0. (*Hint*: Use an AND formula to determine if a person is eligible for a discount, and use an IF formula to check eligibility and to enter the discount amount.) Enter your name in the worksheet footer, save the workbook, preview the worksheet, then submit the worksheet to your instructor.

FIGURE E-31

	A	B	C	D	E	F	G
1	Health Insurance Discount Program Summary						
2							
3	Last Name	Monthly Premium	Age	Smoke	Eligible	Discount	
4	Adams	$170	35	No	TRUE	$8.50	
5	Gurano	$194	64	No	FALSE	$0.00	
6	Greely	$172	30	Yes	FALSE	$0.00	
7	Hanlon	$135	27	Yes	FALSE	$0.00	
8	Perez	$175	59	No	FALSE	$0.00	
9	Medway	$118	24	No	TRUE	$5.90	
10	Merkel	$197	67	Yes	FALSE	$0.00	
11	Star	$119	25	No	TRUE	$5.95	
12	Gonzalez	$127	30	No	TRUE	$6.35	
13							
14							

Managing Workbook Data

CASE Tony Sanchez, the office manager at RMC, asks for your help in analyzing yearly revenue data for the clinic's procedures. When the analysis is complete, he will distribute the workbook for the vice presidents to review.

Unit Objectives

After completing this unit, you will be able to:

- View and arrange worksheets
- Protect worksheets and workbooks
- Save custom views of a worksheet
- Add a worksheet background
- Prepare a workbook for distribution
- Insert hyperlinks
- Save a workbook for distribution
- Group worksheets

Files You Will Need

EMP F-1.xlsx	EMP F-Classifications.xlsx
EMP F-2.xlsx	EMP F-Contact Information.xlsx
EMP F-3.xlsx	EMP F-Dermatology Revenue.xlsx
EMP F-4.xlsx	EMP F-Equipment.xlsx
EMP F-5.xlsx	EMP F-Logo.gif
EMP F-6.xlsx	EMP F-Op Elective.xlsx

View and Arrange Worksheets

Learning Outcomes
- Compare worksheet data by arranging worksheets
- View and hide instances of a workbook

As you work with workbooks made up of multiple worksheets, you might need to compare data in the various sheets. To do this, you can view each worksheet in its own workbook window, called an **instance**, and display the windows in an arrangement that makes it easy to compare data. When you work with worksheets in separate windows, you are working with different views of the same workbook; the data itself remains in one file. **CASE** *Tony asks you to compare the monthly revenue totals for elective and acute procedures. Because the revenue totals are on different worksheets, you want to arrange the worksheets side by side in separate windows.*

STEPS

1. **Start Excel, open the file EMP F-1.xlsx from the location where you store your Data Files, then save it as EMP F-Revenue**

2. **With the Elective sheet active, click the VIEW tab, then click the New Window button in the Window group**

   There are now two instances of the Revenue workbook open. You can see them when you place the mouse pointer over the Excel icon on the task bar: EMP F-Revenue.xlsx:1 and EMP F-Revenue.xlsx:2. The EMP F-Revenue.xlsx:2 window appears in the title bar, indicating that it's the active instance.

3. **Click the Acute sheet tab, click the VIEW tab, click the Switch Windows button in the Window group, then click EMP F-Revenue.xlsx:1**

   The EMP F-Revenue.xlsx:1 instance is active. The Elective sheet is active in the EMP F-Revenue.xlsx:1 workbook, and the Acute sheet is active in the EMP F-Revenue.xlsx:2 workbook.

4. **Click the Arrange All button in the Window group**

   The Arrange Windows dialog box, shown in **FIGURE F-1**, lets you choose how to display the instances. You want to view the workbooks next to each other.

5. **Click the Vertical option button to select it, then click OK**

   The windows are arranged next to each other, as shown in **FIGURE F-2**. The second instance of the workbook opens at a zoom of 100%, not the 120% zoom of the workbook. You can activate a workbook by clicking one of its cells. You can also view only one of the workbooks by hiding the one you do not wish to see.

6. **Scroll horizontally to view the data in the EMP F-Revenue.xlsx:1 workbook, click anywhere in the EMP F-Revenue.xlsx:2 workbook, scroll horizontally to view the data in the EMP F-Revenue.xlsx:2 workbook, then click the Hide button in the Window group**

   When you hide the second instance, only the EMP F-Revenue.xlsx:1 workbook is visible.

7. **In the EMP F-Revenue.xlsx:1 window, click the Unhide button in the Window group; click EMP F-Revenue.xlsx:2 if necessary in the Unhide dialog box, then click OK**

   The EMP F-Revenue.xlsx:2 instance appears.

8. **Close the EMP F-Revenue.xlsx:2 instance, then maximize the Elective worksheet in the EMP F-Revenue.xlsx workbook**

   Closing the EMP F-Revenue.xlsx:2 instance leaves only the first instance open. Its name in the title bar returns to EMP F-Revenue.xlsx.

FIGURE F-1: Arrange Windows dialog box

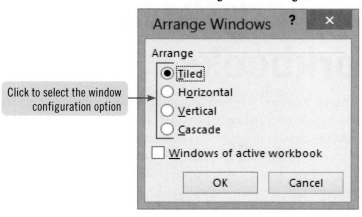

Click to select the window configuration option →

FIGURE F-2: Windows instances displayed vertically

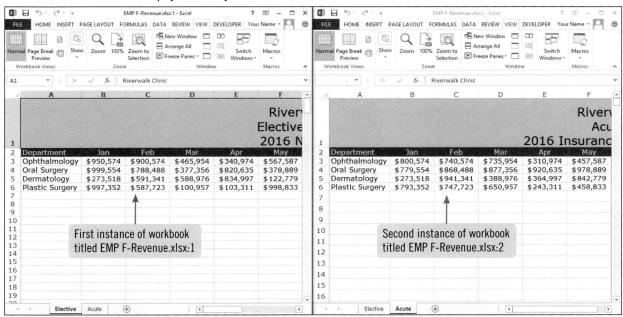

First instance of workbook titled EMP F-Revenue.xlsx:1

Second instance of workbook titled EMP F-Revenue.xlsx:2

Splitting the worksheet into multiple panes

Excel lets you split the worksheet area into vertical and/or horizontal panes, so that you can click inside any one pane and scroll to locate information in that pane while the other panes remain in place, as shown in **FIGURE F-3**. To split a worksheet area into multiple panes, click a cell below and to the right of where you want the split to appear, click the VIEW tab, then click the Split button in the Window group. You can also split a worksheet into only two panes by selecting the row or column below or to the right of where you want the split to appear, clicking the VIEW tab, then clicking Split in the Window group. To remove a split, click the VIEW tab, then click Split in the Window group.

FIGURE F-3: Worksheet split into two horizontal and two vertical panes

Break in column letters indicates split sheet

Break in row numbers indicates split sheet

Worksheet divided into 4 panes

Protect Worksheets and Workbooks

Learning Outcomes
• Protect worksheet data by locking cells
• Create a data entry area on a worksheet by unlocking cells
• Protect a workbook using read-only format

To protect sensitive information, Excel lets you **lock** one or more cells so that other people can view the values and formulas in those cells, but not change it. Excel locks all cells by default, but this locking does not take effect until you activate the protection feature. A common worksheet protection strategy is to unlock cells in which data will be changed, sometimes called the **data entry area**, and to lock cells in which the data should not be changed. Then, when you protect the worksheet, the unlocked areas can still be changed. **CASE** ▶ *Because the elective revenue sales figures for January through March have been finalized, Tony asks you to protect that worksheet area. That way, users cannot change the figures for those months.*

STEPS

QUICK TIP
You can also lock a cell by clicking the Format button in the Cells group of the HOME tab, then clicking Lock Cell on the shortcut menu.

1. **On the Elective sheet, select the range E3:M6, click the HOME tab, click the Format button in the Cells group, click Format Cells, then in the Format Cells dialog box click the Protection tab**

   The Locked check box in the Protection tab is already checked, as shown in **FIGURE F-4**. All the cells in a new workbook start out locked. The protection feature is inactive by default.

2. **Click the Locked check box to deselect it, click OK, click the REVIEW tab, then click the Protect Sheet button in the Changes group**

   The Protect Sheet dialog box opens, as shown in **FIGURE F-5**. The default options protect the worksheet while allowing users to select locked or unlocked cells only. You choose not to use a password.

QUICK TIP
To hide any formulas that you don't want to be visible, select the cells that contain formulas that you want to hide, open the Format Cells dialog box, then click the Hidden check box on the Protection tab to select it. The formula will be hidden after the worksheet is protected.

3. **Verify that Protect worksheet and contents of locked cells is checked, that the password text box is blank, and that Select locked cells and Select unlocked cells are checked, then click OK**

   You are ready to test the new worksheet protection.

4. **Click cell B3, type 1 to confirm that locked cells cannot be changed, click OK, click cell F3, type 1, notice that Excel lets you begin the entry, press [Esc] to cancel the entry, then save your work**

   When you try change a locked cell on a protected worksheet, a dialog box, shown in **FIGURE F-6**, reminds you of the protected cell's status and provides instructions to unprotect the worksheet. These cells are in **read-only format**, which means they can be viewed in the worksheet but not changed. Because you unlocked the cells in columns E through M before you protected the worksheet, these cells are not in read-only format and you can change these cells. You decide to add more protection by protecting the workbook from changes to the workbook's structure, but decide not to require a password.

5. **Click the Protect Workbook button in the Changes group, in the Protect Structure and Windows dialog box, make sure the Structure check box is selected, verify that the password text box is blank, then click OK**

   The Protect Workbook button is a toggle, which means it's like an on/off switch. When it is green, the workbook is protected. Clicking it again removes the green color indicating the protection is removed from the workbook. You are ready to test the new workbook protection.

6. **Right-click the Elective sheet tab**

   The Insert, Delete, Rename, Move or Copy, Tab Color, Hide, and Unhide menu options are not available because the structure is protected. You decide to remove the workbook and worksheet protections.

7. **Click the Protect Workbook button in the Changes group to turn off the protection, then click the Unprotect Sheet button to remove the worksheet protection**

FIGURE F-4: Protection tab in Format Cells dialog box

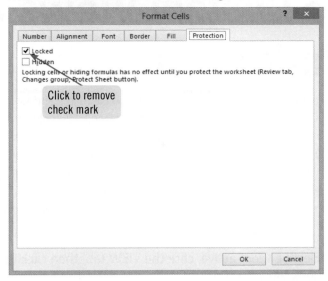

FIGURE F-5: Protect Sheet dialog box

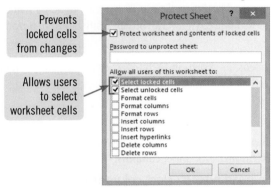

FIGURE F-6: Reminder of protected worksheet status

Freezing rows and columns

As the rows and columns of a worksheet fill up with data, you might want to Freeze panes to hold headers in place so you can see them as you scroll through the worksheet. Freezing panes is similar to splitting panes except that the panes do not move, so you can keep column or row labels in view as you scroll. **Panes** are the columns and rows that **freeze**, or remain in place, while you scroll through your worksheet. To freeze panes, click the first cell in the area you want to scroll, click the VIEW tab, click the Freeze Panes button in the Window group, then click Freeze Panes. Excel freezes the columns to the left and the rows above the selected cell as shown in **FIGURE F-7**. You can also select Freeze Top Row or Freeze First Column to freeze the top row or left worksheet column. To unfreeze panes, click the VIEW tab, click Freeze panes, then click Unfreeze Panes.

FIGURE F-7: Worksheet with top row and left column frozen

	A	F	G	H	I
1	Procedure	Provider	Authorization	Balance	
26	Manual Therapy Tec	Laneighton	Yes	Yes	
27	Therap Proc 4	Toloes	Yes	Yes	
28	Manual Therapy Tec	Laneighton	No	Yes	
29	Therap Proc 3	Sonna	Yes	Yes	
30	Manual Therapy Tec	March	Yes	Yes	
31	Physical Therapy E	Michaels	Yes	Yes	
32	Therapeutic Activity D	March	No	Yes	
33	Therap Proc 4	Michaels	Yes	Yes	
34	Therap Proc 1	Laneighton	Yes	Yes	
35	Physical Therapy E	March	No	Yes	
36	Therapeutic Activity Tec	Toloes	Yes	Yes	
37	Therap Proc 3	March	No	Yes	
38	Manual Therapy Tec	Michaels	No	Yes	
39	Therapeutic Activity B	Michaels	No	Yes	
40	Therap Proc 5	Laneighton	No	Yes	
41	Manual Therapy Tec	March	No	Yes	
42	Therap Proc 5	Toloes	Yes	Yes	
43	Theran Proc 1	Michaels	Yes	Yes	

Break in column letters and row numbers indicates first column and first row are frozen

Save Custom Views of a Worksheet

Learning Outcomes
- Create different views of worksheet data using custom views
- Display different views of worksheet data using custom views

A **view** is a set of display and/or print settings that you can name and save, then access at a later time. By using the Excel Custom Views feature, you can create several different views of a worksheet without having to create separate sheets. For example, if you often hide columns in a worksheet, you can create two views, one that displays all of the columns and another with the columns hidden. You set the worksheet display first, then name the view. Then you can open the view whenever you want. **CASE** ▶ *Because Tony wants to generate a revenue report from the final sales data for January through March, he asks you to save the first-quarter revenue data as a custom view. You begin by creating a view showing all of the worksheet data.*

STEPS

1. **With the Elective sheet active, click the VIEW tab, then click the Custom Views button in the Workbook Views group**

   The Custom Views dialog box opens. Any previously defined views for the active worksheet appear in the Views box. No views are defined for the Elective worksheet. You decide to add a named view for the current view, which shows all the worksheet columns. That way, you can easily return to it from any other views you create.

2. **Click Add**

   The Add View dialog box opens, as shown in **FIGURE F-8**. Here, you enter a name for the view and decide whether to include print settings and hidden rows, columns, and filter settings. You want to include these options, which are already selected.

3. **In the Name box, type Revenue, then click OK**

   You have created a view called Revenue that shows all the worksheet columns. You want to set up another view that will hide the April through December columns.

4. **Drag across the column headings to select columns E through M, right-click the selected area, then click Hide on the shortcut menu**

   You are ready to create a custom view of the January through March sales data.

5. **Click cell A1, click the Custom Views button in the Workbook Views group, click Add, in the Name box type First Quarter, then click OK**

   You are ready to test the two custom views.

6. **Click the Custom Views button in the Workbook Views group, click Revenue in the Views list, then click Show**

   The Revenue custom view displays all of the months' revenue data. Now you are ready to test the First Quarter custom view.

7. **Click the Custom Views button in the Workbook Views group, then with First Quarter in the Custom Views dialog box selected, click Show**

   Only the January through March revenue figures appear on the screen, as shown in **FIGURE F-9**.

8. **Return to the Revenue view, then save your work**

Managing Workbook Data

FIGURE F-8: **Add View dialog box**

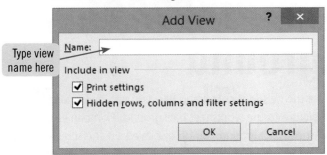

Type view name here →

FIGURE F-9: **First Quarter view**

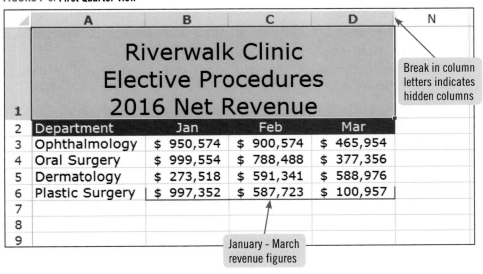

Break in column letters indicates hidden columns

January - March revenue figures

Using Page Break Preview

The vertical and horizontal dashed lines in the Normal view of worksheets represent page breaks. Excel automatically inserts a page break when your worksheet data doesn't fit on one page. These page breaks are **dynamic**, which means they adjust automatically when you insert or delete rows and columns and when you change column widths or row heights. Everything to the left of the first vertical dashed line and above the first horizontal dashed line is printed on the first page. You can manually add or remove page breaks by clicking the PAGE LAYOUT tab, clicking the Breaks button in the Page Setup group, then clicking the

appropriate command. You can also view and change page breaks manually by clicking the VIEW tab, then clicking the Page Break Preview button in the Workbook Views group, or by clicking the Page Break Preview button 📖 on the status bar, then clicking OK. You can drag the blue page break lines to the desired location. Some cells may temporarily display ##### while you are in Page Break Preview. If you drag a page break to the right to include more data on a page, Excel shrinks the type to fit the data on that page. To exit Page Break Preview, click the Normal button in the Workbook Views group.

Add a Worksheet Background

In addition to using a theme's font colors and fills, you can make your Excel data more attractive on the screen by adding a picture to the worksheet background. Companies often use their logo as a worksheet background. A worksheet background will be displayed on the screen but will not print with the worksheet. If you want to add a worksheet background that appears on printouts, you can add a **watermark**, a translucent background design that prints behind your data. To add a watermark, you add the image to the worksheet header or footer. **CASE** ▶ *Tony asks you to add the RMC logo to the printed background of the Elective worksheet. But first he wants to see it as a nonprinting background.*

STEPS

1. **With the Elective sheet active, click the PAGE LAYOUT tab, then click the Background button in the Page Setup group**

   The Insert Pictures dialog box opens.

2. **Click Browse, navigate to the location where you store your Data Files, click EMP F-Logo.gif, then click Insert**

   The RMC logo appears behind the worksheet data. It appears twice horizontally on your screen because the graphic is **tiled**, or repeated, to fill the background.

3. **Click the FILE tab, click Print, view the preview of the Elective worksheet, then click the Back button ⬅ to return to the worksheet**

   Because the logo is only for display purposes, it will not print with the worksheet, so is not visible in the Print preview. You want the logo to print with the worksheet, so you decide to remove the background and add the logo to the worksheet header.

4. **On the PAGE LAYOUT tab, click the Delete Background button in the Page Setup group, click the INSERT tab, then click the Header & Footer button in the Text group**

   The HEADER & FOOTER TOOLS DESIGN tab appears, as shown in **FIGURE F-10**. You can use the buttons in the Header & Footer group to add preformatted headers and footers to a worksheet. The Header & Footer Elements buttons let you add page numbers, the date, the time, the file location, names, and pictures to the header or footer. The Navigation group buttons move the insertion point from the header to the footer and back. You want to add a picture to the header.

5. **Click in the center section of the header to place the insertion point, click the Picture button in the Header & Footer Elements group, click Browse, then navigate to the location where you store your Data Files, click EMP F-Logo.gif, then click Insert**

   A code representing a picture, "&[Picture]", appears in the center of the header.

6. **Click cell A1, then click the Normal button ⊞ on the Status Bar**

   You want to scale the worksheet data to print on one page.

7. **Click the PAGE LAYOUT tab, click the Width list arrow in the Scale to Fit group, click 1 page, click the Height list arrow in the Scale to Fit group, click 1 page, then preview the worksheet**

   Your worksheet should look like **FIGURE F-11**.

8. **Return to the worksheet, click the HOME tab, then save the workbook**

FIGURE F-10: HEADER & FOOTER TOOLS DESIGN tab

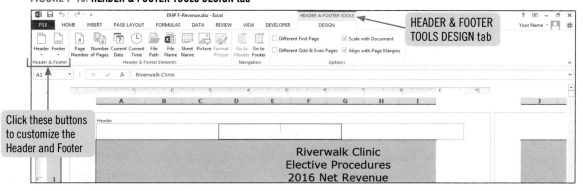

FIGURE F-11: Preview of Elective worksheet with logo in the background

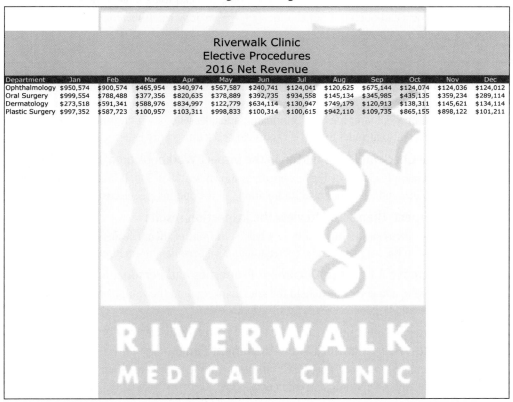

Riverwalk Clinic
Elective Procedures
2016 Net Revenue

Department	Jan	Feb	Mar	Apr	May	Jun	Jul	Aug	Sep	Oct	Nov	Dec
Ophthalmology	$950,574	$900,574	$465,954	$340,974	$567,587	$240,741	$124,041	$120,625	$675,144	$124,074	$124,036	$124,012
Oral Surgery	$999,554	$788,488	$377,356	$820,635	$378,889	$392,735	$934,558	$145,134	$345,985	$435,135	$359,234	$289,114
Dermatology	$273,518	$591,341	$588,976	$834,997	$122,779	$634,114	$130,947	$749,179	$120,913	$138,311	$145,621	$134,114
Plastic Surgery	$997,352	$587,723	$100,957	$103,311	$998,833	$100,314	$100,615	$942,110	$109,735	$865,155	$898,122	$101,211

Working with Screenshots in Excel

You can paste an image of an open file, called a **screenshot**, into an Excel workbook or another Office document. This pastes the screenshot into your document as an image that you can move, copy, or edit. To insert a screenshot, click the INSERT tab, click the Screenshot button in the Illustrations group to see a gallery of other currently open windows, then click on one of the available windows in the gallery. This pastes a screenshot of the window you clicked into the current Excel document. You can also click the Screen Clipping button in the gallery to select and paste an area from an open window. Once you have created a screenshot and positioned it in your worksheet, you can modify it using tools on the PICTURE TOOLS FORMAT tab. This tab appears when the screenshot object is selected. You can change the overall visual style of the image by clicking the More button in the Picture Styles group, then clicking a style. In the Picture Styles group you can also use the Picture Effects button to apply a visual effect to the image, the Picture Border button to enhance the border surrounding the image, and the Picture Layout button to convert the image to a SmartArt Graphic. The Picture Tools tab also has other tools to correct images. For example, you can sharpen and soften an image and make corrections for brightness and contrast by clicking the Corrections button in the Adjust group. Clicking a choice in the Sharpen/Soften section allows you to change the visual acuity of the image and choosing an option in the Brightness/Contrast section adjusts the lightness of an image.

Prepare a Workbook for Distribution

Learning Outcomes
• Add keywords to a worksheet using the Document Panel
• Review a file for problems using the Inspect Document feature
• Protect a workbook by using Mark as Final status

If you are collaborating with others and want to share a workbook with them, you might want to remove sensitive information before distributing the file. On the other hand, you might want to add helpful information, called **properties**, to a file to help others identify, understand, and locate it. Properties might include keywords, the author's name, a title, the status, and comments. **Keywords** are terms users can search for that will help them locate your workbook. Properties are a form of **metadata**, information that describes data and is used in Microsoft Windows document searches. In addition, to ensure that others do not make unauthorized changes to your workbook, you can mark a file as final. This makes it a read-only file, which others can open but not change. **CASE** *Tony wants you to protect the workbook and prepare it for distribution.*

STEPS

1. **Click the FILE tab**

   Backstage view opens, with the Info screen in front. It shows you a preview of your printed worksheet and information about your file. This information includes who has permission to open, copy, or change your workbook. It also includes tools you can use to check for security issues.

2. **Click the Check for Issues button in the Inspect Workbook area, then click Inspect Document**

   The Document Inspector dialog box opens, as shown in **FIGURE F-12**. It lists items from which you can have Excel evaluate hidden or personal information. All the options are selected by default.

3. **Click Inspect, then scroll to view the inspection results**

   Areas with personal information have a red "!" in front of them. Headers and footers is also flagged. You want to keep the file's header and footer and remove personal information.

4. **Click Remove All next to Document Properties and Personal Information, then click Close**

   You decide to add keywords to help the sales managers find the worksheet. The search words "Elective" or "Acute" would be good keywords for this workbook.

5. **Click the File tab if necessary, click the Properties list arrow on the right side of Backstage view, then click Show Document Panel**

   The Document Properties Panel appears at the top of the worksheet, as shown in **FIGURE F-13**. You decide to add a title, status, keywords, and comments.

6. **In the Title text box type Revenue, in the Keywords text box type Elective Acute Revenue, in the Status text box type DRAFT, then in the Comments text box type The first-quarter figures are final., then click the Close button on the Document Properties Panel**

   You are ready to mark the workbook as final.

7. **Click the FILE tab, click the Protect Workbook button in the Info area, click Mark as Final, click OK, then click OK again**

   "[Read-Only]" appears in the title bar indicating the workbook is saved as a read-only file. A yellow bar also appears below the tabs indicating the workbook is marked as final. The yellow bar also has an Edit Anyway button.

8. **Click the HOME tab, click cell B3, type 1 to confirm that the cell cannot be changed, click the Edit Anyway button above the Formula Bar, then save the workbook**

   Marking a workbook as final is not a strong form of workbook protection because a workbook recipient can remove this Final status. By clicking Edit Anyway, you remove the read-only status, which makes the workbook editable again.

FIGURE F-12: Document Inspector dialog box

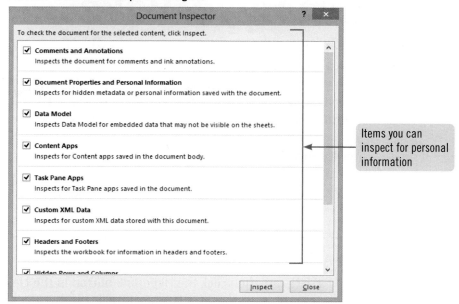

Items you can inspect for personal information

FIGURE F-13: Document Properties Panel

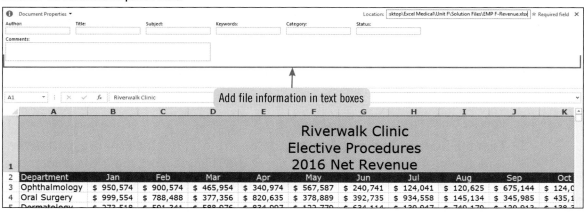

Add file information in text boxes

Sharing a workbook using SkyDrive

Once you set up a Windows Live account you can save your Excel files "to the cloud" (meaning on the Internet) using SkyDrive. This allows you to access your Excel files from any computer and share Excel files with others. When saving an Excel file to the cloud, click the FILE tab, click Save As, then click the SkyDrive, which is the default location and the first location listed under Places on the Save As tab. After you save an Excel file to your SkyDrive, you can share it by clicking the FILE tab, clicking Share, entering the email addresses of the people you wish to invite to share the file, and clicking Share. An email with a link to the Excel file on your SkyDrive will be sent to the addresses you entered. The recipients can open and edit the file using the Excel Web App. The Share option also allows you to get a link to your Excel file on your SkyDrive, post a workbook to social networks, and email your workbook.

Insert Hyperlinks

As you manage the content and appearance of your workbooks, you might want the workbook user to view information that exists in another location. It might be nonessential information or data that is too detailed to place in the workbook itself. In these cases, you can create a hyperlink. A **hyperlink** is an object (a file-name, word, phrase, or graphic) in a worksheet that, when you click it, displays, or "jumps to," another location, called the **target**. The target can also be a worksheet, another document, or a site on the World Wide Web. For example, in a worksheet that lists customer invoices, at each customer's name, you might create a hyperlink to an Excel file containing payment terms for each customer. **CASE** ▶ *Tony wants vice presidents who view the Revenue workbook to be able to view a breakdown of the revenue totals for each elective ophthalmology procedure. He asks you to create a hyperlink at the Ophthalmology heading so that users can click the hyperlink to view the revenue for each elective procedure in that department.*

STEPS

1. **Click cell A3 on the Elective worksheet**

2. **Click the INSERT tab, then click the Hyperlink button in the Links group**
   The Insert Hyperlink dialog box opens, as shown in **FIGURE F-14**. The icons under "Link to" on the left side of the dialog box let you select the type of location to where you want the link to jump: an existing file or Web page, a place in the same document, a new document, or an e-mail address. Because you want the link to display an already-existing document, the selected first icon, Existing File or Web Page, is correct, so you won't have to change it.

3. **Click the Look in list arrow, navigate to the location where you store your Data Files if necessary, then click EMP F-Op Elective.xlsx in the file list**
   The filename you selected and its path appear in the Address text box. This is the document users will see when they click the hyperlink. You can also specify the ScreenTip that users see when they hold the pointer over the hyperlink.

4. **Click the ScreenTip button, type Revenue by Procedure, click OK, then click OK again**
   Cell A3 now contains underlined green text, indicating that it is a hyperlink. The color of a hyperlink depends on the worksheet theme colors. You will change the text color of the hyperlink text so it stands out from the other text.

5. **Click the HOME tab, click the Font Color list arrow ▲ ▾ in the Font group, click the Dark Green, Accent 4, Darker 50% color in the Theme Colors, move the pointer over the Category text, until the pointer turns into the 🖑 pointer, view the ScreenTip, then click once**
   After you click, the EMP F-Op Elective workbook opens, displaying the Ophthalmology elective procedures, as shown in **FIGURE F-15**.

6. **Close the EMP F-Op Elective Sales workbook, click Don't Save if necessary, then save the EMP F-Revenue workbook**

Working with Headers and Footers

You may want to add a different header or footer to the first page of your worksheet. You can do this by clicking the INSERT tab on the Ribbon, clicking the Header & Footer button in the Text group, clicking the HEADER & FOOTER TOOLS DESIGN tab on the Ribbon, then clicking the Different First Page check box in the Options group to select it. A text indicator (that changes to 'First Page Header' from 'Header') appears in the header/footer area on the Page Layout view, indicating that you are creating a different first page header/footer. You can also have different headers or footers on odd and even pages of your worksheet by clicking the Different Odd & Even Pages check box to select it.

FIGURE F-14: **Insert Hyperlink dialog box**

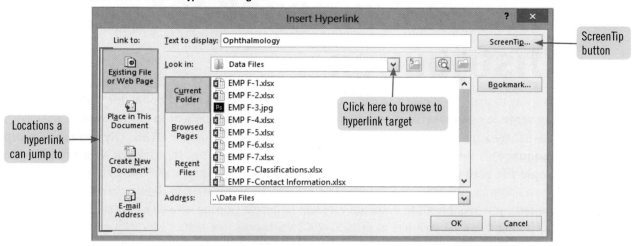

Locations a hyperlink can jump to

ScreenTip button

Click here to browse to hyperlink target

FIGURE F-15: **Target document**

	A	B
1	**Ophthalmology**	
2	**Elective Procedures**	
3	**Procedure**	**2016 Revenue**
4	CK	$98,812
5	Lasik	$1,813,456
6	PRK	$697,425
7	LTK	$1,213,456
8	Intacs	$1,205,187
9		
10		
11		

Using research tools

You can access resources online and locally on your computer using the Research task pane. To open the Research task pane, click the REVIEW tab, then click the Research button in the Proofing group. The Search for text box in the Research pane lets you enter a research topic. The Research pane has a drop-down list of the resources available to search for your topic. You can use this list to access resources such as a thesaurus, a dictionary, financial web sites, and research web sites. You can also access a Thesaurus task pane using the Thesaurus button on the REVIEW tab in the Proofing group.

Save a Workbook for Distribution

**Learning
Outcomes**
• Save a workbook
  in earlier formats
  of Excel
• Save a workbook
  in single file Web
  page format

One way to share Excel data is to place, or **publish**, the data on a network or on the Web so that others can access it using their Web browsers. To publish an Excel document to an **intranet** (a company's internal Web site) or the Web, you can save it in an HTML format. **HTML (Hypertext Markup Language)** is the coding format used for all Web documents. You can also save your Excel file as a **single-file Web page** that integrates all of the worksheets and graphical elements from the workbook into a single file. This file format is called MHTML, also known as MHT. In addition to distributing files on the Web, you might need to distribute your files to people working with an earlier version of Excel. You can do this by saving your files as Excel 97-2003 workbooks. See TABLE F-1 for a list of the most popular formats. **CASE** *Tony asks you to create a workbook version that managers running an earlier Excel version can use. He also asks you to save the EMP F-Revenue workbook in MHT format so he can publish it on the RMC intranet.*

STEPS

1. **Click the FILE tab, click Save As, click Browse, navigate to the location where you store your Data Files, click the Save as type list arrow in the Save As dialog box, click Excel 97-2003 Workbook (*.xls), then click Save**

   The Compatibility Checker dialog box opens. It alerts you to the features that will be lost or converted by saving in the earlier format. Some Excel 2013 features are not available in earlier versions of Excel.

2. **Click Continue, close the workbook, then reopen the EMP F-Revenue.xls workbook**

   "[Compatibility Mode]" appears in the title bar, as shown in FIGURE F-16. Compatibility mode prevents you from including Excel features in your workbook that are not supported in Excel 97-2003 workbooks. To exit compatibility mode, you need to convert your file to the Excel 2013 format.

3. **Click the FILE tab, click Info, click the Convert button, click Save, click Yes if you are asked if you want to replace the existing file, then click Yes to close and reopen the workbook**

   The title bar no longer displays "[Compatibility Mode]" and the file has been changed to the .xlsx format. You still need to save the file for Web distribution.

4. **Click the FILE tab, click Save As, in the Save As dialog box navigate to the location where you store your Data Files if necessary, change the filename to revenue, then click the Save as type list arrow and click Single File Web Page (*.mht, *.mhtml)**

   The Save as type list box indicates that the workbook is to be saved as a Single File Web Page, which is in MHTML or MHT format. To avoid problems when publishing your pages to a Web server, it is best to use lowercase characters, omit special characters and spaces, and limit your filename to eight characters with an additional three-character extension.

5. **Click Save, then click Yes**

   The dialog box indicated that some features may not be retained in the Web page file. Excel saves the workbook as an MHT file in the location you specified. The MHT file is open on your screen. See FIGURE F-17. It's a good idea to open an MHT file in your browser to see how it will look to viewers.

6. **Close the revenue.mht file in Excel, start your browser, open the revenue.mht file by double-clicking it in the location where you store your Data Files, click the Acute sheet tab, then close your browser window**

FIGURE F-16: Workbook in compatibility mode

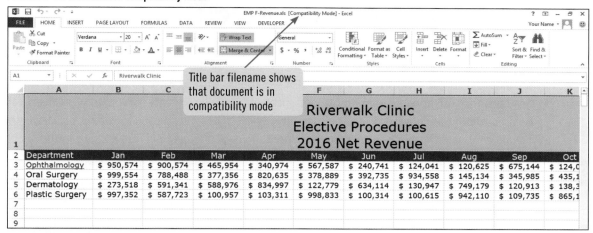

FIGURE F-17: Workbook saved as a single file Web page

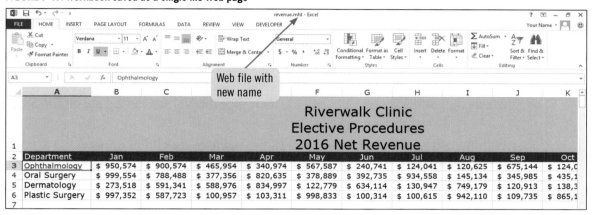

TABLE F-1: Workbook formats

type of file	file extension(s)	used for
Macro-enabled workbook	.xlsm	Files that contain macros
Excel 97 – 2003 workbook	.xls	Working with people using older versions of Excel
Single file Web page	.mht, .mhtml	Web sites with multiple pages and graphics
Web page	.htm, .html	Simple single-page Web sites
Excel template	.xltx	Excel files that will be reused with small changes
Excel macro-enabled template	.xltm	Excel files that will be used again and contain macros
PDF (Portable document format)	.pdf	Files with formatting that needs to be preserved
XML paper specification	.xps	Files with formatting that needs to be preserved and files that need to be shared
OpenDocument spreadsheet	.ods	Files created with OpenOffice

Understanding Excel file formats

The default file format for Excel 2013 files is the Office Open XML format, which supports all Excel features. This has been the default file format of Office files since Microsoft Office 2007. This format stores Excel files in small XML components that are zipped for compression, making the files smaller. The most often used format, .xlsx, does not support macros. **Macros,** programmed instructions that perform tasks, can be a security risk. If your worksheet contains macros, you need to save it with an extension of .xlsm so the macros can function in the workbook. If you use a workbook's text and formats repeatedly, you might want to save it as a template with the extension .xltx. If your template contains macros, you need to save it with the .xltm extension.

Group Worksheets

You can group worksheets to work on them as a collection. When you enter data into one grouped worksheet, that data is also automatically entered into all of the worksheets in the group. This is useful for data that is common to every sheet of a workbook, such as headers and footers, or for column headings that will apply to all monthly worksheets in a yearly summary. Grouping worksheets can also be used to print multiple worksheets at one time. **CASE** ▶ *Tony asks you to add the text "Riverwalk" to the footer of both the Elective and Acute worksheets. You will also add half-inch margins to the top of both worksheets.*

STEPS

1. **Open the EMP F-Revenue.xlsx file from the location where you store your Data Files**

2. **With the Elective sheet active, press and hold [Shift], click the Acute sheet, then release [Shift]**

   Both sheet tabs are selected, and the title bar now contains "[Group]", indicating that the worksheets are grouped together. Now any changes you make to the Elective sheet will also be made to the Acute sheet.

3. **Click the INSERT tab, then click the Header & Footer button in the Text group**

4. **On the HEADER & FOOTER TOOLS DESIGN tab, click the Go to Footer button in the Navigation group, type Riverwalk in the center section of the footer, enter your name in the left section of the footer, click cell A1, then click the Normal button ▦ on the Status Bar**

   You decide to check the footers in Print Preview.

5. **With the worksheets still grouped, click the FILE tab, click Print, preview the first page, then click the Next Page button ▶ to preview the second page**

   Because the worksheets are grouped, both pages contain the footer with "Riverwalk" and your name. The worksheets would look better with a smaller top margin.

6. **Click the Normal Margins list arrow, click Custom Margins, in the Top text box on the Margins tab of the Page Setup dialog box type .5, then click OK**

   You decide to ungroup the worksheets.

7. **Return to the worksheet, right-click the Elective worksheet sheet tab, then click Ungroup Sheets**

8. **Save and close the workbook, exit Excel, then submit the workbook to your instructor**

   The completed worksheets are shown in **FIGURES F-18** and **F-19**.

Adding a digital signature to a workbook

You can digitally sign a workbook to establish its validity and prevent it from being changed. You can obtain a valid certificate from a certificate authority to authenticate the workbook or you can create your own digital signature. To add a signature line in a workbook, click the INSERT tab, then click the Signature Line button in the Text group. In the Signature Setup dialog box, enter information about the signer of the worksheet and then click OK. A signature line with your name under it appears on the worksheet. To add a signature, double-click the signature line, click Yes; if you want to get a digital ID from a Microsoft partner and your browser will open with providers of digital IDs.

FIGURE F-18: Elective worksheet

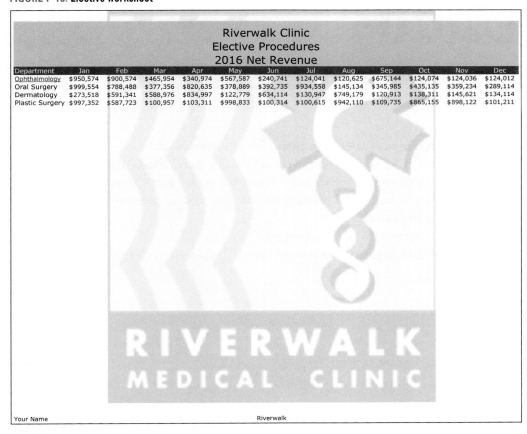

Riverwalk Clinic
Elective Procedures
2016 Net Revenue

Department	Jan	Feb	Mar	Apr	May	Jun	Jul	Aug	Sep	Oct	Nov	Dec
Ophthalmology	$950,574	$900,574	$465,954	$340,974	$567,587	$240,741	$124,041	$120,625	$675,144	$124,074	$124,036	$124,012
Oral Surgery	$999,554	$788,488	$377,356	$820,635	$378,889	$392,735	$934,558	$145,134	$345,985	$435,135	$359,234	$289,114
Dermatology	$273,518	$591,341	$588,976	$834,997	$122,779	$634,114	$130,947	$749,179	$120,913	$138,311	$145,621	$134,114
Plastic Surgery	$997,352	$587,723	$100,957	$103,311	$998,833	$100,314	$100,615	$942,110	$109,735	$865,155	$898,122	$101,211

Your Name   Riverwalk

FIGURE F-19: Acute worksheet

Riverwalk Clinic
Acute Care
2016 Insurance Reimbursements

Department	Jan	Feb	Mar	Apr	May	Jun	Jul	Aug	Sep	Oct	Nov	Dec
Ophthalmology	$800,574	$740,574	$735,954	$310,974	$457,587	$180,741	$654,041	$360,625	$345,144	$344,074	$524,036	$824,012
Oral Surgery	$779,554	$868,488	$877,356	$920,635	$978,889	$472,735	$244,558	$875,134	$115,985	$315,135	$449,234	$589,114
Dermatology	$273,518	$941,341	$388,976	$364,997	$842,779	$364,114	$660,947	$619,179	$330,913	$228,311	$555,621	$444,114
Plastic Surgery	$793,352	$747,723	$650,957	$243,311	$458,833	$350,314	$470,615	$242,110	$669,735	$445,155	$228,122	$771,211

Your Name   Riverwalk

Practice

Concepts Review

1. **Which element do you click to move between instances of a workbook?**
2. **Which element do you click to view and change the way worksheet data is distributed on printed pages?**
3. **Which element do you click to open another instance of the active worksheet in a separate window?**
4. **Which element do you click to name and save a set of display and/or print settings?**
5. **Which element points to a hyperlink?**
6. **Which element points to a ScreenTip for a hyperlink?**
7. **Which element do you click to organize open worksheet windows in a specific configuration?**

FIGURE F-20

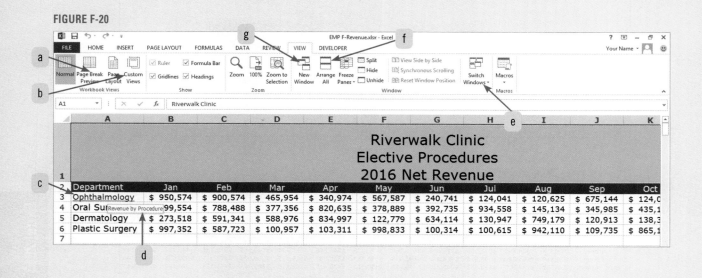

Match each term with the statement that best describes it.

8. **HTML**
9. **Dynamic page breaks**
10. **Hyperlink**
11. **Watermark**
12. **Data entry area**

a. Web page format
b. Portion of a worksheet that can be changed
c. Translucent background design on a printed worksheet
d. An object that when clicked displays another worksheet or a Web page
e. Adjusted automatically when rows and columns are inserted or deleted

Select the best answer from the list of choices.

13. You can establish the validity of a workbook by adding a:

    a. Digital signature.
    c. Custom View.
    b. Template.
    d. Keyword.

14. Which of the following formats means that users can view but not change data in a workbook?

    a. Macro
    c. Web page
    b. Read-only
    d. Template

15. You can group contiguous worksheets by clicking the first sheet, and then pressing and holding _____ while clicking the last sheet tab that you want to group.

    a. [Alt]
    c. [Shift]
    b. [Spacebar]
    d. [F6]

Skills Review

1. View and arrange worksheets.

    a. Start Excel, open the file EMP F-2.xlsx from the location where you store your Data Files, then save it as **EMP F-Budget**.

    b. Open another instance of the workbook in a new window.

    c. Activate the East sheet in the EMP F-Budget.xlsx:1 workbook. Activate the West sheet in the EMP F-Budget.xlsx:2 workbook.

    d. View the EMP F-Budget.xlsx:1 and EMP F-Budget.xlsx:2 workbooks tiled horizontally. View the workbooks in a vertical arrangement.

    e. Hide the EMP F-Budget.xlsx:2 instance, then unhide the instance. Close the EMP F-Budget.xlsx:2 instance, and maximize the EMP F-Budget.xlsx workbook.

2. Protect worksheets and workbooks.

    a. On the East sheet, unlock the expense data in the range C9:F16.

    b. Protect the sheet without using a password.

    c. To make sure the other cells are locked, attempt to make an entry in cell D4 and verify that you receive an error message.

    d. Change the first-quarter mortgage expense in cell C9 to 5500.

    e. Protect the workbook's structure without applying a password. Right-click the East and West sheet tabs to verify that you cannot insert, delete, rename, move, copy, hide, or unhide the sheets, or change their tab color.

    f. Unprotect the workbook. Unprotect the East worksheet.

    g. Save the workbook.

3. Save custom views of a worksheet.

    a. Using the East sheet, create a custom view of the entire worksheet called **Entire East Budget**.

    b. Hide rows 8 through 19, then create a new view called **Income** showing only the income data.

    c. Use the Custom Views dialog box to display all of the data on the East worksheet.

    d. Use the Custom Views dialog box to display only the income data on the East worksheet.

    e. Use the Custom Views dialog box to return to the Entire East Budget view.

    f. Save the workbook.

4. Add a worksheet background.

    a. Add a Physical Therapy Clip Art image as a worksheet background for the East sheet, then delete it. (*Hint*: In the Insert Pictures dialog box, search for "Physical Therapy" in the Office.com Clip Art Search area.)

    b. Add a Physical Therapy Clip Art image to the East header, then preview the sheet to verify that the background will print. (*Hint*: Click Picture on the HEADER & FOOTER TOOLS tab.)

    c. Add your name to the center section of the East worksheet footer, then save the workbook.

Skills Review (continued)

5. Prepare a workbook for distribution.

   a. Inspect the workbook and remove any properties, personal data, and header and footer information.

   b. Use the Document Properties Panel to add a title of **Quarterly Budget**, the keywords **sports** and **medicine**.

   c. Mark the workbook as final and verify that "[Read-Only]" is in the title bar.

   d. Remove the final status, then save the workbook.

6. Insert hyperlinks.

   a. On the East worksheet, make cell B11 a hyperlink to the file **EMP F-Equipment.xlsx** in your Data Files folder.

   b. Test the link and verify that Sheet1 of the target file displays equipment details.

   c. Return to the EMP F-Budget.xlsx workbook, edit the hyperlink in cell B11, adding a ScreenTip that reads **Equipment Details**, then verify that the ScreenTip appears.

   d. On the West worksheet, enter the text **East Budget** in cell A25.

   e. Make the text in cell A25 a hyperlink to cell A1 in the East worksheet. (*Hint*: Use the Place in This Document button and note the cell reference in the Type the cell reference text box.)

   f. Test the hyperlink. Remove the hyperlink in cell A25 of the West worksheet, remove the text in the cell, then save the workbook.

7. Save a workbook for distribution.

   a. Save the EMP F-Budget.xlsx workbook as a single file Web page with the name **budget.mht**.

   b. Close the budget.mht file that is open in Excel, then open the budget.mht file in your Web browser. (If you see an Information bar at the top of the Web page notifying you about blocked content, you can ignore it because your Web page doesn't contain any scripts that need to run.)

   c. Close your browser window, and reopen EMP F-Budget.xlsx.

   d. Save the EMP F-Budget.xlsx workbook as an Excel 97-2003 workbook, and review the results of the Compatibility Checker.

   e. Close the EMP F-Budget.xls file, and reopen the EMP F-Budget.xls file in Compatibility Mode.

   f. Convert the .xls file to .xlsx format, resaving the file with the same name and replacing the previously saved file. This allows the workbook to be closed and reopened.

   g. Save the workbook.

8. Grouping worksheets.

   a. Group the East and West worksheet.

   b. Add your name to the center footer section of the worksheets. Add 1.5" custom margins to the top of both worksheets.

   c. Preview both sheets, verify the Clip Art will not print (it was removed when the file was inspected), then ungroup the sheets.

   d. Save the workbook, comparing your worksheets to **FIGURE F-21**.

   e. Submit your EMP F-Budget.xlsx, coffee.mht, and EMP F-Equipment (the linked file) files to your instructor, close all open files, and exit Excel.

FIGURE F-21

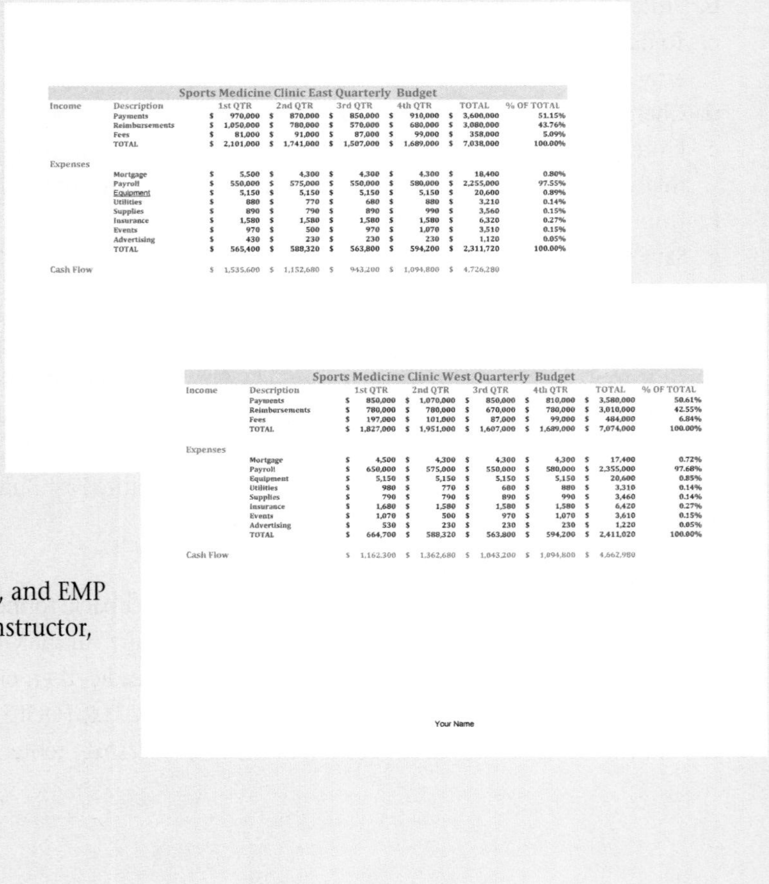

Sports Medicine Clinic East Quarterly Budget

Income	Description	1st QTR	2nd QTR	3rd QTR	4th QTR	TOTAL	% OF TOTAL
	Payments	$ 970,000	$ 870,000	$ 850,000	$ 910,000	$ 3,600,000	51.15%
	Reimbursements	$ 1,050,000	$ 780,000	$ 570,000	$ 680,000	$ 3,080,000	43.76%
	Fees	$ 81,000	$ 91,000	$ 87,000	$ 99,000	$ 358,000	5.09%
	TOTAL	$ 2,101,000	$ 1,741,000	$ 1,507,000	$ 1,689,000	$ 7,038,000	100.00%
Expenses							
	Mortgage	$ 5,500	$ 4,300	$ 4,300	$ 4,300	$ 18,400	0.80%
	Payroll	$ 550,000	$ 575,000	$ 550,000	$ 580,000	$ 2,255,000	97.55%
	Equipment	$ 5,150	$ 5,150	$ 5,150	$ 5,150	$ 20,600	0.89%
	Utilities	$ 880	$ 770	$ 680	$ 880	$ 3,210	0.14%
	Supplies	$ 890	$ 790	$ 890	$ 990	$ 3,560	0.15%
	Insurance	$ 1,580	$ 1,580	$ 1,580	$ 1,580	$ 6,320	0.27%
	Events	$ 970	$ 500	$ 970	$ 1,070	$ 3,510	0.15%
	Advertising	$ 430	$ 230	$ 230	$ 230	$ 1,120	0.05%
	TOTAL	$ 565,400	$ 588,320	$ 563,800	$ 594,200	$ 2,311,720	100.00%
Cash Flow		$ 1,535,600	$ 1,152,680	$ 943,200	$ 1,094,800	$ 4,726,280	

Sports Medicine Clinic West Quarterly Budget

Income	Description	1st QTR	2nd QTR	3rd QTR	4th QTR	TOTAL	% OF TOTAL
	Payments	$ 850,000	$ 1,070,000	$ 850,000	$ 810,000	$ 3,580,000	50.61%
	Reimbursements	$ 780,000	$ 780,000	$ 670,000	$ 780,000	$ 3,010,000	42.55%
	Fees	$ 197,000	$ 101,000	$ 87,000	$ 99,000	$ 484,000	6.84%
	TOTAL	$ 1,827,000	$ 1,951,000	$ 1,607,000	$ 1,689,000	$ 7,074,000	100.00%
Expenses							
	Mortgage	$ 4,500	$ 4,300	$ 4,300	$ 4,300	$ 17,400	0.72%
	Payroll	$ 650,000	$ 575,000	$ 550,000	$ 580,000	$ 2,355,000	97.68%
	Equipment	$ 5,150	$ 5,150	$ 5,150	$ 5,150	$ 20,600	0.85%
	Utilities	$ 980	$ 770	$ 680	$ 880	$ 3,310	0.14%
	Supplies	$ 790	$ 790	$ 890	$ 990	$ 3,460	0.14%
	Insurance	$ 1,680	$ 1,580	$ 1,580	$ 1,580	$ 6,420	0.27%
	Events	$ 1,070	$ 500	$ 970	$ 1,070	$ 3,610	0.15%
	Advertising	$ 530	$ 230	$ 230	$ 230	$ 1,220	0.05%
	TOTAL	$ 664,700	$ 588,320	$ 563,800	$ 594,200	$ 2,411,020	100.00%
Cash Flow		$ 1,162,300	$ 1,362,680	$ 1,043,200	$ 1,094,800	$ 4,662,980	

Your Name

Independent Challenge 1

You manage four pharmacies for City Hospital. You are organizing your first-quarter sales in an Excel worksheet. Because the sheet for the month of January includes the same type of information you need for February and March, you decide to enter the headings for all of the first-quarter months at the same time. You use a separate worksheet for each month and create data for 3 months.

a. Start Excel, then save a new workbook as **EMP F-Pharmacy Sales.xlsx** in the location where you store your Data Files.

b. Name the first sheet **January**, name the second sheet **February**, and name the third sheet **March**.

c. Group the worksheets.

d. With the worksheets grouped, add the title **City Hospital** centered across cells A1 and B1. Enter the label **Pharmacy Reimbursements** in cell B2. Enter wing labels in column A beginning in cell A6 and ending in cell A9. Use the following labels in the range A3:A6: **East Wing**, **West Wing**, **North Wing**, and **South Wing**. Add the label **TOTAL** in cell A7. Enter the formula to sum the reimbursement column in cell B7.

e. Ungroup the worksheets, and enter your own reimbursement data for each of the reimbursement categories in the range B3:B9 in the January, February, and March sheets.

f. Display each worksheet in its own window, then arrange the three sheets vertically.

g. Hide the window displaying the March sheet. Unhide the March sheet window.

h. Split the March window into two panes: the upper pane displaying rows 1 through 4, and the lower pane displaying rows 5 through 7. Scroll through the data in each pane, then remove the split. (*Hint*: Select row 5, click the VIEW tab, then click Split in the Window group Clicking Split again will remove the split.)

i. Close the windows displaying EMP F-Pharmacy Sales.xlsx:2 and EMP F-Pharmacy Sales.xlsx:3, then maximize the EMP F-Pharmacy Sales.xlsx workbook.

j. Add the keywords **pharmacy sales** to your workbook, using the Document Properties Panel.

k. Group the worksheets again.

l. Add headers to all three worksheets that include your name in the left section and the sheet name in the center section. (*Hint*: You can add the sheet name to a header by clicking the Sheet Name button in the Header and Footer Elements group of the HEADER & FOOTER TOOLS DESIGN tab.)

m. With the worksheets still grouped, format the worksheets using the fill and color buttons on the Home tab appropriately.

n. Ungroup the worksheets, then mark the workbook status as final. Close the workbook, reopen the workbook, and enable editing.

o. Save the workbook, submit the workbook to your instructor, then exit Excel.

Independent Challenge 2

As the payroll manager at an occupational therapy center, you decide to organize the weekly timecard data using Excel worksheets. You use a separate worksheet for each week and track the hours for employees with different job classifications. A hyperlink in the worksheet provides pay rates for each classification, and custom views limit the information that is displayed.

a. Start Excel, open the file EMP F-3.xlsx from the location where you store your Data Files, then save it as **EMP F-Timesheets**.

b. Compare the data in the workbook by arranging the Week 1, Week 2, and Week 3 sheets horizontally.

c. Maximize the Week 1 window. Unlock the hours data in the Week 1 sheet and protect the worksheet. Verify that the employee names, numbers, and classifications cannot be changed. Verify that the total hours data can be changed, but do not change the data.

d. Unprotect the Week 1 sheet, and create a custom view called **Complete Worksheet** that displays all the data.

Independent Challenge 2 (continued)

e. Hide column E and create a custom view of the data in the range A1:D22. Name the view **Employee Classifications**. Display each view, then return to the Complete Worksheet view.

f. Add a page break between columns D and E so that the Total Hours data prints on a second page. Preview the worksheet, then remove the page break. (*Hint*: Use the Breaks button on the PAGE LAYOUT tab.)

g. Add a hyperlink to the Classification heading in cell D1 that links to the file EMP F-Classifications.xlsx. Add a ScreenTip that reads Pay Rates, then test the hyperlink. Compare your screen to FIGURE F-22.

h. Save the EMP F-Classifications workbook as an Excel 97-2003 workbook, reviewing the Compatibility Checker information. Close the EMP F-Classifications.xls file.

i. Group the three worksheets in the EMP F-Timesheets.xlsx workbook, and add your name to the center footer section.

j. Save the workbook, then preview the grouped worksheets.

k. Ungroup the worksheets, and add 2-inch top and left margins to the Week 1 worksheet.

l. Hide the Week 2 and Week 3 worksheets, inspect the file and remove all document properties, personal information, and hidden worksheets. Do not remove header and footer information.

FIGURE F-22

	A	B
1	**Occupational Therapist**	
2	Classifications	Pay Rate
3	Assistant	$35
4	Associate	$40
5	Senior	$45
6		

m. Add the keyword **hours** to the workbook, save the workbook, then mark it as final.

n. Close the workbook, submit the workbook to your instructor, then exit Excel.

Independent Challenge 3

One of your responsibilities as the office manager at North Shore Medical Center is to track supplies. You decide to create a spreadsheet to track these orders, placing each month's orders on its own sheet. You create custom views that will focus on the categories of supplies. A hyperlink will provide the supplier's contact information.

a. Start Excel, open the file EMP F-4.xlsx from the location where you store your Data Files, then save it as **EMP F-NSMC**.

b. Arrange the sheets for the 3 months horizontally to compare revenue, then close the extra workbook windows and maximize the remaining window. (*Hint*: If you want to hide the Ribbon to see more of the worksheet, double-click a Ribbon tab. To display the Ribbon later, double-click a tab again.)

c. Create a custom view of the entire January worksheet named **All Revenue**. Hide the Cancer Care, Wellness, and Laboratory revenue data, and create a custom view displaying only the Surgery data. Call the view **Surgery**.

d. Display the Revenue view, group the worksheets, and create a total for the total costs in cell D28 on each month's sheet. If necessary, use the Format Painter to copy the format from cell D26 to cell D28.

e. With the sheets grouped, add the sheet name to the center section of all the sheets' headers and your name to the center section of all the sheets' footers.

f. Ungroup the sheets and use the Compatibility Checker to view the features that are unsupported in earlier Excel formats. (*Hint*: Click the File tab, click Info, click the Check for Issues button, then click Check Compatibility.)

g. Add a hyperlink in cell A4 of the January sheet that opens the file EMP F-Dermatology Revenue.xlsx. Add a ScreenTip of **Procedure Information**. Test the link, viewing the ScreenTip, then return to the EMP F-NSMC.xlsx workbook without closing the EMP F-Dermatology Revenue.xlsx workbook. Save the EMP F-NSMC.xlsx workbook.

h. Hide the EMP F-Dermatology Revenue.xlsx workbook, then unhide it.

Independent Challenge 3 (continued)

i. Freeze worksheet rows one through two on the January Sheet of the EMP F-NSMC.xlsx workbook. (*Hint*: Select row 3, click the VIEW tab, click the Freeze Panes button in the Window group, then click Freeze Panes.) Scroll down in the worksheet to verify the top two rows remain visible.

j. Unfreeze rows one through three. (*Hint*: Click the VIEW tab, click Freeze panes, then click Unfreeze Panes.)

k. Close both the EMP F-Dermatology Revenue.xlsx and the EMP F-NSMC.xlsx workbooks.

l. Submit the workbooks to your instructor, then exit Excel.

Independent Challenge 4: Explore

As the assistant to the director of professional services at a pain management clinic, you review the non-payroll expense sheets submitted by employees for each contract. You decide to create a spreadsheet to track these contract expenses.

a. Start Excel, open the file EMP F-5.xlsx from the location where you store your Data Files, then save it as **EMP F-Invoice** in the location where you store your Data Files.

b. Freeze rows 1 through 5 in the worksheet. Scroll vertically to verify rows 1 through 5 are visible at the top of the worksheet.

c. Research the steps necessary to hide a formula in the Formula Bar of a worksheet. Record these steps in cell A1 on Sheet2 of the workbook, then hide the display of the formula for cell B38 on Sheet1. Check the Formula Bar to verify the formula is hidden. Compare your worksheet to FIGURE F-23.

d. Save your workbook. If you don't have a Microsoft account, research the steps for creating an account and create your Microsoft ID. Use your Microsoft ID to log into your SkyDrive, then save your file on your SkyDrive.

e. Share your workbook with a classmate.

f. Unprotect Sheet1. (Your formula will be displayed.) Add a header that includes your name on the left side of the worksheet (this will unfreeze rows 1 through 5). Using the PAGE LAYOUT tab, scale Sheet1 to fit vertically on one page. Save the workbook, then preview the worksheet.

FIGURE F-23

	A	B
1		**Expenses**
2		
3	Activity:	Pain Management Workshop
4	Contract ID:	WS158
5	Employee Number:	1002
30	Beverage	$ 15.00
31		
32		**Miscellaneous**
33	Miscellaneous item 1	
34	Miscellaneous item 2	
35	Miscellaneous item 3	
36		
37		
38	Total Expenses	$ 1,080.00
39		
40		
41		

g. If you are able to create a folder on the computer you are working on, create a folder named Templates in the location where you store your Data Files. Use the Excel Options menu to change the location where templates are saved to the path of your new template folder. (*Hint*: Click the File menu, click Options, click Save, then enter the path in the Default Personal Templates location text box. You may want to copy the path from the Address bar of a File Explorer window.)

h. Delete the amount values in column B, and save the workbook as an Excel template in the Templates folder you created in the step above.

i. Open a new workbook based on the template. (*Hint*: Click File, click New, then click Personal, then click the template name.)

j. Submit the workbook and template to your instructor, then exit Excel.

Visual Workshop

Start Excel, open the file EMP F-6.xlsx from the location where you store your Data Files, then save it as **EMP F-Study**. Make your worksheet look like the one shown in FIGURE F-24. The text in cell A3 is a hyperlink to the EMP F-Contact Information workbook. Enter your name in the footer, save the workbook, submit the workbook to your instructor, close the workbook, then exit Excel.

FIGURE F-24

	A	B	C	D	E	F	G
1	North Shore Hospital						
2	Blood Pressure Study						
3	Patient Number	Group	Supervising Physician	Begin Date	End Date		
4	1022	Experimental	Miller	1/3/2016	4/4/2016		
5	1561	Control	Jones	1/3/2016	4/4/2016		
6	1987	Control	Carlo	1/3/2016	4/4/2016		
7	1471	Control	Carlo	1/3/2016	4/4/2016		
8	1132	Experimental	Miller	1/3/2016	4/4/2016		
9	1462	Experimental	Miller	1/3/2016	4/4/2016		
10	1024	Experimental	Jones	1/10/2016	4/11/2016		
11	1563	Control	Jones	1/10/2016	4/11/2016		
12	1988	Control	Carlo	1/10/2016	4/11/2016		
13	1478	Experimental	Miller	1/10/2016	4/11/2016		
14	1133	Experimental	Jones	1/10/2016	4/11/2016		
15	1469	Control	Miller	1/17/2016	4/18/2016		
16	1887	Control	Miller	1/18/2016	4/18/2016		
17	1964	Control	Carlo	1/19/2016	4/18/2016		
18	1756	Experimental	Carlo	1/20/2016	4/18/2016		
19							

Managing Data Using Tables

CASE ▶ RMC uses tables to analyze medical data. The office manager, Tony Sanchez, asks you to help him build and manage a table of physical therapy procedure information. You will help by planning and creating a table; adding, changing, finding, and deleting table information; sorting table data, and performing calculations with table data.

Unit Objectives

After completing this unit, you will be able to:

- Plan a table
- Create and format a table
- Add table data
- Find and replace table data

- Delete table data
- Sort table data
- Use formulas in a table
- Print a table

Files You Will Need

EMP G-1.xlsx	EMP G-4.xlsx
EMP G-2.xlsx	EMP G-5.xlsx
EMP G-3.xlsx	EMP G-6.xlsx

Plan a Table

Learning Outcomes
• Plan the data organization for a table
• Plan the data elements for a table

In addition to using Excel spreadsheet features, you can analyze and manipulate data in a table structure. An Excel **table** is an organized collection of rows and columns of similarly structured worksheet data. Tables are a convenient way to understand and manage large amounts of information. When planning a table, consider what information you want your table to contain and how you want to work with the data, now and in the future. As you plan a table, you should understand its most important components. A table is organized into rows called records. A **record** is a table row that contains data about an object, person, or other item. Records are composed of fields. **Fields** are columns in the table; each field describes a characteristic of the record, such as a customer's last name or street address. Each field has a **field name**, which is a column label, such as "Address," that describes its contents. Tables usually have a **header row** as the first row, which contains the field names. To plan your table, use the guidelines below. **CASE** *Tony asks you to compile a table of the January physical therapy procedures. Before entering the procedure data into an Excel worksheet, you plan the table contents.*

DETAILS

As you plan your table, use the following guidelines:

- **Identify the purpose of the table**

  The purpose of the table determines the kind of information the table should contain. You want to use the procedure information table to find all departure dates for a particular procedure and to display the procedures in order of date.

- **Plan the structure of the table**

  In designing your table's structure, determine the fields (the table columns) you need to achieve the table's purpose. You have worked with the physical therapy and finance departments to determine the type of information they record for each procedure. FIGURE G-1 shows a layout sketch for the table. Each row will contain one procedure record. The columns represent fields that contain pieces of financial information you will enter for each procedure, such as the name, date, and amount.

- **Plan your row and column structure**

  You can create a table from any contiguous range of cells on your worksheet. Plan and design your table so that all rows have similar types of information in the same column. A table should not have any blank rows or columns. Instead of using blank rows to separate table headings from data, use a table style, which will use formatting to make column labels stand out from your table data. FIGURE G-2 shows a table, populated with data that has been formatted using a table style.

- **Document the table design**

  In addition to your table sketch, you should make a list of the field names to document the type of data and any special number formatting required for each field. Field names should be as short as possible while still accurately describing the column information. When naming fields it is important to use text rather than numbers because Excel could interpret numbers as parts of formulas. Your field names should be unique and not easily confused with cell addresses, such as the name D2. You want your procedure table to contain eight field names, each one corresponding to the financial details of the procedures. TABLE G-1 shows the documentation of the field names in your table.

FIGURE G-1: Table layout sketch

Procedure	Date	Amount of Adjustment	Insurance Payment	Provider	Patient ID	Balance

Header row will contain field names

Each procedure will be placed in a table row

FIGURE G-2: Formatted table with data

	A	B	C	D	E	F	G	H	
1	Procedure	Date	Amount	Adjustment	Insurance Payment	Provider	Patient ID	Balance	Amo
2	Therap Proc 2		$60.00	$10.12	$0.00	March	1125	Yes	
3	Therap Proc 2		$60.00	$12.73	$0.00	Michaels	1126	Yes	
4	Therap Proc 5		$60.00	$8.22	$8.00	Toloes	1127	Yes	
5	Therapeutic Activity B	1/21/2016	$60.00	$14.93	$10.00	Appleton	1128	Yes	
6	Therap Proc 4	1/14/2016	$57.00	$12.00	$32.00	Toloes	1189	Yes	
7	Therap Proc 5	1/21/2016	$60.00	$17.00	$0.00	Appleton	1129	Yes	
8	Therap Proc 6	1/14/2016	$60.00	$17.00	$24.14	March	1130	Yes	
9	Therap Proc 4		$60.00	$17.86	$24.14	Michaels	1131	Yes	
10	Therap Proc 2		$60.00	$18.77	$24.14	Michaels	1132	Yes	
11	Therapeutic Ac		$60.00	$20.15	$30.07	Toloes	1133	Yes	
12	Therap Proc 4	1/7/2016	$60.00	$22.00	$30.07	Laneighton	1134	Yes	
13	Therap Proc 3	1/4/2016	$60.00	$23.00	$0.00	Appleton	1135	Yes	
14	Therap Proc 1	1/21/2016	$60.00	$23.00	$8.00	Michaels	1136	Yes	
15	Therapeutic Activity B	1/21/2016	$60.00	$23.00	$15.00	Toloes	1137	Yes	
16	Manual Therapy Tec	1/31/2016	$60.00	$23.00	$32.00	Sonna	1138	Yes	
17	Therapeutic Activity D	1/5/2016	$60.00	$23.00	$32.00	March	1139	Yes	

Header row contains field names

Records for each procedure, organized by field name

TABLE G-1: Table documentation

field name	type of data	description of data
Procedure	Text	Name of procedure
Date	Date	Date of procedure
Amount	Currency with 2 decimal places	Procedure cost
Adjustment	Currency with 2 decimal places	Price adjustment for the procedure
Insurance Payment	Currency with 2 decimal places	Amount received from the insurance company
Provider	Text	Person performing the procedure
Patient ID	Number with 0 decimal places	Patient ID number
Balance	Text	Yes: Balance due from patient No: No balance due

© 2014 Cengage Learning

Create and Format a Table

**Learning
Outcomes**
• Create a table
• Format a table

Once you have planned the table structure, the sequence of fields, and appropriate data types, you are ready to create the table in Excel. After you create a table, a TABLE TOOLS DESIGN tab appears, containing a gallery of table styles. **Table styles** allow you to easily add formatting to your table by using preset formatting combinations of fill color, borders, type style, and type color. **CASE** ▶ *Tony asks you to build a table with the January PT procedure data. You begin by entering the field names. Then you enter the procedure data that corresponds to each field name, create the table, and format the data using a table style.*

STEPS

1. **Start Excel, open the file EMP G-1.xlsx from the location where you store your Data Files, then save it as EMP G-PT Procedures**

2. **Beginning in cell A1 of the Practice sheet, enter each field name in a separate column, as shown in FIGURE G-3**

   Field names are usually in the first row of the table.

3. **Enter the information from FIGURE G-4 in the rows immediately below the field names, leaving no blank rows**

   The data appears in columns organized by field name.

4. **Select the range A1:H4, click the Format button in the Cells group, click AutoFit Column Width, then click cell A1**

   Resizing the column widths this way is faster than double-clicking the column divider lines.

5. **With cell A1 selected, click the INSERT tab, click the Table button in the Tables group, in the Create Table dialog box verify that your table data is in the range $A$1:$H$4, and make sure My table has headers is checked as shown in FIGURE G-5, then click OK**

   The data range is now defined as a table. **Filter list arrows**, which let you display portions of your data, now appear next to each column header. When you create a table, Excel automatically applies a table style. The default table style has a dark blue header row and alternating gray and blue data rows. The TABLE TOOLS DESIGN tab appears, and the Table Styles group displays a gallery of table formatting options. You decide to choose a different table style from the gallery.

6. **Click the Table Styles More button ▼, scroll to view all of the table styles, then move the mouse pointer over several styles without clicking**

   The Table Styles gallery on the TABLE TOOLS DESIGN tab has three style categories: Light, Medium, and Dark. Each category has numerous design types; for example, in some of the designs, the header row and total row are darker and the rows alternate colors. The available table designs use the current workbook theme colors so the table coordinates with your existing workbook content. If you select a different workbook theme and color scheme in the Themes group on the PAGE LAYOUT tab, the Table Styles gallery uses those colors. As you point to each table style, Live Preview shows you what your table will look like with the style applied. However, you only see a preview of each style; you need to click a style to apply it.

7. **Click Table Style Medium 28 to apply it to your table, then click cell A1**

   Compare your table to FIGURE G-6.

FIGURE G-3: **Field names entered in row 1**

	A	B	C	D	E	F	G	H	I	J
1	Procedure	Date	Amount	Adjustment	Insurance Payment	Provider	Patient ID	Balance		
2										

FIGURE G-4: **Three records entered in the worksheet**

	A	B	C	D	E	F	G	H
1	Procedure	Date	Amount	Adjustment	Insurance Payment	Provider	Patient ID	Balance
2	Therap Proc 2	1/15/2016	$45.00	$15.35	$0.00	March	1011	Yes
3	Therap Proc 2	1/16/2016	$55.00	$25.35	$20.00	Somma	1031	Yes
4	Therap Proc 5	1/17/2016	$75.00	$35.35	$15.00	Michaels	1111	Yes
5								

FIGURE G-5: **Create Table dialog box**

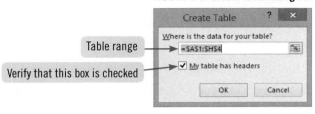

Table range → =$A$1:$H$4

Verify that this box is checked → ✓ My table has headers

FIGURE G-6: **Formatted table with three records**

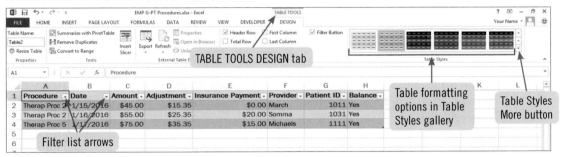

TABLE TOOLS DESIGN tab

Table formatting options in Table Styles gallery

Table Styles More button

Filter list arrows

Changing table style options

You can change a table's appearance by using the check boxes in the Table Styles Options group on the TABLE TOOLS DESIGN tab, shown in **FIGURE G-7**. For example, you can turn on or turn off the following options: Header Row, which displays or hides the header row; Total Row, which calculates totals for each column; **banding**, which creates different formatting for adjacent rows and columns; and special formatting for first and last columns. Use these options to modify a table's appearance either before or after applying a table style. For example, if your table has banded rows, you can select the Banded Columns check box to change the table to be displayed with banded columns as well. Also, you may want to deselect the Header Row check box to hide a table's header row if a table will be included in a presentation where the header row repeats slide labels.

You can also create your own table style by clicking the Table Styles More button, then at the bottom of the Table Styles Gallery, clicking New Table Style. In the New Table Style dialog box, name the style in the Name text box, click a table element, then format selected table elements by clicking Format. You can also set a custom style as the default style for your tables by checking the Set as default table quick style for this document check box. You can click Clear at the bottom of the Table Styles gallery if you want to delete a table style from the currently selected table.

FIGURE G-7: **Table Styles Options**

TABLE TOOLS DESIGN tab

Table Style Options group

Banded rows

Add Table Data

Learning Outcomes
- Add fields to a table
- Add records to a table

You can add records to a table by typing data directly below the last row of the table. After you press [Enter], the new row becomes part of the table and the table formatting extends to the new data. When the active cell is the last cell of a table, you can add a new row by pressing [Tab]. You can also insert rows in any table location. If you decide you need additional data fields, you can add new columns to a table. You can also expand a table by dragging the sizing handle in a table's lower-right corner; drag down to add rows and drag to the right to add columns. **CASE** > *After entering all of the January PT procedure data, Tony is informed that two additional procedures need to be added to the table. He also wants the table to display the amount due for each procedure and whether authorization is required for the procedure.*

STEPS

1. **Click the January sheet tab**

   The January sheet containing the January PT procedure data becomes active.

2. **Scroll down to the last table row, click cell A65, enter the data for the new procedure as shown below, then press [Enter]**

Therap Proc 2	1/5/2016		$54	$10	$30	$	Michaels	1188	Yes

   As you scroll down, the table headers are visible at the top of the table as long as the active cell is inside the table. The new procedure is now part of the table. You want to enter a record about a new procedure above row 6.

3. **Scroll up to and click the inside left edge of cell A6 to select the table row data as shown in FIGURE G-8, click the Insert list arrow in the Cells group, then click Insert Table Rows Above**

   Clicking the left edge of the first cell in a table row selects the entire table row, rather than the entire worksheet row. A new blank row 6 is available for the new record.

4. **Click cell A6, then enter the Yellowstone record shown below**

Therap Proc 4	1/14/2016		$57	$12	$32	$	Toloes	1189	Yes

   The new procedure is part of the table. You want to add a new field that displays the amount a patient owes to the clinic.

5. **Click cell I1, enter the field name Amount Due, then press [Enter]**

   The new field becomes part of the table, and the header formatting extends to the new field as shown in FIGURE G-9. The AutoCorrect menu allows you to undo or stop the automatic table expansion, but in this case you decide to leave this feature on. You want to add another new field to the table to display procedures that require authorization, but this time you will add the new field by resizing the table.

6. **Scroll down until cell I66 is visible, drag the sizing handle in the table's lower-right corner one column to the right to add column J to the table, as shown in FIGURE G-10**

   The table range is now A1:J66, and the new field name is Column1.

7. **Scroll up to and click cell J1, enter Authorization, press [Enter], then widen column J to display the field name**

8. **Click the INSERT tab, click the Header & Footer button in the Text group, enter your name in the center header text box, click cell A1, click the Normal button ⊞ in the status bar, then save the workbook**

FIGURE G-8: **Table row 6 selected**

	Procedure	Date	Amount	Adjustment	Insurance Payment	Provider	Patie
1							
2	Therap Proc 2	1/21/2016	$60.00	$10.12	$0.00	March	11
3	Therap Proc 2	1/12/2016	$60.00	$12.73	$0.00	Michaels	11
4	Therap Proc 5	1/21/2016	$60.00	$8.22	$8.00	Toloes	11
5	Therapeutic Activity B	1/21/2016	$60.00	$14.93	$10.00	Appleton	11
6	Therap Proc 5	1/21/2016	$60.00	$17.00	$0.00	Appleton	11
7	Therap Proc 6	1/14/2016	$60.00	$17.00	$24.14	March	11
8	Therap Proc 4	1/20/2016	$60.00	$17.86	$24.14	Michaels	11
	rap Proc 2	1/3/2016	$60.00	$18.77	$24.14	Michaels	11
	rapeutic Activity Tec	1/6/2016	$60.00	$20.15	$30.07	Toloes	11

Row 6 selected

Pointer over inside left edge of cell selects only the table row

FIGURE G-9: **New table column**

	A Procedure	B Date	C Amount	D Adjustment	E Insurance Payment	F Provider	G Patient ID	H Balance	I Amount Due
2	Therap Proc 2	1/21/2016	$60.00	$10.12	$0.00	March	1125	Yes	
3	Therap Proc 2	1/12/2016	$60.00	$12.73	$0.00	Michaels	1126	Yes	
4	Therap Proc 5	1/21/2016	$60.00	$8.22	$8.00	Toloes	1127		
5	Therapeutic Activity B	1/21/2016	$60.00	$14.93	$10.00	Appleton	1128		
6	Therap Proc 4	1/14/2016	$57.00	$12.00	$32.00	Toloes	1189		
7	Therap Proc 5	1/21/2016	$60.00	$17.00	$0.00	Appleton	1129		
8	Therap Proc 6	1/14/2016	$60.00	$17.00	$24.14	March	1130	Yes	
9	Therap Proc 4	1/20/2016	$60.00	$17.86	$24.14	Michaels	1131	Yes	
10	Therap Proc 2	1/3/2016	$60.00	$18.77	$24.14	Michaels	1132	Yes	
11	Therapeutic Activity Tec	1/6/2016	$60.00	$20.15	$30.07	Toloes	1133	Yes	
12	Therap Proc 4	1/7/2016	$60.00	$22.00	$30.07	Laneighton	1134	Yes	
13	Therap Proc 3	1/4/2016	$60.00	$23.00	$0.00	Appleton	1135	Yes	
14	Therap Proc 1	1/21/2016	$60.00	$23.00	$8.00	Michaels	1136	Yes	
15	Therapeutic Activity B	1/21/2016	$60.00	$23.00	$15.00	Toloes	1137	Yes	
16	Manual Therapy Tec	1/31/2016	$60.00	$23.00	$32.00	Sonna	1138	Yes	
17	Therapeutic Activity D	1/5/2016	$60.00	$23.00	$32.00	March	1139	Yes	

New table column will show amount due for each procedure

New record in row 6

FIGURE G-10: **Resizing a table using the resizing handle**

	Procedure	Date	Amount	Adjustment	Insurance Payr	Provider	Patient ID	Balance	Amount Due	J
61	Physical Therapy E	1/21/2016	$165.00	$83.24	$0.00	Michaels	1183	Yes		
62	Physical Therapy E	1/3/2016	$165.00	$83.24	$65.41	Sonna	1184	Yes		
63	Physical Therapy E	1/5/2016	$165.00	$83.24	$65.41	Sonna	1185	Yes		
64	Physical Therapy E	1/5/2016	$165.00	$83.24	$65.41	Sonna	1186	Yes		
65	Physical Therapy E	1/27/2016	$165.00	$88.33	$65.41	March	1187	Yes		
66	Therap Proc 2	1/5/2016	$54.00	$10.00	$30.00	Michaels	1188	Yes		
67										
68										
69										
70										
71										
72										

Drag sizing handle to add column J to table

Selecting table elements

When working with tables you often need to select rows, columns, and even the entire table. Clicking to the right of a row number, inside column A, selects the entire table row. You can select a table column by clicking the top edge of the header. Be careful not to click a column letter or row number, however, because this selects the entire worksheet row or column. You can select the table data by clicking the upper-left corner of the first table cell. When selecting a column or a table, the first click selects only the data in the column or table. If you click a second time, you add the headers to the selection.

Find and Replace Table Data

Learning
Outcomes
• Find data in a
  table
• Replace data in a
  table

From time to time, you need to locate specific records in your table. You can use the Excel Find feature to search your table for the information you need. You can also use the Replace feature to locate and replace existing entries or portions of entries with information you specify. If you don't know the exact spelling of the text you are searching for, you can use wildcards to help locate the records. **Wildcards** are special symbols that substitute for unknown characters. **CASE** ▶ *In response to a memo from the HR Department that Ms. Laneighton has been married and is now Mrs. Crowley, Tony needs to replace "Laneighton" with "Crowley" in all of the procedure names. He also wants to know how many Physical Therapy E procedures were performed in January. You begin by searching for records with the text "Physical Therapy E".*

STEPS

1. **Click cell A1 if necessary, click the HOME tab, click the Find & Select button in the Editing group, then click Find**

   The Find and Replace dialog box opens, as shown in FIGURE G-11. In the Find what text box, you enter criteria that specify the records you want to find. You want to search for records whose Procedure field contains the label "Physical Therapy E".

2. **Type Physical Therapy E in the Find what text box, then click Find Next**

   A47 is the active cell because it is the first instance of Physical Therapy E in the table.

3. **Click Find Next and examine the record for each Physical Therapy E procedure found until no more matching cells are found in the table and the active cell is A47 again, then click Close**

   There are eight Physical Therapy E procedures.

4. **Return to cell A1, click the Find & Select button in the Editing group, then click Replace**

   The Find and Replace dialog box opens with the Replace tab selected and "Physical Therapy E" in the Find what text box, as shown in FIGURE G-12. You will search for entries containing "Laneighton" and replace them with "Crowley". To save time, you will use the asterisk (*) wildcard to help you locate the records containing Laneighton.

5. **Delete the text in the Find what text box, type La* in the Find what text box, click the Replace with text box, then type Crowley**

   The asterisk (*) wildcard stands for one or more characters, meaning that the search text "La*" will find words such as "lake", "lane", and "lately". Because you notice that there are other table entries containing the text "la" with a lowercase "l" (in the Balance column heading), you need to make sure that only capitalized instances of the letter "L" are replaced.

6. **Click Options >>, click the Match case check box to select it, click Options <<, then click Find Next**

   Excel moves the cell pointer to the cell containing the first occurrence of "Laneighton".

7. **Click Replace All, click OK, then click Close**

   The dialog box closes. Excel made three replacements, in cells F12, F18, and F35. The Balance field heading remains unchanged.

8. **Save the workbook**

FIGURE G-11: Find and Replace dialog box

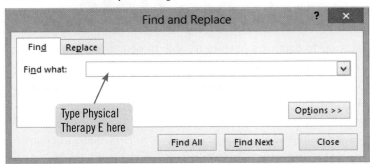

FIGURE G-12: The Replace tab in the Find and Replace dialog box

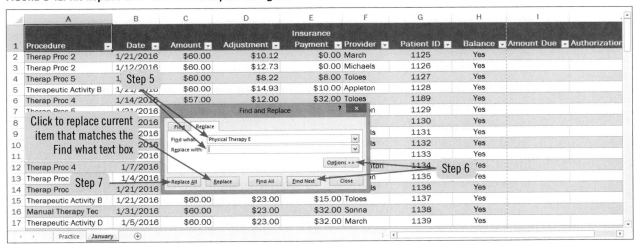

Using Find and Select features

You can also use the Find feature to navigate to a specific place in a workbook by clicking the Find & Select button in the Editing group, clicking Go To, typing a cell address, then clicking OK. Clicking the Find & Select button also allows you to find comments and conditional formatting in a worksheet. You can use the Go To Special dialog box to select cells that contain different types of formulas or objects. Some Go To Special commands also appear on the Find & Select menu. Using this menu, you can also change the mouse pointer shape to the Select Objects pointer so you can quickly select drawing objects when necessary. To return to the standard Excel pointer, press [Esc].

Delete Table Data

To keep a table up to date, you need to be able to periodically remove records. You may even need to remove fields if the information stored in a field becomes unnecessary. You can delete table data using the Delete button in the Cells group or by dragging the sizing handle at the table's lower-right corner. You can also easily delete duplicate records from a table. **CASE** ▶ *Tony informs you that the record for the Manual Therapy Tec procedure on 1/31/2016 must be deleted from the table. You will also remove any duplicate records from the table. Because the authorization requirements are difficult to keep up with, Tony asks you to delete the field with authorization information.*

STEPS

1. **Click the left edge of cell A16 to select the table row data, click the Delete list arrow in the Cells group, then click Delete Table Rows**

   The procedure is deleted, and the Therapeutic Activity D procedure moves up to row 16, as shown in **FIGURE G-13**. You can also delete a table row or a column using the Resize Table button in the Properties group of the TABLE TOOLS DESGIN tab, or by right-clicking the row or column, pointing to Delete on the shortcut menu, then clicking Table Columns or Table Rows. You decide to check the table for duplicate records.

2. **Click the TABLE TOOLS DESIGN tab, then click the Remove Duplicates button in the Tools group**

   The Remove Duplicates dialog box opens, as shown in **FIGURE G-14**. You need to select the columns that will be used to evaluate duplicates. Because you don't want to delete procedures with the same provider but different dates, you will look for duplicate data in all of the columns.

3. **Make sure that "My data has headers" is checked and that all the Columns check boxes (column headers) are checked, then click OK**

   One duplicate record is found and removed, leaving 63 records of data and a total of 64 rows in the table, including the header row. You want to remove the last column, which contains space for visa information.

4. **Click OK, scroll down until cell J64 is visible, drag the sizing handle of the table's lower-right corner one column to the left to remove column J from the table**

   The table range is now A1:I64, and the Visa Required field no longer appears in the table.

5. **Delete the contents of cell J1, return to cell A1, then save the workbook**

	Procedure	Date	Amount	Adjustment	Insurance Pa	Provider	Patient ID	Balance	Amount Due	Authorizatior
7	Therap Proc 5	1/21/2016	$60.00	$17.00	$0.00	Appleton	1129	Yes		
8	Therap Proc 6	1/14/2016	$60.00	$17.00	$24.14	March	1130	Yes		
9	Therap Proc 4	1/20/2016	$60.00	$17.86	$24.14	Michaels	1131	Yes		
10	Therap Proc 2	1/3/2016	$60.00	$18.77	$24.14	Michaels	1132	Yes		
11	Therapeutic Activity Tec	1/6/2016	$60.00	$20.15	$30.07	Toloes	1133	Yes		
12	Therap Proc 4	1/7/2016	$60.00	$22.00	$30.07	Crowley	1134	Yes		
13	Therap Proc 3	1/4/2016	$60.00	$23.00	$0.00	Appleton	1135	Yes		
14	Therap Proc 1	1/21/2016	$60.00	$23.00	$8.00	Michaels	1136	Yes		
15	Therapeutic Activity B	1/21/2016	$60.00	$23.00	$15.00	Toloes	1137	Yes		
16	Therapeutic Activity D	1/5/2016	$60.00	$23.00	$32.00	March	1139	Yes		
17	Therap Proc 2	1/5/2016	$60.00	$24.93	$0.00	Crowley	1140	Yes		
18	Therap Proc 3	1/14/2016	$60.00	$24.93	$0.00	Appleton	1141	Yes		
19	Therap Proc 3	1/21/2016	$60.00	$24.93	$0.00	March	1142	Yes		
20	Therap Proc 1	1/20/2016	$60.00	$24.93	$24.14	Appleton	1143	Yes		
21	Therap Proc 3	1/17/2016	$60.00	$24.93	$24.14	March	1144	Yes		
2		1/19/2016	$60.00	$24.93	$24.14	Sonna	1145	Yes		
2		1/19/2016	$60.00	$24.93	$24.14	Toloes	1146	Yes		
2		1/13/2016	$60.00	$24.93	$24.14	Michaels	1147	Yes		

Row is deleted and procedures move up one row

FIGURE G-14: **Remove Duplicates dialog box**

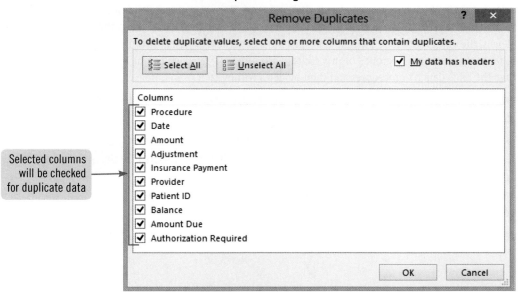

Selected columns will be checked for duplicate data

Sort Table Data

Usually, you enter table records in the order in which you receive information, rather than in alphabetical or numerical order. When you add records to a table, you usually enter them at the end of the table. You can change the order of the records any time using the Excel **sort** feature. Because the data is structured as a table, Excel changes the order of the records while keeping each record, or row of information, together. You can sort a table in ascending or descending order on one field using the filter list arrows next to the field name. In **ascending order**, the lowest value (the beginning of the alphabet or the earliest date) appears at the top of the table. In a field containing labels and numbers, numbers appear first in the sorted list. In **descending order**, the highest value (the end of the alphabet or the latest date) appears at the top of the table. In a field containing labels and numbers, labels appear first. TABLE G-2 provides examples of ascending and descending sorts. **CASE** ▶ *Tony wants the procedure data sorted by date, displaying procedures that were performed the earliest at the top of the table.*

STEPS

1. **Click the Depart Date filter list arrow, then click Sort Oldest to Newest**

   Excel rearranges the records in ascending order by date, as shown in **FIGURE G-15**. The Date filter list arrow has an upward pointing arrow indicating the ascending sort in the field. You can also sort the table on one field using the Sort & Filter button.

2. **Click the HOME tab, click any cell in the Amount column, click the Sort & Filter button in the Editing group, then click Sort Largest to Smallest**

   Excel sorts the table, placing those records with the higher amount at the top. The Amount filter list arrow now has a downward pointing arrow next to the filter list arrow, indicating the descending sort order. You can also rearrange the table data using a **multilevel sort**. This type of sort rearranges the table data using more than one field, where each field is a different level, based on its importance in the sort. If you use two sort levels, the data is sorted by the first field, and the second field is sorted within each grouping of the first field. Since you have many groups of procedures with different dates, you want to use a multilevel sort to arrange the table data by procedures and then by dates within each procedure.

3. **Click the Sort & Filter button in the Editing group, then click Custom Sort**

   The Sort dialog box opens, as shown in **FIGURE G-16**.

4. **Click the Sort by list arrow, click Procedure, click the Order list arrow, click A to Z, click Add Level, click the Then by list arrow, click Date, click the second Order list arrow, click Oldest to Newest if necessary, then click OK**

   FIGURE G-17 shows the table sorted alphabetically in ascending order (A–Z) by Procedure and, within each procedure grouping, in ascending order by the Date.

5. **Save the workbook**

Sorting conditionally formatted data

If conditional formats have been applied to a table, you can sort the table using conditional formatting to arrange the rows. For example, if cells are conditionally formatted with color, you can sort a field on Cell Color, using the color with the order of On Top or On Bottom in the Sort dialog box. If the data is not in a table, you can select a cell in the column of conditionally formatted data you want to sort by, or select the range of cells to be sorted, right-click the selection, point to Sort, then select the font color, highlighted color, or icon that you want to appear on top.

FIGURE G-15: Table sorted by date

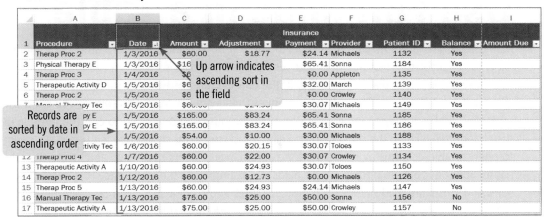

FIGURE G-16: Sort dialog box

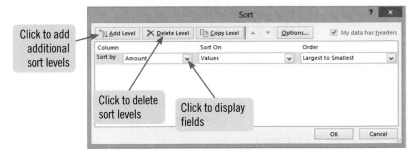

FIGURE G-17: Table sorted using two levels

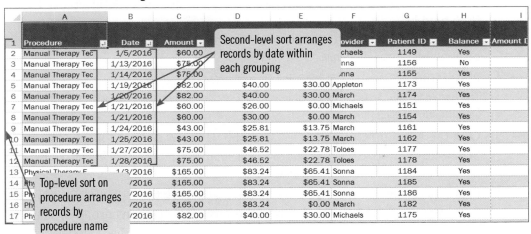

TABLE G-2: Sort order options and examples

option	alphabetic	numeric	date	alphanumeric
Ascending	A, B, C	7, 8, 9	1/1, 2/1, 3/1	12A, 99B, DX8, QT7
Descending	C, B, A	9, 8, 7	3/1, 2/1, 1/1	QT7, DX8, 99B, 12A

Specifying a custom sort order

You can identify a custom sort order for the field selected in the Sort by box. Click the Order list arrow in the Sort dialog box, click Custom List, then click the desired custom order. Commonly used custom sort orders are days of the week (Sun, Mon, Tues, Wed, etc.) and months (Jan, Feb, Mar, etc.); alphabetic sorts do not sort these items properly.

Use Formulas in a Table

**Learning
Outcomes**
• Build a table
  formula
• Use calculated
  columns to display
  formula results
• Use the table style
  options to add
  summary informa-
  tion to a table

Many tables are large, making it difficult to know from viewing them the "story" the table tells. The Excel table calculation features help you summarize table data so you can see important trends. After you enter a single formula into a table cell, the **calculated columns** feature fills in the remaining cells with the formula's results. The column continues to fill with the formula results as you enter rows in the table. This makes it easy to update your formulas because you only need to edit the formula once, and the change will fill in to the other column cells. The **structured reference** feature allows your formulas to refer to table columns by names that are automatically generated when you create the table. These names adjust as you add or delete table fields. An example of a table reference is =[Sales]–[Costs], where Sales and Costs are field names in the table. Tables also have a specific area at the bottom called the **table total row** for calculations using the data in the table columns. The cells in this row contain a dropdown list of functions that can be used for the column calculation. The table total row adapts to any changes in the table size. **CASE** ▶ *Tony wants you to use a formula to calculate the amount due for each procedure. You will also add summary information to the end of the table.*

STEPS

1. **Click cell I2, then type =[**

   A list of the table field names appears, as shown in FIGURE G-18. Structured referencing allows you to use the names that Excel created when you defined your table to reference fields in a formula. You can choose a field by clicking it and pressing [Tab] or by double-clicking the field name.

2. **Click [Amount], press [Tab], then type]**

   Excel begins the formula, placing [Amount] in the cell in blue and framing the Amount data in a blue border.

3. **Type -[, double-click [Adjustment], type], type -[, double-click [Insurance Payment], then type]**

   Excel places [Adjustment] in the cell in red and outlines the Adjustment data in a red border. The insurance payment data displays in purple.

4. **Press [Enter]**

   The formula result, $5.00 is displayed in cell I2. The table column also fills with the formula displaying the amount due for each procedure.

5. **Click the AutoCorrect Options list arrow ▦ ▾ to view options for the column**

   Because the calculated columns option saves time, you decide to leave the feature on. You want to display the amount due for all of the procedures.

6. **Click any cell inside the table to close the menu, click the TABLE TOOLS DESIGN tab, then click the Total Row check box in the Table Style Options group to select it**

   A total row appears at the bottom of the table, and the total amount due, $1,255.56, is displayed in cell I65. You can select other formulas in the total row.

7. **Click cell C65, then click the cell list arrow on the right side of the cell**

   The list of available functions appears, as shown in FIGURE G-19. You want to find the average procedure amount.

8. **Click Average, then save your workbook**

   The average procedure amount, $73.17, appears in cell C65.

FIGURE G-18: Table field names

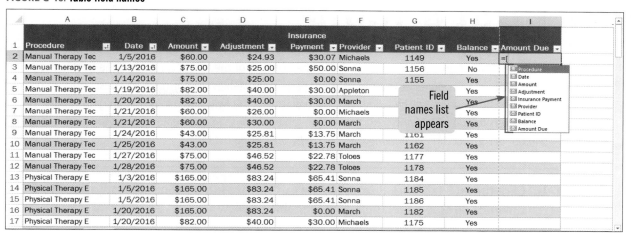

	A	B	C	D	E	F	G	H	I
					Insurance				
1	Procedure	Date	Amount	Adjustment	Payment	Provider	Patient ID	Balance	Amount Due
2	Manual Therapy Tec	1/5/2016	$60.00	$24.93	$30.07	Michaels	1149	Yes	=[
3	Manual Therapy Tec	1/13/2016	$75.00	$25.00	$50.00	Sonna	1156	No	
4	Manual Therapy Tec	1/14/2016	$75.00	$25.00	$0.00	Sonna	1155	Yes	
5	Manual Therapy Tec	1/19/2016	$82.00	$40.00	$30.00	Appleton		Yes	
6	Manual Therapy Tec	1/20/2016	$82.00	$40.00	$30.00	March		Yes	
7	Manual Therapy Tec	1/21/2016	$60.00	$26.00	$0.00	Michaels		Yes	
8	Manual Therapy Tec	1/21/2016	$60.00	$30.00	$0.00	March		Yes	
9	Manual Therapy Tec	1/24/2016	$43.00	$25.81	$13.75	March	1161	Yes	
10	Manual Therapy Tec	1/25/2016	$43.00	$25.81	$13.75	March	1162	Yes	
11	Manual Therapy Tec	1/27/2016	$75.00	$46.52	$22.78	Toloes	1177	Yes	
12	Manual Therapy Tec	1/28/2016	$75.00	$46.52	$22.78	Toloes	1178	Yes	
13	Physical Therapy E	1/3/2016	$165.00	$83.24	$65.41	Sonna	1184	Yes	
14	Physical Therapy E	1/5/2016	$165.00	$83.24	$65.41	Sonna	1185	Yes	
15	Physical Therapy E	1/5/2016	$165.00	$83.24	$65.41	Sonna	1186	Yes	
16	Physical Therapy E	1/20/2016	$165.00	$83.24	$0.00	March	1182	Yes	
17	Physical Therapy E	1/20/2016	$82.00	$40.00	$30.00	Michaels	1175	Yes	

Field names list:
- Procedure
- Date
- Amount
- Adjustment
- Insurance Payment
- Provider
- Patient ID
- Balance
- Amount Due

Field names list appears

FIGURE G-19: Functions in the Total Row

	Procedure	Date	Amount	Adjustment	Insurance Payr	Provider	Patient ID	Balance	Amount Due
55	Therapeutic Activity B	1/21/2016	$60.00	$23.00	$15.00	Toloes	1137	Yes	$22.00
56	Therapeutic Activity B	1/21/2016	$50.00	$32.24	$0.00	Michaels	1168	Yes	$17.76
57	Therapeutic Activity D	1/5/2016	$60.00	$23.00	$32.00	March	1139	Yes	$5.00
58	Therapeutic Activity D	1/17/2016	$82.00	$40.00	$0.00	Michaels	1172	Yes	$42.00
59	Therapeutic Activity D	1/20/2016	$82.00	$32.99	$0.00	March	1170	Yes	$49.01
60	Therapeutic Activity Tec	1/6/2016	$60.00	$20.15	$30.07	Toloes	1133	Yes	$9.78
61	Therapeutic Activity Tec	1/13/2016	$75.00	$25.00	$50.00	Toloes	1158	No	$0.00
62	Therapeutic Activity Tec	1/18/2016	$82.00	$40.00	$30.00	Sonna	1176	Yes	$12.00
63	Therapeutic Activity Tec	1/20/2016	$60.00	$27.00	$24.14	Toloes	1152	Yes	$8.86
64	Therapeutic Activity Tec	1/26/2016	$43.00	$25.81	$0.00	Sonna	1160	Yes	$17.19
65	Total								$1,255.56

Functions available in the Total Row:
- None
- Average
- Count
- Count Numbers
- Max
- Min
- Sum
- StdDev
- Var
- More Functions...

Using structured references

When you create a table from worksheet data, Excel creates a default table name such as Table1. This table name appears in structured references. Structured references make it easier to work with formulas that use table data. You can reference the entire table, columns in the table, or specific data. Structured references are especially helpful to use in formulas because they automatically adjust as data ranges change in a table, so you don't need to edit formulas.

Print a Table

Learning
Outcomes
• Preview a table
• Add print titles
  to a table

You can determine the way a table will print using the PAGE LAYOUT tab. Because tables often have more rows than can fit on a page, you can define the first row of the table (containing the field names) as the **print title**, which prints at the top of every page. Most tables do not have any descriptive information above the field names on the worksheet, so to augment the field name information, you can use headers and footers to add identifying text, such as the table title or the report date. **CASE** ▶ *Tony asks you for a printout of the procedure information. You begin by previewing the table.*

STEPS

1. **Click the FILE tab, click Print, click the Custom Scaling button list arrow, click Fit All Columns on One Page, then view the table preview**
   Below the table you see 1 of 2.

2. **In the Preview window, then click the Next Page button ▶ in the Preview area to view the second page**
   All of the field names in the table fit across the width of page 1. Because the records on page 2 appear without column headings, you want to set up the first row of the table, which contains the field names, as a repeating print title.

3. **Return to the worksheet, click the PAGE LAYOUT tab, click the Print Titles button in the Page Setup group, click inside the Rows to repeat at top text box under Print titles, in the worksheet scroll up to row 1 if necessary, click any cell in row 1 on the table, then compare your Page Setup dialog box to** FIGURE G-20
   When you select row 1 as a print title, Excel automatically inserts an absolute reference to the row that will repeat at the top of each page.

4. **Click the Print Preview button in the Page Setup dialog box, then click ▶ in the preview window to view the second page**
   Setting up a print title to repeat row 1 causes the field names to appear at the top of each printed page. The printout would be more informative with a header to identify the table information.

5. **Return to the worksheet, click the INSERT tab, click the Header & Footer button in the Text group, click the left header section text box, then type January PT Procedures**

6. **Select the left header section information, click the HOME tab, click the Increase Font Size button A˙ in the Font group twice to change the font size to 14, click the Bold button B in the Font group, click any cell in the table, then click the Normal button ▦ in the status bar**

7. **Save the table, preview it, close the workbook, exit Excel, then submit the workbook to your instructor**
   Compare your printed table with FIGURE G-21.

FIGURE G-20: Page Setup dialog box

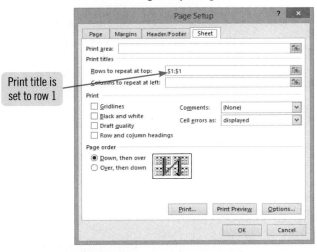

Print title is set to row 1

FIGURE G-21: Printed table

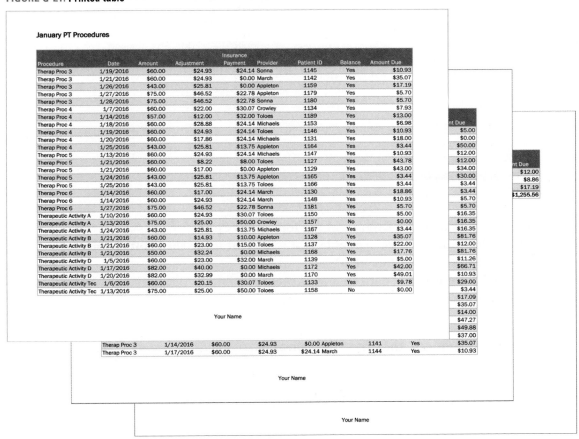

Setting a print area

Sometimes you will want to print only part of a worksheet. To do this, select any worksheet range, click the FILE tab, click Print, click the Print Active Sheets list arrow, then click Print Selection. If you want to print a selected area repeatedly, it's best to define a **print area**, the area of the worksheet that previews and prints when you use the Print command in Backstage view. To set a print area, select the range of data on the worksheet that you want to print, click the PAGE LAYOUT tab, click the Print Area button in the Page Setup group, then click Set Print Area. You can add to the print area by selecting a range, clicking the Print Area button, then clicking Add to Print Area. A print area can consist of one contiguous range of cells, or multiple areas in different parts of a worksheet.

Practice

Concepts Review

FIGURE G-22

	A	B	C	D	E	F	G	H	I
					Insurance				
1	Procedure	Date	Amount	Adjustment	Payment	Provider	Patient ID	Balance	Amount Due
2	Manual Therapy Tec	1/5/2016	$60.00	$24.93	$30.07	Michaels	1149	Yes	$35.07
3	Manual Therapy Tec	1/13/2016	$75.00	$25.00	$50.00	Sonna	1156	No	$50.00
4	Manual Therapy Tec	1/14/2016	$75.00	$25.00	$0.00	Sonna	1155	Yes	$50.00
5	Manual Therapy Tec	1/19/2016	$82.00	$40.00	$30.00	Appleton	1173	Yes	$42.00
6	Manual Therapy Tec	1/20/2016	$82.00	$40.00	$30.00	March	1174	Yes	$42.00
7	Manual Therapy Tec	1/21/2016	$60.00	$26.00	$0.00	Michaels	1151	Yes	$34.00
8	Manual Therapy Tec	1/21/2016	$60.00	$30.00	$0.00	March	1154	Yes	$30.00
9	Manual Therapy Tec	1/24/2016	$43.00	$25.81	$13.75	March	1161	Yes	$17.19
10	Manual Therapy Tec	1/25/2016	$43.00	$25.81	$13.75	March	1162	Yes	$17.19
11	Manual Therapy Tec	1/27/2016	$75.00	$46.52	$22.78	Toloes	1177	Yes	$28.48
12	Manual Therapy Tec	1/28/2016	$75.00	$46.52	$22.78	Toloes	1178	Yes	$28.48
13	Physical Therapy E	1/3/2016	$165.00	$83.24	$65.41	Sonna	1184	Yes	$81.76
14	Physical Therapy E	1/5/2016	$165.00	$83.24	$65.41	Sonna	1185	Yes	$81.76
15	Physical Therapy E	1/5/2016	$165.00	$83.24	$65.41	Sonna	1186	Yes	$81.76
16	Physical Therapy E	1/20/2016	$165.00	$83.24	$0.00	March	1182	Yes	$81.76
17	Physical Therapy E	1/20/2016	$82.00	$40.00	$30.00	Michaels	1175	Yes	$42.00

1. Which element do you click to print field names at the top of every page?
2. Which element do you click to set a range in a table that will print using the Print command?
3. Which element points to a second-level sort field?
4. Which element do you click to sort field data on a worksheet?
5. Which element points to a top-level sort field?

Match each term with the statement that best describes it.

6. Field
7. Sort
8. Record
9. Table
10. Header row

    a. Organized collection of related information in Excel
    b. Arrange records in a particular sequence
    c. Column in an Excel table
    d. First row of a table containing field names
    e. Row in an Excel table

Select the best answer from the list of choices.

11. Which of the following Excel sorting options do you use to sort a table of employee names in order from Z to A?
    a. Ascending
    b. Absolute
    c. Alphabetic
    d. Descending

Managing Data Using Tables

12. Which of the following series appears in descending order?

a. 8, 6, 4, C, B, A

b. 4, 5, 6, A, B, C

c. 8, 7, 6, 5, 6, 7

d. C, B, A, 6, 5, 4

13. You can easily add formatting to a table by using:

a. Table styles.

b. Print titles.

c. Print areas.

d. Calculated columns.

14. When printing a table on multiple pages, you can define a print title to:

a. Include the sheet name in table reports.

b. Include field names at the top of each printed page.

c. Exclude from the printout all rows under the first row.

d. Include gridlines in the printout.

Skills Review

1. Create and format a table.

a. Start Excel, open the file EMP G-2.xlsx from the location where you store your Data Files, then save it as **EMP G-Employees**.

b. Using the Practice sheet, enter the field names in the first row and the first two records in rows two and three, as shown in the table below, adjusting column widths as necessary to fit the text entries.

Last Name	First Name	Years Employed	Department	Full/Part Time	Training Completed
Diaz	Irina	3	Phlebotomy	P	Y
Merril	Doreen	2	Imaging	F	N

c. Create a table using the data you entered.

d. On the Staff sheet, create a table with a header row. Adjust the column widths, if necessary, to display the field names. Enter your name in the center section of the worksheet footer, return to Normal view if necessary, then save the workbook.

e. Apply a table style of Light 16 to the table.

f. Enter your name in the center section of the worksheet footer, return to Normal view if necessary, then save the workbook.

2. Add table data.

a. Add a new record in row seven for **Heather Walker**, a 5-year employee in the Phlebotomy department. Heather works part time and has completed training. Adjust the height of the new row to match the other table rows.

b. Insert a table row above Julie Kosby's record, and add a new record for **Sarah Allen**. Sarah works full time, has worked at the company for 2 years in Imaging, and has not completed training. Adjust the table formatting if necessary.

c. Insert a new data field in cell G1 with a label **Weeks Vacation**. Adjust the column width, and wrap the label in the cell to display the field name with **Weeks** above **Vacation**. (*Hint*: Use the Wrap Text button in the Alignment group on the HOME tab.)

d. Add a new column to the table by dragging the table's sizing handle, and give the new field a label of **Employee #**. Widen the column to fit the label.

e. Save the file.

3. Find and replace table data.

a. Return to cell A1.

b. Open the Find and Replace dialog box and if necessary uncheck the Match case option. Find the first record that contains the text **Imaging**.

c. Find the second and third records that contain the text **Imaging**.

d. Replace all **Imaging** text in the table with **X-Ray**, then save the file.

Skills Review (continued)

4. **Delete table data.**
   a. Go to cell A1.
   b. Delete the record for Irina Diaz.
   c. Use the Remove Duplicates button to confirm that the table does not have any duplicate records.
   d. Delete the Employee # table column, then delete its column header, if necessary.
   e. Save the file.

5. **Sort table data.**
   a. Sort the table by years employed in largest to smallest order.
   b. Sort the table by last name in A to Z order.
   c. Perform a multilevel sort: Sort the table first by Full/Part Time in A to Z order and then by last name in A to Z order.
   d. Check the table to make sure the records appear in the correct order.
   e. Save the file.

6. **Use formulas in a table.**
   a. In cell G2, enter the formula that calculates an employee's vacation time; base the formula on the company policy that employees working at the company less than 3 years have 2 weeks of vacation. At 3 years of employment and longer, an employee has 3 weeks of vacation time. Use the table's field names where appropriate. (*Hint*: The formula is: **=IF([Years Employed]<3,2,3).**)
   b. Check the table to make sure the formula filled into the cells in column G and that the correct vacation time is calculated for all cells in the column.
   c. Add a Total Row to display the total number of vacation weeks.
   d. Change the function in the Total Row to display the maximum number of vacation weeks. Change the entry in cell A8 from Total to **Maximum**.
   e. Compare your table to FIGURE G-23, then save the workbook.

   FIGURE G-23

	A	B	C	D	E	F	G
1	Last Name	First Name	Years Employed	Department	Full/Part Time	Training Completed	Weeks Vacation
2	Allen	Sarah	2	X-Ray	F	N	2
3	Green	Jane	1	Phlebotomy	F	N	2
4	Kosby	Julie	4	X-Ray	F	Y	3
5	Merril	Doreen	2	X-Ray	F	N	2
6	Ropes	Mark	1	X-Ray	P	Y	2
7	Walker	Heather	5	Phlebotomy	P	Y	3
8	Maximum						3
9							

7. **Print a table.**
   a. Add a header that reads **Employees** in the left section, then format the header in bold with a font size of 16.
   b. Add column A as a print title that repeats at the left of each printed page.
   c. Preview your table to check that the last names appear on both pages.
   d. Change the page orientation to landscape, preview the worksheet, then save the workbook.
   e. Submit your workbook to your instructor. Close the workbook, then exit Excel.

Independent Challenge 1

You are the marketing director for a rehabilitation clinic. You decide to organize the results of an outreach program in an Excel worksheet. You will create a table using the data, and analyze the survey results to help focus the clinic's expenses in the most successful areas.

   a. Start Excel, open the file EMP G-3.xlsx from the location where you store your Data Files, then save it as **EMP G-Survey Results**.
   b. Create a table from the worksheet data, and apply Table Style Light 18.

Independent Challenge 1 (continued)

c. Add the two records shown in the table below:

Last Name	First Name	Street Address	City	State	Zip	Area Code	Ad Source
Riley	Cate	81 Apple St.	San Francisco	CA	94177	415	Fitness Center
Jenkins	Sam	307 7th St.	Seattle	WA	98001	206	Newspaper

d. Find the record for Mike Rondo, then delete it.

e. Click cell A1 and replace all instances of **TV** with **Social Media**. Compare your table to FIGURE G-24.

FIGURE G-24

	A	B	C	D	E	F	G	H
1	Last Name	First Name	Street Address	City	State	Zip	Area Code	Ad Source
2	Kahil	Kathy	14 South St.	San Francisco	CA	94177	415	Social Media
3	Johnson	Mel	17 Henley St.	Reading	MA	03882	413	Newspaper
4	Malone	Kris	1 South St.	San Francisco	CA	94177	415	Fitness Center
5	Worthen	Sally	2120 Central St.	San Francisco	CA	93772	415	Fitness Center
6	Herbert	Greg	1192 Dome St.	San Diego	CA	93303	619	Newspaper
7	Chavez	Jane	11 Northern St.	San Diego	CA	92208	619	Social Media
8	Chelly	Yvonne	900 Sola St.	San Diego	CA	92106	619	Fitness Center
9	Smith	Carolyn	921 Lopez St.	San Diego	CA	92104	619	Newspaper
10	Oren	Scott	72 Yankee St.	Brookfield	CT	06830	203	Health Website
11	Warner	Salvatore	100 Westside St.	Chicago	IL	60620	312	Newspaper
12	Roberts	Bob	56 Water St.	Chicago	IL	60618	771	Fitness Center
13	Miller	Hope	111 Stratton St.	Chicago	IL	60614	773	Newspaper
14	Duran	Maria	Galvin St.	Chicago	IL	60614	773	Health Website
15	Roberts	Bob	56 Water St.	Chicago	IL	60614	312	Newspaper
16	Graham	Shelley	989 26th St.	Chicago	IL	60611	773	Education Website
17	Kelly	Janie	9 First St.	San Francisco	CA	94177	415	Newspaper
18	Kim	Janie	9 First St.	San Francisco	CA	94177	415	Health Website
19	Williams	Tasha	1 Spring St.	Reading	MA	03882	413	Newspaper
20	Juarez	Manuel	544 Cameo St.	Belmont	MA	02483	617	Newspaper
21	Masters	Latrice	88 Las Puntas Rd.	Boston	MA	02205	617	Education Website
22	Kooper	Peter	671 Main St.	Cambridge	MA	02138	617	Social Media
23	Kelly	Shawn	22 Kendall St.	Cambridge	MA	02138	617	Education Website
24	Rodriguez	Virginia	123 Main St.	Boston	MA	02007	617	Radio
25	Frei	Carol	123 Elm St.	Salem	MA	01970	978	Newspaper
26	Stevens	Crystal	14 Waterford St.	Salem	MA	01970	508	Radio
27	Ichikawa	Pam	232 Shore Rd.	Boston	MA	01801	617	Newspaper
28	Paxton	Gail	100 Main St.	Woburn	MA	01801	508	Newspaper
29	Spencer	Robin	293 Serenity Dr.	Concord	MA	01742	508	Radio
30	Lopez	Luis	1212 City St.	Kansas City	MO	64105	816	Social Media
31	Nelson	Michael	229 Rally Rd.	Kansas City	MO	64105	816	Education Website

f. Remove duplicate records where all fields are identical.

g. Sort the list by Last Name in A to Z order.

h. Sort the list again by Area Code in Smallest to Largest order.

i. Sort the table first by State in A to Z order, then within the state, by Zip in Smallest to Largest order.

j. Enter your name in the center section of the worksheet footer.

k. Add a centered header that reads **Ad Survey** in bold with a font size of 16.

l. Add print titles to repeat the first row at the top of each printed page.

m. Save the workbook, preview it, then submit the workbook to your instructor.

n. Close the workbook, then exit Excel.

Independent Challenge 2

You manage an orthopedic and podiatry supply firm that sells products to medical offices. The offices purchase items in quantities of 10 or more to have on hand when treating their patients. You decide to plan and build a table of sales information with eight records.

a. Prepare a plan for a table that states your goal, outlines the data you need, and identifies the table elements.

b. Sketch a sample table on a piece of paper, indicating how the table should be built. Create a table documenting the table design including the field names, type of data, and description of the data. You sell four categories of products: Brace, Support, Insert, and Guard.

Independent Challenge 2 (continued)

c. Start Excel, create a new workbook, then save it as **EMP G-Ortho Products** in the location where you store your Data Files. Enter the field names shown in the table below in the designated cells:

cell	field name
A1	Customer
B1	Contact
C1	Category
D1	Quantity
E1	Cost

d. Enter eight data records using your own data. The physician's practice name will be entered in the Customer column and the office manager's name will be entered in the contact column. The categories are Brace, Support, Insert, and Guard.

e. Create a table using the data in the range A1:E9. Adjust the column widths as necessary.

f. Apply the Table Style Light 11 to the table.

g. Add a field named **Total** in cell F1.

h. Enter a formula in cell F2 that calculates the total by multiplying the Quantity field by the Cost field. Check that the formula was filled down in the column.

i. Format the Cost and Total columns using the Accounting Number format. Adjust the column widths as necessary.

j. Add a new record to your table in row 10. Add another record above row 4.

k. Sort the table in ascending order by Category.

l. Enter your name in the worksheet footer, then save the workbook.

m. Preview the worksheet, then submit your workbook to your instructor.

n. Close the workbook, then exit Excel.

Independent Challenge 3

You are a project manager at the office of licensure and certification in a clinic. You are managing your professional development accounts using an Excel worksheet and have decided that a table will provide additional features to help you keep track of the accounts. You will use the table sorting features and table formulas to analyze your account data.

a. Start Excel, open the file EMP G-4.xlsx from the location where you store your Data Files, then save it as **EMP G-Accounts**.

b. Create a table with the worksheet data, and apply a table style of your choice. Adjust the column widths as necessary.

c. Sort the table on the Budget field using the Smallest to Largest order.

d. Sort the table using two fields, by Contact in A to Z order, then by Budget in Smallest to Largest order. Compare your table to FIGURE G-25. (Your table style may differ.)

FIGURE G-25

	A	B	C	D	E	F	G
1	Seminar	Date	Code	Budget	Expenses	Contact	Balance
2	Electronic Medical Records	3/3/2016	AA1	$100,000	$30,000	Cathy Brown	$70,000
3	Health Care Corporate Compliance	3/14/2016	C43	$200,000	$170,000	Cathy Brown	$30,000
4	Electronic Medical Records	3/11/2016	V13	$390,000	$400,000	Cathy Brown	-$10,000
5	Confidentiality of Medical Records	3/18/2016	C21	$450,000	$400,000	Cathy Brown	$50,000
6	Electronic Medical Records	3/23/2016	C43	$100,000	$150,000	Jane Atkins	-$50,000
7	Confidentiality of Medical Records	3/21/2016	V53	$200,000	$210,000	Jane Atkins	-$10,000
8	HIPAA Compliance	3/16/2016	V51	$300,000	$320,000	Jane Atkins	-$20,000
9	HIPAA Compliance	3/1/2016	AA5	$500,000	$430,210	Jane Atkins	$69,790
10	Health Care Corporate Compliance	3/7/2016	A3A	$200,000	$210,000	Kim Jess	-$10,000
11	HIPAA Compliance	3/9/2016	B12	$810,000	$700,000	Kim Jess	$110,000

Independent Challenge 3 (continued)

e. Add the new field label **Balance** in cell G1, and adjust the column width as necessary.

f. Enter a formula in cell G2 that uses structured references to table fields to calculate the balance on an account as the Budget minus the Expenses.

g. Add a new record for a seminar named **Confidentiality of Medical Records** with a date of **3/2/2016**, a code of **AB2**, a budget of **$300,000**, expenses of **$150,000**, and a contact of **Cathy Brown**.

h. Verify that the formula accurately calculated the balance for the new record.

i. Replace all of the Jane Smith data with **Jane Atkins**.

j. Find the record with a code of V51 and delete it.

k. Delete the Code field from the table.

l. Add a total row to the table and display the totals for appropriate columns. Adjust the column widths as necessary.

m. Enter your name in the center section of the worksheet footer, add a center section header of **Accounts** using formatting of your choice, change the page orientation to landscape, then save the workbook.

n. Preview your workbook, submit the workbook to your instructor, close the workbook, then exit Excel.

Independent Challenge 4: Explore

As the Director of Community Services at a public health department, you supervise employees' expense accounts in an immunization outreach program. You decide to highlight accounts that are over budget for the monthly meeting.

a. Start Excel, open the file EMP G-5.xlsx from the location where you store your Data Files, then save it as **EMP G-Associates**.

b. Create a table with the worksheet data, and apply the table style of your choice. Adjust the column widths as necessary.

c. Sort the table on the Balance field using the Smallest to Largest order.

d. Use conditional formatting to format the cells of the table containing negative balances with a green fill with dark green text.

e. Sort the table using the Balance field with the order of no cell color on top.

f. Format the table to emphasize the Balance column, and turn off the banded rows. (*Hint*: Use the Table Style Options on the TABLE TOOLS DESIGN tab.)

g. Research how to print nonadjacent areas on a single page. (Excel prints nonadjacent areas of a worksheet on separate pages by default.) Enter the result of your research on Sheet2 of the workbook.

h. Return to Sheet1 and create a print area that prints only the Account Number, Associate, and Balance columns of the table on one page.

i. Compare your table with FIGURE G-26. Save the workbook.

j. Preview your print area to make sure it will print on a single page.

k. Enter your name in the worksheet footers, then save the workbook.

l. Submit the workbook to your instructor, close the workbook, then exit Excel.

FIGURE G-26

	A	B	F
1	Account Number	Associate	Balance
2	96634	Kris Lowe	$ 5,000
3	32577	George Well	$ 10,000
4	15334	Janet Colby	$ 19,790
5	98661	Judy Makay	$ 25,000
6	84287	Joe Wood	$ 345,000
7	78441	Nancy Allen	$ 600,000
8	41557	Judy Makay	$ (15,000)
9	21889	Nancy Allen	$ (10,000)
10	57741	George Well	$ (10,000)
11	38997	Janet Colby	$ (5,000)

Visual Workshop

Start Excel, open the file EMP G-6.xlsx from the location where you store your Data Files, then save it as **EMP G-Cardiology**. Create the table and sort the data as shown in FIGURE G-27. (*Hint*: The table is formatted using Table Style Medium 5.) Add a worksheet header with the sheet name in the center section that is formatted in bold with a size of 14. Enter your name in the center section of the worksheet footer. Save the workbook, preview the table, close the workbook, submit the workbook to your instructor, then exit Excel.

FIGURE G-27

	Order Number	Order date	Amount	Shipping	Sales Rep
1					
2	1587	4/30/2016	$ 200,000	Air	Ellie Cranson
3	1032	11/15/2016	$ 210,000	Air	Ellie Cranson
4	1111	3/15/2016	$ 230,000	Air	Ellie Cranson
5	1251	2/15/2016	$ 300,000	Air	Ellie Cranson
6	1533	10/10/2016	$ 450,000	Air	Ellie Cranson
7	2001	1/15/2016	$ 100,000	Ground	Gene Coburn
8	2113	2/1/2016	$ 130,000	Air	Gene Coburn
9	2187	9/30/2016	$ 300,000	Ground	Gene Coburn
10	2257	6/1/2016	$ 500,000	Ground	Gene Coburn
11	2357	7/10/2016	$ 390,000	Ground	Neil Boxer
12	2588	12/15/2016	$ 810,000	Ground	Neil Boxer

Analyzing Table Data

CASE ▶ RMC's office manager, Tony Sanchez, asks you to display insurance reimbursement information from a table of the first quarter January Physical Therapy procedures. You will prepare these reports using various filters, subtotals, and Excel functions.

Unit Objectives

After completing this unit, you will be able to:

- Filter a table
- Create a custom filter
- Filter a table with the Advanced Filter
- Extract table data

- Look up values in a table
- Summarize table data
- Validate table data
- Create subtotals

Files You Will Need

EMP H-1.xlsx	EMP H-5.xlsx
EMP H-2.xlsx	EMP H-6.xlsx
EMP H-3.xlsx	EMP H-7.xlsx
EMP H-4.xlsx	

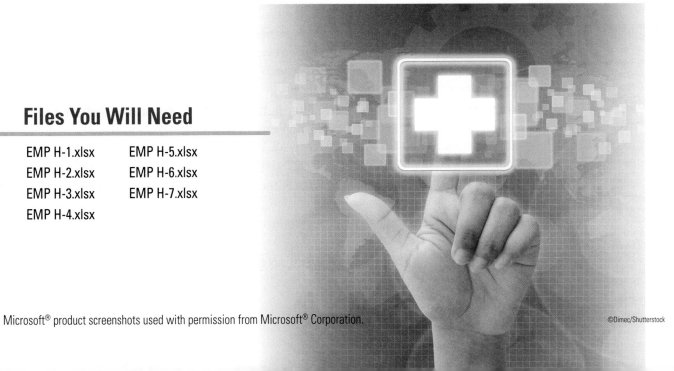

Filter a Table

Learning Outcomes
• Filter records using AutoFilter
• Filter records using search criteria

An Excel table lets you easily manipulate large amounts of data to view only the data you want, using a feature called **AutoFilter**. When you create a table, arrows automatically appear next to each column header. These arrows are called **filter list arrows**, **AutoFilter list arrows**, or **list arrows**, and you can use them to **filter** a table to display only the records that meet criteria you specify, temporarily hiding records that do not meet those criteria. For example, you can use the filter list arrow next to the Procedure field header to display only records that contain Therapeutic Activity B in the Procedure field. Once you filter data, you can copy, chart, and print the displayed records. You can easily clear a filter to redisplay all the records. **CASE** ▶ *Tony asks you to display only the records for the Therapeutic Activity B. He also asks for information about the procedures that are the most expensive and the procedures that were scheduled in March.*

STEPS

1. **Start Excel, open the file EMP H-1.xlsx from the location where you save your Data Files, then save it as EMP H-Procedures**

2. **Click the Procedure list arrow**

   Sort options appear at the top of the menu, advanced filtering options appear in the middle, and at the bottom is a list of the procedure data from column A, as shown in FIGURE H-1. Because you want to display data for only the Therapeutic Activity B procedures, your **search criterion** (the text you are searching for) is Therapeutic Activity B. You can select one of the Procedure data options in the menu, which acts as your search criterion.

QUICK TIP
You can also filter the table to display only the Therapeutic Activity B procedures information by clicking the Procedure list arrow, entering "Therapeutic Activity B" in the Search text box on the menu options below Text Filters, then clicking OK.

3. **In the list of procedures for the Procedure field, click Select All to clear the check marks from the procedures, scroll down the list of procedures, click Therapeutic Activity B, then click OK**

   Only those records containing "Therapeutic Activity B" in the Procedure field appear, as shown in FIGURE H-2. The row numbers for the matching records change to blue, and the list arrow for the filtered field has a filter icon. Both indicate that there is a filter in effect and that some of the records are temporarily hidden.

4. **Move the pointer over the Procedure list arrow**

   The ScreenTip Procedure: Equals "Therapeutic Activity B" describes the filter for the field, meaning that only the Therapeutic Activity B records appear. You decide to remove the filter to redisplay all of the table data.

5. **Click the Procedure list arrow, then click Clear Filter From "Procedure"**

   You have cleared the Therapeutic Activity B filter, and all the records reappear. You want to display the most expensive procedures, those in the top five percent.

QUICK TIP
You can also filter or sort a table by the color of the cells if conditional formatting has been applied.

6. **Click the Amount list arrow, point to Number Filters, click Top 10, select 10 in the middle box, type 5, click the Items list arrow, click Percent, then click OK**

   Excel displays the records for the top five percent in the number of Amount field, as shown in FIGURE H-3. You decide to clear the filter to redisplay all the records.

7. **On the HOME tab, click the Sort & Filter button in the Editing group, then click Clear**

   You have cleared the filter and all the records reappear. You can clear a filter using either the AutoFilter menu command or the Sort & Filter button on the HOME tab. The Sort & Filter button is convenient for clearing multiple filters at once. You want to find all of the procedures that were scheduled in March.

8. **Click the Date list arrow, point to Date Filters, point to All Dates in the Period, then click March**

   Excel displays the records for only the procedures that were scheduled in March. You decide to clear the filter and display all of the records.

QUICK TIP
You can also clear a filter by clicking the Clear button in the Sort & Filter group on the DATA tab.

9. **Click the Sort & Filter button in the Editing group, click Clear, then save the workbook**

FIGURE H-1: Worksheet showing AutoFilter options

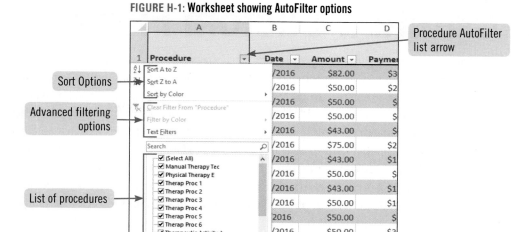

Procedure AutoFilter list arrow

Sort Options

Advanced filtering options

List of procedures

FIGURE H-2: Table filtered to show Therapeutic Activity B procedures

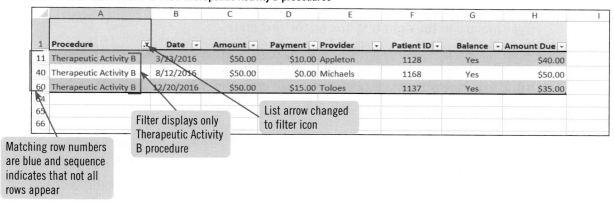

	A	B	C	D	E	F	G	H	I
1	Procedure	Date	Amount	Payment	Provider	Patient ID	Balance	Amount Due	
11	Therapeutic Activity B	3/23/2016	$50.00	$10.00	Appleton	1128	Yes	$40.00	
40	Therapeutic Activity B	8/12/2016	$50.00	$0.00	Michaels	1168	Yes	$50.00	
60	Therapeutic Activity B	12/20/2016	$50.00	$15.00	Toloes	1137	Yes	$35.00	
64									
65									
66									

List arrow changed to filter icon

Filter displays only Therapeutic Activity B procedure

Matching row numbers are blue and sequence indicates that not all rows appear

FIGURE H-3: Table filtered with top 5% of Amount

	A	B	C	D	E	F	G	H	I
1	Procedure	Date	Amount	Payment	Provider	Patient ID	Balance	Amount Due	
19	Physical Therapy E	5/18/2016	$165.00	$0.00	March	1182	Yes	$165.00	
20	Physical Therapy E	5/20/2016	$165.00	$65	Table filtered with top 5% in this field	87	Yes	$99.59	
31	Physical Therapy E	6/27/2016	$165.00	$0		83	Yes	$165.00	
44	Physical Therapy E	8/29/2016	$165.00	$65.41	Sonna	1184	Yes	$99.59	
45	Physical Therapy E	9/11/2016	$165.00	$65.41	Sonna	1185	Yes	$99.59	
46	Physical Therapy E	9/12/2016	$165.00	$65.41	Sonna	1186	Yes	$99.59	
47	Physical Therapy E	9/14/2016	$165.00	$65.41	Sonna	1169	Yes	$99.59	
64									

Create a Custom Filter

While AutoFilter lists can display records that are equal to certain amounts, you will often need more detailed filters. You can use more complex filters with the help of options in the Custom AutoFilter dialog box. For example, your criteria can contain comparison operators such as "greater than" or "less than" that let you display values above or below a certain amount. You can also use **logical conditions** like And and Or to narrow a search even further. You can have Excel display records that meet a criterion in a field *and* another criterion in that same field. This is often used to find records between two values. For example, by specifying an **And logical condition**, you can display records for customers with incomes between $40,000 *and* $70,000. You can also have Excel display records that meet either criterion in a field by specifying an Or condition. The **Or logical condition** is used to find records that satisfy either of two values. For example, in a table of book data you can use the Or condition to find records that contain either Beginning *or* Introduction in the title name. **CASE** ▶ *Tony wants to locate manual and physical procedure records for patients at the RMC Physical Therapy clinic. He also wants to find procedures that are scheduled between February 15, 2016, and April 15, 2016. He asks you to create custom filters to find the procedures satisfying these criteria.*

STEPS

1. **Click the Procedure list arrow, point to Text Filters, then click Contains**

   The Custom AutoFilter dialog box opens. You enter your criteria in the text boxes. The left text box on the first line currently displays "contains." You want to display procedures that contain the word "manual" in their names.

2. **Type manual in the right text box on the first line**

   You want to see entries that contain either manual or physical.

3. **Click the Or option button to select it, click the left text box list arrow on the second line, scroll to and select contains, then type physical in the right text box on the second line**

   Your completed Custom AutoFilter dialog box should match **FIGURE H-4**.

4. **Click OK**

   The dialog box closes, and only those records having "manual" or "physical" in the Procedure field appear in the worksheet. You want to find all procedures scheduled between February 15, 2016 and April 15, 2016.

5. **Click the Procedure list arrow, click Clear Filter From "Procedure", click the Date list arrow, point to Date Filters, then click Custom Filter**

   The Custom AutoFilter dialog box opens. The word "equals" appears in the left text box on the first line. You want to find the dates that are between February 15, 2016 and April 15, 2016 (that is, after February 15 *and* before April 15).

6. **Click the left text box list arrow on the first line, click is after, then type 2/15/2016 in the right text box on the first line**

   The And condition is selected, which is correct.

7. **Click the left text box list arrow on the second line, select is before, type 4/15/2016 in the right text box on the second line, then click OK**

   The records displayed have dates between February 15, 2016, and April 15, 2016. Compare your records to those shown in **FIGURE H-5**.

8. **Click the Date list arrow, click Clear Filter From "Date", then add your name to the center section of the footer**

   You have cleared the filter, and all the procedure records reappear.

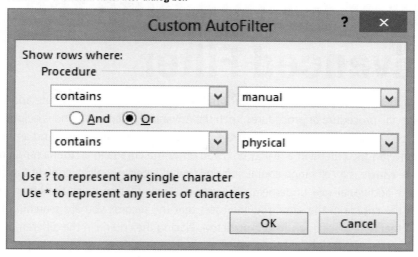

	A	B	C	D	E	F	G	H	I
1	Procedure	Date	Amount	Payment	Provider	Patient ID	Balance	Amount Due	
6	Therap Proc 3	2/22/2016	$43.00	$0.00	Appleton	1159	Yes	$43.00	
7	Therap Proc 3	2/28/2016	$75.00	$22.78	Appleton	1179	Yes	$52.22	
8	Therap Proc 4	3/13/2016	$43.00	$13.75	Appleton	1164	Yes	$29.25	
9		3/19/2016	$50.00	$0.00	Appleton	1129	Yes	$50.00	
10		3/20/2016	$43.00	$13.75	Appleton	1165	Yes	$29.25	
11	Therapeutic Activity B	3/23/2016	$50.00	$10.00	Appleton	1128	Yes	$40.00	
12	Therap Proc 2	4/8/2016	$50.00	$0.00	Crowley	1140	Yes	$50.00	
13	Therap Proc 4	4/11/2016	$50.00	$30.07	Crowley	1134	Yes	$19.93	
64									
65									

Dates are between 2/15 and 4/15 →

A1 ▾ : ✕ ✓ ƒx Procedure

Excel 2013

Using more than one rule when conditionally formatting data

You can apply conditional formatting to table cells in the same way that you can format a range of worksheet data. You can add multiple rules by clicking the HOME tab, clicking the Conditional Formatting button in the Styles group, then clicking New Rule for each additional rule that you want to apply. You can also add rules using the Conditional Formatting Rules Manager, which displays all of the rules for a data range. To use the Rules Manager, click the HOME tab, click the Conditional Formatting button in the Styles group, click Manage Rules, then click New Rule for each rule that you want to apply to the data range. After you have applied conditional formatting such as color fills, icon sets, or color scales to a numeric table range, you can use AutoFilter to sort or filter based on the colors or symbols.

Filter a Table with the Advanced Filter

Learning
Outcomes
• Filter records using
  a criteria range
  and the And
  condition
• Filter records using
  a criteria range
  and the Or
  condition

If you would like to see more specific information in a table, such as view date and insurance information for a specific procedure or procedures, then the Advanced Filter command is helpful. Using the Advanced Filter, you can specify data that you want to display from the table using And and Or conditions. Rather than entering the criteria in a dialog box, you enter the criteria in a criteria range on your worksheet. A **criteria range** is a cell range containing one row of labels (usually a copy of the column labels) and at least one additional row underneath the row of labels that contains the criteria you want to match. Placing the criteria in the same row indicates that the records you are searching for must match both criteria; that is, it specifies an **And condition**. Placing the criteria in the different rows indicates that the records you are searching for must match only one of the criterion; that is, it specifies an **Or condition**. With the criteria range on the worksheet, you can easily see the criteria by which your table is sorted. You can also use the criteria range to create a macro using the Advanced Filter feature to automate the filtering process for data that you filter frequently. Another advantage of the Advanced Filter is that you can move filtered table data to a different area of the worksheet or to a new worksheet, as you will see in the next lesson. **CASE** ▶ *Tony wants to identify procedures performed after 6/1/2016 by the provider Michaels. He asks you to use the Advanced Filter to retrieve these records. You begin by defining the criteria range.*

STEPS

1. **Select table rows 1 through 6, click the Insert list arrow in the Cells group, click Insert Sheet Rows; click cell A1, type Criteria Range, then click the Enter button ☑ on the Formula bar**

   Six blank rows are added above the table. Excel does not require the label "Criteria Range", but it is useful to see the column labels as you organize the worksheet and use filters.

2. **Select the range A7:H7, click the Copy button in the Clipboard group, click cell A2, click the Paste button in the Clipboard group, then press [Esc]**

   Next, you want to insert criteria that will display records for only those procedures scheduled after June 1, 2016 and that are performed by Michaels.

3. **Click cell B3, type >6/1/2016, click cell E3, type Michaels, then click ☑**

   You have entered the criteria in the cells directly beneath the Criteria Range labels, as shown in **FIGURE H-6**.

4. **Click any cell in the table, click the DATA tab, then click the Advanced button in the Sort & Filter group**

   The Advanced Filter dialog box opens, with the table (list) range already entered. The default setting under Action is to filter the table in its current location ("in-place") rather than copy it to another location.

5. **Click the Criteria range text box, select the range A2:H3 in the worksheet, then click OK**

   You have specified the criteria range and used the filter. The filtered table contains fourteen records that match both criteria—the date is after 6/1/2016 and the provider is Michaels, as shown in **FIGURE H-7**. You'll filter this table even further in the next lesson.

FIGURE H-6: Criteria in the same row indicating an and condition

	A	B	C	D	E	F	G	H	I	J
1	Criteria Range									
2	Procedure	Date	Amount	Payment	Provider	Patient ID	Balance	Amount Due		
3		>6/1/2016			Michaels					
4										
5										
6										
7	Procedure ▼	Date ▼	Amount ▼	Payment		ID ▼	Balance ▼	Amount Due ▼		
8	Manual Therapy Tec	1/12/2016	$82.00	$30.00	Appleton	1173	Yes	$52.00		
9	Therap Proc 1	1/13/2016	$50.00	$24.14	Appleton	1143	Yes	$25.86		
10	Therap Proc 3	1/19/2016	$50.00	$0.00	Appleton	1135	Yes	$50.00		
11	Therap Proc 3	1/21/2016	$50.00	$0.00	Appleton	1141	Yes	$50.00		

Filtered records will match these criteria

FIGURE H-7: Filtered table

	A	B	C	D	E	F	G	H	I
7	Procedure	Date	Amount	Payment	Provider	Patient ID	Balance	Amount Due	
34	Manual Therapy Tec	6/12/2016	$50.00	$30.07	Michaels	1149	Yes	$19.93	
35	Manual Therapy Tec	6/18/2016	$50.00	$0.00	Michaels	1151	Yes	$50.00	
36	Physical Therapy E	6/20/2016	$82.00	$30.00	Michaels	1175	Yes	$52.00	
37	Physical Therapy E	6/27/2016	$165.00	$0.00	Michaels	1183	Yes	$165.00	
38	Therap Proc 1	7/2/2016	$50.00	$8.00	Michaels	1136	Yes	$42.00	
39	Therap Proc 2	7/7/2016	$50.00	$24.14	Michaels	1132	Yes	$25.86	
40	Therap Proc 2	7/9/2016	$52.00	$30.00	Michaels	1188	Yes	$22.00	
41	Therap Proc 2	7/11/2016	$50.00	$0.00	Michaels	1126	Yes	$50.00	
42	Therap Proc 4	7/12/2016	$50.00	$24.14	Michaels	1153	Yes	$25.86	
43	Therap Proc 4	7/12/2016	$50.00	$24.14	Michaels	1131	Yes	$25.86	
44	Therap Proc 5	7/27/2016	$50.00	$24.14	Michaels	1147	Yes	$25.86	
45	Therapeutic Activity A	8/11/2016	$43.00	$13.75	Michaels	1167	Yes	$29.25	
46	Therapeutic Activity B	8/12/2016	$50.00	$0.00	Michaels	1168	Yes	$50.00	
47	Therapeutic Activity D	8/20/2016	$82.00	$0.00	Michaels	1172	Yes	$82.00	

Dates are after 6/1/2016

Provider is Michaels

Using advanced conditional formatting options

You can emphasize top- or bottom-ranked values in a field using conditional formatting. To highlight the top or bottom values in a field, select the field data, click the Conditional Formatting button in the Styles group on the HOME tab, point to Top/Bottom Rules, select a Top or Bottom rule, if necessary enter the percentage or number of cells in the selected range that you want to format, select the format for the cells that meet the top or bottom criteria, then click OK. You can also format your worksheet or table data using icon sets and color scales based on the cell values. A **color scale** uses a set of two, three, or four fill colors to convey relative values. For example, red could fill cells to indicate they have higher values and green could signify lower values. To add a color scale, select a data range, click the HOME tab, click the Conditional Formatting

button in the Styles group, then point to Color Scales. On the submenu, you can select preformatted color sets or click More Rules to create your own color sets. **Icon sets** let you visually communicate relative cell values by adding icons to cells based on the values they contain. An upward-pointing green arrow might represent the highest values, and downward-pointing red arrows could represent lower values. To add an icon set to a data range, select a data range, click the Conditional Formatting button in the Styles group, then point to Icon Sets. You can customize the values that are used as thresholds for color scales and icon sets by clicking the Conditional Formatting button in the Styles group, clicking Manage Rules, clicking the rule in the Conditional Formatting Rules Manager dialog box, then clicking Edit Rule.

Extract Table Data

Whenever you take the time to specify a complicated set of search criteria, it's a good idea to extract the matching records, rather than filtering it in place. When you **extract** data, you place a copy of a filtered table in a range that you specify in the Advanced Filter dialog box. This way, you won't accidentally clear the filter or lose track of the records you spent time compiling. To extract data, you use an Advanced Filter and enter the criteria beneath the copied field names, as you did in the previous lesson. You then specify the location where you want the extracted data to appear. **CASE** *Tony needs to filter the table one step further to reflect only the Therap Proc 1 and Therap Proc 2 procedures in the current filtered table. He asks you to complete this filter by specifying an Or condition, which you will do by entering two sets of criteria in two separate rows. You decide to save the filtered records by extracting them to a different location in the worksheet.*

STEPS

1. **In cell A3, enter Therap Proc 1, then in cell A4, enter Therap Proc 2**

   The new sets of criteria need to appear in two separate rows, so you need to copy the previous filter criteria to the second row.

2. **Copy the criteria in B3:E3 to B4:E4**

   The criteria are shown in FIGURE H-8. When you use the Advanced Filter this time, you indicate that you want to copy the filtered table to a range beginning in cell A75, so that Tony can easily refer to the data, even if you use more filters later.

3. **If necessary, click the DATA tab, then click Advanced in the Sort & Filter group**

4. **Under Action, click the Copy to another location option button to select it, click the Copy to text box, then type A75**

   The last time you filtered the table, the criteria range included only rows 2 and 3, and now you have criteria in row 4.

5. **Edit the contents of the Criteria range text box to show the range $A$2:$H$4, click OK, then if necessary scroll down until row 75 is visible**

   The matching records appear in the range beginning in cell A75, as shown in FIGURE H-9. The original table, starting in cell A7, contains the records filtered in the previous lesson.

6. **Press [Ctrl][Home], then click the Clear button in the Sort & Filter group**

   The original table is displayed starting in cell A7, and the extracted table remains in A75:H79.

7. **Save the workbook**

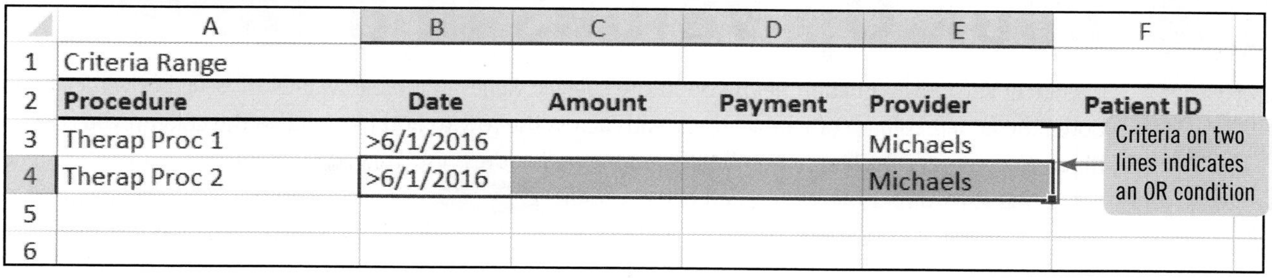

⁄	A	B	C	D	E	F
1	Criteria Range					
2	**Procedure**	**Date**	**Amount**	**Payment**	**Provider**	**Patient ID**
3	Therap Proc 1	>6/1/2016			Michaels	Criteria on two
4	Therap Proc 2	>6/1/2016			Michaels	lines indicates
5						an OR condition
6						

FIGURE H-9: Extracted data records

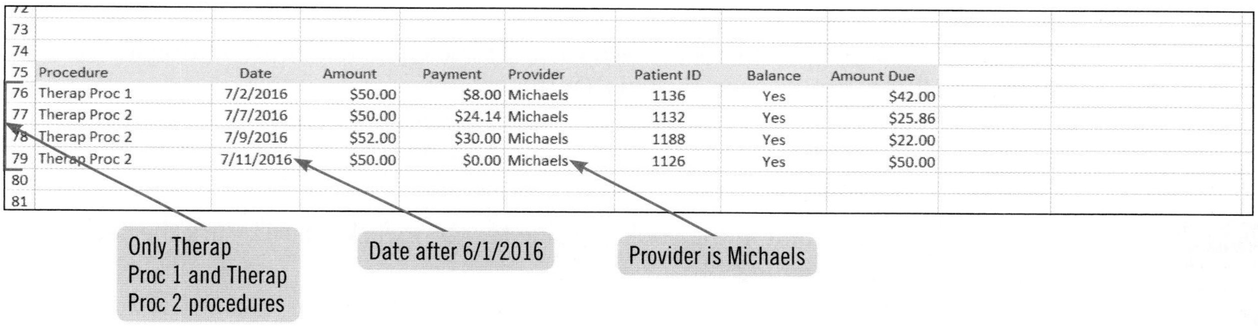

73								
74								
75	Procedure	Date	Amount	Payment	Provider	Patient ID	Balance	Amount Due
76	Therap Proc 1	7/2/2016	$50.00	$8.00	Michaels	1136	Yes	$42.00
77	Therap Proc 2	7/7/2016	$50.00	$24.14	Michaels	1132	Yes	$25.86
78	Therap Proc 2	7/9/2016	$52.00	$30.00	Michaels	1188	Yes	$22.00
79	Therap Proc 2	7/11/2016	$50.00	$0.00	Michaels	1126	Yes	$50.00
80								
81								

Only Therap Proc 1 and Therap Proc 2 procedures

Date after 6/1/2016

Provider is Michaels

Understanding the criteria range and the copy-to location

When you define the criteria range and the copy-to location in the Advanced Filter dialog box, Excel automatically creates the range names Criteria and Extract for these ranges in the worksheet. The Criteria range includes the field names and any criteria rows underneath them. The Extract range includes just the field names above the extracted table. You can select these ranges by clicking the Name box list arrow, then clicking the range name. If you click the Name Manager button in the Defined Names group on the FORMULAS tab, you will see these new names and the ranges associated with each one.

Look Up Values in a Table

Learning Outcomes
- Use table references in a VLOOKUP formula
- Find table information using VLOOKUP

The Excel VLOOKUP function helps you locate specific values in a table. VLOOKUP searches vertically (V) down the far left column of a table, then reads across the row to find the value in the column you specify, much as you might look up a number in a name and address list: You locate a person's name, then read across the row to find the phone number you want. **CASE** *Tony wants to be able to find a procedure destination by entering the procedure code. You will use the VLOOKUP function to accomplish this task. You begin by viewing the table name so you can refer to it in a lookup function.*

STEPS

QUICK TIP

You can change table names to better represent their content so they are easier to use in formulas. Click the table in the list of names in the Name Manager text box, click Edit, type the new table name in the Name text box, then click OK.

1. **Click the Lookup sheet tab, click the FORMULAS tab in the Ribbon, then click the Name Manager button in the Defined Names group**

   The named ranges for the workbook appear in the Name Manager dialog box, as shown in **FIGURE H-10**. The Criteria and Extract ranges appear at the top of the range name list. At the bottom of the list is information about the three tables in the workbook. Table1 refers to the table on the 2016 Procedures sheet, Table2 refers to the table on the Lookup sheet, and Table3 refers to the table on the Subtotals worksheet. The Excel structured reference feature automatically created these table names when the tables were created.

2. **Click Close**

   You want to find the procedure represented by the code 677Y. The VLOOKUP function lets you find the procedure name for any procedure code. You will enter a procedure code in cell M1 and a VLOOKUP function in cell M2.

3. **Click cell M1, enter 677Y, click cell M2, click the Lookup & Reference button in the Function Library group, then click VLOOKUP**

   The Function Arguments dialog box opens, with boxes for each of the VLOOKUP arguments. Because the value you want to find is in cell M1, M1 is the Lookup_value. The table you want to search is the table on the Lookup sheet, so its assigned name, Table2, is the Table_array.

QUICK TIP

If you want to find only the closest match for a value, enter TRUE in the Range_lookup text box. However, this can give misleading results if you are looking for an exact match. If you use FALSE and Excel can't find the value, you see an error message.

4. **With the insertion point in the Lookup_value text box, click cell M1, click the Table_array text box, then type Table2**

   The column containing the information that you want to find and display in cell M2 is the second column from the left in the table range, so the Col_index_num is 2. Because you want to find an exact match for the value in cell M1, the Range_lookup argument is FALSE.

5. **Click the Col_index_num text box, type 2, click the Range_lookup text box, then enter FALSE**

   Your completed Function Arguments dialog box should match **FIGURE H-11**.

6. **Click OK**

   Excel searches down the far-left column of the table until it finds a procedure code that matches the one in cell M1. It then looks in column 2 of the table range and finds the procedure for that record, Therap Proc 1, and displays it in cell M2. You use this function to determine the procedure for one other procedure code.

7. **Click cell M1, type 543Y, then click the Enter button ✓ on the formula bar**

   The VLOOKUP function returns the value of Physical Therapy E in cell M2.

8. **Press [Ctrl][Home], then save the workbook**

Finding records using the DGET function

You can also use the DGET function to find a record in a table that matches specified criteria. When using DGET, you need to include [#All] after your table name in the formula to include the column labels that are used for the criteria range. Unlike VLOOKUP, you do not have the option of using a Range_Lookup value of TRUE to find an approximate match.

FIGURE H-10: Named ranges in the workbook

Created by Advanced Filter

Tables in the workbook

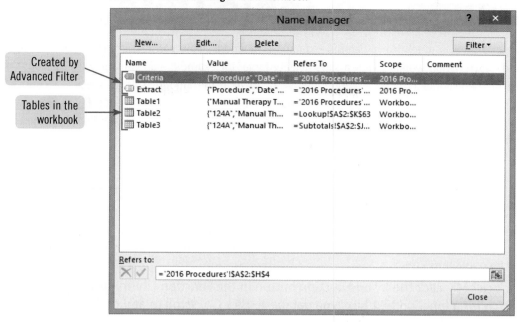

FIGURE H-11: Completed Function Arguments dialog box for VLOOKUP

Location of value you want to search for

Range name of table to search

Number of column to search

Finds exact match

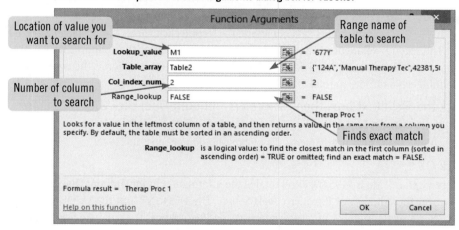

Using the HLOOKUP and MATCH functions

The VLOOKUP (Vertical Lookup) function is useful when your data is arranged vertically, in columns. When your data is arranged horizontally in rows, use the HLOOKUP (Horizontal Lookup) function. HLOOKUP searches horizontally across the upper row of a table until it finds the matching value, then looks down the number of rows you specify. The arguments for this function are identical to those for the VLOOKUP function, with one exception. Instead of a Col_index_number, HLOOKUP uses a Row_index_number, which indicates the location of the row you want to search. For example, if you want to search the fourth row from the top of the table range, the Row_index_number should be 4. You can use the MATCH function when you want the position of an item in a range. The MATCH function uses the syntax: MATCH (lookup_value,lookup_array,match_ type) where the lookup_value is the value you want to match in the lookup_array range. The match_type can be 0 for an exact match, 1 for matching the largest value that is less than or equal to lookup_value, or −1 for matching the smallest value that is greater than or equal to the lookup_value.

Excel 2013

Summarize Table Data

Learning Outcomes
- Summarize table data using DSUM
- Summarize table data using DCOUNT or DCOUNTA

Because a table acts much like a database, database functions allow you to summarize table data in a variety of ways. When working with a sales activity table, for example, you can use Excel to count the number of client contacts by sales representative or to total the amount sold to specific accounts by month. **TABLE H-1** lists database functions commonly used to summarize table data. **CASE** > *Tony is reviewing procedures performed in 2016. He needs your help in determining the procedures performed by certain providers.*

STEPS

1. **Review the criteria range for the provider Sonna in the range L5:L6**

   The criteria range in L5:L6 tells Excel to summarize records with the entry "Sonna" in the Provider column. The functions will be in cells M8 and M9. You use this criteria range in a DSUM function to sum the amount due for only Sonna's patients.

2. **Click cell M8, click the Insert Function button in the Function Library group, in the Search for a function text box type database, click Go, scroll to and click DSUM under Select a function, then click OK**

   The first argument of the DSUM function is the table, or database.

3. **In the Function Arguments dialog box, with the insertion point in the Database text box, move the pointer over the upper-left corner of cell A1 until the pointer becomes ↘, click once, then click again**

   The first click selects the table's data range, and the second click selects the entire table, including the header row. The second argument of the DSUM function is the label for the column that you want to sum. You want to total the amount due. The last argument for the DSUM function is the criteria that will be used to determine which values to total.

4. **Click the Field text box, then click cell J1, Amount Due; click the Criteria text box and select the range L5:L6**

   Your completed Function Arguments dialog box should match **FIGURE H-12**.

5. **Click OK**

   The result in cell M8 is $195.09. Excel totaled the information in the Amount Due column for those records that meet the criterion of Provider equals Sonna. The DCOUNT and the DCOUNTA functions can help you determine the number of records meeting specified criteria in a database field. DCOUNTA counts the number of nonblank cells. You will use DCOUNTA to determine the number of procedures scheduled.

6. **Click cell M9, click the Insert Function button 𝑓ₓ on the formula bar, in the Search for a function text box type database, click Go, select DCOUNTA from the Select a function list, then click OK**

7. **With the insertion point in the Database text box, move the pointer over the upper-left corner of cell A1 until the pointer becomes ↘, click once, click again to include the header row, click the Field text box and click cell B1, click the Criteria text box and select the range L5:L6, then click OK**

   The result in cell M9 is 10, and it indicates that there are ten procedures performed by Sonna. You also want to display the total amount due and number of procedures for Appleton.

8. **Click cell L6, type Appleton, then click the Enter button ✓ on the formula bar**

   FIGURE H-13 shows that $177.84 is due for a total of ten procedures by Appleton.

FIGURE H-12: Completed Function Arguments dialog box for DSUM

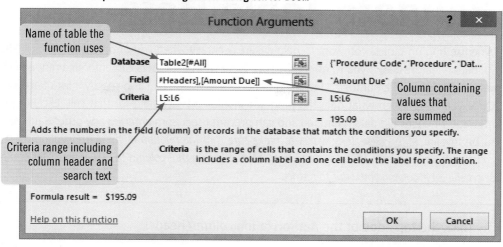

FIGURE H-13: Result generated by database functions

	E	F	G	H	I	J	K	L	M	N	O
1	Adjustment	Insurance Payment	Provider	Patient ID	Balance	Amount Due	Authorization	Procedure Code	543Y		
2	$19.93	$30.07	Michaels	1149	No	$0.00	Yes	Procedure	Physical Therapy E		
3	$25.00	$50.00	Sonna	1156	No	$0.00	Yes				
4	$25.00	$0.00	Sonna	1155	Yes	$50.00	No	Provider Information			
5	$40.00	$30.00	Appleton	1173	Yes	$12.00	Yes	Provider			
6	$40.00	$30.00	March	1174	Yes	$12.00	Yes	Appleton			
7	$21.00	$0.00	Michaels	1151	Yes	$29.00	No				
8	$25.00	$0.00	March	1154	Yes	$25.00	Yes	Amount Due	$177.84		
9	$25.81	$13.75	March	1161	Yes	$3.44	Yes	Number of procedures	10		
10	$25.81	$13.75	March	1162	Yes	$3.44	Yes				
11	$46.52	$22.78	Toloes	1177	Yes	$5.70	Yes				
12	$46.52	$22.78	Toloes	1178	Yes	$5.70	Yes				

Information for Provider Appleton

TABLE H-1: Common database functions

function	result
DGET	Extracts a single record from a table that matches criteria you specify
DSUM	Totals numbers in a given table column that match criteria you specify
DAVERAGE	Averages numbers in a given table column that match criteria you specify
DCOUNT	Counts the cells that contain numbers in a given table column that match criteria you specify
DCOUNTA	Counts the cells that contain nonblank data in a given table column that match criteria you specify

Excel 2013

Validate Table Data

Learning Outcomes
- Use data validation to restrict data entry to specified values
- Insert table data using data validation

When setting up tables, you want to help ensure accuracy when you or others enter data. The Excel data validation feature allows you to do this by specifying what data users can enter in a range of cells. You can restrict data to whole numbers, decimal numbers, or text. You can also specify a list of acceptable entries. Once you've specified what data the program should consider valid for that cell, Excel displays an error message when invalid data is entered and can prevent users from entering any other data that it considers to be invalid. **CASE** *Tony wants to make sure that information in the Authorization column is entered consistently in the future. He asks you to restrict the entries in that column to two options: Yes and No. First, you select the table column you want to restrict.*

STEPS

1. **Click the top edge of the Authorization column header**

   The column data is selected.

2. **Click the DATA tab, click the Data Validation button in the Data Tools group, click the Settings tab if necessary, click the Allow list arrow, then click List**

   Selecting the List option lets you type a list of specific options.

QUICK TIP

To specify a long list of valid entries, type the list in a column or row elsewhere in the worksheet, then type the list range in the Source text box.

3. **Click the Source text box, then type Yes, No**

   You have entered the list of acceptable entries, separated by commas, as shown in FIGURE H-14. You want the data entry person to be able to select a valid entry from a drop-down list.

4. **Click the In-cell dropdown check box to select it if necessary, then click OK**

   The dialog box closes, and you return to the worksheet.

TROUBLE

If you get an invalid data error, make sure that cell K1 is not included in the selection. If K1 is included, open the Data Validation dialog box, click Clear All, click OK, then begin with Step 1 again.

5. **Click the HOME tab, click any cell in the last table row, click the Insert list arrow in the Cells group, click Insert Table Row Below, click the last cell in the Authorization column, then click its list arrow to display the list of valid entries**

   The drop-down list is shown in FIGURE H-15. You could click an item in the list to have it entered in the cell, but you want to test the data restriction by entering an invalid entry.

6. **Click the list arrow to close the list, type Maybe, then press [Enter]**

   A warning dialog box appears and prevents you from entering the invalid data, as shown in FIGURE H-16.

7. **Click Cancel, click the list arrow, then click Yes**

   The cell accepts the valid entry. The data restriction ensures that records contain only one of the two correct entries in the Authorization column. The table is ready for future data entry.

8. **Delete the last table row, add your name to the center section of the footer, then save the workbook**

Restricting cell values and data length

In addition to providing an in-cell drop-down list for data entry, you can use data validation to restrict the values that are entered into cells. For example, if you want to restrict cells in a selected range to values less than a certain number, date, or time, click the DATA tab, click the Data Validation button in the Data Tools group, and on the Settings tab, click the Allow list arrow, select Whole number, Decimal, Date, or Time, click the Data list arrow, select less than, then in the bottom text box, enter the maximum value. You can also limit the length of data entered into cells by choosing Text length in the Allow list, clicking the Data list arrow and selecting less than, then entering the maximum length in the Maximum text box.

FIGURE H-14: Creating data restrictions

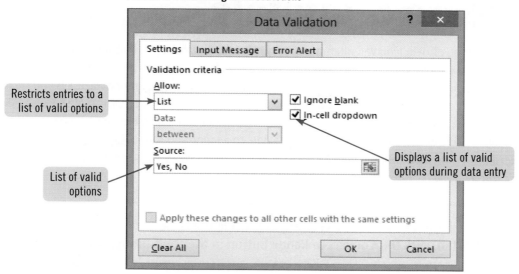

Restricts entries to a list of valid options

List of valid options

Displays a list of valid options during data entry

FIGURE H-15: Entering data in restricted cells

	Adjustment	Insurance Pa	Provider	Patient	Balance	Amount Due	Authorization
61	$25.00	$50.00	Toloes	1158	No	$0.00	Yes
62	$40.00	$30.00	Sonna	1176	Yes	$12.00	Yes
63	$22.00	$24.14	Toloes	1152	Yes	$3.86	Yes
64					No	$0.00	
65							Yes
66							No
67							
68							
69							
70							
71							
72							

Dropdown list

FIGURE H-16: Invalid data warning

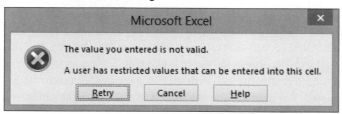

Microsoft Excel

The value you entered is not valid.

A user has restricted values that can be entered into this cell.

Retry · Cancel · Help

Adding input messages and error alerts

You can customize the way data validation works by using the two other tabs in the Data Validation dialog box: Input Message and Error Alert. The Input Message tab lets you set a message that appears when the user selects that cell. For example, the message might contain instructions about what type of data to enter. On the Input Message tab, enter a message title and message, then click OK. The Error Alert tab lets you set one of three alert levels if a user enters invalid data. The Information level displays your message with the information icon but allows the user to proceed with data entry. The Warning level displays your information with the warning icon and gives the user the option to proceed with data entry or not. The Stop level, which you used in this lesson, displays your message and only lets the user retry or cancel data entry for that cell.

Create Subtotals

Learning Outcomes
- Summarize worksheet data using subtotals
- Use outline symbols
- Convert a table to a range

In a large range of data, you will often need ways to perform calculations that summarize groups within the data. For example, you might need to subtotal the sales for several sales reps listed in a table. The Excel Subtotals feature provides a quick, easy way to group and summarize a range of data. It lets you create not only subtotals using the SUM function, but other statistics as well, including COUNT, AVERAGE, MAX, and MIN. However, subtotals cannot be used in an Excel table, nor can it rearrange data. Before you can add subtotals to table data, you must first convert the data to a range and sort it. **CASE** ▶ *Tony wants you to group data by procedure, with subtotals for the insurance payments and the amount due for the procedures. You begin by converting the table to a range.*

STEPS

1. **Click the Subtotals sheet tab, click any cell inside the table, click the TABLE TOOLS DESIGN tab, click the Convert to Range button in the Tools group, then click Yes**

    The filter list arrows and the TABLE TOOLS DESIGN tab no longer appear. Before you can add the subtotals, you must first sort the data. You decide to sort it in ascending order, first by procedure and then by date.

2. **Click the DATA tab, click the Sort button in the Sort & Filter group, in the Sort dialog box click the Sort by list arrow, click Procedure, click the Add Level button, click the Then by list arrow, click Date, verify that the order is Oldest to Newest, then click OK**

    You have sorted the range in ascending order, first by procedure, then by date within each procedure grouping.

3. **Click any cell in the data range if necessary, then click the Subtotal button in the Outline group**

    The Subtotal dialog box opens. Here you specify the items you want subtotaled, the function you want to apply to the values, and the fields you want to summarize.

4. **Click the At each change in list arrow, click Procedure if necessary, click the Use function list arrow, click Sum; in the "Add subtotal to" list, click the Insurance Payment and Amount Due check boxes to select them, if necessary, then click any other selected check boxes to deselect them**

5. **If necessary, click the Replace current subtotals and Summary below data check boxes to select them**

    Your completed Subtotal dialog box should match FIGURE H-17.

6. **Click OK, then scroll down so you can see row 76**

    The subtotaled data appears after each procedure grouping, showing the calculated subtotals and grand total in columns E and F, as shown in FIGURE H-18. Excel displays an outline to the left of the worksheet, with outline buttons to control the level of detail that appears. The button number corresponds to the detail level that is displayed. You want to show the second level of detail, the subtotals and the grand total.

    > **QUICK TIP**
    > You can click the ⊟ button to hide or the ⊞ button to show a group of records in the subtotaled structure.

7. **Click the outline symbol** 2

    Only the subtotals and the grand total appear.

    > **QUICK TIP**
    > You can remove subtotals in a worksheet by clicking the Subtotal button and clicking Remove All. The subtotals no longer appear, and the Outline feature is turned off automatically.

8. **Add your name to the center section of the footer, preview the worksheet, click the No Scaling list arrow, click Fit Sheet on One Page to scale the worksheet to print on one page, then save the workbook**

9. **Close the workbook, exit Excel, then submit the workbook to your instructor**

FIGURE H-17: Completed Subtotal dialog box

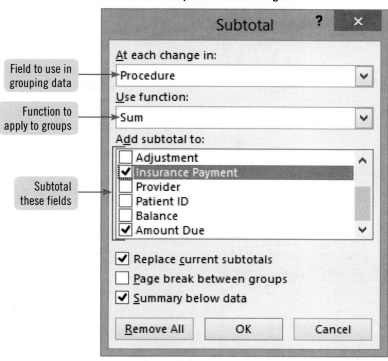

Field to use in grouping data

Function to apply to groups

Subtotal these fields

FIGURE H-18: Portion of subtotaled table

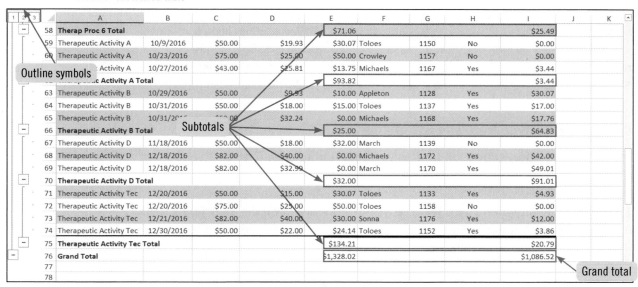

Outline symbols

Subtotals

Grand total

Excel 2013

Practice

Put your skills into Practice with **SAM**! If you have a SAM account, go to www.cengage.com/sam2013 to access SAM assignments for this unit.

Concepts Review

FIGURE H-19

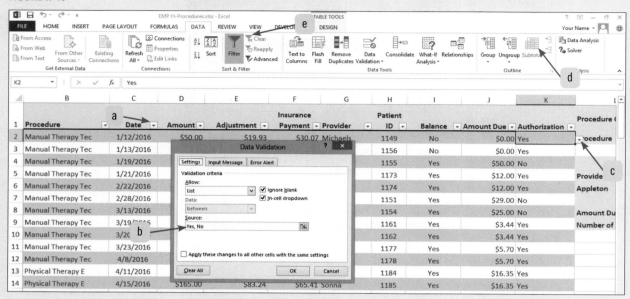

1. Which element points to an in-cell drop-down list arrow?
2. Which element would you click to remove a filter?
3. Which element points to a field's list arrow?
4. Which element do you click to group and summarize data?
5. Where do you specify acceptable data entries for a table?

Match each term with the statement that best describes it.

6. Table_array
7. Extracted table
8. Data validation
9. Criteria range
10. DSUM

a. Cell range when Advanced Filter results are copied to another location
b. Range in which search conditions are set
c. Restricts table entries to specified options
d. Name of the table searched in a VLOOKUP function
e. Function used to total table values that meet specified criteria

Select the best answer from the list of choices.

11. The _____ logical condition finds records matching both listed criteria.
   a. True
   b. Or
   c. And
   d. False

12. What does it mean when you select the Or option when creating a custom filter?
   a. Both criteria must be true to find a match.
   b. Neither criterion has to be 100% true.
   c. Either criterion can be true to find a match.
   d. A custom filter requires a criteria range.

13. What must a data range have before subtotals can be inserted?

a. Enough records to show multiple subtotals

b. Sorted data

c. Formatted cells

d. Grand totals

14. Which function finds the position of an item in a table?

a. VLOOKUP

b. MATCH

c. DGET

d. HLOOKUP

Skills Review

1. Filter a table.

a. Start Excel, open the file EMP H-2.xlsx from the location where you store your Data Files, then save it as **EMP H-Compensation**.

b. With the Compensation sheet active, filter the table to list only records for employees in the Radiology Department.

c. Clear the filter, then add a filter that displays the records for employees in the Radiology and Cardiology Departments.

d. Redisplay all employees, then use a filter to show the three employees with the highest annual salary.

e. Redisplay all the records.

2. Create a custom filter.

a. Create a custom filter showing employees hired before 1/1/2013 or after 12/31/2013.

b. Create a custom filter showing employees hired between 1/1/2013 and 12/31/2013.

c. Enter your name in the worksheet footer, then preview the filtered worksheet.

d. Redisplay all records.

e. Save the workbook.

3. Filter and extract a table with the Advanced Filter.

a. You want to retrieve a list of employees who were hired before 1/1/2014 and who have an annual salary of more than $75,000 a year. Define a criteria range by inserting six new rows above the table on the worksheet and copying the field names into the first row.

b. In cell D2, enter the criterion **<1/1/2014**, then in cell G2 enter **>75000**.

c. Click any cell in the table.

d. Open the Advanced Filter dialog box.

e. Indicate that you want to copy to another location, enter the criteria range **A1:J2**, verify that the List range is $A$7:$J$17, then indicate that you want to place the extracted list in the range starting at cell **A20**.

f. Confirm that the retrieved list meets the criteria as shown in FIGURE H-20.

g. Save the workbook, then preview the worksheet.

FIGURE H-20

Skills Review (continued)

4. **Look up values in a table.**

   a. Click the Summary sheet tab. Use the Name Manager to view the table names in the workbook, then close the dialog box.

   b. You will use a lookup function to locate an employee's annual compensation; enter the Employee Number **2214** in cell A17.

   c. In cell B17, use the VLOOKUP function and enter **A17** as the Lookup_value, **Table2** as the Table_array, **10** as the Col_index_num, and **FALSE** as the Range_lookup; observe the compensation displayed for that employee number, then check it against the table to make sure it is correct.

   d. Replace the existing Employee Number in cell A17 with **4177**, and view the annual compensation for that employee.

   e. Format cell B17 with the Accounting format with the $ symbol and no decimal places.

   f. Save the workbook.

5. **Summarize table data.**

   a. You want to enter a database function to average the annual salaries by branch, using the Emergency Medical Department as the initial criterion. In cell E17, use the DAVERAGE function, and click the upper-left corner of cell A1 twice to select the table and its header row as the Database, select cell G1 for the Field, and select the range D16:D17 for the Criteria. Verify that the average Emergency Medical Department salary is 91480.

   b. Test the function further by entering the text **Radiology** in cell D17. When the criterion is entered, cell E17 should display 58500.

   c. Format cell E17 in Accounting format with the $ symbol and no decimal places.

   d. Save the workbook.

6. **Validate table data.**

   a. Select the data in column E of the table, and set a validation criterion specifying that you want to allow a list of valid options.

   b. Enter a list of valid options that restricts the entries to **Radiology, Cardiology**, and **Emergency Medicine**. Remember to use a comma between each item in the list.

   c. Indicate that you want the options to appear in an in-cell drop-down list, then close the dialog box.

   d. Add a row to the table. Go to cell E12, then select Cardiology in the drop-down list.

   e. Select the data in column F in the table, and indicate that you want to restrict the data entered to only whole numbers. In the Minimum text box, enter **1000**; in the Maximum text box, enter **10000**. Close the dialog box.

   f. Click cell F12, enter **15000**, then press [Enter]. You should get an error message.

   g. Click Cancel, then enter **7000**.

   h. Complete the new record by adding an Employee Number of **1119**, a First Name of **Cate**, a Last Name of **Smith**, a Hire Date of **2/1/2016**, and Retirement Contribution of **$5000**. Format the range F12:J12 as Accounting with no decimal places and using the $ symbol. Compare your screen to FIGURE H-21.

   i. Add your name to the center section of the footer, save the worksheet, then preview the worksheet.

FIGURE H-21

	A	B	C	D		E	F	G	H	I	J
1	Employee Number	First Name	Last Name	Hire Date		Department	Monthly Salary	Annual Salary	Retirement Contribution	Benefits Dollars	Annual Compensation
2	1210	Maria	Lawson	2/12/2013	Radiology		$ 4,600	$ 55,200	$ 1,350	$ 12,696	$ 69,246
3	4510	Laurie	Warton	4/1/2014	Cardiology		$ 5,900	$ 70,800	$ 5,700	$ 16,284	$ 92,784
4	4177	Donna	Donnolly	5/6/2012	Emergency Medicine		$ 7,500	$ 90,000	$ 15,000	$ 20,700	$ 125,700
5	2571	Maria	Marlin	12/10/2013	Radiology		$ 8,500	$ 102,000	$ 18,000	$ 23,460	$ 143,460
6	2214	John	Greeley	2/15/2013	Radiology		$ 2,900	$ 34,800	$ 570	$ 8,004	$ 43,374
7	6587	Peter	Erickson	3/25/2013	Cardiology		$ 2,775	$ 33,300	$ 770	$ 7,659	$ 41,729
8	2123	Erin	Mallo	6/23/2012	Cardiology		$ 3,990	$ 47,880	$ 2,500	$ 11,012	$ 61,392
9	4439	Martin	Meng	8/3/2015	Emergency Medicine		$ 6,770	$ 81,240	$ 5,000	$ 18,685	$ 104,925
10	9807	Harry	Rumeriz	9/29/2014	Emergency Medicine		$ 8,600	$ 103,200	$ 14,000	$ 23,736	$ 140,936
11	3944	Joyce	Roberts	5/12/2013	Radiology		$ 3,500	$ 42,000	$ 900	$ 9,660	$ 52,560
12	1119	Cate	Smith	2/1/2016	Cardiology		$ 7,000	$ 84,000	$ 5,000	$ 19,320	$ 108,320
13											
14											
15											
16	Employee Number	Annual Compensation			Department	Average Annual Salary					
17	4177	$ 125,700			Radiology	$ 58,500					
18											
19											

Skills Review (continued)

7. Create subtotals.

a. Click the Subtotals sheet tab.

b. Use the Department field list arrow to sort the table in ascending order by department.

c. Convert the table to a range.

d. Group and create subtotals of the Annual Compensation data by department, using the SUM function.

e. Click the 2 outline button on the outline to display only the subtotals and the grand total. Compare your screen to FIGURE H-22.

f. Enter your name in the worksheet footer, save the workbook, then preview the worksheet.

g. Save the workbook, close the workbook, exit Excel, then submit your workbook to your instructor.

FIGURE H-22

		A	B	C	D	E	F	G	H	I	J	K	L
	1	Employee Number	First Name	Last Name	Hire Date	Department	Monthly Salary	Annual Salary	Retirement Contribution	Benefits Dollars	Annual Compensation		
+	5					Cardiology Total					$ 195,905		
+	9					Emergency Medicine Total					$ 371,561		
+	14					Radiology Total					$ 308,640		
−	15					Grand Total					$ 876,107		
	16												

Independent Challenge 1

As the manager of Boston Dental, a dental supply distributor, you spend a lot of time managing your inventory. To help with this task, you have created an Excel table that you can extract information from using filters. You also need to add data validation and summary information to the table.

a. Start Excel, open the file EMP H-3.xlsx from the location where you store your Data Files, then save it as **EMP H-Dental**.

b. Using the table data on the Inventory sheet, create a filter to display information about only the product bond refill. Clear the filter.

c. Use a Custom Filter to generate a list of products with a quantity greater than 15. Clear the filter.

d. Copy the labels in cells A1:F1 into A16:F16. Type **Retention Pins** in cell A17, and type **Small** in cell C17. Use the Advanced Filter with a criteria range of A16:F17 to extract a table of small retention pins to the range of cells beginning in cell A20. Enter your name in the worksheet footer, save the workbook, then preview the worksheet.

e. On the Summary sheet tab, select the table data in column B. Open the Data Validation dialog box, then indicate you want to use a validation list with the acceptable entries of **Barnes, Blake, Lyon, Maxwell**. Make sure the In-cell dropdown check box is selected.

f. Test the data validation by trying to change a cell in column B of the table to **Lane**.

g. Using FIGURE H-23 as a guide, enter a function in cell E18 that calculates the total quantity of bond refill available in your inventory. Enter your name in the worksheet footer, preview the worksheet, then save the workbook.

h. On the Subtotals sheet, sort the table in ascending order by product. Convert the table to a range. Insert subtotals by product using the Sum function, then select Quantity in the "Add Subtotal to" box. Remove the check box for the Total field, if necessary. Use the appropriate button on the outline to display only the subtotals and grand total. Save the workbook, then preview the worksheet.

i. Submit the workbook to your instructor. Close the workbook, then exit Excel.

FIGURE H-23

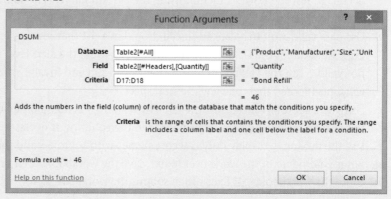

Independent Challenge 2

You work for a laboratory supply company that sells supplies to area clinics and hospitals. Customers work with sales representatives in both the Boston and Salem locations. You have put together an invoice table to track sales for the month of October. Now that you have this table, you would like to manipulate it in several ways. First, you want to filter the table to show only invoices over a certain amount with certain order dates. You also want to subtotal the total column for each office. To prevent data entry errors you will restrict entries in the Order Date column. Finally, you would like to add a database and lookup functions to your worksheet to efficiently retrieve data from the table.

a. Start Excel, open the file EMP H-4.xlsx from the location where you store your Data Files, then save it as **EMP H-Lab Supplies**.

b. Use the Advanced Filter to show invoices with amounts more than $3,500 ordered before 10/15/2016, using cells A27:B28 to enter your criteria and extracting the results to cell A33. (*Hint*: You don't need to specify an entire row as the criteria range.) Enter your name in the worksheet footer.

c. Use the Data Validation dialog box to restrict entries to those with order dates between 10/1/2016 and 6/31/2016. Test the data restrictions by attempting to enter an invalid date in cell D25.

d. Enter **23721** in cell G28. Enter a VLOOKUP function in cell E28 to retrieve the total based on the invoice number entered in cell D28. Make sure you have an exact match with the invoice number. Format E28 using Accounting format with two decimal places. Test the function with the invoice number 23718.

e. Enter the date **10/1/2016** in cell G28. Use the database function, DCOUNT, in cell H28 to count the number of invoices for the date in cell G28. Save the workbook, then preview the worksheet.

f. On the Subtotals worksheet, sort the table in ascending order by Office, then convert the table to a range. Create subtotals showing the totals for Boston and Salem offices. Adjust the column widths if necessary to display the totals. Display only the subtotals for the Boston and Salem offices along with the grand total.

g. Save the workbook, preview the worksheet, close the workbook, then exit Excel. Submit the workbook to your instructor.

Independent Challenge 3

As the office manager for a physical therapy clinic, you keep track of patients' reimbursement data. The therapists work on teams at the clinic and you have been asked to supply information for each team on a monthly basis. You will manipulate a table with September appointment data using database functions and subtotals.

a. Start Excel, open the file EMP H-5.xlsx from the location where you store your Data Files, then save it as **EMP H-PT Clinic**.

b. On the Schedule worksheet, create an advanced filter that extracts records with the following criteria to cell A42: reimbursed amounts greater than $1500 having dates either before 9/10/2016 or after 9/19/2016. (*Hint*: Recall that when you want records to meet one criterion or another, you need to place the criteria on separate lines.)

c. Use the DSUM function in cell H2 to let worksheet users find the total reimbursed amounts for the team entered in cell G2. Format the cell containing the total reimbursed using the Accounting format with the $ symbol and no decimals. Test the DSUM function using the D team name. (The sum for the D team should be $9,148.) Preview the worksheet.

d. Use data validation to create an in-cell drop-down list that restricts team entries to "A", "B", "C", and "D". Use the Error Alert tab of the Data Validation dialog box to set the alert level to the Warning style with the message "Data is not valid." Test the validation in the table with valid and invalid entries. Save the workbook, enter your name in the worksheet footer, then preview the worksheet.

e. Using the Subtotals sheet, sort the table by team in ascending order. Convert the table to a range, and add Subtotals to the reimbursed amounts by team. Widen the columns, if necessary.

f. Use the outline to display only category names with subtotals and the grand total.

g. Enter your name in the worksheet footer, save the workbook, then preview the worksheet.

h. Close the workbook, exit Excel, then submit the workbook to your instructor.

Independent Challenge 4: Explore

You are an assistant to an optician where you track the inventory of eye products in an Excel worksheet. You would like to use conditional formatting in your worksheet to help track the products that need to be reordered as well as your inventory expenses. You would also like to prevent data entry errors using data validation. Finally, you would like to add an area to quickly lookup prices and quantities for customers.

a. Start Excel, open the file EMP H-6.xlsx from the location where you store your Data Files, then save it as **EMP H-Eyewear**.

b. Use conditional formatting to add icons to the quantity field using the following criteria: quantities greater than or equal to 300 are formatted with a green circle, quantities greater than or equal to 100 but less than 300 are formatted with a yellow circle, and quantities less than 100 are formatted with a red circle. If your icons are incorrect, select the data in the Quantity field, click the Conditional Formatting button in the Styles group of the HOME tab, click Manage Rules, click the Show formatting for list arrow, select Current Selection, then double click Icon Set and compare your formatting rule to FIGURE H-24. (*Hint*: You may need to click in the top Value text box for the correct value to display for the red circle.)

c. Conditionally format the Total data using Top/Bottom Rules to emphasize the cells containing the top 30 percent with red text.

d. Add another rule to format the bottom 20 percent in the Total column with purple text.

e. Restrict the Wholesale Price field entries to decimal values between 0 and 100. Add an input message of **Prices must be less than $100**. Add a Warning-level error message of **Please check price**. Test the validation entering a price of $105 in cell D3 and allow the new price to be entered.

f. Below the table, create a product lookup area with the following labels in adjacent cells: **Product Number**, **Wholesale Price**, **Quantity**.

g. Enter 1544 under the label Product Number in your products lookup area.

h. In the product lookup area, enter lookup functions to locate the wholesale price and quantity information for the product number that you entered in the previous step. Make sure you match the product number exactly. Format the wholesale price with the Accounting format with the $ symbol and two decimal places.

i. Enter your name in the center section of the worksheet header, save the workbook then preview the worksheet comparing it to FIGURE H-25.

j. Close the workbook, exit Excel, then submit the workbook to your instructor.

FIGURE H-24

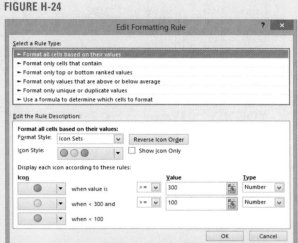

FIGURE H-25

Product Number	Category	Vendor	Wholesale Price		Quantity	Total
			Your Name			
			American Eyewear			
1122	Reading Glasses	Berkley	$105.00		125	$13,125.00
1132	Reading Glasses	Mallory	$10.66		68	$724.88
1184	Sports Eyewear	Bromen	$18.21		187	$3,405.27
1197	Sunglasses	Lincoln	$32.22		210	$6,766.20
1225	Frames	Berkley	$33.99		87	$2,957.13
1267	Frames	Mallory	$34.19		240	$8,205.60
1298	Sports Eyewear	Berkley	$21.97		375	$8,238.75
1345	Reading Glasses	Lincoln	$21.88		105	$2,297.40
1367	Safety Goggles	Lincoln	$17.18		168	$2,886.24
1398	Sports Eyewear	Bromen	$30.39		97	$2,947.83
1422	Sunglasses	Lincoln	$25.19		157	$3,954.83
1436	Cases	Mallory	$5.12		81	$414.72
1445	Sunglasses	Rand	$45.20		150	$6,780.00
1456	Custom	Berkley	$82.33		377	$31,038.41
1498	Safety Goggles	Rand	$19.22		51	$980.22
1521	Cases	Lincoln	$7.84		87	$682.08
1531	Lenses	Lincoln	$40.34		197	$7,946.98
1544	Reading Glasses	Bromen	$23.01		472	$10,860.72
1556	Frames	Bromen	$45.06		12	$540.72
1569	Sports Eyewear	Rand	$17.36		178	$3,090.08
1578	Sunglasses	Mallory	$63.22		35	$2,212.70
1622	Reading Glasses	Mallory	$25.33		874	$22,138.42
1634	Cases	Berkley	$18.47		501	$9,253.47
1657	Sunglasses	Bromen	$34.55		10	$345.50
1688	Safety Goggles	Rand	$18.66		73	$1,362.18
1723	Reading Glasses	Rand	$8.64		534	$4,613.76
1736	Sports Eyewear	Bromen	$25.66		15	$384.90
1798	Sports Eyewear	Mallory	$32.78		640	$20,979.20
1822	Cases	Mallory	$17.44		86	$1,499.84

Product Number	Wholesale Price	Quantity
1544	$ 23.01	472

Visual Workshop

Open the file EMP H-7.xlsx from the location where you save your Data Files, then save it as **EMP H-Schedule**. Complete the worksheet as shown in FIGURE H-26. An in-cell drop-down list has been added to the data entered in the Room field. The range A18:G21 is extracted from the table using the criteria in cells A15:A16. Add your name to the worksheet footer, save the workbook, preview the worksheet, then submit the workbook to your instructor.

FIGURE H-26

	A	B	C	D	E	F	G	H
1				**Prenatal Yoga Classes**				
2								
3	**Class Code**	**Class**	**Time**	**Day**	**Room**	**Fee**	**Instructor**	
4	YOG100	Basics	7:30 AM	Monday	Mat Room	$15	Malloy	
5	YOG101	Power	8:00 AM	Tuesday	Equipment Room	$20	Gregg	
6	YOG102	Hatha	9:00 AM	Wednesday	Mat Room	$15	Malloy	
7	YOG103	Kripalu	10:00 AM	Monday	Mat Room	$15	Brent	
8	YOG104	Basics	11:00 AM	Friday	Mat Room	$15	Paulson	
9	YOG105	Power	12:00 PM	Saturday	Equipment Room	$20	Dally	
10	YOG106	Hatha	12:00 PM	Tuesday	Mat Room	$15	Rand	
11	YOG107	Power	2:00 PM	Monday	Equipment Room	$20	Walton	
12	YOG108	Basics	4:00 PM	Tuesday	Mat Room	15	Malloy	
13					Please select Mat Room or Equipment Room			
14								
15	**Class**							
16	**Basics**							
17								
18	**Class Code**	**Class**	**Time**	**Day**	**Room**	**Fee**	**Instructor**	
19	YOG100	Basics	7:30 AM	Monday	Mat Room	$15	Malloy	
20	YOG104	Basics	11:00 AM	Friday	Mat Room	$15	Paulson	
21	YOG108	Basics	4:00 PM	Tuesday	Mat Room	$15	Malloy	
22								

Analyzing Table Data

Working in the Cloud

CASE ▶ In your job for the Vancouver branch of Quest Specialty Travel, you travel frequently, you often work from home, and you also collaborate online with colleagues and clients. You want to learn how you can use SkyDrive with Office 2013 to work in the Cloud so that you can access and work on your files anytime and anywhere. (*Note*: SkyDrive and Office Web Apps are dynamic Web pages, and might change over time, including the way they are organized and how commands are performed. The steps and figures in this appendix reflect these pages at the time this book was published.)

Unit Objectives

After completing this unit, you will be able to:

- Understand Office 2013 in the Cloud
- Work Online
- Explore SkyDrive
- Manage Files on SkyDrive

- Share Files
- Explore Office Web Apps
- Complete a Team Project

Files You Will Need

WEB-1.pptx
WEB-2.docx

Understand Office 2013 in the Cloud

Learning
Outcomes
• Describe Office
2013 Cloud
Computing
features
• Define SkyDrive
• Define Office
Web Apps

The term **cloud computing** refers to the process of working with files and apps online. You may already be familiar with Web-based e-mail accounts such as Gmail and outlook.com. These applications are **cloud-based**, which means that you do not need a program installed on your computer to run them. Office 2013 has also been designed as a cloud-based application. When you work in Office 2013, you can choose to store your files "in the cloud" so that you can access them on any device connected to the Internet. **CASE** ➤ *You review the concepts related to working online with Office 2013.*

DETAILS

- **How does Office 2013 work in the Cloud?**

  When you launch an Office application such as Word or Excel, you might see your name and maybe even your picture in the top right corner of your screen. This information tells you that you have signed in to Office 2013, either with your personal account or with an account you are given as part of an organization such as a company or school. When you are signed in to Office and click the FILE tab in any Office 2013 application such as Word or Excel, you see a list of the files that you have used recently on your current computer and on any other connected device such as a laptop, a tablet or even a Windows phone. The file path appears beneath each filename so that you can quickly identify its location as shown in FIGURE WEB-1. Office 2013 also remembers your personalized settings so that they are available on all the devices you use.

- **What are roaming settings?**

  A **roaming setting** is a setting that travels with you on every connected device. Examples of roaming settings include your personal settings such as your name and picture, the files you've used most recently, your list of connected services such as Facebook and Twitter, and any custom dictionaries you've created. Two particularly useful roaming settings are the Word Resume Reading Position setting and the PowerPoint Last Viewed Slide setting. For example, when you open a PowerPoint presentation that you've worked on previously, you will see a message similar to the one shown in FIGURE WEB-2.

- **What is SkyDrive?**

  SkyDrive is an online storage and file sharing service. When you are signed in to your computer with your Microsoft account, you receive access to your own SkyDrive, which is your personal storage area on the Internet. On your SkyDrive, you are given space to store up to 7 GB of data online. A SkyDrive location is already created on your computer as shown in FIGURE WEB-3. Every file you save to SkyDrive is synced among your computers and your personal storage area on SkyDrive.com. The term **synced** (which stands for synchronized) means that when you add, change or delete files on one computer, the same files on your other devices are also updated.

- **What are Office Web Apps?**

  Office Web Apps are versions of Microsoft Word, Excel, PowerPoint, and OneNote that you can access online from your SkyDrive. An Office Web App does not include all of the features and functions included with the full Office version of its associated application. However, you can use the Office Web App from any computer that is connected to the Internet, even if Microsoft Office 2013 is not installed on that computer.

- **How do SkyDrive and Office Web Apps work together?**

  You can create a file in Office 2013 using Word, Excel, PowerPoint, or OneNote and then save it to your SkyDrive. You can then open the Office file saved to SkyDrive and edit it using your Office 2013 apps. If you do not have Office 2013 installed on the computer you are using, you can edit the file using your Web browser and the corresponding Office Web App. You can also use an Office Web App to create a new file, which is saved automatically to SkyDrive while you work and you can download a file created with an Office Web App and work with the file in the full version of the corresponding Office application.

FIGURE WEB-1: FILE tab in Microsoft Excel

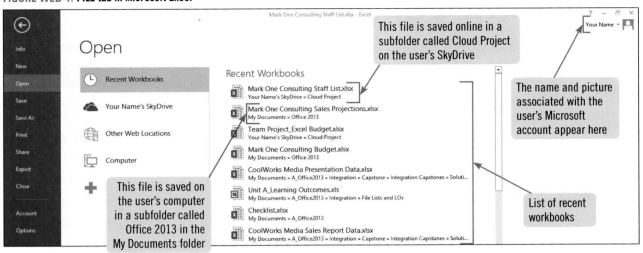

FIGURE WEB-2: PowerPoint Last Viewed Slide setting

FIGURE WEB-3: Saving a Word file on SkyDrive

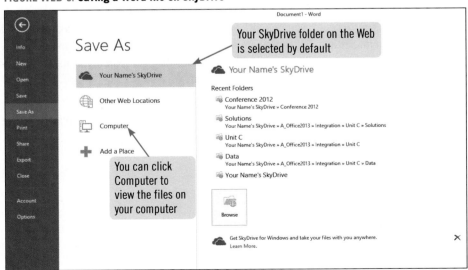

Work Online

When you work on your own computer, you are usually signed in to your Microsoft account automatically. When you use another person's computer or a public computer, you will be required to enter the password associated with your Microsoft account to access files you have saved on Windows SkyDrive. You know you are signed in to Windows when you see your name and possibly your picture in the top right corner of your screen. *Note*: To complete the steps below, you need to be signed in to your Microsoft account. If you do not have a Microsoft account, see "Getting a Microsoft account" in the yellow box. **CASE** ▶ *You explore the settings associated with your account, learn how to switch accounts, and sign out of an account.*

STEPS

1. **Sign in to Windows, if necessary, launch Word, click Blank document, then verify that your name appears in the top right corner of your screen**

2. **Click the list arrow to the right of your name, as shown in FIGURE WEB-4, then click About me and sign in if prompted**

   Internet Explorer opens and your Profile page appears. Here, you can add or edit your contact information and information about your workplace. You can also change the name and picture that appear in the top right corner of your window.

3. **Click the list arrow next to Profile in the top left corner of your screen, above the picture**

   The tiles representing the services your Windows account is connected to appear as shown in FIGURE WEB-5. Note that if you have connected your Microsoft account to accounts in other services such as Facebook, LinkedIn, or outlook.com, you will see these connections in the appropriate app. For example, your connections to Facebook and LinkedIn appear in the People app.

4. **Click a blank area below the apps tiles, click Your Name in the top right corner, then click Account settings**

   Either you are taken directly to the Microsoft account screen or, depending on your security settings, a Sign in screen appears. To make changes to your account, you might need to enter the password associated with your account. You can also choose to sign in with a different Microsoft account. Once you sign in, you can change the information associated with your account such as your name, email address, birth date, and password. You can also choose to close your Microsoft account, which deletes all the data associated with it.

5. **Click the Close button ✕ in the upper right corner of the window to remove the Sign-in window, click Close all tabs to return to Word, then click the list arrow ▼ next to Your Name in the top right corner of the Word window**

   To sign out of your account, you can click Sign Out at the top of the Accounts dialog box that appears when you click Account Settings. When you are working on your own computers, you will rarely need to sign out of your account. However, if you are working on a public computer, you may want to sign out of your account to avoid having your files accessible to other users.

6. **Click Switch account**

   You can choose to sign into another Microsoft account or to an account with an organization.

7. **Click the Close button ✕**

   You are returned to a blank document in Word.

8. **Exit Word**

FIGURE WEB-4: Viewing Windows account options in Word

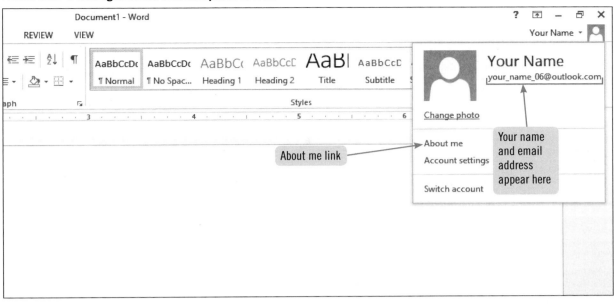

FIGURE WEB-5: Connected services associated with a Profile

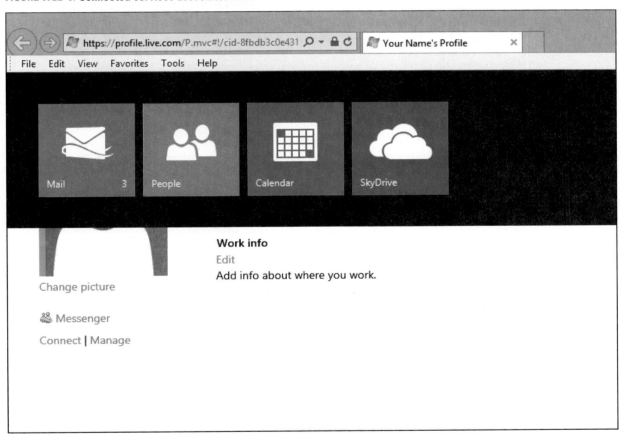

Getting a Microsoft account

If you have been working with Windows and Office 2013, you might already have a Microsoft account, which was previously referred to as a Windows Live ID. You also have an account if you use outlook.com (formerly Hotmail), SkyDrive, Xbox LIVE, or have a Windows Phone. A Microsoft account consists of an email address and a password. If you wish to create a new Microsoft account, go to https://signup.live.com/ and follow the directions provided.

Explore SkyDrive

Learning Outcomes
• Save a file to SkyDrive
• Create a folder on SkyDrive

SkyDrive works like the hard drive on your computer. You can save and open files from SkyDrive, create folders, and manage your files. You can access the files you save on SkyDrive from any of your connected devices and from anywhere you have a computer connection. **CASE** ▶ *You open a PowerPoint presentation, save the file to your SkyDrive, then create a folder.*

STEPS

1. **Start PowerPoint, then open the file WEB-1.pptx from the location where you store your Data Files**

QUICK TIP
If you are signed in with your own account, you will see Your Name's Sky-Drive (for example, "Tom's SkyDrive").

2. **Click the FILE tab, click Save As, then click Your Name's SkyDrive (top selection) if it is not already selected**

3. **Click the Browse button**

    The Save As dialog box opens, showing the folders stored on your SkyDrive. You may have several folders already stored there or you may have none.

4. **Click New folder, type Cengage, then press [Enter]**

5. **Double-click Cengage, select WEB-1.pptx in the File name text box, type WEB-QST Vancouver 1 as shown in** FIGURE WEB-6, **then click Save**

    The file is saved to the Cengage folder on the SkyDrive that is associated with your Microsoft account. The PowerPoint window reappears.

6. **Click the FILE tab, click Close, click the FILE tab, then click Open**

    WEB-QST Vancouver 1.pptx appears as the first file listed in the Recent Presentations list, and the path to your Cengage folder on your SkyDrive appears beneath it.

7. **Click WEB-QST Vancouver 1.pptx to open it, then type your name where indicated on the title slide**

8. **Click Slide 2 in the Navigation pane, select 20% in the third bullet, type 30%, click the FILE tab, click Save As, click Cengage under Current Folder, change the file name to WEB-QST Vancouver 2, then click Save**

9. **Exit PowerPoint**

    A new version of the presentation is saved to the Cengage folder that you created on SkyDrive.

How to disable default saving to Skydrive

You can specify how you want to save files from Office 2013 applications. By default, files are saved to locations you specify on your SkyDrive. You can change the default to be a different location. In Word, PowerPoint, or Excel, click the FILE tab, then click Options. Click Save in the left sidebar, then in the Save section, click the Save to Computer by default check box, as shown in FIGURE WEB-7. Click OK to close the PowerPoint Options dialog box. The Save options you've selected will be active in Word, PowerPoint, and Excel, regardless of which application you were using when you changed the option.

FIGURE WEB-6: Saving a presentation to SkyDrive

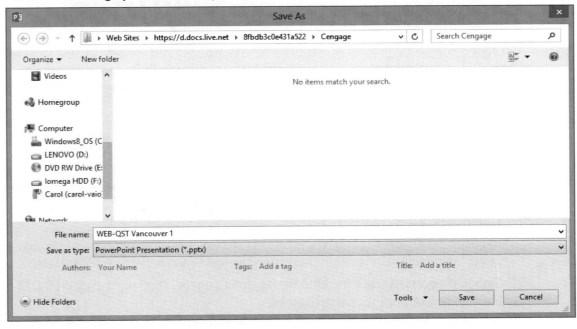

FIGURE WEB-7: Changing the default Save location in PowerPoint

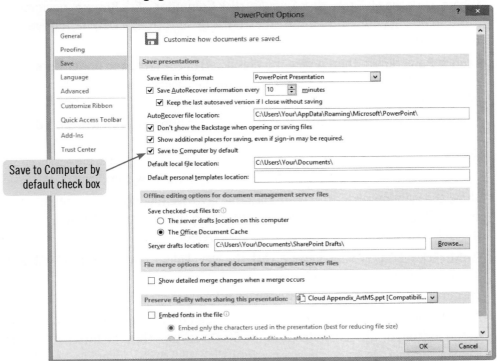

Save to Computer by default check box

Manage Files on SkyDrive

You are automatically connected to SkyDrive when you sign into your Microsoft account and launch an Office 2013 application. You can also access SkyDrive through your Web browser or from the SkyDrive App in Windows 8. When you start the SkyDrive App, you can upload and download files, create folders, and delete files. You can also download the SkyDrive app to your tablet or other mobile device so you can access files wherever you have an Internet connection. When you access SkyDrive from Internet Explorer, you can do more file management tasks, including renaming and moving files. **CASE** ▶ *You explore how to work with SkyDrive from your Web browser and from the SkyDrive App.*

1. **Launch Internet Explorer or another Web browser, type** skydrive.com **in the Address box, then press [Enter]**

   If you are signed in to your Microsoft account, your SkyDrive opens. If you are not signed in, the login page appears where you can enter the email address and password associated with your Microsoft account.

2. **Sign in if necessary, click the blue tile labeled** Cengage, **then right-click WEB-QST Vancouver 1.pptx as shown in** FIGURE WEB-8

   You can open the file in the PowerPoint Web App or in PowerPoint, download the file to your computer, share it, embed it, and perform other actions such as renaming and deleting.

3. **Click** Download, **click** Open **in the bar at the bottom of the screen, then click** Enable Editing

   The presentation opens in PowerPoint where you can save it to your computer hard drive or back to SkyDrive.

4. **Click the** DESIGN **tab, click the** More button **☰ in the Themes group, select the** Wisp **theme, click the** FILE **tab, click** Save As, **click** Computer, **click** Browse, **navigate to a location on your computer or on an external drive such as a USB flash drive, click** Save, **then exit PowerPoint**

5. **Launch PowerPoint, then notice the files listed in the left pane under Recent**

   The file you just saved to your computer or external drive appears first and the file saved to the Cengage folder on SkyDrive appears second.

6. **Click the second listing, notice that the file is not updated with the Wisp design, then exit PowerPoint**

   When you download a file from SkyDrive, changes you make are not saved to the version on SkyDrive. You can also access SkyDrive from your Windows 8 screen by using the SkyDrive app.

7. **Show the Windows 8 Start screen, click the** SkyDrive **tile, open the Cengage folder, right-click WEB-QST Vancouver 1, view the buttons on the taskbar as shown in** FIGURE WEB-9, **click the** Delete **button on the taskbar, then click** Delete

8. **Right-click WEB-QST Vancouver 2, click the** New Folder **button on the taskbar, type Illustrated, then click** Create folder

   You can rename and move files in SkyDrive through Internet Explorer.

9. **Move the mouse pointer to the top of the screen until it becomes the hand pointer, drag to the bottom of the screen to close the SkyDrive App, click the** Internet Explorer **tile on the Start screen, go to** skydrive.com, **right-click WEB-QST Vancouver 2 on the SkyDrive site, click** Move to, **click the** ▶ **next to Cengage, click Illustrated, then click** Move

FIGURE WEB-8: File management options on SkyDrive

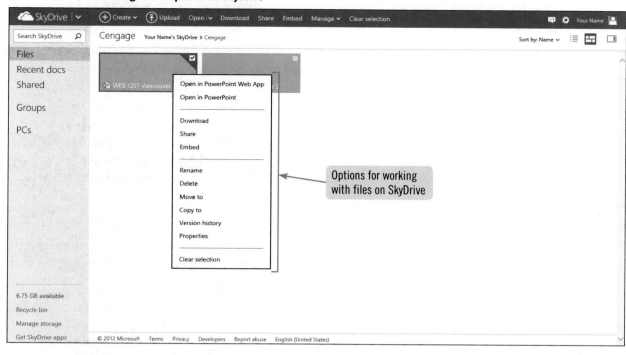

Options for working with files on SkyDrive

FIGURE WEB-9: File management options on SkyDrive App

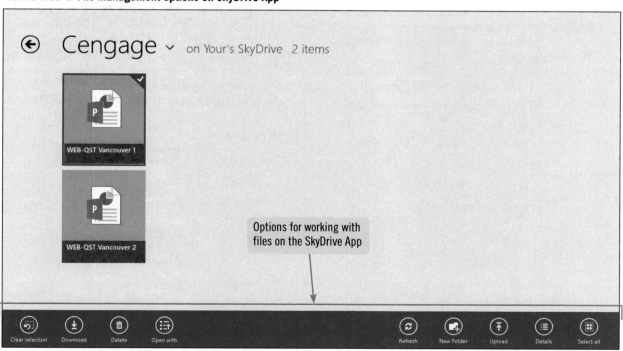

Options for working with files on the SkyDrive App

Share Files

One of the great advantages of working with SkyDrive is that you can share your files with others. Suppose, for example, that you want a colleague to review a presentation you created in PowerPoint and then add a new slide. You can, of course, e-mail the presentation directly to your colleague who can then make changes and e-mail the presentation back. Alternatively, you can share the PowerPoint file directly from SkyDrive. Your colleague can edit the file using the PowerPoint Web App or the full version of PowerPoint, and then you can check the updated file on SkyDrive. In this way, you and your colleague are working with just one version of the presentation that you both can update. **CASE** *You have decided to share files in the Illustrated folder that you created in the previous lesson with another individual. You start by sharing files with your partner and your partner can share files with you.*

STEPS

1. **Identify a partner with whom you can work, and obtain his or her e-mail address; you can choose someone in your class or someone on your e-mail list, but it should be someone who will be completing these steps when you are**

2. **Right-click the Illustrated folder, then click Sharing as shown in** FIGURE WEB-10

3. **Type the e-mail address of your partner**

4. **Click in the Include a personal message box, then type Here's the presentation we're working on together as shown in** FIGURE WEB-11

5. **Verify that the Recipients can edit check box is selected, then click Share**

   Your partner will receive a message advising him or her that you have shared the WEB-QST Vancouver 2.pptx file. If your partner is completing the steps at the same time, you will receive an e-mail from your partner.

6. **Check your e-mail for a message advising you that your partner has shared a folder with you**

   The subject of the e-mail message will be "[Name] has shared documents with you."

7. **If you have received the e-mail, click the Show content link that appears in the warning box, if necesary, then click WEB-QST Vancouver 2.pptx in the body of the e-mail message**

   The PowerPoint presentation opens in the Microsoft PowerPoint Web App. You will work in the Web App in the next lesson.

Co-authoring documents

You can work on a document, presentation, or workbook simultaneously with a partner. First, save the file to your SkyDrive. Click the FILE tab, click Share, then click Invite People. Enter the email addresses of the people you want to work on the file with you and then click Share. Once your partner has received, opened, and started editing the document, you can start working together. You will see a notification in the status bar that someone is editing the document with you. When you click the notification, you can see the name of the other user and their picture if they have one attached to their Windows account. When your partner saves, you'll see his or changes in green shading which goes away the next time you save. You'll have an opportunity to co-author documents when you complete the Team Project at the end of this appendix.

FIGURE WEB-10: **Sharing a file from SkyDrive**

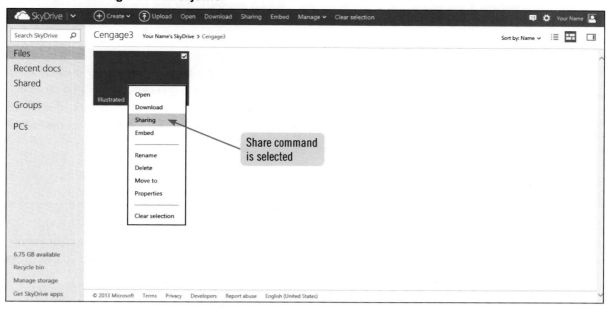

FIGURE WEB-11: **Sharing a file with another person**

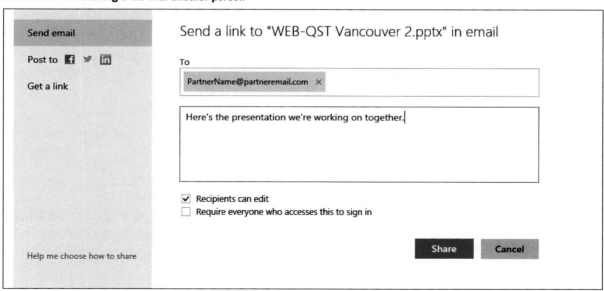

Explore Office Web Apps

**Learning
Outcomes**
- Edit a presentation
  with PowerPoint
  Web App
- Open a presenta-
  tion from
  PowerPoint
  Web App

As you have learned, a Web App is a scaled-down version of an Office program. Office Web Apps include Word, Excel, PowerPoint, and OneNote. You can use the Office Web Apps to create and edit documents even if you don't have Office 2013 installed on your computer and you can use them on other devices such as tablets and smartphones. From SkyDrive, you can also open the document in the full Office application if the application is installed on the computer you are using. **CASE** ▶ *You use the PowerPoint Web App and the full version of PowerPoint to edit the presentation.*

STEPS

1. **Click EDIT PRESENTATION, then click Edit in PowerPoint Web App**

   Presentations opened using the PowerPoint Web App have the same look and feel as presentations opened using the full version of PowerPoint. However, like all of the Office Web Apps, the PowerPoint Web App has fewer features available than the full version of PowerPoint.

2. **Review the Ribbon and its tabs to familiarize yourself with the commands you can access from the PowerPoint Web App**

   TABLE WEB-1 summarizes the commands that are available.

   TROUBLE
   You need to click the
   text first, click it
   again, then drag to
   select it.

3. **Click Slide 3, click the text Hornby Island, click it again and select it, then type Tofino so the bullet item reads Tofino Sea Kayaking**

4. **Click outside the text box, click the DESIGN tab, then click the More Themes list arrow ▼ to show the selection of designs available**

   A limited number of designs are available on the PowerPoint Web App. When you want to use a design or a command that is not available on the PowerPoint Web App, you open the file in the full version of PowerPoint.

5. **Click on a blank area of the slide, click OPEN IN POWERPOINT at the top of the window, then click Yes in response to the message**

6. **Click the DESIGN tab, click the More button ▼ in the Themes group to expand the Themes gallery, select the Quotable design as shown in FIGURE WEB-12, click the picture on Slide 1, then press [Delete]**

7. **Click the Save button 🖫 on the Quick Access toolbar**

   The Save button includes a small icon indicating you are saving to SkyDrive and not to your computer's hard drive or an external drive.

8. **Click the Close button ✖ to exit PowerPoint**

   You open the document again to verify that your partner made the same changes.

9. **Launch PowerPoint, click WEB-QST Vancouver 2.pptx at the top of the Recent list, verify that the Quotable design is applied and the picture is removed, then exit PowerPoint**

Exploring other Office Web Apps

Three other Office Web Apps are Word, Excel, and OneNote. You can share files on SkyDrive directly from any of these applications using the same method you used to share files from PowerPoint. To familiarize yourself with the commands available in PowerPoint. To familiarize yourself with the commands available

in an Office Web App, open the file and then review the commands on each tab on the Ribbon. If you want to perform a task that is not available in the Web App, open the file in the full version of the application.

FIGURE WEB-12: Selecting the Quotable design

TABLE WEB-1: Commands on the PowerPoint Web App

tab	category/group	options
FILE	Info	• Open in PowerPoint (also available on the toolbar above the document window)
		• Previous Versions
	Save As	• Where's the Save Button?: In PowerPoint Web App, the presentation is being saved automatically so there is no Save button
		• Download: use to download a copy of the presentation to your computer
	Print	• Create a printable PDF of the presentation that you can then open and print
	Share	• Share with people - you can invite others to view and edit your presentation
		• Embed - include the presentation in a blog on Web site
	About	• Try Microsoft Office, Terms of Use, and Privacy and Cookies
	Help	• Help with PowerPoint questions, Give Feedback to Microsoft, and modify how you can view the presentation (for example, text only)
	Exit	• Close the presentation and exit to view SkyDrive folders
HOME	Clipboard	• Cut, Copy, Paste, Format Painter
	Delete	• Delete a slide
	Slides	• Add a new slide, duplicate a slide, hide a slide
	Font	• Change the font, size, style, and color of selected text
	Paragraph	• Add bullets and numbering, indent text, align text, and change text direction
	Drawing	• Add text boxes and shapes, arrange them on the slide, apply Quick Styles, modify shape fill and outline, and duplicate a shape
INSERT	Slides	• Add new slides with selected layout
	Images	• Add pictures from your computer, online pictures, or screen shots
	Illustrations	• Add shapes, SmartArt, or charts
	Links	• Add links or actions to objects
	Text	• Add comments, text boxes, headers and footers, and other text elements
	Comments	• Add comments
DESIGN	Themes	• Apply a limited number of themes to a presentation and apply variants to a selected theme
		• Apply variants to a selected theme
ANIMATIONS	Animation	• Apply a limited number of animation effects to a slide element and modify existing timings
TRANSITIONS	Transitions to This Slide	• Apply a limited number of transition effects to slides and chose to apply the effect to all slides
VIEW	Presentation Views	• You can view the slide in Editing View, Reading View, Slide Show View, and Notes View and you can show any comments made by users who worked on PowerPoint using the full version

Team Project

Introduction

From SkyDrive, you can easily collaborate with others to produce documents, presentations, and spreadsheets that include each user's input. Instead of emailing a document to colleagues and then waiting for changes, you can both work on the document at the same time online. To further explore how you can work with SkyDrive and Office 2013, you will work with two other people to complete a team project. The subject of the team project is the planning of a special event of your choice, such as a class party, a lecture, or a concert. The special event should be limited to a single afternoon or evening.

Follow the guidelines provided below to create the files required for the team project. When you have completed the project, the team will submit a Word document containing information about your project, as well as three files related to the project: a Word document, a PowerPoint presentation, and an Excel workbook.

Project Setup

As a team, work together to complete the following tasks.

a. Share email addresses among all three team members.

b. Set up a time (either via email, an online chat session, Internet Messaging, or face to face) when you will get together to choose your topic and assign roles.

c. At your meeting, complete the table below with information about your team and your special event.

Team Name (last name of one team member or another name that describes the project.)
Team Members
Event type (for example, party, lecture, concert, etc.)
Event purpose (for example, fundraiser for a specific cause, celebrate the end of term, feature a special guest, etc.)
Event location, date, and time
Team Roles indicate who is responsible for each of the following three files (one file per team member)
Word document:
Excel workbook:
PowerPoint presentation:

Document Development

Individually, complete the tasks listed below for the file you are responsible for. You need to develop appropriate content, format the file attractively, and then be prepared to share the file with the other team members.

Word Document

The Word document contains a description of your special event and includes a table listing responsibilities and a time line. Create the Word document as follows:

1. Create a Cloud Project folder on your SkyDrive, then create a new Word document and save it as **Cloud Project_ Word Description** to the Cloud Project folder.

Document Development (continued)

2. Include a title with the name of your project and a subtitle with the names of your team members. Format the title with the Title style and the subtitle with the Subtitle style.

3. Write a paragraph describing the special event—its topics, purpose, the people involved, etc. You can paraphrase some of the information your team discussed in your meeting.

4. Create a table similar to the table shown below and then complete it with the required information. Include up to ten rows. A task could be "Contact the caterers" or "Pick up the speaker." Visualize the sequence of tasks required to put on the event.

Task	Person Responsible	Deadline

5. Format the table using the table style of your choice.

6. Save the document to your SkyDrive. You will share the document with your team members and receive feedback in the next section.

Excel Workbook

The Excel workbook contains a budget for the special event. Create the Excel workbook as follows:

1. Create a new Excel workbook and save it as **Cloud Project_Excel Budget** to the Cloud Project folder on your SkyDrive.

2. Create a budget that includes both the revenues you expect from the event (for example, ticket sales, donations, etc.) and the expenses. Expense items include advertising costs (posters, ads, etc.), food costs if the event is catered, transportation costs, etc. The revenues and expenses you choose will depend upon the nature of the project.

3. Make the required calculations to total all the revenue items and all the expense items.

4. Calculate the net profit (or loss) as the revenue minus the expenses.

5. Format the budget attractively using fill colors, border lines, and other enhancements to make the data easy to read.

6. Save the workbook to your SkyDrive. You will share the workbook with your team members and receive feedback in the next section.

PowerPoint Presentation

The PowerPoint presentation contains a presentation that describes the special event to an audience who may be interested in attending. Create the PowerPoint presentation as follows:

1. Create a new PowerPoint presentation and save it as **Cloud Project_PowerPoint Presentation** to the Cloud Project folder on your SkyDrive.

2. Create a presentation that consists of five slides including the title slide as follows:

   a. Slide 1: Title slide includes the name of the event and your team members

   b. Slide 2: Purpose of the party or event

   c. Slide 3: Location, time, and cost

   d. Slide 4: Chart showing a breakdown of costs (to be supplied when you co-author in the next section)

   e. Slide 5: Motivational closing slide designed to encourage the audience to attend; include appropriate pictures

3. Format the presentation attractively using the theme of your choice.

4. Save the presentation to your SkyDrive. You will share the presentation with your team members and receive feedback.

Co-Authoring on Skydrive

You need to share your file, add feedback to the other two files, then create a final version of your file. When you read the file created by the other two team members, you need to add additional data or suggestions. For example, if you created the Excel budget, you can provide the person who created the PowerPoint presentation with information about the cost breakdown. If you created the Word document, you can add information about the total revenue and expenses contained in the Excel budget to your description. You decide what information to add to each of the two files you work with.

1. Open the file you created.
2. Click the **FILE tab**, click **Share**, then click **Invite People**.
3. Enter the email addresses of the other two team members, then enter the following message: **Here's the file I created for our team project. Please make any changes, provide suggestions, and then save it. Thanks!** See FIGURE WEB-13.

FIGURE WEB-13

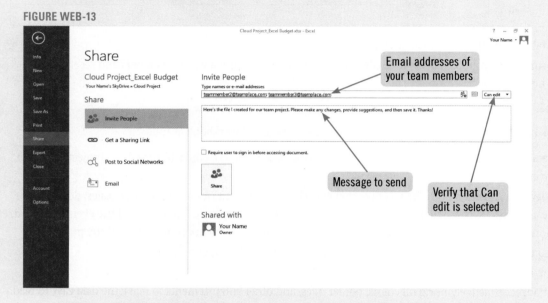

4. Click the **Share button**.
5. Allow team members time to add information and comments to your file. Team members should save frequently. When the file is saved, it is saved directly to your SkyDrive. Note that you can work together on the document or you can work separately. You can also choose to make changes with the full version of the Office 2013 applications or with the Office Web Apps. When someone is working on your file, you will see their user name on the status bar.
6. Decide which changes you want to keep, make any further changes you think are needed to make the document as clear as possible, then save a final version.

Project Summary

When you are pleased with the contents of your file and have provided feedback to your team members, assign a team member to complete the following tasks and then complete your portion as required.

1. Open **WEB-2.docx** from the location where you save your Data Files, then save it to your Cloud Project folder on your SkyDrive as **Cloud Project_Summary**.
2. Read the directions in the document, then enter your name as Team Member 1 and write a short description of your experience working with SkyDrive and Office 2013 to complete the team project.
3. Share the file with your team members and request that they add their own names and descriptions.
4. When all team members have finished working on the document, save all the changes.
5. Make sure you store all four files completed for the project in the Cloud Project appendix on your SkyDrive, then submit them to your instructor on behalf of your team.

Glossary

3-D reference A worksheet reference that uses values on other sheets or workbooks, effectively creating another dimension to a workbook.

Absolute cell reference In a formula, a cell address that refers to a specific cell and does not change when you copy the formula; indicated by a dollar sign before the column letter and/or row number. *See also* Relative cell reference.

Active The currently available document, program, or object; on the taskbar, when more than one program is open, the button for the active program appears slightly lighter.

Active cell The cell in which you are currently working.

Alignment The placement of cell contents in relation to a cell's edges; for example, left-aligned, centered, or right-aligned.

And logical condition A filtering feature that searches for records by specifying that all entered criteria must be matched.

Argument Information necessary for a formula or function to calculate an answer.

Arithmetic operators In a formula, symbols that perform mathematical calculations, such as addition (+), subtraction (–), multiplication (*), division (/), or exponentiation (^).

Ascending order In sorting an Excel field (column), the lowest value (the beginning of the alphabet, or the earliest date) appears at the beginning of the sorted data.

AutoFill Feature activated by dragging the fill handle; copies a cell's contents or continues a series of entries into adjacent cells.

AutoFill Options button Button that appears after using the fill handle to copy cell contents; enables you to choose to fill cells with specific elements (such as formatting) of the copied cell if desired.

AutoFilter A table feature that lets you click a list arrow and select criteria by which to display certain types of records; *also called* filter.

AutoFilter list arrows *See* Filter List arrows.

AutoFit A feature that automatically adjusts the width of a column or the height of a row to accommodate its widest or tallest entry.

Backstage view Appears when then FILE tab is clicked. The navigation bar on the left side contains commands to perform actions common to most Office programs, such as opening a file, saving a file, and closing the file.

Backward-compatible Software feature that enables documents saved in an older version of a program to be opened in a newer version of the program.

Banding Worksheet formatting in which adjacent rows and columns are formatted differently.

Calculated columns In a table, a column that automatically fills in cells with formula results, using a formula entered in only one other cell in the same column.

Calculation operators Symbols in a formula that indicate what type of calculation to perform on the cells, ranges, or values.

Category axis Horizontal axis in a chart, usually containing the names of data categories; in a 2-dimensional chart, also known as the x-axis.

Cell The intersection of a column and a row in a worksheet or table.

Cell address The location of a cell, expressed by cell coordinates; for example, the cell address of the cell in column A, row 1 is A1.

Cell pointer Dark rectangle that outlines the active cell.

Cell styles Predesigned combinations of formats based on themes that can be applied to selected cells to enhance the look of a worksheet.

Chart sheet A separate sheet in a workbook that contains only a chart, which is linked to the workbook data.

Charts Pictorial representations of worksheet data that make it easier to see patterns, trends, and relationships; *also called* graphs.

Clip A media file, such as a graphic, sound, animation, or movie.

Clip art A graphic image, such as a corporate logo, a picture, or a photo, that can be inserted into a document.

Clipboard A temporary Windows storage area that holds the selections you copy or cut.

Cloud computing Work done in a virtual environment using data, applications, and resources stored on servers and accessed over the Internet or a company's internal network rather than on users' computers.

Color scale In conditional formatting, a formatting scheme that uses a set of two, three, or four fill colors to convey relative values of data.

Column heading Box that appears above each column in a worksheet; identifies the column letter, such as A, B, etc.

Combination chart Two charts in one, such as a column chart combined with a line chart, that together graph related but dissimilar data.

Comparison operators In a formula, symbols that compare values for the purpose of true/false results.

Compatibility The ability of different programs to work together and exchange data.

Complex formula A formula that uses more than one arithmetic operator.

Conditional formatting A type of cell formatting that changes based on the cell's value or the outcome of a formula.

Consolidate To combine data on multiple worksheets and display the result on another worksheet.

Contextual tab A tab that is displayed only when a specific task can be performed: they appear in an accent color and close when no longer needed.

Criteria range In advanced filtering, a cell range containing one row of labels (usually a copy of column labels) and at least one additional row underneath it that contains the criteria you want to match.

Data entry area The unlocked portion of a worksheet where users are able to enter and change data.

Data marker A graphical representation of a data point in a chart, such as a bar or column.

Data point Individual piece of data plotted in a chart.

Data series The selected range in a worksheet whose related data points Excel converts into a chart.

Delimiter A separator such as a space, comma, or semicolon between elements in imported data.

Descending order In sorting an Excel field (column), the order that begins with the letter Z, the highest number, or the latest date of the values in a field.

Dialog box launcher An icon you can click to open a dialog box or task pane from which to choose related commands.

Document window Most of the screen in any given program, where you create a document, slide, or worksheet.

Dynamic page breaks In a larger workbook, horizontal or vertical dashed lines that represent the place where pages print separately. They also adjust automatically when you insert or delete rows or columns, or change column widths or row heights.

Edit To make a change to the contents of an active cell.

Electronic spreadsheet A computer program used to perform calculations and analyze and present numeric data.

Embedded chart A chart displayed as an object in a worksheet.

Exploding Visually pulling a slice of a pie chart away from the whole pie chart in order to add emphasis to the pie slice.

External reference indicator The exclamation point (!) used in a formula to indicate that a referenced cell is outside the active sheet.

Extract To place a copy of a filtered table in a range you specify in the Advanced Filter dialog box.

Field In a table (an Excel database), a column that describes a characteristic about records, such as first name or city.

Field name A column label that describes a field.

File A stored collection of data.

Filter list arrows List arrows that appear next to field names in an Excel table; used to display portions of your data. *Also called* AutoFilter list arrows.

Flash Fill An Excel feature that automatically fills in column or row data based on calculations you enter.

Font The typeface or design of a set of characters (letters, numbers, symbols, and punctuation marks).

Font size The size of characters, measured in units called points.

Font style Format such as bold, italic, and underlining that can be applied to change the way characters look in a worksheet or chart.

Format The appearance of a cell and its contents, including font, font styles, font color, fill color, borders, and shading. *See also* Number format.

Formula A set of instructions used to perform one or more numeric calculations, such as adding, multiplying, or averaging, on values or cells.

Formula bar The area above the worksheet grid where you enter or edit data in the active cell.

Formula prefix An arithmetic symbol, such as the equal sign (=), used to start a formula.

Freeze To hold in place selected columns or rows when scrolling in a worksheet that is divided in panes. *See also* Panes.

Function A special, predefined formula that provides a shortcut for a commonly used or complex calculation, such as SUM (for calculating a sum) or FV (for calculating the future value of an investment).

Gallery A visual collection of choices you can browse through to make a selection. Often available with Live Preview.

Gridlines Evenly spaced horizontal and/or vertical lines used in a worksheet or chart to make it easier to read.

Groups Each tab on the Ribbon is arranged into groups to make features easy to find.

Header row In an Excel table, the first row; it contains field (column) names.

HTML (Hypertext Markup Language) The format of pages that a Web browser can read.

Hyperlink An object (a filename, a word, a phrase, or a graphic) in a worksheet that, when you click it, displays another worksheet or a Web page called the target. *See also* Target.

Hypertext Markup Language *See* HTML.

Icon sets In conditional formatting, groups of images that are used to visually communicate relative cell values based on the values they contain.

Insertion point A blinking vertical line that appears when you click in the formula bar or in an active cell; indicates where new text will be inserted.

Instance A worksheet in its own workbook window.

Integrate To incorporate a document and parts of a document created in one program into another program; for example, to incorporate an Excel chart into a PowerPoint slide, or an Access table into a Word document.

Interface The look and feel of a program; for example, the appearance of commands and the way they are organized in the program window.

Intranet An internal network site used by a group of people who work together.

Keywords Terms added to a workbook's Document Properties that help locate the file in a search.

Labels Descriptive text or other information that identifies data in rows, columns, or charts, but is not included in calculations.

Landscape Page orientation in which the contents of a page span the length of a page rather than its width, making the page wider than it is tall.

Launch To open or start a program on your computer.

Legend In a chart, information that identifies how data is represented by colors or patterns.

Linking The dynamic referencing of data in the same or in other workbooks, so that when data in the other location is changed, the references in the current location are automatically updated.

List arrows *See* AutoFilter list arrows.

Live Preview A feature that lets you point to a choice in a gallery or palette and see the results in the document without actually clicking the choice.

Lock To secure a row, column, or sheet so that data in that location cannot be changed.

Logical conditions Using the operators And and Or to narrow a custom filter criteria.

Logical formula A formula with calculations that are based on stated conditions.

Logical test The first part of an IF function; if the logical test is true, then the second part of the function is applied; if it is false, then the third part of the function is applied.

Macros Programmed instructions that perform tasks in a workbook.

Major gridlines In a chart, the gridlines that represent the values at the tick marks on the value axis.

Metadata Information that describes data and is used in Microsoft Windows document searches.

Minor gridlines In a chart, the gridlines that represent the values between the tick marks on the value axis.

Mixed reference Cell reference that combines both absolute and relative cell addressing.

Mode indicator An area on the left end of the status bar that indicates the program's status. For example, when you are changing the contents of a cell, the word 'Edit' appears in the mode indicator.

Multilevel sort A reordering of table data using more than one column (field) at a time.

Name box Box to the left of the formula bar that shows the cell reference or name of the active cell.

Navigate To move around in a worksheet; for example, you can use the arrow keys on the keyboard to navigate from cell to cell, or press [Page Up] or [Page Down] to move one screen at a time.

Normal view Default worksheet view that shows the worksheet without features such as headers and footers; ideal for creating and editing a worksheet, but may not be detailed enough when formatting a document.

Number format A format applied to values to express numeric concepts, such as currency, date, and percentage.

Object Independent element on a worksheet (such as a chart or graphic) that is not located in a specific cell or range; can be moved and resized and displays handles when selected.

Office Web Apps Versions of the Microsoft Office applications with limited functionality that are available online. Users can view documents online and then edit them in the browser using a selection of functions. Office Web Apps are available for Word, PowerPoint, Excel, and One Note.

Online collaboration The ability to incorporate feedback or share information across the Internet or a company network or intranet.

Or logical condition A filtering feature that searches for records by specifying that only one entered criterion must be matched.

Order of precedence Rules that determine the order in which operations are performed within a formula containing more than one arithmetic operator.

Page Break Preview A worksheet view that displays a reduced view of each page in your worksheet, along with page break indicators that you can drag to include more or less information on a page.

Page Layout view Provides an accurate view of how a worksheet will look when printed, including headers and footers.

Panes Sections into which you can divide a worksheet when you want to work on separate parts of the worksheet at the same time; one pane freezes, or remains in place, while you scroll in another pane until you see the desired information.

Paste Options button Button that appears onscreen after pasting content; enables you to choose to paste only specific elements of the copied selection, such as the formatting or values, if desired.

Plot area In a chart, the area inside the horizontal and vertical axes.

Point A unit of measure used for font size and row height. One point is equal to 1/72nd of an inch.

Portrait Page orientation in which the contents of a page span the width of a page, so the page is taller than it is wide.

Previewing Prior to printing, seeing onscreen exactly how the printed document will look.

Print area A portion of a worksheet that you can define using the Print Area button on the Page Layout tab; after you select and define a print area, the Quick Print feature prints only that worksheet area.

Print title In a table that spans more than one page, the field names that print at the top of every printed page.

Properties File characteristics, such as the author's name, keywords, or the title, that help others understand, identify, and locate the file.

Publish To place an Excel workbook or worksheet on a Web site or an intranet in HTML format so that others can access it using their Web browsers.

Quick Access toolbar A small toolbar on the left side of a Microsoft application program window's title bar, containing icons that you click to quickly perform common actions, such as saving a file.

Quick Analysis tool An icon that is displayed below and to the right of a range that lets you easily create charts and other elements.

Range A selection of two or more cells, such as B5:B14.

Read-only format Describes cells that display data but that cannot be changed in a protected worksheet.

Record In a table (an Excel database), data about an object or a person.

Reference operators In a formula, symbols which enable you to use ranges in calculations.

Relative cell reference In a formula, a cell address that refers to a cell's location in relation to the cell containing the formula and that automatically changes to reflect the new location when the formula is copied or moved; default type of referencing used in Excel worksheets. *See also* Absolute cell reference.

Return In a function, to display a result.

Ribbon Appears beneath the title bar in every Office program window, and displays commands you're likely to need for the current task.

Scope In a named cell or range, the worksheet(s) in which the name can be used.

Screen capture An electronic snapshot of your screen, as if you took a picture of it with a camera, which you can paste into a document.

Screenshot An image of an open file that is pasted into an Excel document; you can move, copy, and edit the image.

Scroll bars Bars on the right edge (vertical scroll bar) and bottom edge (horizontal scroll bar) of the document window that allow you to move around in a document that is too large to fit on the screen at once.

Search criterion In a workbook or table search, the text you are searching for.

Secondary axis In a combination chart, an additional axis that supplies the scale for one of the chart types used.

Sheet tabs Identify the sheets in a workbook and let you switch between sheets; located below the worksheet grid.

Sheet tab scrolling buttons Allow you to navigate to additional sheet tabs when available; located to the left of the sheet tabs.

Sizing handles Small series of dots at the corners and edges of a chart indicating that the chart is selected; drag to resize the chart.

SkyDrive An online storage and file sharing service. Access to SkyDrive is through a Microsoft account. Up to 25 GB of data can be stored in a personal SkyDrive, with each file a maximum size of 300 MB.

SmartArt graphics Predesigned diagram types for the following types of data: List, Process, Cycle, Hierarchy, Relationship, Matrix, and Pyramid.

Sparkline A quick, simple chart located within a cell that serves as a visual indicator of data trends.

Stated conditions In a logical formula, criteria you create.

Status bar Bar at the bottom of the Excel window that provides a brief description about the active command or task in progress.

Structured reference Allows table formulas to refer to table columns by names that are automatically generated when the table is created.

Suite A group of programs that are bundled together and share a similar interface, making it easy to transfer skills and program content among them.

Table An organized collection of rows and columns of similarly structured data on a worksheet.

Table styles Predesigned formatting that can be applied to a range of cells or even to an entire worksheet; especially useful for those ranges with labels in the left column and top row, and totals in the bottom row or right column. *See also* Table.

Table total row A row you can add to the bottom of a table for calculations using the data in the table columns.

Tabs Organizational unit used for commands on the Ribbon. The tab names appear at the top of the Ribbon and the active tab appears in front.

Target The location that a hyperlink displays after you click it.

Template A predesigned, formatted file that serves as the basis for a new workbook; Excel template files have the file extension .xltx.

Text annotations Labels added to a chart to draw attention to or describe a particular area.

Text concatenation operators In a formula, symbols used to join strings of text in different cells.

Theme A predefined set of colors, fonts, line and fill effects, and other formats that can be applied to an Excel worksheet and give it a consistent, professional look.

Tick marks Notations of a scale of measure on a chart axis.

Title bar Appears at the top of every Office program window: displays the document name and program name.

User interface A collective term for all the ways you interact with a software program.

Value axis In a chart, the axis that contains numerical values; in a 2-dimensional chart, also known as the y-axis.

Values Numbers, formulas, and functions used in calculations.

View A method of displaying a document window to show more or fewer details or a different combination of elements that makes it easier to complete certain tasks, such as formatting or reading text.

Watermark A translucent background design on a worksheet that is displayed when the worksheet is printed. A watermark is a graphic file that is inserted into the document header.

What-if analysis A decision-making tool in which data is changed and formulas are recalculated, in order to predict various possible outcomes.

Wildcard A special symbol that substitutes for unknown characters in defining search criteria in the Find and Replace dialog box. The most common types of wildcards are the question mark (?), which stands for any single character, and the asterisk (*), which represents any group of characters.

Workbook A collection of related worksheets contained within a single file which has the file extension xlsx.

Worksheet A single sheet within a workbook file; also, the entire area within an electronic spreadsheet that contains a grid of columns and rows.

Worksheet window Area of the program window that displays part of the current worksheet; the worksheet window displays only a small fraction of the worksheet, which can contain a total of 1,048,576 rows and 16,384 columns.

X-axis The horizontal axis in a chart; because it often shows data categories, such as months or locations, *also called* Category axis.

XML Acronym that stands for eXtensible Markup Language, which is a language used to structure, store, and send information.

Y-axis The vertical axis in a chart; because it often shows numerical values, *also called* Value axis.

Z-axis The third axis in a true 3-D chart, lets you compare data points across both categories and values.

Zooming in A feature that makes a document appear larger but shows less of it on screen at once; does not affect actual document size.

Zooming out A feature that shows more of a document on screen at once but at a reduced size; does not affect actual document size.

Index

SPECIAL CHARACTERS
< (left angle bracket), EX 117
> (right angle bracket), EX 117
(hash mark), EX 8, EX 58
$ (dollar sign), EX 8, EX 38
% (percent sign), EX 7
* (asterisk), EX 7, EX 180
+ (plus sign), EX 7, EX 8
− (minus sign), EX 7, EX 8
/ (forward slash), EX 7
= (equal sign), EX 8, EX 12, EX 28, EX 111, EX 117
? (question mark), EX 160, EX 180
@ (at sign), EX 8
^ (caret), EX 7
_ (underscore), EX 114

A
About command, PowerPoint Web App, CL 13
absolute cell references, EX 34
 copying formulas with, EX 38–39
Access, OFF 2, OFF 3
 filename and file extension, OFF 8
active cell, EX 4
Add Chart Element button, EX 84
Add View dialog box, EX 134, EX 135
addition operator (+), EX 7
Advanced Filter command, EX 182–183
Advanced Filter dialog box, EX 185
alignment
 axis labels and titles, changing, EX 91
 buttons, EX 57
 labels and values, EX 56, EX 57
analyzing data, EX 3
AND function, EX 118–119
And logical condition, EX 180, EX 182
Animation command, PowerPoint Web
 App, CL 13
ANIMATIONS tab, PowerPoint Web App, CL 13
annotations, charts, EX 92, EX 93
app(s), launching, OFF 4–5
applications
 cloud-based, CL 2
 Office Web Apps. *See* Office Web Apps

Apps for Office feature, EX 26
area charts, EX 81
arguments, EX 8
arithmetic operators, EX 7, EX 12, EX 26, EX 27
Arrange Windows dialog box, EX 130, EX 131
arrow keys, navigating worksheets, EX 9
ascending order, EX 164, EX 165
asterisk (*)
 multiplication operator, EX 7
 wildcard, EX 180
at sign (@), value entries, EX 8
Auto Fill Options button, EX 36
AutoFilter feature, EX 178–179
AutoFilter list arrows, EX 178, EX 179
AutoFit Column Width command, EX 58
AutoFit feature, EX 58
AutoSum button, EX 28
AVERAGEIF function, EX 108

B
background, adding to worksheets, EX 136–137
Backstage view, OFF 6, OFF 7
backward compatibility, OFF 11
banding, tables, EX 157
bar charts, EX 81
Between dialog box, EX 65
borders, EX 62, EX 88

C
calculated columns feature, EX 166
calculation(s), EX 2, EX 3
 entering, EX 8
calculation operators, EX 12
callouts, annotating charts, EX 92, EX 93
Cancel button, EX 8
canceling entries, EX 8
capitalization as sort criterion, EX 164
caret (^), exponent operator, EX 7
category axis, EX 80, EX 81
cell(s), EX 4
 active, EX 4
 deleting, EX 33
 inserting, EX 33
 locking, EX 132

cell addresses, EX 4
cell contents
   copying, EX 32, EX 33
   moving, EX 32, EX 33
   pasting specific components, EX 36
   selecting using keyboard, EX 10
cell entries
   editing, EX 10–11
   indenting, EX 57
   rotating, EX 57
cell pointer, EX 4, EX 5
cell references, EX 12
   absolute. *See* absolute cell references
   circular, correcting, EX 113
   mixed, EX 35
   relative. *See* relative cell references
   3-D, EX 110
cell styles, EX 62, EX 63
cell values, restricting, EX 190
Change Chart Type dialog box,
   EX 86, EX 87
chart(s), EX 2, EX 3, EX 79–95
   annotating, EX 92, EX 93
   area, EX 81
   bar, EX 81
   changing design, EX 86–87
   column, EX 81
   combination, EX 86
   creating, EX 82–83
   data labels, EX 89
   deleting, EX 84
   drawing on, EX 92, EX 93
   elements, EX 80, EX 81
   embedded. *See* embedded charts
   formatting, EX 88–91
   line, EX 81
   moving, EX 84, EX 85
   pie, EX 81, EX 94–95
   placeholder text, EX 82
   planning, EX 80–81
   previewing, EX 90
   resizing, EX 84, EX 85
   scatter, EX 81
   3-D, EX 87
   types, EX 81
chart sheets, EX 82
CHART TOOLS DESIGN tab, EX 82, EX 86, EX 88
   Add Chart Element button, EX 84
   Move Chart button, EX 85
CHART TOOLS FORMAT tab, EX 82, EX 84, EX 90
Choose a SmartArt Graphic dialog box, EX 93
circular references, correcting, EX 113
Clear button, EX 56, EX 83
Clipboard (Office), OFF 5
Clipboard (Windows), OFF 13
Clipboard command, PowerPoint Web
   App, CL 13

cloud computing, OFF 9
   definition, CL 2
   SkyDrive. *See* SkyDrive
cloud-based applications, CL 2. *See also*
   Office Web Apps
Collapse Dialog Box button, EX 106, EX 188
color(s), EX 62
   filtering tables by, EX 178
   sorting tables by, EX 178
color scale, EX 183
column(s). *See* table columns; worksheet columns
Column button, EX 83
column charts, EX 81
column headings, EX 58
column resize pointer, EX 11
Column Width command, EX 58
combination charts, EX 86
comments, EX 61
Comments command, PowerPoint Web App, CL 13
comparison operators, EX 12, EX 117
compatibility, OFF 2
compatibility mode, EX 142, EX 143, OFF 11
complex formulas, EX 26–27
CONCATENATE function, EX 106
conditional formatting, EX 64–65
   advanced options, EX 183
   modifying rules, EX 64
   multiple rules, EX 181
   sorting data, EX 164
Conditional Formatting button, EX 64
Conditional Formatting Rules Manager
   dialog box, EX 64
consolidating data
   using formulas, EX 110–111
   using named ranges, EX 114
copy pointer, EX 11
copying
   cell entries, EX 32, EX 33
   formulas with absolute cell references, EX 38–39
   formulas with relative cell references, EX 36–37
   items, using Office Clipboard, OFF 5
   worksheets, EX 67
COUNT function, EX 30
COUNTA function, EX 30
COUNTIF function, EX 108
Create Table dialog box, EX 156, EX 157
criteria range, EX 182, EX 185
currency formats, EX 52
Current Date button, EX 14
Current Time button, EX 14
Custom AutoFilter dialog box, EX 180, EX 181
custom filters, EX 180–181
Custom Format button, EX 64
custom sort order, specifying, EX 165
Custom Views dialog box, EX 134
Customize Quick Access Toolbar button, OFF 12
cutting items, Office Clipboard, OFF 5

D

data entry area, EX 132
data labels, charts, EX 89
data markers, EX 80, EX 81
data points, EX 80
data series, EX 80, EX 81
DATA tab
    Remove Duplicates button, EX 162
    Text to Columns button, EX 107
databases, functions, EX 189
Date & Time button, EX 109
date and time functions, EX 109
DATE function, EX 109
DAVERAGE function, EX 189
DCOUNT function, EX 189
DCOUNTA function, EX 189
decimal places, EX 52
Default Width command, EX 58
Define Name button, EX 12
Delete button, EX 61
Delete command, PowerPoint Web App, CL 13
deleting. *See also* removing
    cells, EX 33
    charts, EX 84
    columns, EX 60, EX 61
    data in tables, EX 162–163
    rows, EX 60, EX 61
    views from active worksheet, EX 134
    worksheets, EX 66, EX 67
delimiters, EX 107
descending order, EX 164, EX 165
DESIGN tab, PowerPoint Web App, CL 13
Desktop, saving files to, OFF 8
DGET function, EX 186, EX 189
dialog box launcher, OFF 6, OFF 7
digital signatures, EX 144
displaying hidden worksheets, EX 130
distribution
    preparing workbooks for, EX 138–139
    saving workbooks for, EX 142–143
#DIV/0 error value, EX 113
division operator (/), EX 7
document(s), OFF 12. *See also* file(s)
    co-authoring, CL 10
Document Inspector dialog box, EX 138, EX 139
Document Properties Panel, EX 138, EX 139
Document Recovery pane, EX 10, OFF 15
document window, OFF 6, OFF 7
documenting table design, EX 80, EX 81
dollar sign ($)
    absolute cell references, EX 38
    value entries, EX 8
Drawing command, PowerPoint Web App, CL 13
drawing on charts, EX 92, EX 93

DSUM function, EX 189
duplicates, removing from worksheet data, EX 162
dynamic page breaks, EX 135

E

Edit Comment button, EX 61
Edit Formatting Rule dialog box, EX 64
editing
    cell entries, EX 10–11
    comments, EX 61
    formulas, EX 12, EX 13
    text in chart or axis titles, EX 88
electronic spreadsheets, EX 2
emailing workbooks, EX 68
embedded charts, EX 82
    moving to sheets, EX 85
enlarging areas of worksheet, EX 16
equal sign (=)
    calculations, EX 8
    formula prefix, EX 12
    function prefix, EX 28
    linking data between workbooks, EX 111
    value entries, EX 8
equal to operator (=), EX 117
equation(s), inserting into worksheets, EX 119
EQUATION TOOLS DESIGN tab, mathematical symbols, EX 119
error(s), checking formulas for, EX 112–113
error alerts, EX 191
ERROR value, EX 112
Excel, OFF 2, OFF 3
    filename and file extension, OFF 8
    Office Web App, CL 12
    starting, EX 4
    uses, EX 3
Excel window, EX 4–5
Exit command, PowerPoint Web App, CL 13
Expand Dialog Box button, EX 188
exploding pie charts, EX 94, EX 95
exponent operator (^), EX 7
Export button, EX 142
exporting Excel files into another format, EX 142
external reference indicators, EX 110
extracting table data, EX 184–185

F

field(s), tables, EX 80
field names, EX 80
file(s), OFF 10, OFF 11. *See also* document(s)
    blank, creating, OFF 8

creating, OFF 8, OFF 9
definition, OFF 8
integrating, OFF 2
names, OFF 8
opening, OFF 10, OFF 11
recovering, OFF 15
saving. *See* saving files
sharing, SkyDrive, CL 10–11
file extensions, OFF 8
file formats, workbooks, EX 143
file management, SkyDrive, CL 8–9
FILE tab, CL 2, CL 3, OFF 7
Export button, EX 142
PowerPoint Web App, CL 13
Save As button, EX 139
Share button, EX 139
Fill button, EX 38
fill handle, sequential text or values, EX 39
fill handle pointer, EX 11
filter list arrows, EX 156, EX 178
filtering tables, EX 178–183
Advanced Filter command, EX 182–183
AutoFilter feature, EX 178–179
by color, EX 178
custom filters, EX 180–181
Find & Select button, EX 161
Find and Replace dialog box, EX 68, EX 69, EX 160, EX 161
finding data in tables, EX 160–161
flash fill feature, EX 2
font(s), EX 54, EX 55
Font command, PowerPoint Web App, CL 13
font size, EX 54
font styles, EX 56, EX 57
buttons, EX 57
overuse, EX 56
footers, EX 140
adding, EX 168
Format button, EX 58, EX 61, EX 64
Format Cells dialog box, EX 64
Format Chart Area pane, EX 87
Format Data Series command, EX 94
formatting
entire rows, EX 54
keyboard shortcuts, EX 56
tables, EX 156, EX 157
using text functions, EX 106–107
worksheets. *See* conditional formatting; formatting worksheets
formatting worksheets, EX 51–65
borders, EX 62, EX 63
colors, EX 62, EX 63
column width, EX 58–59
conditional formatting. *See* conditional formatting
font and font size, EX 54–55
font styles and alignment, EX 56–57
inserting/deleting rows and columns, EX 60–61

patterns, EX 62, EX 63
as table, EX 53
values, EX 52–53
formula(s), EX 6–7
absolute cell references, EX 38–39
checking for errors, EX 112–113
complex, EX 26–27
consolidating data, EX 110–111
constructing using named ranges, EX 114
editing, EX 12, EX 13
entering, EX 12, EX 13
hiding, EX 132
logical. *See* logical formulas
printing, EX 16
tables, EX 166–167
Formula AutoComplete, EX 40
formula bar, EX 4, EX 5
formula prefix (=), EX 12
FORMULAS tab
Date & Time button, EX 109
Define Name button, EX 12
Name Manager button, EX 115, EX 185
Show Formulas button, EX 16
forward slash (/), division operator, EX 7
freezing rows and columns, EX 133
function(s), EX 8, EX 28–29
database, common, EX 189
information, EX 28
text, EX 106–107
typing, EX 30–31
Function Arguments dialog box, EX 108, EX 188, EX 189
moving, EX 106
function prefix (=), EX 28
FV argument, PMT function, EX 120
FV function, EX 121

G

greater than operator (>), EX 117
gridlines, EX 80, EX 81
hiding, EX 168
major and minor, EX 88
printing, EX 168
group(s), OFF 6
group worksheets, EX 144–145

H

hash mark (#)
column too narrow to display values, EX 58
value entries, EX 8
header(s), EX 140
adding, EX 168

Header & Footer button, EX 140
HEADER & FOOTER TOOLS DESIGN tab, EX 14, EX 140
header rows, tables, EX 80
headings
   hiding, EX 168
   printing, EX 168
Help button, OFF 14
Help command, PowerPoint Web App, CL 13
Help window, OFF 14, OFF 15
Hide command, EX 58
hiding
   formulas, EX 132
   gridlines, EX 168
   headings, EX 168
   rows and columns, EX 61
   worksheets, EX 130
Highlight Cells Rules submenu, EX 64
HLOOKUP function, EX 187
HOME tab
   Clear button, EX 56
   Copy button, EX 32
   Cut button, EX 32
   Fill button, EX 38
   Format button, EX 58, EX 61
   Insert Sheet button, EX 67
   Paste button, EX 32
   PowerPoint Web App, CL 13
horizontal axis, EX 80, EX 81
HOUR function, EX 109
HTML (Hypertext Markup Language), EX 142
hyperlinks
   inserting, EX 140–141
   removing, EX 140
Hypertext Markup Language. *See* HTML (Hypertext Markup
   Language)

I

I-beam pointer, EX 11
icon sets, EX 64, EX 183
IF functions
   building logical formulas with, EX 116–117
   nested, EX 116
Illustrations command, PowerPoint Web App, CL 13
images, EX 55
Images command, PowerPoint Web App, CL 13
indenting cell entries, EX 57
Info command, PowerPoint Web App, CL 13
input messages, EX 191
Insert dialog box, EX 60, EX 61
Insert Function dialog box, EX 28, EX 29
Insert Hyperlink dialog box, EX 140, EX 141
Insert Sheet button, EX 67

INSERT tab, EX 26, EX 92
   Column button, EX 83
   Header & Footer button, EX 140
   Line button, EX 83
   Pictures button, EX 55
   PowerPoint Web App, CL 13
   Shapes button, EX 92, EX 93
   Signature Line button, EX 144
   Text Box button, EX 119
   Win/Loss button, EX 83
inserting cells, EX 33
insertion point, EX 10, OFF 8
instances, EX 130
integrating files, OFF 2
interface, OFF 2
intranets, EX 142

K

keyboard
   enabling function keys, EX 10
   selecting cell contents, EX 10
keyboard shortcuts, formatting, EX 56
keywords, EX 55, EX 138

L

labels, EX 8
   alignment, EX 56, EX 57, EX 91
landscape orientation, EX 16
launching apps, OFF 4–5
left angle bracket (<), less than
   operator, EX 117
legends, EX 80, EX 81
   moving, EX 84
less than operator (<), EX 117
Line button, EX 83
line charts, EX 81
linking. *See also* hyperlinks
   data between workbooks, EX 110, EX 111
Links command, PowerPoint Web App, CL 13
list arrows, EX 178
Live Preview, OFF 6, OFF 7
locking cells, EX 132
logical conditions, filtering tables, EX 180
logical formulas
   building with AND function, EX 118–119
   building with IF function,
     EX 116–117
logical tests, EX 116
looking up values, tables, EX 186–187
LOWER function, EX 107

M

macros, EX 143
major gridlines, EX 88
MATCH function, EX 187
mathematical symbols, equations, EX 119
metadata, EX 138
.mht files, EX 143
.mhtml files, EX 143
Microsoft account
  new, creating, CL 5
  signing in to, CL 4
  signing out of, CL 4
Microsoft Accounts, OFF 9
Microsoft Office. *See also* Access; Excel;
  PowerPoint; Word
  benefits, OFF 2
  launching apps, OFF 4–5
  moving between programs, OFF 4
  user interface, OFF 6
Microsoft Office 365, OFF 3
Microsoft Office 365 Home Premium
  edition, OFF 3
minor gridlines, EX 88
minus sign (–)
  subtraction operator, EX 7
  value entries, EX 8
MINUTE function, EX 109
mixed cell references, EX 35
mode indicator, EX 4, EX 5, EX 8
Move Chart button, EX 85
Move Chart dialog box, EX 85
move pointer, EX 11
moving
  cell entries, EX 32, EX 33
  charts, EX 84, EX 85
  embedded charts to sheets, EX 85
  Function Arguments dialog box, EX 106
  legends, EX 84
  titles, EX 88
  worksheets, EX 66, EX 67
multilevel sorts, EX 164
multiplication operator (*), EX 7

N

#NA error value, EX 113
name(s), tables, changing, EX 186
Name box, EX 4, EX 5
Name Manager button, EX 115, EX 185
Name Manager dialog box, EX 115
named ranges, EX 12
  consolidating data, EX 114

  constructing formulas using, EX 114–115
  navigating using, EX 114
navigating
  between sheets, EX 66
  using named cells and ranges, EX 114
  worksheets, EX 9
nested IF functions, EX 116
New Comment button, EX 61
New Name dialog box, EX 114, EX 115
New Table Style dialog box, EX 157
noncontiguous worksheets, grouping, EX 144
normal pointer, EX 11
Normal view, EX 14
NOT function, EX 118
NOW function, EX 109
#NUM! error value, EX 113
number format, EX 52

O

object(s), EX 84
object pointers, EX 85
.ods files, EX 143
Office Clipboard, OFF 5
Office Open XML format, EX 143
Office Web Apps, CL 2, CL 12–13, EX 5
OneNote, Office Web App, CL 12
online collaboration, OFF 2, OFF 9
online pictures, EX 55
Open as Copy option, Open dialog box, OFF 10
Open dialog box, OFF 10, OFF 11
opening files, OFF 10, OFF 11
Open-Read-Only option, Open dialog
  box, OFF 10
operators
  arithmetic, EX 7, EX 12, EX 26, EX 27
  calculation, EX 12
  comparison, EX 12, EX 117
  order of precedence, EX 26, EX 27
  reference, EX 12
  text concatenation, EX 12
OR function, EX 118
Or logical condition, EX 180, EX 182
order of precedence, EX 26, EX 27
organizing data, EX 3

P

page break(s)
  dynamic, EX 135
  previewing, EX 135
Page Break Preview button, EX 135
Page Break view, EX 14, EX 15

PAGE LAYOUT tab, EX 16
  Print check boxes, EX 110
  Themes button, EX 63
  Width and Height settings, EX 17
Page Layout view, EX 14, EX 15
Page Setup dialog box, EX 168, EX 169
panes, EX 133
  splitting worksheets into, EX 131
Paragraph command, PowerPoint Web App, CL 13
Paste Options button, EX 36
Paste Preview feature, EX 37
pasting items, Office Clipboard, OFF 5
patterns, EX 62
payments
  calculating with FV function, EX 121
  calculating with PMT function, EX 120–121
.pdf files, EX 143
percent sign (%), percent operator, EX 7
Picture Border button, EX 137
Picture Effects button, EX 137
Picture Layout button, EX 137
PICTURE TOOLS FORMAT tab
  Picture Border button, EX 137
  Picture Effects button, EX 137
  Picture Layout button, EX 137
Pictures button, EX 55
pie charts, EX 81, EX 94–95
  exploding, EX 94, EX 95
placeholder text, charts, EX 82
planning
  charts, EX 80–81
  tables, EX 154–155
plot area, EX 80, EX 81
plus sign (+)
  addition operator, EX 7
  value entries, EX 8
PMT function, EX 120–121
point(s), EX 54
pointers, EX 11
portrait orientation, EX 16, EX 17
pound sign. *See* hash mark (#)
PowerPoint, OFF 2, OFF 3
  filename and file extension, OFF 8
  Office Web App, CL 12–13
PowerPoint Last Viewed Slide setting, CL 2
Presentation Views command, PowerPoint
  Web App, CL 13
previewing
  charts, EX 90
  documents, OFF 12
  page breaks, EX 135
  worksheets, EX 110
print area, setting, EX 169
Print command, PowerPoint Web App, CL 13
Print layout view, OFF 12
print titles, EX 168

printers, active, changing, EX 16
printing
  formulas, EX 16
  gridlines, EX 168
  headings, EX 168
  tables, EX 168–169
PROPER function, EX 106
properties, EX 138
Protect Sheet dialog box, EX 132, EX 133
publishing, EX 142

Q

question mark (?), wildcard, EX 160, EX 180
Quick Access toolbar, OFF 6, OFF 7
  customizing, OFF 12
Quick Analysis tool, EX 2, EX 4, EX 28, EX 64
Quick Print button, EX 16

R

range(s), EX 4, EX 5
  named. *See* named ranges
  selecting, EX 28, EX 52
range names, EX 114
read-only format, EX 132
recalculating, EX 2, EX 8
records, tables, EX 154
recovering unsaved changes to workbook files, EX 10
reference(s). *See also* absolute cell references; cell references;
  relative cell references
  structured, EX 166, EX 167
reference operators, EX 12
relative cell references, EX 34, EX 35
  copying formulas with, EX 36–37
Remove Duplicates button, EX 162
Remove Duplicates dialog box, EX 162, EX 163
removing. *See also* deleting
  hyperlinks, EX 140
renaming worksheets, EX 66, EX 67
replacing data in tables, EX 160–161
reports, EX 3
Research button, EX 141
Research task pane, EX 141
research tools, EX 141
Resize table button, EX 158
resizing
  charts, EX 84, EX 85
  tables, EX 158
return, EX 118
reversing actions, EX 10
REVIEW tab
  Delete button, EX 61
  Edit Comment button, EX 61

New Comment button, EX 61
Research button, EX 141
Show All Comments button, EX 61
Ribbon, OFF 6, OFF 7
right angle bracket (>), greater than operator, EX 117
roaming settings, CL 2
rotating cell entries, EX 57
ROUND function, EX 40–41
rows. *See* table rows; worksheet rows
Rule Manager, EX 64

S

Save As button, EX 139
Save As command, PowerPoint Web
    App, CL 13
Save As dialog box, OFF 8, OFF 9, OFF 10, OFF 11
saving
    custom views of worksheets, EX 134–135
    files. *See* saving files
    workbooks for distribution, EX 142–143
saving files, OFF 8, OFF 9, OFF 10, OFF 11
    SkyDrive, OFF 9
    to SkyDrive, default, disabling, CL 6, CL 7
scaling data to fit worksheet, EX 17
scatter charts, EX 81
scope, EX 114
screen captures, OFF 13
screenshots, EX 137
scroll bars, EX 4, EX 5
secondary axis, EX 86
security, worksheets and workbooks, EX 132–133
selecting
    cell contents, EX 10
    ranges, EX 4, EX 5, EX 28, EX 52
    table elements, EX 159
sequential text or values, fill handle for, EX 38
shadows, EX 88
Shapes button, EX 92, EX 93
Share button, EX 139
Share command, PowerPoint Web App, CL 13
sharing files, SkyDrive, CL 10–11
sheet tab(s), EX 4, EX 5
sheet tab scrolling buttons, EX 4, EX 5
shortcut keys, OFF 4
Show All Comments button, EX 61
Show Formulas button, EX 16
signature(s), digital, EX 144
Signature Line button, EX 144
single-file Web pages, EX 142
sizing handles, EX 82
SkyDrive, CL 2, CL 6–7, EX 5
    accessing, CL 8
    default saving to, disabling, CL 6, CL 7
    file management, CL 8–9

sharing files, CL 10–11
sharing workbooks, EX 139
Slides command, PowerPoint Web App, CL 13
SmartArt graphics, EX 93
SMARTART TOOLS DESIGN tab, Text Pane
    button, EX 93
Snipping Tool, OFF 13
Sort dialog box, EX 164, EX 165
sort feature, EX 164
sorting
    custom sort order, EX 165
    data in tables, EX 164–165
    tables by color, EX 178
sparkline(s), EX 83
SPARKLINE TOOLS DESIGN tab, Clear button, EX 83
spell checking, EX 68–69
Spelling dialog box, EX 68, EX 69
start screen, OFF 4, OFF 5
starting Excel, EX 4
stated conditions, EX 116
status bar, EX 4, EX 5
**Stop Automatically Creating Calculated
    Columns button**, EX 166
structured references, EX 166, EX 167
styles
    cell styles, EX 62, EX 63
    font styles. *See* font styles
    table styles, EX 53
subscriptions, Microsoft Office 365, OFF 3
SUBSTITUTE function, EX 107
subtotal(s), tables, EX 192–193
Subtotal dialog box, EX 192, EX 193
subtraction operator (-), EX 7
suites, OFF 2
SUM function, EX 28
SUMIF function, EX 108, EX 109
summarizing table data, EX 188–189
summary information, viewing, EX 138
switching worksheet views, EX 14–15
Synchronous Scrolling button, EX 130
syncing, CL 2

T

tab(s), OFF 6, OFF 7
table(s), EX 153–169
    adding data, EX 158–159
    changing names, EX 186
    creating, EX 156, EX 157
    deleting data, EX 162–163
    extracting data, EX 184–185
    filtering. *See* filtering tables
    finding and replacing data,
        EX 160–161

formatting, EX 156, EX 157
formatting worksheets as, EX 53
formulas, EX 166–167
looking up values, EX 186–187
planning, EX 154–155
printing, EX 168–169
resizing, EX 158
selecting elements, EX 159
sorting data, EX 164–165
structure, EX 80
subtotals, EX 192–193
summarizing data, EX 188–189
validating data, EX 190–191
table columns
calculated, EX 166
structure, EX 80
table rows
header rows, EX 80
structure, EX 80
total row, EX 166
table styles, EX 53, EX 156, EX 157
Table Styles gallery, EX 156
Table Styles More button, EX 157
TABLE TOOLS DESIGN tab
Resize table button, EX 158
Table Styles gallery, EX 156
table total row, EX 166
target, hyperlink, EX 140
templates, EX 2, EX 41, OFF 4
text
chart or axis titles, editing, EX 88
sequential, fill handle for, EX 38
text annotations, EX 92, EX 93
text box(es), charts, EX 92, EX 93
Text Box button, EX 119
Text command, PowerPoint Web App, CL 13
text concatenation operators, EX 12
text functions, EX 106–107
Text Pane button, EX 93
Text to Columns button, EX 107
themes, EX 63, OFF 2
Themes button, EX 63
Themes command, PowerPoint Web
App, CL 13
3-D charts, EX 87
3-D references, EX 110
tick marks, EX 80
tiling graphics, EX 136
TIME function, EX 109
title(s)
changing alignment, EX 91
editing text, EX 88
moving, EX 88
title bar, OFF 6, OFF 7
TODAY function, EX 109

touch mode, enabling, OFF 15
Touch Mode button, OFF 15
TRANSITIONS tab, PowerPoint Web App, CL 13
Transitions to This Slide command, PowerPoint Web App, CL 13
Type argument, PMT function, EX 120

U

underscore (_), range names, EX 114
Undo button, EX 10
Undo Calculated Column button, EX 166
Unhide command, EX 58
unhiding rows and columns, EX 61
UPPER function, EX 107
user interface, OFF 2

V

validating table data, EX 190–191
value(s), EX 8
alignment, EX 56, EX 57
sequential, fill handle for, EX 38
value axis, EX 80, EX 81
#VALUE! error value, EX 113
vertical axis, EX 80, EX 81
view(s), OFF 12–13
custom, saving, EX 134–135
worksheets, switching, EX 14–15
View buttons, OFF 12
View Side by Side button, EX 130
VIEW tab, OFF 12
PowerPoint Web App, CL 13
viewing, OFF 12, OFF 13
summary information for a file, EX 138
worksheets, EX 130, EX 131
VLOOKUP function, EX 186–187

W

watermarks, EX 136
Web pages, single-file, EX 142
what-if analysis, EX 2, EX 3
wildcards
asterisk (*), EX 180
question mark (?), EX 160, EX 180
Windows Live ID, CL 5. *See also* Microsoft account
Windows 7, starting apps, OFF 4, OFF 5
Win/Loss button, EX 83
Word, OFF 2, OFF 3
filename and file extension, OFF 8
Office Web App, CL 12

Word Resume Reading Position setting, CL 2
WordArt styles, EX 90
workbooks, EX 2
 emailing, EX 68
 file formats, EX 143
 linking data between, EX 110, EX 111
 names, managing, EX 115
 preparing for distribution, EX 138–139
 protecting, EX 132–133
 recovering unsaved changed, EX 10
 saving for distribution, EX 142–143
 sharing using SkyDrive, EX 139
working online, CL 4–5
worksheet(s), EX 2, EX 3
 active, deleting views, EX 134
 adding, EX 67
 adding background, EX 136–137
 arranging, EX 130, EX 131
 columns. *See* worksheet columns
 copying, EX 67
 deleting, EX 66, EX 67
 enlarging areas, EX 16
 formatting. *See* formatting worksheets
 group, EX 144–145
 hiding, EX 130
 inserting equations, EX 119
 moving, EX 66, EX 67
 navigating, EX 9
 noncontiguous, grouping, EX 144
 previewing, EX 110
 protecting, EX 132–133
 renaming, EX 66, EX 67
 rows. *See* worksheet rows
 saving custom views, EX 134–135
 scaling data to fit, EX 17
 scaling to fit on one page, EX 136
 size, EX 14
 splitting into multiple panes, EX 131
 switching views, EX 14–15
 viewing, EX 130, EX 131
worksheet columns
 adjusting width, EX 58–59
 freezing, EX 133
 hiding and unhiding, EX 61
 inserting and deleting, EX 60, EX 61
worksheet rows
 changing height, EX 59
 freezing, EX 133
 hiding and unhiding, EX 61
 inserting and deleting, EX 60, EX 61
worksheet window, EX 4, EX 5

X

x-axis, EX 80, EX 81
.xls files, EX 143
.xlsm files, EX 143
.xltm files, EX 143
.xltx files, EX 143
.xps files, EX 143

Y

y-axis, EX 80, EX 81
YEAR function, EX 109
Your Profile page, CL 4

Z

z-axis, EX 80, EX 87
Zoom button, OFF 6
Zoom slider, EX 16
zooming in and out, OFF 6